WHERE EMPIRES COLLIDED

WHERE EMPIRES COLLIDED

Russian and Soviet Relations with Hong Kong, Taiwan, and Macao

Michael Share

The Chinese University Press

Where Empires Collided: Russian and Soviet Relations with Hong Kong, Taiwan, and Macao
By Michael Share

ISBN-10: 962–996–306–X
ISBN-13: 978–962–996–306–4

THE CHINESE UNIVERSITY PRESS
The Chinese University of Hong Kong
SHA TIN, N.T., HONG KONG
Fax: +852 2603 6692
+852 2603 7355
E-mail: cup@cuhk.edu.hk
Web-site: www.chineseupress.com

Printed in Hong Kong

To Priscilla,
without whom none of this project
would have been possible

Contents

Foreword

This book on the past relationship between Russia and Hong Kong, Macao, and Taiwan represents the fruit of many years' hard labor by Dr. Michael Share, one of the few Hong Kong scholars studying Russia's relations with the countries and regions of East Asia. The author has done outstanding work in the Russian archives, making this a fundamental and even unique study: the first book of its kind to explore the policies of Tsarist Russia, the Soviet Union, and the Russian Federation toward these three Chinese enclaves. It is an easy and exciting read, combining a wide historical perspective, deep political analysis, and an intriguing plot. One may not agree with all Dr. Share's deliberations and conclusions, but they deserve careful attention from all those interested in Asian and Pacific issues.

Until recently Russia's links with the Chinese periphery attracted only marginal academic attention, but coincidentally, as the Russian Federation actively increases its presence in the Asia-Pacific region, this topic is now winning growing interest from historians. The Asia-Pacific region is a top priority in the Russian Federation's multifaceted foreign policy, and not merely because two-thirds of Russia's territory lies in Asia. Russia has always been and remains an influential power center, while its recently strengthened international posture has enhanced the country's role as one of Asia's key regional players. Objectively, on the other hand, the stable development of the Russian economy must ultimately bring greater participation by the Russian Far East in the process of economic integration in the Asia-Pacific region, which has become one of the world's most dynamic and growing centers of power. These are the reasons why Russian regional policy has become so assertive. By participating in existing regional multilateral mechanisms, Russia seeks to establish a multipolar system of security and cooperation, equal and collaborative in nature. Moscow is enthusiastically promoting bilateral relations with its major partners in the Asia-Pacific region: China, Japan, the Republic of Korea, and the ASEAN (Association of Southeast Asian Nations) member-states. Nor, given its interest in the region, can Russia neglect the huge potential of cooperation with such important Asia-Pacific territories as Hong Kong, Macao, and Taiwan.

Russian interest in the South China periphery has a long heritage. In August 1793, the Chinese rejected the request of Lord McCartney, head of the British official delegation to Beijing, to open Chinese ports to trade and to authorize free navigation in the Pearl River Delta area. Interestingly, as long ago as November 1805, two Russian ships, the *Nadezhda* and *Neva*, commanded by two famous Russian sailors, Admiral Ivan Kruzenshtern and Captain-Lieutenant Yuri Lisiansky, dropped anchor in the Bay of Aomen, Macao, in South China, where they unloaded their cargo, sold Russian goods, and investigated the possibilities of developing commerce in Siberian furs. Paradoxically, the Russian traders never returned to South China, while the British eventually established what later became a very successful colony in Hong Kong.

Not until the mid-1850s did Russian strategists rediscover the significance of South China. In 1857, Admiral Evfim Putyatin was instructed to negotiate an agreement on trade with Hong Kong, and in 1860 the first Russian Consulate was established in the territory. The Consulate-General of the Russian Empire, which functioned until the early 1920s, was centrally located in Hong Kong, next to St. John's Cathedral, on a site now occupied by the Court of Final Appeal building. After the Communists came to power in Russia, Tsarist diplomats refused to serve the new authorities and emigrated to Great Britain, France, and other Western countries. The Consulate was closed, and its archives disappeared, their whereabouts still unknown today, though perhaps the publication of this book will prompt someone to provide the missing piece in this intriguing puzzle. The ensuing years represented a period of near complete vacuum in official Russian–Hong Kong ties, though between the wars some Comintern operatives were based in the colony. Understandably, before World War II Soviet diplomacy in East Asia assigned Hong Kong a fairly low priority, perceiving the territory and its affairs primarily in the context of Soviet relations with China, Japan, and Great Britain. During the Cold War the colony simply remained closed to citizens of the USSR for all but the briefest of visits.

Soon after the disintegration of the Soviet Union in 1991, the political authorities of the new successor entity, the Russian Federation, faced the question of how to restore Russia's diplomatic presence in Hong Kong. In October 1993, I was privileged to be one of a group of Russian diplomats led by Mr. V. Vorobiev, Minister-Counsellor of the Russian Embassy in Beijing, sent to Hong Kong on "a reconnaissance mission." At that time Russians were still rare guests in the British colony, but we received a very warm welcome, meeting in the government offices on Lower Albert Road with Mr. Vivian Warrington, Chief of the Protocol Division of the Hong Kong Government Secretariat, and Mr. William Ehrman, then Political Adviser to the Governor, now British Ambassador in Beijing. The colonial administration welcomed Russian interest in Hong Kong. On returning home we submitted a report containing optimistic conclusions on the vast prospects for Russian–Hong Kong cooperation, and endorsing previous arguments in favor of an earlier opening of the Consulate-General there. In October 1994, the new Russian Consul-General presented his credentials to Christopher Patten, Governor of Hong Kong.

At the Hong Kong handover ceremony on July 1, 1997 Russia was represented by Foreign Minister Yevgeniy Primakov, who later became Prime Minister of the Russian Federation. Congratulating his Chinese hosts on this occasion, Dr. Primakov wished the people of Hong Kong further prosperity and expressed his hopes for even closer cooperation between the territory and the Russian Federation, since from then onward Hong Kong, now under PRC jurisdiction, would be a close neighbor of ours. History is still being made before our eyes, since everything in Russian–Hong Kong relations, including mutual high-level political visits, sets a new precedent. In July 2002, Mr. Igor Ivanov, then Russian Foreign Minister, paid an official visit to Hong Kong. Mr. Donald Tsang, then Hong Kong's Chief Secretary for Administration, visited Russia in May 2004, becoming the first top Hong Kong official to step onto Russian soil. When he became Chief Executive the following year Mr. Tsang, like his predecessor Mr. Tung Chee-hwa, the first Chief Executive, also received a standing invitation to visit Russia. Such contacts are designed to give additional political impetus to the relationship between Russia and Hong Kong.

At the commercial and cultural level, the new relationship between

Hong Kong and Russia developed apace. For over ten years passenger planes of the Russian air company Aeroflot have been flying from Moscow to Hong Kong. Today this is a very busy route, with three to four flights a week depending on the season of the year, carrying tens of thousands of passengers, businessmen, tourists, journalists, and officials, whose numbers continue to grow. Cooperation between Russia and Hong Kong is not limited merely to trade exchanges. Our law enforcement agencies cooperate in fighting international terrorism, organized crime, and money laundering. The recent SARS pandemic made Russian and Hong Kong public health authorities realize the need for closer exchanges in the field of medical science. We also cooperate successfully within the framework of the Asia-Pacific Economic Conference, an important international forum of which both Russia and Hong Kong are members.

Macao—the place where two centuries ago Russians first encountered South China—is currently among the responsibilities of the Consulate-General of the Russian Federation in Hong Kong. The participation of Russian Deputy Foreign Minister Mr. Grigory Karasin in the Macao handover ceremony on December 20, 1999 was a symbolic manifestation of my country's interest in its relationship with this territory. During his July 2002 visit to Hong Kong, Igor Ivanov also visited Macao, and held talks with Mr. Edmund Ho, Chief Executive of the Administration of Macao Special Administrative Region. The two officials eagerly expressed their commitment to strengthening bilateral cooperation between Russia and Macao and also outlined various concrete measures by which this might be achieved.

The history of Russia's ties with Taiwan is relatively short by comparison with Russian links with Hong Kong and Macao. Although the Soviet Union and Japan were not formally at war, during World War II, some Soviet volunteer pilots based in Chinese territory nonetheless made audacious flights from Chongqing to Taiwan to bomb Japanese military bases. My country does, however, have very unusual ties to Taiwan. In his youth Mr. Chiang Ching-kuo, who from 1972 to 1988 headed the Taiwanese administration, studied and worked in the Soviet Union under the Russian name "Yelizarov." At that time he even joined the VKP (b)—All-Soviet Bolshevik Communist Party—and married a Russian girl, Faina Vahreva, who later became Taiwan's first lady.

After the PRC emerged in 1949 the Soviet Union unequivocally stated that Taiwan was a part of China, a position to which Moscow steadfastly adhered from then onward, never questioning the "one China" principle even at times of severe confrontation between the USSR and the PRC. The fact that in 1971 the Soviet Union wholeheartedly supported the application of the PRC to replace Taipei and represent China in the UN spoke for itself. Today non-official Russian-Taiwanese ties should be regarded as an integral part of Russia's overall policy toward China, whose crux is to strengthen Russian-Chinese strategic partnership on the basis of the 2001 Treaty of Good-Neighborliness and Friendly Cooperation. Understandably, the Russian Federation's MID keeps tight control over non-official contacts with Taiwan, which it coordinates. Within this framework, and with the support of appropriate organizational and legal infrastructure, the tireless efforts of many enthusiasts for Russian-Taiwanese exchanges on both sides have put flesh and blood on the bones of cooperation between Russia and the "Beautiful Island," so that today it encompasses practical ties in such areas as trade, investment, banking, transportation, science and technology, education, and culture.

Dr. Share's book will enable the reader to learn more of the history and future prospects of Russian relations with the "Greater China" area, Hong Kong, Macao, and Taiwan. Dr. Share's research is characterized by a solid scientific approach, scrupulous fact-finding and, most valuable of all, balanced assessments. It is to be hoped that this knowledgeable and talented scholar will continue his pathbreaking research for many years into the future.

Kirill M. Barsky, Ph.D.
Minister Counselor, Russian Embassy, Jakarta, Indonesia
(Former Chief of the Division of Chinese Foreign Policy,
Regional Problems, Taiwan, and Hong Kong)

Preface

This book has been several years in the making, and represents a personal long march through numerous archives in three different continents. Even so, it is in many ways a preliminary study that can in no sense claim to be the last word on Russian and Soviet relations with China's eastern periphery, but is only a first attempt to elucidate a fascinating yet in many ways still obscure topic. At best, the picture it gives is partial, reflecting the limitations of many of the archival resources involved. After the collapse of the Soviet Union in 1991, most Soviet archives were for the first time made available to scholars. I sought to take advantage of this situation to mine the relevant archives and gather information on a topic on which no earlier scholars had written. Almost every year from 1998, I went to Moscow to work in various archives for a month or two at a time. Initially, my research focused on the Soviet Union, Hong Kong, and the Cold War, investigating Soviet policy toward the former British crown colony of Hong Kong from 1945 to 1970.

This project relies mostly on Soviet and Russian archival records. Over time, I examined materials from assorted Russian archives. First and most obviously, I sought relevant documents in files from the AVP RF. Upon my very first visit to that archive, the Director of the Reading Room told me that there was probably little or nothing on this topic. Eventually, matters proved very different, and over time I have examined over 100 relevant files or *dela* there. With generous assistance from the Russian Consulate-General in Hong Kong and from friends and colleagues within the MID itself, I was granted exceptionally wide access to the records in the AVP RF, where archivists allowed me to examine materials dated as recently as 1987. In contrast, most Western archives, such as the American and the British, have a 30-year rule, making it virtually impossible for scholars to gain access to newer materials. Although one must remember that the MID was by no means the only agency involved in making foreign policy, this study does give a fairly comprehensive picture of its policies toward Hong Kong almost until the Soviet Union ended in 1991.

Besides the MID, the International Section of the CPSU also helped to formulate foreign policy, often even dictating policies to the MID. Each had different concerns and constituencies. On the whole, the MID tended to support the interests and needs of Soviet companies, professional diplomats, and academics, while the International Department of the CPSU was generally more representative of the preoccupations of the military and the KGB. CPSU records are held in two archives: the RGASPI (formerly known as RTsKhIDNI) for materials prior to 1952, and the RGANI (formerly known as TsKhSD) for materials after 1952, or the post-Stalin era. I never gained access to any materials from the RGANI for any year beyond 1961. Despite numerous requests, most recently in May 2004, I was informed that files from the 1960s and 1970s are still classified. This means that to date the record of the International Department of the CPSU regarding Hong Kong, Taiwan, and Macao remains closed. I also requested, but was denied access to both the TsA FSB *Rossii* (formerly known as TsA KGB SSSR), where I wished to examine potential files, especially those in the foreign intelligence section, from agents stationed in Hong Kong, Taiwan, and Macao, and the AP RF, which contains the files of the Soviet Politburo and national leaders from Lenin through Gorbachev. Without access to these two very important archives, this picture of Russian and Soviet foreign policy and activities toward the China periphery must inevitably remain incomplete until all the archives are fully open. It is impossible to predict when this is likely to occur, especially given that over the past two years, it has become significantly more difficult to gain access to certain archival materials, especially where files relating to Taiwan are concerned.

To supplement materials gleaned from Moscow, I collected numerous documents, most of which were generated by the United States Department of State and the American Consulate in Hong Kong, from the NA. I also consulted relevant Foreign Office and Colonial Office materials at the PRO.

I spent the summer of 1998 at Harvard University's Davis Center for

Russian and Eurasian Studies, where I wrote an article based on my research on Hong Kong during the Cold War era.[1] In 1999, my growing interest in this topic and appreciation of its potential impelled me to broaden my work both chronologically and geographically. I first explored Soviet and then Russian policy toward Hong Kong prior to the Cold War, as far back as the colony's very inception in the mid-nineteenth century. As I went through the Hong Kong collections in the archives, I unearthed materials—substantial for Taiwan, naturally much sparser for tiny Macao—relating to each, encouraging me to expand my work to cover those territories too. The few existing articles on Soviet policy toward Taiwan were largely based on newspaper accounts and tended to be speculative. During the late 1970s, when most of these articles were published, Soviet archival materials remained absolutely closed to all foreigners, making me the first foreigner and often the first person to work on these files. During the summers of 1999, 2000, and 2001, I went through relevant files at various Russian archives, including the AVP RI, supplementing these with materials collected from the NA as well as the PRO. From the late nineteenth century until 1917, imperial Russia had a consulate in the then Japanese colony of Formosa. Since 2003, however, all files relating to Formosa (Taiwan) have been unavailable at the AVP RI. The Director of the Reading Room informed me all their files were being microfilmed. Thus, my picture of early Taiwan-Russian relations perforce remains decidedly incomplete.[2]

Besides using materials from the Russian, British, and American archives, in 2001 and 2002, I paid a visit to Taiwan and examined relevant files at the Foreign Ministry Archive, Taipei, which granted me access to some documents, though none newer than 1962, from which, unfortunately, I learned nothing of any great significance. I also inquired whether relevant files might exist in the Ministry of National Defense, ROC Archive and the Kuomintang Party Archive, but was told that they possessed no such materials. Only when the Soviet and Taiwanese archives are each completely open will scholars be able to elucidate and understand fully the Soviet policies toward Taiwan and responses and initiatives from Taiwan that encouraged the thawing of relations between the two states.

During spring 2004, I finally went through materials at the AHM, which gave me access to materials from the Portuguese Foreign and Colonial Ministries, as well as the records of the colonial government of

Macao. They possessed no files more recent than 1943, and their extremely helpful staff believed that all relevant materials for the past 60 years had been returned to Lisbon before Macao was handed over to China in December 1999. In June 2004, I also finally inspected materials at the HK PRO, including the Hong Kong government and police records, as well as its special Carl Smith Collection. By that point, I had examined all the available relevant archival sources for this project.

Without the assistance of institutions and individuals from several countries, I could not have completed this project. In terms of financial support, I am especially grateful to the University of Hong Kong Research and Conference Grants Committee and the Hsu Long-sing Fund of the Faculty of Arts, the University of Hong Kong, for awarding me four generous grants, which allowed me to conduct research in relevant archives in several countries. Without their financial assistance, this project involving archival research done in half a dozen cities around the world would not have been possible.

I wish to thank the following institutions and their gracious staff, all of whom proved extremely helpful. I am particularly grateful to the excellent and usually overworked staff of the various Russian archives I consulted, which included the GARF; the RGASPI for its CPSU files up to 1952, and the Comintern files; the RGANI for its CPSU files after 1952; the AVP RI; the AVP RF; the RGAE; and the IFES. In Britain, staff and archivists of the PRO, and the British Library, London ably assisted me. In the United States, I relied upon the staff and archivists of the NA; the Davis Center for Russian and Eurasian Studies Collection of the H. C. Fung Library at Harvard University; the Widener Library at Harvard University; and the Memorial Library at the University of Wisconsin in Madison. In Taiwan, thanks are due to the staff of the Foreign Ministry Archive, Taipei and the Kuomintang Party Archive, Taipei. In Hong Kong, I made much use of the HK PRO and the Main Library at the University of Hong Kong. While in Macao, I received hospitable and informed assistance from the staff of the AHM.

The Russian Consulate-General in Hong Kong and the MID itself both provided invaluable assistance and support. The Russian Consulate wrote a letter of introduction, which opened doors for me to both the AVP RI and AVP RF. I am especially grateful to the former Consul-General, Dr. Konstantin Vnukov, since December 2004 Director of the Far East Department of the MID; his cultural attaché, Dr. Vladimir Shin, now Second Secretary of the Russian Embassy in Singapore; the current Consul-General in Hong Kong, Andrei N. Smorodin; and his attaché, Dmitri Prosvirkin. All have shown themselves true friends to historical scholarship and research. When I encountered some access problems, Vladislav Lukyanchuk, who worked both at the MID and at the Presidential Administration, quickly resolved them.

In Moscow, I had the good fortune to work with several outstanding research assistants: Ivan Sventsitsky, Peter Mironenko, Alexei Dokuchaev, and Olga Livshina, who helped me navigate the vagaries of the Russian archives and skim through thousands of pages of documents, and then translated innumerable materials for me. In Macao, I was blessed with another excellent research assistant, Dr. Carlos Alves, who translated Portuguese documents for me.

At the University of Hong Kong, I would like to thank my colleagues in the Department of History, especially Professor Chan Lau Kit-ching, the then head of the department, who was more than kind in permitting me to take leave for several successive years in May and June, allowing me to conduct vital research before the Russian archives closed during July for their summer break. Professor Chan also read and most insightfully critiqued several chapters.

I must express my great appreciation to the Davis Center for Russian and Eurasian Studies of Harvard University, Cambridge, Massachusetts, which very kindly made me a Visiting Associate at the Center from 1998 through 2005. Particular thanks are due especially to the Director, Professor Timothy Colton, Associate Director, Professor Marshall Goldman, and Alexei Bulanov, for all their help, and for allowing me to present some of my findings at a special seminar cohosted by Harvard University's Davis and Fairbank Centers during the summer of 2002. The Moscow office of the Davis Center also provided me with visa support, helped me gain access to the various archives and libraries, located accommodation within Moscow, and provided office support. My personal thanks are due to its Moscow Director, Ms. Maria Tarasova, for her tireless assistance.

Several individuals most generously read and made insightful comments on the manuscript at various stages: Professors Walter Pintner, Edward Judge, Vladimir Wozniuk, David Pomfret, Cathy Potter, Alexander Mansourov, Robert Koehl, Minh Ling, Richard Stites, Frank Dikötter, and Dr. Steven Luk, Director of The Chinese University Press, who has waited most patiently for this manuscript. I am grateful to the Cold War International History Project and the editors of the following journals, which published earlier drafts of chapters as articles: *Cold War History, Diplomacy & Statecraft, Tamkang Journal of International Affairs, Europe-Asia Studies* (formerly *Soviet Studies*), *The Round Table,* and *Journal of the Royal Asiatic Society*. Finally, I wish to thank the organizers of seminars at the Woodrow Wilson International Center for Scholars, Harvard University, the University of Hong Kong, the Academia Sinica, Taipei, the Association of Third World Studies, and the annual Russian-American seminars held in St. Petersburg, Russia, who allowed me to present research findings and papers, and all those participants who provided useful comments and feedback on my work in progress. All errors in fact and interpretation are nonetheless solely my own.

Last but decidedly not least, I wish to extend warm thanks to my colleague Dr. Priscilla Roberts, who first suggested this topic to me back in 1996, following a conference on the Cold War in Asia held at the University of Hong Kong. She then acted as my mentor, and assisted me in obtaining several grants to help defray my research and writing costs. As the project progressed, Dr. Roberts kindly read through each and every chapter, suggesting numerous changes, which helped to make the text both more readable and analytical. Without her assistance this book would not have been possible, and I therefore take great pleasure in dedicating it to her.

Abbreviations

AHM	*Arquivo Histórico de Macau* (Macao Historical Archive)
AP RF	Archive of the President of the Russian Federation
AVP RF	Archive of Foreign Policy of the Russian Federation
AVP RI	Archive of Foreign Policy of the Russian Empire
CCP	Chinese Communist Party
CIA	Central Intelligence Agency
COC	Chinese National Olympic Committee
CPF	Communist Party of Formosa
CPJ	Communist Party of Japan
CPSU	Communist Party of the Soviet Union
FRG	Federal Republic of Germany / West Germany
GARF	State Archive of the Russian Federation, Moscow
GDR	German Democratic Republic / East Germany
GRU	Russian-language acronym for Main Intelligence Directorate
HK PRO	Hong Kong Public Records Office
IAAF	International Association of Athletics Federations
IOC	International Olympic Committee
ILO	International Labor Organization
KGB	Russian-language abbreviation for Committee for State Security
KMT	Kuomintang / Nationalist Party
MID	Ministry of Foreign Affairs of Russia
NA	National Archives II at College Park, Maryland
NATO	North Atlantic Treaty Organization
PLA	People's Liberation Army

PRO	Public Records Office, London
PRC	People's Republic of China
RGAE	Russian State Archive of the Economy
RGANI	Russian State Archive of Contemporary History
RGASPI	Russian State Archive of Socio-Political History
ROC	Republic of China / Taiwan
SAR	Special Administrative Region
TsA FSB *Rossii*	Central Archive of the Federal Security Service
UN	United Nations
UNCHR	United Nations Commission on Human Rights
UNESCAP	United Nations Economic and Social Commission for Asia and the Pacific
UNESCO	United Nations Educational, Scientific and Cultural Organization
UNGA	United Nations General Assembly
UNSC	United Nations Security Council
USIS	United States Information Service
USSR	Union of Soviet Socialist Republics / Soviet Union (1922–1991)
VOKS	All-Union Society for Cultural Relations Abroad

List of Illustrations

Greater China and Its East Asian Neighbors

Introduction: Russian and Soviet Policy toward the China Periphery—Hong Kong, Macao, and Taiwan

Russian and Soviet dealings with the China eastern periphery—Hong Kong, Taiwan, and Macao—in the 150 years from the British capture of Hong Kong in 1841 to the collapse of the Soviet Union in 1991 were always intimately and inextricably linked to the broader international relationships among Russia, China, Great Britain, Japan, and the United States. Careful scrutiny of Russian and Soviet policies toward the periphery reveals that, far from being marginal, from the historical perspective those territories, separated and removed from the administrative control of the mainland Chinese government, serve as prisms. The light refracted through them illuminates our understanding of broader relationships among the great powers, and deepens our comprehension of such issues as competing nineteenth-century imperialisms, the evolution of early Soviet international policies toward an often hostile world, the interrelationships and conflicts among the assorted Communist Bloc powers, and great power dealings in Asia during the Cold War.

For the purposes of this volume, I have defined the China periphery, or, in more precise terms, the Chinese eastern periphery, as Hong Kong, Macao, and Taiwan. Although populated predominantly by Han Chinese and considered parts of greater China, during most of the twentieth century, all were not ruled by a mainland Chinese government, whether imperial, republican, or Communist. All are maritime territories, long exposed to international commerce and the outside world, that for much of the last century were colonies of foreign empires: Taiwan of Japan, Hong Kong of Britain, and Macao of Portugal. For each, these unique characteristics have made their history and international dealings quite different from those of China, something historians to date have rather neglected. The histories and characteristics of China's other peripheral areas—the western in Tibet and Xinjiang, and the northern in Mongolia and Manchuria—have by contrast been quite different, and should be the subject of separate studies.

At first glance, the lengthy Russian and Soviet involvement with the missing territories on China's eastern fringes might appear, despite being a source of many splendid anecdotes, almost entirely peripheral. Close examination, however, makes apparent several leading themes: the nature and limitations of nineteenth-century Russian Far Eastern imperialism; Western reactions toward the Bolshevik Revolution, both immediate and long-term; the soaring ambitions of Communist revolutionary internationalism during the 1920s and 1930s, and the manner in which, by 1930, the pursuit of narrower Soviet national bureaucratic rivalries, in the 1920s between the Comintern and the Foreign Office, during the Cold War between the Ministry of Trade and the Foreign Office, affected the making of foreign policy; the dynamics of Soviet relations with Mao's China, as the demands of that increasingly acrimonious relationship and the constraints of Communist ideological solidarity inhibited Soviet ability to exploit to the full the potential benefits to itself of China's lost territories or encourage their permanent separation from China; and the evolution, especially after Nikita Khrushchev adopted policies of peaceful coexistence, of Soviet Cold War policies toward ideologically divided states, not just China, but also Vietnam, Korea, and Germany.

Throughout their history, the Russian Empire and the successor Soviet Union understandably devoted much attention to China, Russia's largest neighbor, with a common border of some 2,000 miles. Throughout the past 200 years, trade has been a significant feature of Russian and Soviet policy. During the seventeenth century Russia expanded eastward to the Pacific Ocean and then south to Korea and the Sea of Japan, and by the mid-nineteenth century it had taken over hundreds of thousands of square miles of territory that China claimed. These lands are still sparsely populated today, and the prospect that China might reclaim that territory or massive numbers of Chinese might simply flood over the border makes Russian officials very apprehensive. While neither Tsarist Russia nor its

Soviet successor has ever fought outright wars against China, the two powers have waged military battles, most recently in 1969. The MIDs of both imperial Russia and the Soviet Union habitually devoted much of their energy and personnel to China. The Russian Embassy in China is one of the largest in the world, with an estimated approximately one thousand diplomats and their families living and working in the huge compound in central Beijing. As Russia has entered a new century, its attention to China can only be expected to increase.

Russian and Western historians alike have produced innumerable books and articles on Russian and Soviet relations with China. In 2004, the library catalog of Harvard University listed more than 1,220 separate entries on the subject in Chinese, English, Russian, German, French, Italian, and other languages. Certain topics have attracted particular attention: the influence of the CPSU on the early history of the CCP and its rival the KMT during the 1920s[1]; Soviet activities during the successive Sino-Japanese War, World War II, and Chinese Civil War[2]; the Alliance period of the 1950s[3]; and the causes of the momentous split between the two Communist giants that opened in the late 1950s and continued until the 1980s.[4] Less scholarly attention has been given to relations between Tsarist Russia and China, with most such studies devoted to the "unequal treaties" that Russia pressured Qing China to sign during the mid-nineteenth century.[5] One reason for the scarcity of books describing Tsarist relations with China may be because at this time both empires were in decline. Another reason is the shortage of Western scholars possessing the necessary linguistic abilities in both Russian and Chinese.

In both Russian and Soviet foreign affairs, the eastern periphery of China was a fairly low priority. The status of the various China periphery territories was, moreover, always somewhat anomalous. The foreign ministry of one nation usually communicates directly with its counterparts in other states. Both the MIDs of imperial Russia and the Soviet Union, for example, generally dealt with their Chinese equivalent, which during the nineteenth and twentieth centuries was usually, though not always, located in Beijing. Both Tsarist Russia and the subsequent Soviet Union, therefore, almost always recognized only one existing official government for all China—the "one China" principle—which until 1911 and after 1949 was based in Beijing, though between those years the situation was more fluid. While the Tsarist government accepted that Hong Kong and Macao were under colonial rule, Russia wistfully though unavailingly contemplated seizing the former from Britain during the Crimean War and again in the mid-1880s, ambitions reflecting broader Russian imperial designs in Asia. The Soviet Union, by contrast, never officially recognized the colonial status of Macao, Hong Kong, or Taiwan, nor after 1949 that Taiwan was independent of China. Soviet officials always treated Hong Kong and Macao as illegitimate relics of Western imperialism, condemning with equal opprobrium Great Britain's fairly recent great empire and the more historically remote but once impressive empire of Portugal. In the early decades of the twentieth century Taiwan, too, was a colony, ruled by Japan, an aggressive neighbor of Russia, that posed an increasing threat first to the Tsarist Empire, then to the interwar Soviet Union. After 1949, the island was considered a renegade province, ruled by a discredited and illegitimate regime that had lost a civil war and been driven from the mainland. Consequently, the Soviet Union never had official relations with or an embassy or consulate in Hong Kong, Macao, or Taiwan.

Perhaps reflecting the low priority in Russian and Soviet foreign policy of relations with the neglected area of the China periphery, Russian and Western historians have published very little on the subject. During the Soviet period, the Russian relationship with Taiwan was too sensitive a subject for scholarly speculation or study, and even today political constraints remain compelling. Current specialists on the island, such as Alexander Larin, Yuri Galenovich, Peter Ivanov, and Vladimir Miasnikov, restrict themselves to writing on political developments in Taiwan, and then only within certain bounds. While broadly sympathetic to Taiwan, none feels able publicly to suggest that Taiwan might become an independent nation.[6] Russia possesses even fewer specialists on Hong Kong history. Only Ivanov has written a somewhat limited full-length history of Hong Kong, which contains little on either Russian or Soviet relations with Hong Kong or the Russian community within Hong Kong, and no information whatever on the Soviet Union and Hong Kong after 1920. While Ivanov utilized the AVP RI, he was unable to examine the AVP RF, the RGANI, and the RGAE, leaning heavily for source material on the annual yearbooks published by the Hong Kong government.[7] Perhaps predictably, since the tiny enclave played so small a role in either Russian or Soviet foreign policy, Russian and Western historians have produced little or nothing on Macao. Historians have virtually ignored the development of Russian and Soviet relations with both Hong Kong and Macao, believing, like most Russians, that no such ties existed.[8] About 30 years ago, when the world became conscious of a thaw in relations between the Soviet Union and Taiwan, a few Americans wrote accounts of this development, but these were largely speculative, based primarily on newspaper articles.[9]

The present book attempts to fill the existing void and discuss the following questions. First of all, was there any discernible trend or pattern in Russian and Soviet activities and policies toward Hong Kong, Macao, and Taiwan? Was there ever a region-wide policy, or was Russian and Soviet policy more localized toward each specific territory? To what extent did Russian and Soviet contacts with Hong Kong, Taiwan, and Macao serve as examples or case studies of the manner in which an individual nation deals with another state entity, when one does not even recognize the other's existence? How and why did Russian and then Soviet policy toward the China periphery and each state change over time? How did Russian and then Soviet policy toward China impact on Russian and Soviet policies toward Hong Kong, Macao, and Taiwan, and vice versa? How did Russian and Soviet policies toward Britain impact on Russian and Soviet policies toward Hong Kong? What role did such factors as ideology, strategy, geopolitics, and economics play in affecting Russian and Soviet policy toward each state within the China periphery?

Hong Kong has been far more than just a typical colony or Chinese treaty port. From a rocky, almost deserted outpost in the mid-nineteenth century, Hong Kong's crucial location enabled the territory to develop into one of the world's most significant ports and financial centers. Its bilingual English and Chinese identity allowed Hong Kong to serve as a meeting-point for Western and Asian ideas and cultures. Its hardworking, well-educated, and predominantly middle-class population has made Hong Kong arguably one of the world's great cities. Hong Kong has also had a unique identity as a city-state under the rule of a distant colonial power, having had to coexist with and confront a huge neighboring, often unstable, and up to now, a very poor China. In that position, during the Cold War, Hong Kong served as a Western listening post so that Britain and the United States could gather otherwise unavailable intelligence on China. In contrast, Macao, while much smaller and poorer than Hong Kong, has had a long proud history dating back some 500 years. While the Soviet Union had no official diplomatic relations with either colony, comparing its *unofficial* economic, political, and cultural ties to each colony has proven fascinating. Both Hong Kong and Macao have served as case studies of Soviet policies and activities toward colonial states. Naturally, Russian and Soviet relations with each territory were impacted by Russian and Soviet relations with China, as well as Russian and Soviet relations with the colonial powers, Britain and Portugal.

Developing a relationship with Taiwan proved even more troublesome for Soviet policy makers. While much richer, more populous, and self-sufficient than either Macao or Hong Kong, Taiwan for years represented the other China, a non-Communist capitalist alternative to the PRC. How Soviet leaders managed from the 1970s to balance the often conflicting demands of ideological constraints with the potentially great economic and perhaps more problematic geopolitical rewards better relations with Taiwan seemed to promise is also a fascinating story. Torn between these opposing pressures, Soviet policy was often contradictory and unable to take full advantage of promising opportunities. During the long grim years of virtually nonexistent relations between the two Communist giants, the Soviets could have used greater ties with Taiwan as a weapon against China, but did not utilize these to anything like the degree they might have. The reasons for their failure to do so are another fascinating aspect of this little known story. Thus, while neglected, the topic of Russian and Soviet relations with the China periphery of Hong Kong, Macao, and Taiwan is a very significant story that needs telling.

Russian, Chinese, and Western historians all debate the nature of Tsarist relations with Qing China, a subject on which nineteenth-century Russian ambitions toward Hong Kong, though ultimately fruitless, shed interesting light, largely confirming the recent skeptical views of non-Russian historians. Was the relationship a friendly one, and did the series of treaties that Russia signed with China during the mid-nineteenth century differ from those treaties China signed with other European states at that time, including the agreements that ceded Hong Kong to Great Britain? Soviet and post-1991 modern Russian historians argued that, unlike the other Western powers, Russia maintained good relations with China, and in fact, claimed that Russia tried to protect China from over-reaching itself to satisfy the Western powers. Following several wars China fought, largely against Britain and France, Russia acted as a friendly intermediary and attempted to broker the best possible peace terms for a defeated China. Gratitude led China in return voluntarily to cede hundreds of thousands of square miles of territory in East Asia, including the Vladivostok area, to the Russian Empire and grant Russia numerous privileges in Manchuria, Outer Mongolia, and the northwestern Chinese province of Xinjiang.[10] Chinese and Western historians, by contrast, contend that China only reluctantly ceded that huge and rich territory to Russia. China did not voluntarily grant Russia these sweeping economic concessions. Russia's mid-nineteenth century treaties with Qing China were just as unequal as those agreements Qing China made with the other European powers.[11]

Most historians agree that China's new Republican leader, Sun Yat-sen, welcomed the Bolshevik Revolution as a new beginning in China's relations with Western powers. Sun and others in the new government hoped that the radical new Russian regime could provide a model of rapid economic development for backward China, which was also experiencing revolutionary change. A major European power was prepared to accord China equal status, a subject of particular concern to China's government given the rise of Chinese nationalism following decades of European exploitation. In 1918, the new Soviet Ambassador, Lev Karakhan, signed a treaty with China repudiating all of Russia's privileges in Manchuria, Outer Mongolia, Xinjiang province, and China proper, an agreement the Soviet government soon afterwards quietly ignored and set aside. Historians debate whether or not the Soviets ever meant to observe the terms embodied in Karakhan's treaty to seek a new relationship with China based on true equality, or whether the agreement was made merely for propaganda purposes at a time when the new Soviet regime was isolated and insecure. Soviet historians contend that Republican China, grateful for Soviet economic and military assistance and also its diplomatic help in expelling the "Western imperialists," granted the Soviets numerous special privileges in return. Bruce A. Elleman attacks these arguments as a series of myths propagated by Soviet historians, in defiance of the reality that the Soviet Union secretly extorted privileges from a divided and weak China resembling those exacted by imperial Russia half a century earlier.[12]

The 1920s were a decade of very heavy Soviet involvement in Chinese affairs. Historians still debate the degree to which the newly formed CCP was an indigenous organization, as opposed to one created by the Soviet government and its sister organization, the Comintern; and whether the CCP remained independent or was a Soviet satellite essentially following Soviet orders. Some historians, notably Conrad Brandt and Allen S. Whiting, held Moscow totally responsible for its birth,[13] while the British historian S. A. Smith followed the approach of Benjamin Isadore Schwartz and Maurice J. Meisner in the late 1960s and stressed the CCP's indigenous origins, arguing that various factors permitted the CCP to maintain extensive autonomy vis-à-vis the Soviet government and the Comintern.[14] Using recently opened Soviet archives, the Norwegian Odd Arne Westad and the Russian Alexander Pantsov followed this perspective, and both argued that throughout the decade, Soviet control over the CCP was tenuous.[15] On the other hand, John W. Garver contended that up to 1935, the Comintern effectively controlled the CCP. In fact, Garver argued that CCP policy followed every twist and turn the Comintern dictated, regardless of how those directives affected China.[16] Virtually all historians conceded that Soviet control or influence was catastrophic for the CCP. In 1926 and 1927, Soviet operatives ordered and financed uprisings in several Chinese cities, all of which failed and brought the deaths of more than 100,000 workers and Party activists and leaders, almost causing the destruction of the CCP. During this crucial formative decade, Soviet foreign policy turned inward and sought to promote Soviet national interests, even when these might conflict with or even prove detrimental to Chinese revolutionary interests.

Between the world wars, the twists and turns of evolving Soviet foreign policy intimately affected Communist attitudes toward and activities in Hong Kong, a colonial city Soviet officials initially viewed as a promising revolutionary base, then more in the light of a venue for trade and investment, and eventually as a useful potential bastion against hostile Japanese power. This progression apparently rather neatly encapsulated the changing faces of broader Soviet international policy between the wars, as Soviet national interests came to bulk ever larger under Josef Stalin and ideological considerations lost their initial salience. During the 1920s, Soviet operatives were undoubtedly active in Hong Kong, and played some role in the turbulent strikes of that decade, developments which were also related to broader Chinese resentment of Western colonialism and special privileges elsewhere in China. Comintern operatives also sought, largely unavailingly, to encourage revolutionary activities in Japanese-controlled Taiwan. At no time between the wars, however, were either the British officials who controlled Hong Kong, their Portuguese counterparts in nearby Macao, or the Japanese in Taiwan, particularly sympathetic to or tolerant of Soviet activities within those territories, and suspected Communists, whether indigenous or Soviet-trained, faced harsh repression. Even so, between the wars Hong Kong served as something of a haven for radical young Chinese, including Soong Ching-ling (Madame Sun Yat-sen) and those Moscow-leaning radicals associated with her, and, for a while, Ho Chi Minh and other future Southeast Asian Communist leaders.[17]

During the 1930s, the Soviet Union faced the increasingly militaristic and expansionist policies of Nazi Germany and the Japanese Empire, while China's efforts to defend itself against an aggressive Japan had by 1937 erupted into a full-scale war. That same year the Soviet Union and the Comintern pressured the Chinese Communists, who had reorganized under Mao Zedong, into a new anti-Japanese alliance with the Nationalist government headed by Chiang Kai-shek. Garver contended that, while Mao agreed to an alliance with the Nationalists, by 1935, he had successfully broken the bonds of Soviet control over the CCP, and from that date on, the CCP acted largely as an independent nationalistic Communist party. Mao repeatedly defied Comintern policies, while presenting a public image of loyalty. A German historian, Dieter Heinzig, also stressed that the CCP began its independent course by adapting Soviet-style Marxism-Leninism to exhibit Chinese characteristics, a development especially marked when for years CCP leaders had few or no communications with the Soviets. Heinzig further pointed out that Stalin and Mao differed over the crucial issue of how hard to hit the Japanese. Stalin urged that Mao concentrate entirely on fighting the Japanese in order to expel them from China, whereas Mao believed he should preserve his military strength for the inevitable battle against the Nationalists.[18] In September 1939, Germany invaded Poland and ignited full-scale war in Europe. In December 1941, the European and Asian conflicts merged into World War II, pitting Germany, Italy, and Japan against the United States, Great Britain, the Soviet Union, and China.

When World War II ended in 1945, China quickly became embroiled in civil war between the Nationalists and the Communists, from which the CCP emerged victorious, expelled the Nationalists from the mainland to Taiwan, and founded the PRC in 1949. Some historians argued that the Communist victory was due to a popular rebellion against social injustice, misgovernment, and foreign domination. Professor Odd Arne Westad, however, noted that the historiography of the Chinese Revolution neglected the role international relations, particularly the emerging Cold

War and the Soviet-American rivalry, played in the Communist victory. Their competition in China was one of many arenas in the global conflict. One major finding in his book was the importance of foreign policy in the revolutionary strategy of the CCP.[19] Professor Westad's recent work, *Decisive Encounters*, focused on the Civil War period. He contended that the KMT possessed numerous advantages over the CCP in 1945. However, within a few years, the KMT squandered most of its advantages, while Mao managed to survive, and then, taking advantage of Chiang's failures, launched his military attacks. During the late 1940s, Soviet influence increased considerably in the structure of the CCP. Soviet advisers and weaponry played a major role in the Communist victory in 1949.[20] At that time, Soviet officials expected and even encouraged the Chinese Communists to take Hong Kong and Macao from Britain and Portugal, advice that Mao Zedong and his followers rejected.

Until the 1960s Chinese and Soviet historians alike stressed the absence of any conflicts or problems between the CCP and the Soviet Union, which, they alleged, led them to conclude a "firm and unshakable alliance" in February 1950. Heinzig has utilized Soviet archives extensively to refute this "myth," pointing out that ever since the 1920s significant differences had existed between the two Communist parties. According to Heinzig, rather than giving exclusive support to the CCP, after World War II ended, the Soviets continued to accord diplomatic recognition, as well as financial and military aid, to the Nationalists, an action that infuriated Mao. China learned not to side too closely with any great power, so that no great power would be able to manipulate China.[21] Well before the conclusion of the Sino-Soviet Treaty of Friendship and Alliance in 1950, therefore, the groundwork for the later split between the two Communist superpowers had been laid.[22]

Whatever their nationality, most historians consider the relatively short period from 1953 to 1956 or 1957 as the high-water mark of Sino-Soviet relations. During this period, the Soviets sent China large amounts of financial, military, and technical assistance and, while some problems arose, both sides made great efforts to collaborate. Yet, discord once more emerged between the two Communist giants, and the "unshakeable and glorious alliance" soon exhibited serious problems.[23] While far from the only factor involved, events on the Chinese periphery had something to do with this. While historians still differ as to the details, there seems little doubt that the Second Taiwan Strait Crisis (1958–1959) contributed substantially to the Sino-Soviet split, as the Chinese first provoked a major international crisis that threatened nuclear war with the United States and, having obtained Soviet support, afterwards backed down. Concurrently, Nikita Khrushchev's readiness to consider recognizing the existence of two Chinese states, the mainland and Taiwan, a tactic he also contemplated with respect to Vietnam, Korea, and Germany, irritated and alarmed Mao Zedong's government.[24]

The rift, first secret and then overt, that developed between the Soviet Union and China was one of the most significant events in the post–World War II world. Historians have debated which country and leader bore greater responsibility for the collapse of the alliance. Russian historians have generally blamed Mao and his "reckless policies," whereas Chinese scholars have usually blamed the Soviet Union and its leader, Nikita Khrushchev. Most Western historians believed that the Soviet Union and the PRC enjoyed sufficient ideological affinities to make them natural allies, but that as each came to recognize their own national interests, they drifted apart, and the traditional pattern of rivalry and mistrust between China and the Soviet Union reemerged.[25] Heinzig believed the breakdown was due to the coincidence of several factors: a poor personal relationship between Mao and Khrushchev; conflicts over how best to handle India, Taiwan, and the United States, with Mao favoring a more uncompromising hard-line policy; ideological differences that emerged after the Soviet Union began its campaign of de-Stalinization in 1956; and nationalism within each country.[26] Westad placed most of the blame for the alliance's collapse on Mao Zedong. "Understanding Mao's ideological development is essential to grasp how, when, and why the split occurred. Mao increasingly believed the progress of socialism was sabotaged in China, and that he had to jettison the close alliance if his ideas of continuous revolution were to triumph in China."[27] While the Soviet Union attempted to ease relations with the West, Mao radicalized the Chinese Revolution, embarking first on the Great Leap Forward economic campaign of the late 1950s, and then, from the mid-1960s, on the Cultural Revolution. By 1963, the breakdown had become irreversible and very public, as the two states presented their dispute to the outside world as a clash of two competing Marxist-Leninist ideologies. By 1969, military forces from each side were engaged in significant clashes along their long border, and, at one stage, full-scale war seemed not just possible, but highly likely. Whatever some Sovietologists may have wished, no longer could Western specialists describe Communism as a monolithic movement, as both countries denounced each other as revisionist and worse, both competing for the allegiances of Communist parties worldwide.

Post-1960 Soviet policies toward Hong Kong and Taiwan provide additional illumination on the Sino-Soviet split, and the limitations upon Soviet freedom of action that the demands of ideological solidarity imposed. Although, during the 1960s, Khrushchev and Soviet publications repeatedly condemned China for failing to recapture colonial Hong Kong, Soviet officials nonetheless refused to recognize British control of the territory, even as they rather ineffectively explored opportunities for trade and investment there. The British, whose Cold War policies were in any case anti-Soviet, were moreover unwilling to follow any policies that might gratuitously irritate the mainland Chinese government, and therefore actively discouraged any significant Soviet involvement or presence in Hong Kong. Although the ROC government in Taiwan was willing to flirt with the Soviets in the 1970s and 1980s and showed some responsiveness to overtures regarding enhanced trade and investment, Taiwan leaders were not prepared to jettison their relationship, however strained, with the United States, still their greatest patron, while the Soviets were likewise never willing to ignore ideological solidarity with China to the point of contemplating anything approaching official recognition of either British control of Hong Kong or the KMT government of Taiwan.

Throughout the 1970s Sino-Soviet relations remained icy. Only during the 1980s did their relations begin to revive, due to several factors, especially, most historians agree, the switch in both countries to more pragmatic leaders, Deng Xiaoping and Mikhail Gorbachev, each of whom sought to ease international tensions and improve his country's relations around the globe. Gorbachev reduced the huge Soviet troop levels along the Sino-Soviet border, withdrew all Soviet forces from Afghanistan, repudiated the Soviet policy of intervention against "renegade Communist states" expressed in the 1968 Brezhnev Doctrine, and sought to treat China as an equal. China under Deng focused primarily upon economic development. By the time the Soviet Union collapsed in late 1991, Russian relations with China had returned to normal. At present, they are at their best in almost half a century. The Cold War thaw and improving Sino-Russian relations both greatly facilitated much enhanced Soviet involvement in Hong Kong and Macao, including the opening of a consulate in Hong Kong and growing investment in both territories, and substantially increased Soviet trade with Taiwan.

While Russian and Soviet relations with the China periphery have been somewhat neglected, they were nonetheless significant. Newly opened Russian sources, where 200 files of varying sizes contain more than 1,000 documents within several archives devoted to Hong Kong, Macao, and Taiwan, present a Russian perspective on various developments in Hong Kong, Taiwan and Macao, and disprove past beliefs that those places played virtually no role in Russian and Soviet foreign policy in East Asia, and vice versa. Russian interest in the region was deep, dating back 200 years, to the early nineteenth century. For economic, political, and military reasons alike, Russian policy makers demonstrated significant interest in and concern with the activities of the British, Portuguese, Japanese, Americans, and Chinese in the China periphery. These newly available materials also add a new chapter in the history of the Cold War, revealing certain continuities between Russian and Soviet policy in the region, regardless of ideology. Informed study of Russian and Soviet relations toward Hong Kong, Macao, and Taiwan, the only ethnic Chinese territories not ruled by the PRC during the Cold War, "demarginalizes" the China periphery, suggesting how Russo-Chinese relations in these three territories intersected with the larger and much better known historical narrative.

1

Along the Fringes of "The Great Game": Imperial Russia and Hong Kong, 1841–1914

Hong Kong, nestled along the southeast coast of the South China Sea, has long been renowned as an exotic locale, a major port for British naval and merchant ships, and an entrepôt for trade between Britain and South China. Increasing trade with Guangzhou (Canton) and the surrounding Guangdong province, which began in the late eighteenth century, led Great Britain to seek a permanent presence in the region for its ships and merchants. Victory over China during the First Opium War from 1839 to 1842 brought Britain the small island of Hong Kong. In 1860, a second military victory over China won Britain the Kowloon Peninsula, immediately across Hong Kong harbor, which protected its control of Hong Kong Island. Finally, in 1898, during the Qing dynasty's last decline, by an unequal treaty imposed on China, Britain forced the cession of a 99-year lease of the much larger New Territories and numerous offshore islands. In all, the tiny crown colony amounted to no more than 500 square miles, but its significance and fame greatly surpassed its minuscule dimensions, as it became one of Asia's and the world's most renowned cities, multilingual, multicultural, and unique.[1]

Russian relations with British Hong Kong dated back virtually to its foundation. The nineteenth-century relationship between Tsarist Russia and British Hong Kong in some ways paralleled that of the post-1945 period. Until the end of the nineteenth century, liberal Britain was arguably Russia's foremost enemy, just as 50 years later the United States emerged as the new ideological rival to the Soviet Union. The ideological differences separating British and Tsarist political cultures undoubtedly had an impact even as far afield as Hong Kong. By the late nineteenth century, as the electoral franchise in Great Britain expanded to include virtually all adult males, British political leaders could not ignore public opinion. An increasingly literate British public read numerous anti-Russian newspaper articles, which led many in Britain and its colonies to abhor Russia's political system and consider the Tsarist regime a stifling, secretive, and intolerant autocracy ruling over a huge mass of drunken, ignorant peasants and bent on the ceaseless pursuit of an expansionist foreign policy that often challenged established British colonies and interests.[2] An ideological dimension developed, in which a liberal, capitalist, and largely democratic power confronted an autocratic, predominantly state-driven, still semi-feudal economy. Again an observer notes the parallels to a century later, with British perspectives on the Soviet Union's government and people. As Tsarist Russia continued its expansionist policy in East Asia, in the words of an American President nearly a hundred years later, Britain increasingly viewed it as an "evil empire." Indeed, the continuities between British attitudes toward Tsarist Russia and the Soviet Union over the past two centuries were matched by similar trends in Tsarist and Soviet policies toward Britain.

The Russian government routinely sent all its embassies and consulates the names of thousands of foreigners who should be denied visas to enter the Russian Empire. Most were Austrians, Italians, Turks, Persians, and Germans, from countries with which Tsarist Russia had poor relations during the late nineteenth and early twentieth centuries. The lists also included political opponents of Russia, such as known anarchists and socialists, and social undesirables, such as foreign prostitutes. Each list, which usually numbered anything from 50 to several hundred names, gave the age, name, occupation, and a brief description of each banned individual. Some Chinese were included, among them possibly individuals resident in Hong Kong, though these documents never identified their precise place of origin or the reason for denying them a visa.[3] The British government held that the existence of these lengthy lists of alleged undesirables only enhanced the Russian Empire's already unfavorable reputation.

In many respects, a Cold War raged a century ago on the political, ideological, economic, military, and cultural fronts between the leader of the liberal "Free World" and an essentially pre-capitalist and authoritarian Russian state which was perceived as threatening British imperial interests in India and elsewhere in Asia.[4] Late nineteenth-century Russian expansion in East Asia seriously alarmed Britain, just as Soviet expansion in East Asia subsequently did. During the mid-nineteenth century, Hong Kong even feared the Russian Far East Fleet might launch a sea-borne invasion. However, during the Cold War's height in the late 1940s and 1950s, never again did Hong Kong believe it faced such a potential Russian or Soviet threat. From the later nineteenth to the late twentieth centuries, Russian visitors to Hong Kong were often accused of spying, and carefully scrutinized by the Royal Hong Kong Police.[5] Only growing fear of Germany persuaded Britain to sign the Anglo-Russian Convention of 1907 settling the two countries' colonial disputes.

There was one major difference between British Hong Kong's relationship with Tsarist Russia and that with the Soviet Union. From 1860 onward Tsarist Russia had a consulate in Hong Kong, which reported regularly to St. Petersburg. Although the Soviet Union made several attempts to do so, it never opened a consulate in Hong Kong or established a permanent diplomatic presence there, forcing it to observe developments there and even—after the Sino-Soviet split brought the closing of its consulate in Guangzhou in the mid-1960s—in South China from a distance. This naturally made for a qualitative difference in the nature of Tsarist and Soviet reporting on Hong Kong, with imperial Russian dispatches from Hong Kong normally providing more substantive, detailed, and informed material than was consistently available to Soviet bureaucrats. Russian officials based in Hong Kong demonstrated considerable interest in the territory, commenting frequently to St. Petersburg in numerous reports on the colony's geopolitical value, strategic location, and active commercial functions.[6] The Hong Kong section of records from the Russian Consulate in Hong Kong covers the period 1857 to 1921, but concentrates heavily on the early twentieth century. Simply browsing through the fairly thin Hong Kong catalog at the AVP RI can be very revealing. Only three files cover the first 40 years of Russian relations with Hong Kong, whereas hundreds deal with the next two decades, an index of growing Russian interest in East Asia. The nineteenth-century Tsarist files cover Russian problems with the Royal Hong Kong Police, trade issues, proclamations from the MID of imperial Russia, and consular reports. Their twentieth-century counterparts deal with momentous events, including the Russo-Japanese War, World War I, the Revolution of 1917, and the Russian Civil War.[7] Two or three files from the large London Russian Embassy collection also raise certain Hong Kong–related matters, including plagues, overcrowded living conditions, and British policies in the territory.[8]

From the time Hong Kong Island was annexed in the mid-nineteenth century, the great powers, including Britain and Russia, were trying to open up China and Japan.[9] In June 1853, Rear Admiral Evfim Putyatin, on his way to Japan as head of a mission to establish Russian influence there, stopped in Hong Kong for two weeks to rest and organize his expedition. In 1854, Count Nikolai Muraviev located the mouth of the Amur River.[10] Less than a dozen years after Great Britain took Hong Kong, it was at war with the Russian Empire. While most of the fighting took place in the Black Sea region, especially the Crimean Peninsula, the conflict also had a Pacific theater. Britain considered the outbreak of war an opportunity to counter and undermine Russian influence in East Asia. The combined British and French fleet enjoyed significant superiority over the Russian Far East Fleet, and could menace Russian positions. Upon the declaration of war in spring of 1854, a British squadron left Hong Kong to move against Russian territories in Northeast Asia in the Amur River basin and Kamchatka. In August 1854, the Anglo-French fleet mounted a disastrously unsuccessful attack on the Russian garrison on the Kamchatka Peninsula northeast of Japan, suffering large losses.[11] Hong Kong, almost the only British outpost in East Asia, was left virtually undefended. Soon after the British warships departed, Hong Kong received word that a large Russian fleet was in the area. Defenses were quickly erected, and signal stations constructed at each end of the island to give some advance warning should Russian ships approach the territory. A volunteer militia, mostly drawn from the small British civilian male population, which could if necessary support the even smaller 400-man British garrison on Hong Kong, was formed, trained, and armed. Meanwhile, Governor John Bowring appealed to the Foreign Office to station more troops and at least one permanent warship to protect the colony. Although the Russian fleet never attacked the territory, the uncertainty made many residents extremely nervous, and Hong Kong's relative defenselessness led some inhabitants—both British and Chinese—to hide their valuables.[12] Several months later, on February 11, 1855, British settlers held a public meeting on how best to bolster the war effort. They drew up a petition of support, signed by several hundred British men in Hong Kong and other cities along the China coast, including Guangzhou and Shanghai, and also decided to send London a monetary contribution of some 6,800 pounds sterling.[13]

Once the war had ended, relations soon improved. Only a dozen years after Hong Kong's establishment, the Russian Empire, recognizing Hong Kong's potential significance, sought to open commercial and diplomatic ties with the territory. In 1857, Admiral Putyatin returned there to negotiate a treaty with the British to grant Russia free trade access. Hostile to Britain and one of a group of proponents of a strong Russian naval presence in East Asia, Putyatin was perhaps not the ideal choice to handle this mission, but he nonetheless won for Russian merchants the same free trade provisions Britain had earlier granted to French and Americans.[14] In addition, even though Hong Kong was still only a rocky outpost inhabited by a few thousand people, Russia already sought a formal diplomatic presence there. On April 23, 1859, the MID proposed establishing a full consulate.

Interestingly, the first Russian consuls in Hong Kong were Americans, not Russians, and until the late nineteenth century all Russian consuls there were non-Russian nationals, either Americans or Germans, mostly businessmen, reflecting Russia's good relations with those two countries. From 1860 to 1890, the first 30 years of the formal Russian presence in Hong Kong, not one Russian became Consul. Russian records gave no reason for this situation, which at this time was by no means unique to Russia. Many states appointed non-citizens to act as consuls, often in an honorary and unpaid capacity, more in prestigious recognition of good service than as a professional diplomatic assignment.[15] The first Russian Consul was Silas E. Burrows, who had intervened on behalf of Russian sailors captured by the British and interned in Hong Kong during the Crimean War. A letter addressed to the Far East Department of the imperial Russia's MID spoke well of Burrows and declared he had even been granted the honor of a personal meeting with Emperor Alexander II. "While Burrows was old and infirm, it would be a good idea to make him consul. Burrows wanted very badly to serve Russia once more. He wants no reward or salary, and would consider it a great service to serve Alexander II."[16] Responding to this strong recommendation, in April 1860, the MID of imperial Russia appointed Burrows Russia's first Consul, simultaneously naming as Vice Consul George F. Heard, another

American who ran a trading company in Hong Kong. Until the century ended non-Russians continued to serve as consuls and vice consuls. Not until April 7, 1900, did an ethnic Russian, Mikhail Ustinov, become Consul, followed in 1903 by another Russian, Count Bologovsky. The last Tsarist Consul, another Baltic German nobleman, Vladimir Ottonovich von Ettingen (also spelled d'Oettigen), appointed in 1910, remained in post for the next tumultuous decade, only leaving the territory in 1920.[17]

Despite their high initial hopes, the Russian presence in the territory remained very small. The 1880 census recorded Hong Kong's total population as 160,402, of whom only 8,000 were Westerners and a mere seven Russians.[18] The territory's geographical remoteness from Western Europe also impeded efforts by the essentially European Russian government to project its influence there. On October 12, 1884, the Consul remarked how difficult he found it in Hong Kong to obtain news and orders from either the Russian Embassy in London or the MID in St. Petersburg. He therefore unavailingly requested the MID to shorten the lengthy lines of communication by transferring jurisdiction over the Consulate from the London Embassy to the Russian Mission in Beijing.[19] The Russian Consul's main duties were to increase trade between Hong Kong and Russia, and to handle any problems arising when Russian ships and sailors visited Hong Kong. In reports to St. Petersburg, consuls frequently noted the important role Hong Kong already played in general East Asian trade, but regretted the limited nature of the Russian Empire's own commercial dealings with Hong Kong.[20] Not until 1909 did a Russian trading company, *Vostok*, establish an office in Hong Kong. Only seven of 745 ships that arrived in Hong Kong the previous year were Russian. In the early twentieth century, Russian consuls argued that an increase in trade with enterprises in Hong Kong would be highly advantageous to Russia, but warned that existing Russian businesses there amounted to little more than a few Russian restaurants.[21]

Besides promoting trade between Russia and Hong Kong, handling problems that Russians might encounter in the territory, and issuing visas, within Hong Kong the Russian Consulate publicized developments inside Russia to members of Hong Kong's foreign community. The other European representatives in Hong Kong showed Russia appropriate respect. For example, in March 1881, after Alexander II was assassinated in St. Petersburg, the Russian Consul held a memorial service, which all foreign consuls attended.[22] On a happier occasion, Governor Frederick Lugard sent the Russian Consul a letter of congratulations on the name day of the new Tsar, Nicholas II.[23]

Even if the Russian presence in Hong Kong was limited, the Russian government nonetheless demonstrated appreciable interest in political, social, and economic developments in the colony. Overall, each year the Russian Consul sent St. Petersburg several detailed eight- to ten-page reports on events likely to interest the Russian government, enclosing clippings from the English language Hong Kong press and occasionally translations into Russian of accounts from the Hong Kong Chinese press. The Ministry of the Interior and the MID sometimes asked the Consulate for specific information, especially data on periodic outbreaks of plague and the increase of opium smoking in the territory. In 1901, for example, the Russian government requested information on the Black Death epidemic in Hong Kong, including the number of cases and deaths, the medical treatment, and the colony's general situation at that time.[24] Both then and again during another plague outbreak in 1908, the Consul reported back that overall its high temperatures and humidity made the territory a very unhealthy place to reside. In a revealing commentary on racist attitudes toward the Chinese, the Consulate only compiled lists of the casualty rates among Westerners, even though most infected individuals were Chinese, which the Consul ascribed to the very crowded housing conditions in Chinese districts, further suggesting that the Chinese contracted the plague by eating infected rats.[25]

Another disturbing development the Russian Consul mentioned was the growth of opium smoking in the territory. While most opium users were Chinese, increasing numbers of Europeans also used the drug, and by 1909 about 13 percent of the entire population regularly smoked opium. According to Consul Tiedemann, the British government opposed the spread of opium use and even passed laws restricting its use, while whenever possible the Royal Hong Kong Police shut down opium dens.[26] Another potential concern for the Consulate regarding Russian relations with Britain was the large number of Chinese emigrants boarding Russian ships in Hong Kong bound for the United States and the Caribbean in 1874, whom the British stated should not be allowed to travel without proper documentation.[27]

Despite encountering occasional problems in British-controlled territory, and even though their country's economic stake there remained small, from an early date Russian officials believed that in strategic terms Hong Kong had potential to be both valuable and significant to their country, and some undoubtedly at least fantasized of seizing the territory. Russian interest aroused genuine British concern. In 1872, Thomas Francis Wade, the British Minister in Beijing, warned London: "There is one place on this side of the world, which in the event of a misunderstanding, Russia would deal a very serious blow to our interests, I do mean not in India, but in Hong Kong."[28] He subsequently suggested that, should Britain and Russia go to war, Russian warships would almost certainly enter Hong Kong harbor and "levy a 'contribution' on the Hong Kong banks." Wade therefore urged that the British government, in order to adequately protect the colony from attack and conquest by the Russian Far East Fleet, seize more Chinese territory across from Hong Kong Island, augment the small garrison, and station a permanent fleet in Hong Kong. Wade, who had spent years in Hong Kong as an adviser to the colonial government, urged that, unless Britain could adequately protect Hong Kong, it should return the territory to China. Foreign Secretary Lord Kimberley, however, disagreed entirely with this view, and declared that in no circumstances should Britain consider restoring Hong Kong to China.[29]

In an effort to improve relations, from September 1872 until the following April, Grand Duke Alexis Aleksandrovich, the fourth son of Emperor Alexander II and a career naval officer, paid a lengthy visit to Hong Kong and Southeast Asia. He first arrived in Hong Kong on the imperial steamer *Svetlana* on September 12, staying at Government House for ten days as the guest of Governor Sir Arthur Kennedy, who wined and dined him and two accompanying Russian admirals in a "series of receptions, dinners, and fetes." According to the American Consul, the Grand Duke spoke warmly of the United States and his earlier stay there.[30] In mid-January, the Grand Duke and his party spent another two weeks in Hong Kong at Government House, leaving on January 30 for Manila in the Philippines, but returning yet again from February 17 until March 3, when they finally left Hong Kong for good, bound for Shanghai and other ports in East and Southeast Asia. Governor Kennedy reported "his highness was treated with every mark of respect by the inhabitants of Hong Kong during his stay."[31] His repeated return visits to the colony suggest that, despite the often-strained relations between Britain and Russia, high-ranking individual visitors could enjoy a stay and be well entertained.

Such high-profile social contacts notwithstanding, British fears of a potential Russian attack were not entirely groundless. Reporting in March 1880 to the MID, Consul Reimers noted that Hong Kong's excellent strategic position would make it a fine base for the Russian navy. He further noted that, except for the occasional presence of the British fleet, Hong Kong was largely defenseless; that its defensive fortifications were still under construction; and as yet there was no large British garrison.[32] Hong Kong officials remained suspicious of Russian activities in the territory. On one occasion, in March 1882, the Hong Kong government claimed, without supplying any evidence, that Russian agents kidnapped Chinese coolies and then shipped them overseas.[33]

In 1885, a growing British-Russian dispute over Afghanistan and Central Asia adversely affected the situation in Hong Kong. Deteriorating British relations with Russia "caused great excitement in the colony." Fearing a possible naval attack, the British government urged the naval and military authorities in Hong Kong to take defensive measures. Two suspected Russian spies left Hong Kong, one for Singapore, the other for Japan, causing the Hong Kong government to send a telegram to Singapore alerting the authorities there.[34] Urging that reason prevail, Hong Kong Governor Sir George Bowen refused to credit Russians with "almost satanic astuteness and malevolence" and believed most of his countrymen exaggerated in thinking all Russian visitors and residents in the territory to be spies. Reporting to the Colonial Office in 1885, Bowen nonetheless discussed the Hong Kong military position should war erupt between Russia and Britain. He warned that the garrison consisted of only 1,000 British troops and 200 Sikhs, and that the existing British warships in Hong Kong harbor would not suffice to defend it against a Russian fleet including two ironclads, four corvettes, and four gunboats.[35] During this tense period, Bowen stated "most leading figures in China and Japan also recognized that Russia was their main enemy. If British power was reduced in East Asia, then China and Japan would be exposed to fresh aggression from the north (Russia)." He further noted that the Japanese closely monitored the movements of the Russian fleet operating out of Vladivostok. Affirming that war could be near, Acting Russian Consul Max Grôte informed the Hong Kong Governor that the entrance to Vladivostok harbor was closed, and non-Russian ships must use Russian pilots to enter the port. Revealing the depth of poor relations, Governor Bowen sent a further note to the Colonial Office enclosing an English translation of an extremely negative Chinese-language Hong Kong newspaper article on Russia and the Russian people, which he stated was highly typical of the average Hong Kong Chinese view of the Russian government.[36]

Some Russian intellectuals were equally critical of their own government's colonial endeavors in the Far East. A few years later, in October 1890, the Russian writer Anton Chekhov visited Hong Kong for 80 hours, as he returned by sea from a lengthy fact-finding trip to the island of Sakhalin, then a Russian penal colony, followed by a stay in Vladivostok. According to one source, while in Hong Kong Chekhov patronized a brothel and availed himself of the services of a cheerful Japanese prostitute.[37] Russian colonial administration of its Far Eastern territories had not impressed Chekhov, as he told a friend, complaining "of our eastern coast in general, with its fleets, tasks, and Pacific reveries, I have just one thing to say: scandalous poverty—poverty, ignorance, and meanness that can drive a person to despair! One honest man for every ninety-nine thieves sullying the Russian name." Hong Kong, by contrast, he admired, writing later of his experiences there:

> The harbor was just lovely, and I had never before seen so much sea traffic, not even in pictures. Splendid roads, horse-drawn trams, a railway up the mountain, museums, botanical gardens, and everywhere you look you see evidence of the Britons' tender concern for the welfare of their employees; there is even a seamen's club. I rode *jinrikshas*, bought all kinds of junk from Chinamen, and felt indignant when I heard my fellow Russian travelers censure the British for exploiting other nationalities. I thought, yes, the British are exploiting the Chinese and Indians, but they have given them roads, plumbing, museums, and Christianity, while you exploit people too, but what have you given them?[38]

Over 50 years later, the Soviet-era editors of the 20-volume collected edition of Chekhov's works published between 1944 and 1951 considered these sensitive reflections by a major writer, together with those relating his sexual experiences, so controversial and unflattering to Russian pride that they were omitted from this supposedly inclusive collection.[39]

Just as before, with war eventually averted and relations improved, reconciliation was once again marked by the descent of a second Russian royal prince on Hong Kong. On April 4–5 (Old Style March 23–24), 1891, the Tsarevich Nicholas (the future Nicholas II) visited Hong Kong as part of a grand tour of East Asia. The future Tsar was accompanied by his cousin, Crown Prince George of Greece, and an entourage including Prince Esper Ukhtomskii, whose extensive diary describing their travels was later published in Russian, French, and English. On April 4 (Old Style March 23), as the Grand Duke Nicholas's party steamed in by sea from Saigon aboard the Russian naval vessel *Pamiat Azova*, the British authorities and a Japanese gunboat welcomed them with thunderous gun salutes. Three officials from the Russian embassy in Beijing, Staff Colonel D. V. Pootiata, and two younger diplomats who were scholarly experts on China, immediately came on board, to accompany Nicholas on his travels in China. The governor, Sir Charles des Voeux, and Major General Digby Barker, commander of the British garrison, both arrived to pay their respects, as did the commanders of two Chinese gunboats that had been detailed to escort Nicholas during his travels in China. Nicholas and his entourage stayed the night at Government House, to which he was escorted by an honor guard of the Argyll and Sutherland Highlanders, before traveling onward to Guangzhou, passing Macao en route.[40]

Ukhtomskii, a strong proponent of an expanded Russian presence in the Pacific region, ideally as the protector of the Chinese Empire, commented rather enviously how Hong Kong, "that creation of Western energy in the seas of the Far East, presents a combination of luxury on shore with an unusual animation in the harbour." He found the city's commercial prosperity outstanding. "It is enough to say that the annual commercial transactions of the place amount to forty-five million pounds sterling, while more than half of the vessels that come here fly the British flag. The income of the colony is increasing, not daily, but hourly." He further noted how, even though businessmen of all nationalities were "free to carry on business in Hong-kong, yet it is only its clever and masterful founders that hold economic sway in it." British merchants handled four times as much trade as all other nationalities combined. "[E]nergetic, industrial England had been the first to fasten on China and exploit her natural riches in all ways." He noted that the city was garrisoned by 4,000 troops and protected by a powerful British naval squadron, supported by a specially constructed yard, wharf, and arsenal, while in recent years the British authorities had spent £400,000 to improve its defenses. Yet, even though the harbor on the north side of the island was considered "impregnable," an enemy expedition could land on its south side. Uhktomskii also believed that, while racial relations were superficially peaceful, Chinese resentment of foreigners was "still smouldering under the ashes," so that in Hong Kong itself "the police carefully watch the harbour at night to see that no boat should take passengers without showing its number and marks, for there have been too many sudden attacks and brutal murders committed for purposes of robbery by rowers taking careless foreigners on board steamers." He recounted various earlier episodes of "enmity between the Chinese and the Europeans" from the 1850s onward, one reason why the British authorities relied on "several hundred energetic and devoted Sikhs" and had introduced police boats to pursue "criminals and smugglers." Even so, Ukhtomskii believed that a mass rising of the Chinese in Hong Kong against the Europeans, who would be either "poisoned or starved," would probably "take place sooner or later."[41]

Ideally, Ukhtomskii would have wished for a personal meeting and interview between the Chinese emperor and the future Tsar, the young Grand Duke Nicholas, since he thought that "between us and China there should be no barriers of a narrow, formal character." Earlier on this voyage, he had already "reflect[ed] in what a marked degree we Russians, as regards our prestige in Asia, voluntarily resign to every comer from Europe our historical part and our inherited mission as leaders of the East." European colonists had, he believed, "dethroned and oppressed the East," yet they could never be truly at home there, whereas "any Asiatic borderland soon becomes a home for a Russian." For 200 years, he claimed, Russia had deliberately eschewed "using Asia as a tool for the advancement of the selfish interests of modern, so-called civilized, mankind, [which] was repugnant to us." He anticipated "the coming supremacy of Russia in the greatest and most populous of continents," suggesting that his country had an almost mystical world role to play, especially as it settled Siberia and became an ever expanding presence on the Pacific. He believed that ultimately the Asian peoples would rebel against western rule and turn for protection to Russia, which would then become "a great power uniting the West with the East."[42]

Ukhtomskii's outlook suggests that late nineteenth-century British fears of Russian designs on Hong Kong were by no means unfounded, apprehensions the publication—with Nicholas II's approval—of his diary in English in 1896 may well have reinforced. Admittedly, in February 1894, the Colonial Secretary, the colony's second highest ranking British official, informed the Russian Consul that all existing restrictions on the number of Russian warships and transports allowed into Hong Kong harbor were now removed.[43] Even so, strains and tensions informed Hong

Kong's relations with Russia. As the nineteenth century ended, British concern over Russian expansion in East Asia, especially into China and Korea, was rekindled. After ten years of planning, Russian construction of the Trans-Siberian Railroad began in 1891. Britain realized this would enable Russia to move supplies and troops quickly from Europe to East Asia. The railroad was also clear evidence of Russia's growing interest in the region.[44]

As suspicions over Russian intentions in the region intensified, in spring 1896 Russians were again charged with spying. Three Russian officers, from the large warship *Vladimir Monomakh*, were arrested for sketching defense fortifications protecting Hong Kong. Reporting to the Colonial Office, Governor Sir William Robinson noted that the Russians had been treated relatively leniently and only accused of the minor offense of trespass rather than the far more serious charge of espionage. Russian Consul Michaelsen protested strongly to the governor, complaining the Royal Hong Kong Police had maltreated these officers, allegations Robinson investigated and denied, stating that the men had been properly detained in appropriate quarters and well-fed from a nearby hotel.[45] British officials sought to play down this incident, because at this time several foreign dignitaries, including Li Hung Chang, Grand Secretary of China, and Prince Fushimi Sadanaru of Tokyo, were passing through Hong Kong en route to the forthcoming coronation of Nicholas II. Despite a raging bubonic plague epidemic, Governor Robinson extended full hospitality to each party and planned a special program for them.[46] Such diplomatic courtesies notwithstanding, by this date the Consulate undoubtedly financed Russian secret agents or spies in Hong Kong. When the money on hand was insufficient for their expenses, the Consulate was forced to request additional funds from St. Petersburg.[47]

The presence of such Russian operatives in Hong Kong was symptomatic of the constantly expanding Tsarist interest in the region, which alarmed both Britain and Japan, as did the Franco-Russian alliance concluded in 1893.[48] One symptom of such apprehensions was the serialized publication, between October 9–16, 1897, in the Hong Kong newspaper *The China Mail* of "The Back Door," a fictionalized anonymous account of a supposedly successful joint French and Russian invasion of Hong Kong in 1897, subsequently reissued in December as a pamphlet that was forwarded to the British Colonial Office. Probably written by a local journalist or military officer and an exercise in scare tactics, "The Back Door" posited that such an invasion would succeed in three and a half days. The pamphlet, which though supposedly fiction featured numerous well-known Hong Kong personalities, was apparently intended to bolster an ongoing campaign by *The China Mail* to boost British defenses in Hong Kong by encouraging additional civilians to attend the impending annual camp of The Hong Kong Volunteers, and by persuading the government in London to provide adequate funding for gunboats, blockhouses, reserve batteries, additional troops, better roads and communications, harbor defenses, and siege provisions. When the camp took place, *The China Mail* reported prominently on it, and with its rival *The Hong Kong Daily Press* also published articles highlighting potential Russian threats to India, Manchuria, Mongolia, and the rest of Asia, as well as following up on the calls to enhance Hong Kong defenses. Subsequent correspondence in the two newspapers on this subject also urged the acquisition or seizure from China of land to the north of the existing Kowloon Peninsula, on the Chinese mainland opposite Hong Kong Island, as a means of providing defense in depth against a potential seaborne foreign invasion. This recommendation became reality in summer 1898, when the British government acquired the New Territories on a 99-year lease from the Chinese Empire, an agreement that paradoxically paved the way for Hong Kong's ultimate return to China in 1997.[49]

Fears of Russia were a major reason motivating the British government to negotiate the cession of the New Territories. Russian expansionism was more alarming to Britain than that of Japan, which went to war with China in 1894 and took Taiwan, but whose demands on China Britain was prepared to tolerate, believing that Japan's growing military power would serve to check Russia. Their shared apprehensions of Russia were a major factor impelling Britain and Japan to conclude the first Anglo-Japanese Alliance in 1902. British and other diplomats believed Russian policy makers sought predominance in China.[50] Most Russian weapons bound for Vladivostok passed through Hong Kong, one of East Asia's preeminent ports, where the government duly noted their quantity and quality.[51] The Russian acquisition of Port Arthur in 1898, just before the Boxer Rebellion, threatened the East Asian balance of power, especially since Russia soon intended to construct branches of the Trans-Siberian Railroad across Manchuria, east to Vladivostok and south to Port Arthur. Furthermore, Russian banks, including the newly created

Russian-Chinese Bank, competed with British rivals for loans and economic influence over a weakening Chinese Empire.[52]

As the nineteenth century closed, British and other officials increasingly believed that war between Russia and Japan was inevitable.[53] In a 1899 dispatch from Hong Kong to Washington, the American Consul-General Rounsevelle Wildman argued "there would be a war between Russia and Japan within one year," declaring that "it was commonly accepted along the China coast there would be an early war." He thought no foreign nations would intervene, that Russia would be totally outclassed in any future war, and Japan would emerge victorious, commenting that Japan had the best transport system in the world and could land 150,000 troops in Korea within one month of a declaration of war.[54] Except for the precise timing of war, which began not one but almost five years later, the American Consul's prediction was remarkably accurate. Tensions increased between Russia and Japan over each country's expansionist policies in Manchuria, Korea, and China itself. Finally, without declaring war, on February 8, 1904, Japanese warships attacked and largely destroyed the Russian Far East Fleet in Port Arthur, following a lengthy and costly battle for both sides.

While the Anglo-Japanese Alliance did not obligate Britain to join Japan in its war against Russia, it was undoubtedly a major reason why British neutrality in that war was not strictly impartial, but tilted toward Japan. Upon the formal declaration of war, on February 12, 1904, Hong Kong Governor Francis Henry May publicly affirmed a policy of strict British neutrality toward the conflict. Britain forbade its subjects to enlist in either the Japanese or the Russian army or navy. No warship from either side could dock in Hong Kong harbor, and any warships currently there were ordered to leave within 24 hours. Only minimal amounts of coal, food, and other provisions would be supplied to either belligerent.[55] In April, the MID issued a proclamation declaring that products deemed useful to Japan's war effort, including arms, munitions, explosives, military equipment and clothing, ships, fuel, and numerous other items were contraband and liable to seizure and confiscation from all neutral ships carrying such items to Japan. Neutral ships not carrying contraband could peacefully conduct trade and shipping unhindered, even with Japan. Russia also pledged to abide by that period's existing rules of war.[56] In response, Japan declared a blockade along the China coast, running from the Liaotung Peninsula near Port Arthur south to Pulantun, and published its own list enumerating contraband goods which might not be exported to Russia, including all those products on the Russian list and also gold, silver, timber, and telephones.[57]

The British did treat Russian sailors wounded in the war humanely. After numerous Russian warships, including the large destroyer *Burni*, were sunk in the Tsushima Strait, ships in the area, including British vessels, rescued some wounded Russian sailors, who were brought for treatment to Hong Kong, the nearest non-belligerent port. The Japanese government acquiesced provided that the sailors would not be returned to Russia before the war ended, a request the Russian government accepted. While in Hong Kong, both officers and men were well-housed and fed, nursed back to health, and allowed to wander unsupervised around the territory on parole.[58]

Its formal public statements and such humanitarian actions notwithstanding, Britain favored a Japanese victory in the Russo-Japanese War and barely maintained its neutrality during the conflict, allowing frequent transshipments of contraband through Hong Kong to Japan and often interpreting the laws of neutrality to Japan's advantage. After each such incident, the Russian Consul, Count Bologovsky, protested formally to the Hong Kong government. In May 1904, for example, he complained that the Hong Kong authorities had allowed a ship bound for Japan to take on a supply of dynamite, an item of military importance on the Russian contraband list. Governor May responded that this action did not violate British neutrality, and the Hong Kong Attorney General ruled "our subjects may sell freely to either belligerent subject to capture by the other side." So long as Hong Kong merchants accepted the risk, they could continue to trade as they had before the war began. When 12,000 cases of dynamite and their detonator caps were loaded on another ship destined for Japan, the Russian Consul again protested, causing the Hong Kong government to respond that he "was mistaken in thinking that this government was bound to prevent the inhabitants of Hong Kong from selling contraband to each side."[59] On several further occasions the Russian Consul again complained of the transportation of potential contraband through Hong Kong, in August 1904, for example, when a Belgian ship docked in Hong Kong carrying coal, together with some 2,500 tons of rifles and munitions, but in each case the British ignored his protests.[60]

Both on the battlefield and domestically, the Russo-Japanese War proved disastrous for Russia, prompting a thorough reexamination of Russia's foreign policy. Russia transferred its attention from East Asia to the Balkans, where its main rivals would be the weak Ottoman Empire and Austria-Hungary, a policy far less antagonistic to Britain. Furthermore, both Britain and Russia recognized that Germany posed a greater threat to each of them than the other did. The new British Liberal government that came to power in 1905 noted that the Russian Revolution of that same year for the first time granted the Russian people basic freedoms, and might well move autocratic Russia toward reform and even a British-style constitutional monarchy. Russia's liberal party, the Constitutional Democrats, even modeled itself on its British counterpart. In this climate of growing détente, Russia and Britain resolved differences over Afghanistan, Persia, and Tibet which had separated them for decades, and signed the Anglo-Russian Convention of 1907 dividing Persia into British, Russian, and neutral spheres of influence. Britain retained its predominance in Afghanistan and Tibet, which Russia recognized lay outside its own sphere. In 1908 King Edward VII of Britain marked this new spirit of cooperation by visiting Russia, a visit Nicholas II returned the following year. British public opinion and media coverage also became more favorable.

While differences still divided Britain and Russia, as war with Germany loomed on the horizon, their relations thawed markedly to reach near complete reconciliation, a development encouraged by France, their mutual ally. The Anglo-Russian Convention that became one of the pillars of the Triple Entente, which in turn would form one of the major armed blocs in World War I, also dissipated at least Hong Kong's past fears of seaborne Russian invasion and allowed Britain's East Asian outpost to relax its earlier suspicions of the Tsarist state. In a warm 1907 letter to the Russian Consul celebrating Tsar Nicholas II's name day, Governor Sir Frederick Lugard of Hong Kong mentioned the "increasing friendship between the two nations" and the "ending of ancient grounds of misunderstanding between Russia and Britain."[61] In this more genial climate, Russian officials even played a role in the first decade of the University of Hong Kong, then the colony's only university. In 1912, Russian Consul Vladimir Ottonovich von Ettingen attended the foundation ceremony. His dispatches described speeches given at the ceremony by individuals who had donated money to the new institution, such as M. N. Mody, a wealthy Parsee, and the address Governor Francis Henry

May, officiating as Chancellor, delivered there in September 1912. Von Ettingen's report to St. Petersburg included a diagram of the Main Building and a poster for the inauguration ceremony.[62]

The Russo-Japanese War and subsequent Russian Revolution of 1905 inflicted two hard successive blows upon the Russian monarchy. As Peter Stolypin, Prime Minister from 1906 until his assassination in 1911 and one of its leading statesmen, conceded, Russia needed 20 years of peace to consolidate his reforms and secure the monarchy.[63] The ending of colonial disputes with Great Britain due to the Anglo-Russian Convention of 1907 should have helped promote that requisite calm. Britain, Russia, and France, however, all concurred that Germany was their major enemy, whose ambitions must therefore be curbed. Consequently, a very loose alliance became tighter by the year, dividing Europe into two armed camps and before long depriving Russia of its coveted two decades of peace and tranquility. In war and revolution as in peace, the role of Hong Kong would loom surprisingly large in Russian affairs.

2

Dawn of a New Age: War and Revolution—Russia and Hong Kong, 1914–1921

The Great War that began in August 1914 soon encompassed a Pacific theater, in which both Russia and Hong Kong played significant roles.[1] British ties to France and the Russo-French alliance meant that Russia and Great Britain became allies when World War I erupted in August 1914. Japan, now allied to both Britain and Russia, joined the Entente in the conflict without ever becoming a formal member. The major contribution of Japan was to allow Russia and Britain to focus their attention on the European fronts during the war. Japanese entry into the war gave Russia military security along its long, sparsely populated, and poorly defended Eastern Front, while allowing Japan to acquire German colonial possessions in China and the northern Pacific. Japan also provided Russia with huge and badly needed supplies of arms. As the war ended in 1918, Japan also hoped the weakness of the new and still shaky Bolshevik regime, engaged in civil war with anti-Communist Russian forces, would give it an opportunity to annex substantial Russian territories in Asia.

The substantial role that Hong Kong, Asia's largest deep-water port, played not just in relation to Russia, but overall in the World War I Pacific theater, has been largely ignored in the historical literature on the period.[2] Following the Russo-Japanese War the British greatly enlarged their docks; however they reduced their military and naval garrisons in Hong Kong in a cost-cutting measure. In November 1913, there were a total of 2,751 British troops in the colony, of whom 1,916 were British, and the remaining 815 were Indians. That was a drop from the previous year. In

December the British government planned a further reduction in ground forces. Governor May declared that withdrawal of British troops was "highly unwise due to precarious conditions in Kwantung (Guangdong) province, including Canton." In March 1914, May sent a telegram to the Foreign Office declaring the situation in Guangdong had only worsened. Finally Foreign Secretary Sir Edward Grey relented and kept the troop levels in Hong Kong stable.[3] Furthermore, when World War I began in August 1914, Britain's one battleship in the Hong Kong fleet was out of commission and needed major repairs. Shortly before the war began, the German Consul and some German reservists left Hong Kong on an American ship. Two German nationals who remained in Hong Kong were later arrested for spying.[4] Although no previous studies have examined either the contribution of Hong Kong to Russia's ability to continue fighting the war, Hong Kong's role in provisioning and aiding financially the return home of Russian revolutionaries in 1917, or its part in the subsequent anti-Bolshevik Allied interventions, Hong Kong's dealings with Russia were significant to both World War I and the Russian Revolution of 1917. The policies of the Hong Kong government also affected the status of the Russian Volunteer Fleet during the war and the Revolution, as its ships were effectively held hostage until the British government finally opened diplomatic relations with the new Soviet regime.

Hong Kong played a little-known but vital role in bolstering World War I Russian defenses. Assisted by its ally Japan, Britain shipped crucial minerals, fuel, and munitions from Hong Kong via Japan to the Russian port of Vladivostok, for transportation along the Trans-Siberian Railroad to European Russia. Those essential supplies quite possibly prolonged Russian involvement in the war, enabling the French and British to resist German military pressure along the Western Front. To facilitate these endeavors, the British authorities in Hong Kong collaborated closely with Russian officials. When the war began, Russian Consul Vladimir Ottonovich von Ettingen, a member of a prominent Russian family—ironically enough, of German origin—that had settled in the Volga region in the early nineteenth century, was empowered to issue or refuse visas for entry into and passage through Russia for all Hong Kong applicants, including British subjects. When applying, individuals had to attest to their nationality and state when, where, and why they sought to travel to wartime Russia. The Russian Consulate also issued lists of contraband items, closely resembling those during the Russo-Japanese War a decade earlier. The Consulate also listed items that could be shipped from Hong Kong without breaking any import regulations, including cereals, flour, vegetables, salt, meat, wood, coal, and sugar, all much needed by the increasingly hungry and cold Russian people.[5] Unfortunately, Russian archives give no precise figures on the quantity of such exports, which constituted only part of the supplies Russia obtained through Hong Kong, whose major contribution to the Russian war effort was economic rather than purely military.

It is nonetheless clear that sizable shipments of crucial supplies, including tin, antimony, sesame seeds, and lumber, all vital to Russia's ability to wage war, traveled from China through Hong Kong and via Japan to Russia. Writing to the Hong Kong Superintendent of Imports and Exports on September 30, 1915, for example, von Ettingen stated: "I have the honor to inform you that over eight tons of tin will be shipped to Japan, then on to Vladivostok destined for military purposes."[6] China was Russia's main source of the glass-like chemical element antimony, used to harden lead needed for munitions.[7] Various subsequent letters reported shipments of 700 packages of antimony, weighing 70 tons, on May 11, 1915, eight tons of tin on the SS *Seattle Maru*, and another shipment of 50 tons of antimony, all destined for Vladivostok via Japan. A letter from the Japanese firm *Mitsui Kaisha* asked the Consul "to grant a certificate of origin on 50 tons of antimony, which we are going to ship to Vladivostok via Kobe on the SS *Ceylon Maru* on June 16, 1915."[8] Governor May informed the Colonial Office that the Russian Ambassador to Japan sought permission for *Mitsui*'s Hong Kong branch to send some ten tons of antimony to Osaka for ultimate export to Russia.[9] Chinese labor, often shipped from Hong Kong, also went to Russia to work in Eastern Siberia, where years earlier many coolies had helped to build the Trans-Siberian Railroad. Silk went from Guangzhou to Vladivostok via Hong Kong. In 1916, over 200 tons of Burmese lead went from the Straits Settlement (Malaya) to Vladivostok, once again via Hong Kong and Japan. When a cash-strapped Russian government complained about difficulties in paying for the high-grade lead, the British government promised to purchase it on Russia's behalf in Hong Kong.[10] Sometimes conditions were attached to Russian purchases. When the Russian government requested high-speed steel, a crucial commodity in short supply, the British declared that permission should not be granted unless the British-owned steel firm could produce a certificate from the Russian government that this batch of steel was required for the war effort.[11]

While the Russian government greatly appreciated the Allied assistance, the authoritarian regime always found incomprehensible the freedom its British partner permitted its people, even in colonial territories in time of war. Von Ettingen was repeatedly enraged to read articles in the Hong Kong press critical of the shortcomings of the Russian war effort. The Consul was justified in complaining over articles describing the seaworthiness and defensive capabilities of warships in Russia's Far East Fleet. While the British colonial government expressed sympathy toward the Russian diplomat's protests, it could do little to censor accurate press reports that Russia was losing the war. Such episodes revealed that, their common war effort against Germany notwithstanding, Russia and Britain still differed enormously politically and ideologically. The Russian government believed that the Hong Kong media could, as in Russia, be readily censored. After Austrian and German forces in Galicia inflicted numerous military defeats on Russia in spring 1915, von Ettingen sent a handwritten note to Colonel H. W. Iles, the local British commander in charge of military censorship, stating that, while he had no objection to "authentic war news," the *Hong Kong Telegraph* had carried "exaggerated reports."[12]

Russian officials in China also resented Hong Kong press freedoms. In September 1915, the Russian Consul in Beijing complained to von Ettingen about Hong Kong press reports of recent Russian military defeats, asking him to investigate the matter. Around the same time, the Guangzhou Russian Consulate complained to the British Mission in Beijing about Hong Kong press reports on ship movements from Vladivostok, which had given the name of each ship and the number of guns it carried. Russian authorities contended that, had those newspaper accounts described British ships, British military censors would have banned them for effectively apprising the enemy of the locations and defense capabilities of vital vessels. Von Ettingen made repeated though unsuccessful appeals to the Hong Kong authorities to force local newspapers to refrain from printing information on the movements and military capabilities of specific Russian warships. "Once again," he proclaimed angrily in September 1915, "the papers in Hong Kong publish confidential information about Russian munitions orders and means of defense, which are prejudicial to our interests." The offending articles, one in the Hong Kong–based *South China Morning Post,* and the other published simultaneously in the Manchurian-based *Harbin Vedomosti*, provided details of Russian orders in Japanese munitions factories. While stating that he did not wish to interfere with the Hong Kong press, von Ettingen asked Colonel Iles to request local newspapers not to publish "details of war orders, of railway material, and of ammunition going into Vladivostok."[13] In response, the British reaffirmed that the Hong Kong press was not subject to formal censorship. According to Colonel Iles: "The custom in Hong Kong is to *ask editors to exercise restraint* on articles." (italics added) Iles added that "some editors are careful, others are not," but agreed that the information should not have been published, and that the Consul "rightly took exception" to the articles. "Had we known, we would not have allowed these reports to have been published." Iles then requested that in future newspaper editors not publish information on munitions orders and shipments.[14] Von Ettingen also begged the British commander in East Asia, Sir Thomas Jerram, to block any subsequent offending articles, but Sir Thomas merely repeated Iles' statement that "there is no special law in Hong Kong stopping those articles, but that he would do what he could."[15]

A year later, the Consul again complained about negative stories in the press, describing, for example, the steam trials a Russian battleship, the *Peresviet*, underwent to determine its seaworthiness after necessary repairs. Other articles dealt with the type and quantity of munitions supplied to Russia from Japan, the launching of several new Russian naval vessels, and Russian ship movements in the Western Pacific Ocean. On September 9, 1916, the *South China Morning Post*, Hong Kong's premier English-language newspaper, published an article reporting that the battleship *Peresviet* was under repair in Japan, and would return to service in Vladivostok on September 19. The newspaper further stated that the Russian Baltic Fleet had gained three new capital ships, whose acquisition would make essential German troop transfers to German-occupied Courland (present-day Latvia) difficult.[16] While no formal punitive sanction existed, the British government once more agreed "it was highly undesirable that particular movements of battleships should be mentioned in its colony's press." William Donaldson, editor of the *South China Morning Post*, wrote apologetically to assure the authorities this would not happen again. Governor Sir Francis May nonetheless told the Consul that the Hong Kong government could control neither the Hong Kong nor the Japanese press, where the piece had originally appeared. "It does no good to block publication of warship movements from the Hong Kong press when identical reports already appeared in the Japanese press, as well as in the widely read American daily *New York Herald*." Governor May essentially repeated the earlier statements of Colonel Iles and other British commanders to von Ettingen. The Consul also complained about a *South China Morning Post* article on the amount and type of munitions shipped to Russia from Japan, and yet another piece on three new ships destined for the Russian Baltic Fleet. Despite requests by the Hong Kong government and British military commanders, as well as demands from the Russian Consulate, the *South China Morning Post* and other Hong Kong newspapers continued to publish indiscreet information on the Russian war effort. The *South China Morning Post*, for example, reported on September 19, 1916, that the total value of arms to date purchased by Russia from Japan was more than 200 million yen. The authoritarian Russian government found it incomprehensible that, despite being a colony and at war, Hong Kong still maintained press freedom.[17]

Wartime reverses were a major factor in precipitating yet another revolution, in February 1917, that replaced Russia's archaic, conservative, and authoritarian monarchy with a fairly democratic liberal Provisional Government. In March 1917, the newly installed Provisional Government sent telegrams to all Russian embassies and consulates notifying them of the change of government, and asking all diplomatic officials to inform local newspapers of the alteration of regime in Russia. The MID declared that any Russian living in China or Hong Kong must immediately obtain a new passport. In Hong Kong, the MID retained Vladimir Ottonovich von Ettingen as Consul-General.[18] This correspondence was almost certainly typical of the instructions the new Russian government issued to its consulates around the world.

Britain swiftly recognized the Provisional Government and urged it to continue the Russian war effort. Britain even initially thought the liberal and well-meaning Provisional Government would prove a better and more efficient ally than the Tsarist regime, whose conduct of the war British officials believed had been corrupt and incompetent. During 1917, the British government became ever more pessimistic over the state of Russia and the course of the war on the Eastern Front. In September 1917, Hong Kong's Governor and Colonial Secretary both requested information from von Ettingen on the confused but deteriorating and apparently desperate situation in Russia. The Consul responded that, while a crisis did exist in Russia, newspaper reports received in Hong Kong were exaggerated and inaccurate, and that foreigners "did not understand the Russian reality,"[19] an oft-repeated claim. Ironically, Consul von Ettingen himself failed to understand Russian realities, especially the new government's inability to solve Russia's manifold problems or to satisfy popular demands for an end to the war, land reform, jobs, and food. Seeking to appease the Russian political left and demonstrate some independence from its Western Allies, on October 24, 1917, the Provisional Government unilaterally denounced an unfavorable commercial treaty with Britain signed in January 1859, following the Crimean War. The treaty's abrogation after the statutory one-year's notice would allow a radicalizing Russian government to revise its commercial relations with other countries.[20]

In the revolution's early months, Hong Kong played an important, though little-known, role in transporting revolutionaries back to Russia, where they radicalized the revolution. On March 13, 1917, the Russian Mission in Beijing instructed von Ettingen to assist political émigrés and their families seeking to return to Russia via Hong Kong in every way possible, including financial. Von Ettingen was ordered to obtain loans from Hong Kong and British banks if necessary. "The important thing was to get the émigrés back as soon as possible." If too few Russian ships were available, he could hire vessels flying other countries' flags. The files described in considerable detail some individual Russians who traveled from Manila or Vietnam through Hong Kong, covering their requests for travel documents, tickets, money, and even warm clothes, since most essentially impoverished émigrés carried very little. Most émigrés arriving in Hong Kong came from Australia, in large groups of 50 to 100 people, from each of which one or two representatives were delegated to come to the Consulate, bringing a full list of the émigrés, the numbers in their families, and their needs. The Russian Embassy in London instructed von Ettingen to screen each group carefully, since only political émigrés should receive money and other assistance, and some émigrés might be common criminals. On August 1, as the revolution deepened and radicalized, Alexander Kerensky, who had emerged as leader of the Provisional Government, revoked many of the privileges granted the political émigrés to ease their passage to Russia. He also ruled that young and healthy émigrés must join the Russian army upon their return and serve in the increasingly unpopular war. The MID asked von Ettingen to verify that applicants were genuine Russian nationals, not foreign radicals or revolutionaries. To facilitate security and to control their entry, the MID asked that parties be limited to a maximum of 150 individuals. Despite these restrictions, thousands of political émigrés returned to Russia through Hong Kong.[21]

The new Provisional Government proved unable to stem the tide of revolution, and was in its turn easily overthrown on November 7, 1917 (New Style) by the radical Bolsheviks, who established the world's first Communist government. Russia quickly became embroiled in a civil war between the Communist and non-Communist forces. The British government was unsympathetic to the new regime and, after the Bolshevik Revolution, the Hong Kong government soon established new passport regulations for Russians. Fearing the free entry of potential Russian Communist revolutionaries, the British demanded that "every Russian proposing to enter Hong Kong must present a passport and a visa granted in the country where the holder first starts his journey to Hong Kong."[22] From that date to the present, all Russian citizens visiting Hong Kong for tourism, business, or any other reason had first to obtain a visa, usually from the British Embassy in Moscow. During the entire Soviet period each request was carefully examined, with positive or negative decisions normally made at the highest level of the British government in London, by either the Foreign Secretary or the Colonial Secretary. Requests were granted very sparingly, never more than a handful each year. Thus, travel to Hong Kong became almost impossible for virtually all Soviet citizens.

Such regulations did not inhibit the passage of anti-Communist Russians through Hong Kong back to their own country, to join anti-Bolshevik forces, or out of Russia as refugees. While the Russian archives did not list any well-known or interesting individuals, who passed through Hong Kong in 1917, during the Russian Civil War one prominent anti-Communist leader, Admiral Alexander Kolchak, stayed briefly in Hong Kong in 1918 on his way to the Russian Far East. His presence in Hong Kong was symptomatic of the way in which, in a relatively short time, British hostility to the Bolsheviks deepened, as Britain gradually severed all diplomatic and cultural ties with the new Soviet state. During the Civil War, Hong Kong also played a significant role in transporting anti-Bolshevik Russians from Russia to the West. New émigrés from the old middle and upper classes, together with some

White Army Commanders, flooded into most cities along the China coast, including Hong Kong, where they formed large and active White Russian communities. One 1918 MID file described in great detail a secret mission by a Captain Ambrasanzeft, a captain in the cavalry guard, dispatched by the White Russian (anti-Bolshevik) General Staff to win help from the Allies in Western Europe. Since Bolshevik forces already controlled the shorter route out through European Russia, he had to make a lengthy, circuitous journey through Asia, including Hong Kong.[23] Unfortunately, the White Guard officer was unable to obtain more assistance from the Allies than had already been promised. One may well speculate that the reason the archive contained such detailed information was to furnish the MID a case study of Hong Kong's role in aiding the anti-Communist cause during the Civil War raging throughout Russia at the time.

The British government gave even more substantial assistance to anti-Bolshevik forces in Russia when in mid-1918 it dispatched British troops to Siberia. In mid-1918, Hong Kong served as a staging post and transit point for such forces as they departed to join the Allied military interventions in Russia. By late 1917 the British, Canadians, and Americans had growing concerns over their ally Japan's drive to ship troops to Vladivostok, ostensibly to safeguard the large stores of Allied war matériel, estimated at over 700,000 tons of goods, and to keep the critical port out of Bolshevik hands. Allied leaders feared that the opportunistic Japanese sought territorial gains at Russian expense.[24] Furthermore, the British Foreign Office received reports from its Consul in Harbin that the Bolsheviks were murdering British and French residents, including women and children, in several Siberian cities. While these allegations later proved highly inaccurate, in light of them, the British War Cabinet and General Sir William Robertson, Chief of the Imperial General Staff, on January 1, 1918 recommended shipping two British infantry companies from their base in Hong Kong to Vladivostok. The Cabinet also ordered the cruiser HMS *Suffolk* to sail immediately from Hong Kong to the Russian port to help guard the British Consulate there, and it reached Vladivostok on January 14, 1918.[25] After the Allied decision for intervention against Russia had been taken in mid-1918, two battalions of the Middlesex Regiment numbering some 1,500 troops were placed on full alert in Hong Kong. They left the colony on August 3, 1918, reaching Vladivostok soon afterwards, and receiving an impressive welcome from

White Russian and Czech troops. They remained in Russia until September 1919, taking part in skirmishes in the Vladivostok-Khabarovsk region and performing guard and ceremonial duties in Omsk, Western Siberia. The 1/9th Cyclist Battalion of the Hampshire Regiment also stopped in Hong Kong in November 1918, on its way from India to Vladivostok. Since many of the men were suffering from severe influenza, its commander, Colonel R. A. Johnson, unavailingly requested that his battalion remain in Hong Kong until they recovered. Instead the battalion traveled onward to Vladivostok, and they too remained in Russia until November 1919. Supposedly intended only to protect the Allied supplies and the Russian railway lines in Siberia, in practice this intervention quickly became an anti-Bolshevik exercise, although an unsuccessful one, as Allied troops cooperated with White Russian forces. The memory of the British efforts to aid the Whites during the Russian Civil War would poison Anglo-Soviet relations for many years to come.[26]

Meanwhile, the emergence of the Bolshevik government posed dilemmas for both the British authorities and Russian diplomatic representatives in Hong Kong. After the overthrow of the Provisional Government in October 1917, Consul von Ettingen effectively found himself unemployed, as the government that had appointed him no longer existed. Von Ettingen refused to recognize the existence of the new Soviet regime, maintaining that the Provisional Government was still the only legitimate Russian government. Because Great Britain also refused to recognize the Bolshevik government, it treated von Ettingen as the legal representative of Russia. His refusal to assist Communist Russian sailors whom the Royal Hong Kong Police had arrested effectively symbolized the divisions of the civil war.

The Bolshevik Revolution affected British treatment of Russian merchant shipping. In 1890, the Russian Volunteer Fleet, founded in 1878 in St. Petersburg during the Russo-Turkish War, had began sailing from Odessa to Vladivostok. A group of Russian merchants agreed to contribute funds to purchase fast steamships that could be converted into commerce raiders in the event of war, whence came the name "Volunteer" Fleet. For several years, the Volunteer Fleet served as something of a second navy, as conservatives within the Russian government used it as a counterweight to the regular Russian navy, then led by liberal-minded Grand Duke Konstantin Nikolaevich. In peacetime, it ran subsidized services, and in wartime, for example during the Russo-Japanese War, provided auxiliary cruisers.[27] Volunteer Fleet vessels journeyed throughout Southeast Asian waters and frequently visited Hong Kong, where the company maintained an office, regularly taking on passengers and cargo bound for Vladivostok. Only when epidemics afflicted Hong Kong, notably in 1908 and 1909, did such ships avoid Hong Kong.[28] On May 2, 1912, Dmitri Afanasievich Liukhmanov arrived in Hong Kong, and was appointed the Head of the Hong Kong Office for the Russian Volunteer Fleet.[29] Previously, a German trading house handled its affairs.

Passenger and cargo services continued during World War I, and after the Tsarist regime fell, the Provisional Government maintained the fleet's services as before. On January 26, 1918, the new Soviet government nationalized the fleet, but since the British government did not recognize the Soviet government, it refused to accept this action, and responded by declaring that all Russian Volunteer Fleet vessels currently in British ports would be requisitioned, to be returned to Russian control only after the war ended, or once a government recognized by Britain held power in Russia. "Until then, the ships should be placed under British flag."[30] The British government explained this situation to Ivan Nabokov, the Provisional Government's chargé d'affaires in London, where Maxim Litvinov, the Soviet government's Plenipotentiary, was still denied British recognition.[31] The British government took great pains to ensure that telegrams from consuls representing the former Russian government should not reach Litvinov by mistake. When, for example, Consul von Ettingen sent a telegram to the Russian Ambassador in London in 1918, the British Colonial Office specified that the use of the cypher was for Nabokov, not Litvinov, to "whom the Admiralty was desirous messages not be sent."[32]

Since Hong Kong was a British port, and vessels from the Russian Volunteer Fleet were in Hong Kong waters, the stage was set for a confrontation, which soon occurred. In January 1918, British authorities seized three vessels of the Russian Volunteer Fleet then in port, the SS *Tobolsk*, the SS *Indigirka*, and the SS *Simbirsk*. Through Boris Nikolaevich Shnitnitkov, its acting agent in Hong Kong, the Russian government[33] formally protested the British requisition and requested the order's annulment. Shnitnitkov declared the British action illegal and demanded the ships' return, together with payment of an indemnity for any loss or damage.[34] The Hong Kong government removed and transferred the SS *Tobolsk*'s cargo of rice to a British ship, which took over the contract for its transport to Japan. Meanwhile, 12 officers and 84 sailors from the ships were interned in Lai Chi Kok in Kowloon, awaiting repatriation to Russia. Consul von Ettingen asked that any sailors who wished to serve under British command should be allowed to remain on the ships. He also requested that the vessels should proceed on their original mission, to deliver supplies to Kamchatka, still under anti-Communist control, since unless these ships provisioned them, the residents of that remote peninsula north of Japan would starve.[35]

Since many sailors were pro-Bolshevik, the Hong Kong government considered them potential spies, and placed them under close military guard. Those pro-Bolshevik sailors not yet under arrest held a meeting, their own *Soviet* or assembly, and elected three representatives to meet with von Ettingen, to ask him to request their release from the British Hong Kong authorities. Even though he represented an old and supplanted regime, to these pro-Bolshevik sailors von Ettingen apparently still remained an official personage who could intercede on their behalf. The Consul refused to meet either the three *Soviet* representatives, or British officials on their behalf, stating that he was only prepared to meet with their ship's anti-Bolshevik captain. When the three representatives again tried to see von Ettingen, he once again rebuffed them, stating that he must observe British laws in Hong Kong, and "as the British did not recognize any Soviet organizations, I would not either."[36] The infuriated sailors then contacted the Far East Department of the MID located in Khabarovsk, and urged that von Ettingen be forced to resign. Nikolai Lubarsky, Regional Commissar for Foreign Affairs in the Far East, agreed, cabling the Commissariat of Foreign Affairs in Petrograd: "We request the immediate resignation of Consul von Ettingen, details will come by regular mail."[37]

Not recognizing the new Soviet government's authority, von Ettingen disregarded the demand for his resignation, and simply continued as before as Consul-General for the Provisional Government of the Russian Republic, a government that no longer existed. As in years past, he sought to promote Russian language and culture in Hong Kong. During the University of Hong Kong's first decade, Russian was one of the languages offered at the university, though this is no longer the case. F. D. Redmond, the Examination Secretary, wrote to von Ettingen in 1918: "The University has instructed me to approach you with the request that you will kindly consent to act as Examiner in Russian for the matriculation examination in December 1918." The Consul replied on

November 8, that he "considered it a duty and a pleasure to assist in the upcoming examination."[38] Several ethnic Russians from Russian communities in Manchuria and along the China coast attended the English-language University of Hong Kong. The Russian archives still contain several examples of these matriculation examinations, including passages of some difficulty for translation from Russian to English and from English to Russian. In 1920, N. T. Macintosh, University Registrar, again requested von Ettingen to continue as examiner in Russian, to which the Consul agreed.[39] This was the last time he performed this service. Soon afterwards he faced the reality that he was representing a now defunct country, the Russian Empire, a situation that could not continue indefinitely. Recognizing, however reluctantly, that neither the Tsarist monarchy nor the provisional government would regain power, in 1920 he therefore closed the Consulate and sold its assets. Even today, the location of the Consulate's archives remains a mystery. In early 1921, when it had become clear that the Red Army would defeat anti-Communist forces, Vladimir Ottonovich von Ettingen left Hong Kong permanently, sailing for Marseilles and on to Paris. No details are known of his subsequent career.[40] His departure marked the end of any full-time Russian diplomatic presence in Hong Kong for over 70 years.

Meanwhile, after the successful Bolshevik Revolution in Petrograd in November 1917, the Russian Volunteer Fleet moved its headquarters from the old capital, first to Feodosia, a port on the Black Sea coast, then to Istanbul, and finally to Paris. The Hong Kong branch office remained under the control of the Paris-based board of directors. The Bolsheviks appointed a rival board based in Moscow, which in 1921 sent a new representative, J. Leonidov, to Hong Kong, to claim control over all Russian Volunteer Fleet ships entering Hong Kong waters. The British government still thought it desirable to deny the fleet to the Bolsheviks, a policy completely endorsed by the Russian Ambassador to Japan, who represented the long defunct provisional government. He sought to transfer the fleet's general administration from Hong Kong to Vladivostok, still in the White Russians' hands and housing thousands of Japanese troops. To keep the fleet's 13 vessels under anti-Communist control, the Foreign Office agreed to the request, and transmitted its decision to the Hong Kong government.[41] By 1922, five of the disputed Russian steamers still sailed frequently along the Chinese and Indochinese coasts and into Hong Kong under the French flag: the SS *Georgii*, the SS *Tobolsk*, the SS *Indigirka*, the SS *Simferopol*, and the SS *Simbirsk*.[42] Acting on behalf of the Bolshevik board, Leonidov officially terminated the services of each ship's captain for refusing to recognize Soviet control.[43] In 1923, after the Soviet Union and Great Britain established diplomatic relations, those ships were delivered to Leonidov.[44] The Paris-based board, having no remaining jurisdiction, soon dissolved.

The Soviet authorities nationalized not just banks and the Russian Volunteer Fleet, but also all foreign-owned property, companies, and other possessions within Russia, including all assets belonging to British subjects and Chinese people in Hong Kong. The British government proclaimed: "All persons, firms, and companies should record their claims with the Colonial Secretary's Office in Hong Kong."[45] Although the Hong Kong government could not guarantee claimants any definite hope of success, it assured them that the British government would seek restitution from the Soviet government during any negotiations to restore diplomatic relations. Five years later, during talks to reestablish diplomatic relations, the Colonial Secretary in London requested particulars of claims by British nationals against the Russian government, classified into loans, debts, bonds, and industrial, mining, oil, and other properties.[46] These claims, together with the large Tsarist foreign debt, were never repaid.

One still unresolved mystery is the whereabouts of the archives of the old imperial Russian Consulate in Hong Kong. After its closure in 1920, Consul von Ettingen sold off all the Consulate's property, except its archives, which he deposited before leaving the colony in the safekeeping of the local branch of the Russo-Asiatic Bank.[47] The bank's vaults held some eight cases, containing records from the consulates in Hong Kong and Guangzhou, one shield of the Russian Imperial Arms, one certified copy of the lease of a plot of land in Guangzhou, and one sealed envelope bearing von Ettingen's name on the outside.[48] During the early 1920s, Soviet relations with the West remained at best frosty. Only in early 1924 did the Soviet Union and Great Britain establish formal relations. Soon afterwards, the Soviet government requested that Britain transfer the files and any other possessions from the imperial Consulate's records to the rightful successor-state, the Soviet Union. After checking, the Hong Kong government reported back to the British Foreign Office that they had failed to locate any property from the old Consulate, including the archives. The Soviet chargé d'affaires in London, M. Berzin, informed

Prime Minister and Foreign Secretary J. Ramsay MacDonald that this information was incorrect. "According to information received by his government, the archives of the late Russian Consulate-General in Hong Kong had been given by Tsarist Consul von Ettingen into the charge of the Russo-Asiatic Bank in Hong Kong." Three weeks later, on October 9, the Foreign Office responded by declaring that if the archives were in truth in the bank, they should be handed over to the Soviet government.[49]

The story did not end there. In the wake of a scandal, diplomatic relations between the USSR and Great Britain worsened within months of their debut. Four days before the October 29, 1924, British elections, the Conservative Party published what it alleged were instructions from the head of the Comintern, Grigory Zinoviev, to the British Communist Party, urging British Communists to step up their revolutionary activities and infiltrate the British Army. Although the "Zinoviev Letter" was a forgery concocted by anti-Soviet British Foreign Office functionaries with ties to the Conservative Party, the governing Labour Party, already attracting severe criticism for recognizing the Soviet Union, was soundly defeated in the elections. Upon taking office, the Conservative government denounced the treaties Labour had negotiated with Moscow. For several years diplomatic relations between Moscow and London were suspended, to be reestablished only after Labour returned to office in 1929.

Predictably, with relations between the two states frozen, the archives deposited in the Russo-Asiatic Bank were never transferred to the Soviet Union. In late 1926 the Russo-Asiatic Bank itself entered into liquidation, an operation in which the large Hong Kong accounting firm, Johnson, Stokes, and Master, was involved.[50] Its employee, John Fleming, who became the Bank's Special Manager, discovered the archives in the bank's vaults and sought guidance from Hong Kong's Colonial Secretary (present-day Chief Secretary), at that time the second highest-ranking official in the Hong Kong government, as to how he should dispose of them. On November 26, 1926, E. W. Hamilton replied on behalf of the Colonial Secretary that the Hong Kong government was prepared to accept custody of the archives. The next day Fleming informed the Colonial Secretary that "eight boxes of Russian Consulate archives left in the safe custody of the Bank had today been transferred to the care of the Colonial Treasurer." Once again the Soviet chargé d'affaires in London, M. Rozengol'ts, requested the archives be transferred to Soviet authorities, as provided years earlier, and until then be sealed for safe keeping. On

March 5, 1927, British Foreign Secretary Austen Chamberlain agreed to the Soviet request. The last dispatch on this matter was a letter Hong Kong Governor Cecil Clementi sent on March 25, 1927, to the Foreign Office in London, acknowledging receipt of his Foreign Office's request, and reporting that the Hong Kong Colonial Treasurer now held eight boxes of archives, a coat of arms, one consular sword, and one signboard.[51]

Nothing more is known of the fate of the former Russian Consulate's remaining property. The only existing Soviet report on the subject dealt with the liquidation of the Russo-Asiatic Bank in Hong Kong, which had held the archives for safekeeping. This document never mentioned the Tsarist records, but only stated that its authors were uncertain whether the Hong Kong branch of the bank was ever finally liquidated.[52] Was the property ever transferred to the Soviet Union as requested? Was it simply kept in Hong Kong, perhaps remaining hidden there to this day? Was it perhaps destroyed, inadvertently or otherwise, by the Japanese who occupied Hong Kong during World War II? The newly established Russian Consulate-General in Hong Kong encouraged the author to try to solve this mystery, but repeated attempts at the AVP RF in Moscow and the PRO in London have proved fruitless. The whereabouts of the old imperial Russian Consulate's archives remains unknown to this day.

In the late nineteenth and early twentieth centuries Hong Kong began its transition from a small, sleepy foreign concession to a large metropolitan port, its products flowing to all the continents. As Hong Kong entered the modern world, and grew in size and importance, Russian interest in the colony grew in tandem, and would remain strong until the end of the Russian monarchy and beyond. Although the Russian community was always small, through the Russian Consulate, Russia maintained an active and vigorous presence in the colony right up through the end of the monarchy and subsequent civil war. The Russian Consulate in Hong Kong also promoted Russian economic and cultural activities in the territory.

British policy toward first Tsarist and then revolutionary Russia, and Russian attitudes toward British-controlled Hong Kong, proved crucially important during the early twentieth century in fostering trade, communications, and defense capabilities in East Asia in general, and China in particular. On the whole, despite the impact on Hong Kong of earlier longstanding tensions between Britain and Russia up to 1907, as part of the Allied coalition, Hong Kong sympathized strongly with Russian efforts during World War I. During the conflict, products crucial to the war effort, such as antimony and tin, were shipped from Hong Kong to Russian ports. Without such products from China and Indochina, Russia might have collapsed even earlier.

Nevertheless, Hong Kong had no real understanding of the Russian Revolution of 1917 and its causes. The economic and political elite in Hong Kong, both British and Chinese, was and remained hostile to the Bolsheviks who took over the Russian government in November 1917. When Tsarist Russia collapsed in 1917, to be succeeded first by a democratic republic and then at the end of the year by a Communist state, the Soviet Union, the last imperial Consul predictably though inaccurately informed the Hong Kong government that the crisis was less grave than the Hong Kong press portrayed it. In 1917, thousands of exiled Russian political émigrés returned to Russia through Hong Kong, to contribute to making the revolution, which they helped to radicalize.[53] During the subsequent civil war, which lasted until 1921, Hong Kong facilitated British military intervention in Siberia, which quickly became an anti-Bolshevik exercise; assisted White Russian representatives who sought to overthrow the Bolshevik government; and withheld Russian Volunteer Fleet vessels from Soviet control. Until the civil war ended, the status of the Russian official presence in Hong Kong remained confused. The old imperial Russian Consul, Vladimir Ottonovich von Ettingen, still remained in Hong Kong representing a Russian state that no longer existed, whether as the Russian Empire or the Russian Provisional Republic, until, finally recognizing the reality that his government was gone forever, he left Hong Kong in 1921, disappearing into obscurity. From then until 1994, after the Soviet Union collapsed and during the last few years of British rule, Russia would have no formal diplomatic presence in Hong Kong, and Soviet relations with the British authorities in Hong Kong would be characterized by deep mutual suspicions and antagonisms at both the ideological and strategic levels.

3

Clash of Worlds: The Comintern, British Hong Kong, and Chinese Nationalism, 1921–1929

Introduction

British Hong Kong, with a population of around 500,000, was a fraction of its current size just after World War I. Even then, though, the British crown colony was the largest port in East Asia facing out on an increasingly important Pacific Ocean, and by far the most significant listening post for the West on developments in a rapidly changing China, undergoing the throes of civil war and revolution. Hong Kong also had the largest and most politically conscious working class, one that the revolutionary, new Soviet government saw as offering an opportunity for a potential socialist revolution in a heartland of the world's greatest capitalist empire. The Soviet Union also recognized that Hong Kong constituted a threat. While much smaller numerically, British forces were far better-armed, better-trained, and therefore militarily stronger than any possible Chinese army that might be a Soviet ally.

The 1920s was a crucial time for Soviet diplomacy and revolutionary activities, which often but not always coincided. Newly-released Soviet documents reveal the increasing attention that the East Asian specialists of the MID devoted to British Hong Kong and the importance they ascribed to it. One place affected the other, as developments in Hong Kong and Nationalist-controlled but ever more chaotic South China increasingly intersected.

This chapter examines the interactions and issues arising from the collision of British Hong Kong, the Soviet Union, and China during the

1920s. These issues include the following: the differences between the Comintern and the MID regarding Soviet policy toward South China and Hong Kong; the extent of Soviet involvement in Hong Kong and South China; why the Communist movement collapsed so drastically in Hong Kong and South China; and Hong Kong's broader significance to Soviet policy toward China and toward colonial empires in general. One can argue that, for Britain at least, the Cold War conflict with the Soviet Union for influence in developing countries, such as China, and within its colonies, such as Hong Kong, began in the early 1920s. During the 1920s, Soviet agents posed a significant threat to British rule in Hong Kong. Soviet policy sought to foment revolution in South China. Hong Kong constituted a potential base to promulgate that revolution, with the added advantage that British imperialism could be opposed and undermined in one of its crucial trading areas. It also gave rise to a protracted Soviet conflict between the broad ideological objectives of the international Communist movement and the more narrow strategic interests of the Soviet Union itself. Following the catastrophic impact of the events of 1927 on Communists in South China, the latter considerations triumphed among Soviet foreign policy makers.

The Comintern View of Hong Kong and Revolution

The Leninist theory of socialist revolution held that, wherever revolution first occurred, similar revolutions would inevitably follow elsewhere, since revolution was a universal phenomenon, and every country must observe the same laws of history and succession of societies until it achieved Communism, the final stage of historical development. Other countries around the world faced economic and social problems resembling Russia's, and Vladimir Lenin, the first Bolshevik leader of Russia, hoped they too, especially the war-ravaged and weakened autocratic empires of Germany and Austria, would follow suit. Lenin suggested that, as the era of socialist revolution approached, the capitalist stage of world history was rapidly drawing to a close. The Bolsheviks saw themselves as part of the advance guard of international socialism. The First International, the International Workingmen's Association, had collapsed in 1876 due to an ideological dispute between Mikhail Bakunin, the founder of modern anarchism, and Karl Marx. The Second International, founded in 1889, excluded anarchists, but collapsed in 1916, during World War I. In

March 1919, the new Third International or Comintern, designed to exclude such ideological differences and weaknesses and to operate under complete Soviet control, held its first Congress in Moscow, with Bolshevik ideas predominating throughout. Its focus was to spread revolution throughout Europe, especially in the defeated German and Austro-Hungarian Empires.[1]

Post–World War I efforts at Communist revolutions proved unsuccessful in Europe, impelling Comintern leaders to look eastward, especially to China and other parts of East and Southeast Asia, where they believed their prospects of instigating a Communist revolution by exploiting those areas' traditionally harsh poverty and resentment of foreign domination were far more promising. To mark this turn to Asia, in September 1920, the first Congress of the Peoples of the East was held in Baku, Azerbaijan. Bolshevik slogans and promises of national self-determination offered great hope to Asian colonized and semi-colonized peoples. Yet as early as the Second Comintern Congress, held in Moscow in July and August 1920, tensions arose over the issues of whether, and to what extent, Communist parties in colonial and semi-colonial areas, such as China, should cooperate with local bourgeois and nationalist forces; what form any such collaboration should take; and the role of the small urban working class in shaping national liberation struggles, especially in relation to the far more numerous but generally less politically conscious peasantry. Both Congresses decided that temporary agreements and alliances between Communists and nationalist forces should be encouraged in colonial and semi-colonial areas.[2]

Concrete steps toward forming a Communist party in China only began in early 1920, when Grigori Voitinsky, a Comintern agent, arrived in China.[3] In July 1921, the founding meeting of the CCP was held secretly in Shanghai, attended by some 12 delegates. From its inception the CCP was divided into two factions, one taking the European Marxist view that the working class would be the main engine of revolution in China, while the other, reflecting China's overwhelmingly rural nature, stressed the importance of China's peasantry in making any revolution. The Bolshevik Revolution also prompted a reorganization of the KMT, whose leader, Sun Yat-sen, found new inspiration in the Bolshevik Revolution and sought to model the KMT on the Bolsheviks and utilize Communist ties with grassroots urban workers' and peasants' movements. Believing that the father of China's own revolution was converting to

Bolshevism, Soviet officials concluded a golden revolutionary moment was developing. In August 1922, the Comintern dispatched Adolf Ioffe to China to further cooperation among the Soviet Union, the KMT, and the CCP.[4] That same month the Comintern stated that the CCP should submerge itself in a KMT-dominated United Front. In a January 1923 accord, Sun and Ioffe formalized this decision to seek immediate national independence from Western domination and to unify China's disparate regions, then controlled by numerous warlords.[5] Reluctantly and provisionally, fearing their party might be absorbed in the process, the CCP acquiesced in the Comintern directive. The CCP did not dissolve itself and Communists only entered the United Front as individuals. Some CCP members nonetheless perceived the United Front as an opportunity to take over the KMT from inside. Communists headed several crucial departments within the United Front, including propaganda, labor, peasant affairs, and student affairs.

The Comintern and the Soviet government, already increasingly dominated by Josef Stalin in a vicious and evolving power struggle initially precipitated by Lenin's declining health and intensified by his death in 1924, regarded China as an experimental area where they could implement Stalin's theory of revolution in colonial and semi-colonial regions, that in any struggle to oust Western imperialists and their local "feudal lackeys," the local bourgeoisie would play a central role. The ever warmer ties between the Soviet Union and the United Front led to the dispatch of thousands of Soviet military and political advisers to China, among whom was an experienced diplomat, Mikhail Borodin, whose mission was to help Sun reorganize the KMT.[6] The British government in Hong Kong was consistently antagonistic toward the presence of such Soviet operatives in Hong Kong and China alike. Since he had no desire to apply for a visa and alert the British to his presence, Borodin specifically avoided stopping in Hong Kong.[7] General Vasily Blyukher, a noted Civil War commander, was sent to reorganize the army. Meanwhile Sun sent a young commander, Chiang Kai-shek, to the Soviet Union to study its military system. Upon his return in 1925, Chiang became Commandant of the Huangpu (Whampoa) Military Academy outside the southern city of Guangzhou (Canton), established to provide Chinese military officers with professional training. Sun's leftist KMT-CCP United Front government, based in Guangzhou, which became the center of KMT power, received full support from the Soviet Union, which hoped the

KMT would win control of all China. To further Chinese revolutionaries' ideological training, on January 25, 1926, the Soviet Union founded Moscow Sun Yat-sen University. The university's first intake comprised 250 Chinese students, all talented KMT members, who studied a variety of subjects, mostly related to East Asia.[8]

Soviet ability to maneuver in China was intimately bound up with the state of Soviet relations with Great Britain, and these in turn closely informed the attitudes and policies of the British government in Hong Kong toward the Soviet government and its representatives. For much of the interwar period, each country regarded the other as its major enemy. During the 1920s, Soviet-British relations oscillated from outright hostility in 1920, to a more hopeful establishment of first commercial, then diplomatic relations by 1924. Subsequently, within months, the British government suspended all ties, but dealings between Britain and the Soviet Union concluded on a hopeful note with the reestablishment of commercial and diplomatic relations at the close of the decade. The British sought the repayment of debts incurred during the Tsarist era, the ending of Soviet propaganda directed at people within the British Empire and at home, and enhanced trade and commerce. The Soviet Union sought legitimacy from Europe's still preeminent capitalist power, trade with Britain, and access to its huge colonial market. While the British Labour Party tended to be more sympathetic toward the Soviet Union, at no time during this decade could the relationship between Britain and the Soviet Union be described as cordial or warm. Given the prevailing mutual distrust and fear, many observers have written that the Cold War that raged between East and West actually began in 1921, soon after the Bolshevik Revolution triumphed throughout Russia. This underlying coolness informed British attitudes toward Soviet activities in Hong Kong and elsewhere in South China throughout the 1920s.[9]

Fundamentally poor Soviet-British relations had a major impact on the Soviets' ability to maneuver in South China. The overall situation in and around Hong Kong was unfavorable to the promotion of Comintern and Soviet objectives in South China. As early as 1919, the "Bolshevik threat" alarmed the British and Hong Kong governments, causing the British War Office to compile a list of alleged Bolshevik agents in South China and Hong Kong.[10] The British nonetheless still tended to minimize the gravity of such dangers. In 1919, the Acting British Consul in Guangzhou declared that, scandalous working conditions in that city notwithstanding, he thought it unlikely that Bolshevism, a foreign ideology, would recruit many Chinese.[11]

Britain made serious efforts to prevent the spread of either Communist or KMT influence in the South China region, undertakings greatly facilitated by its possession of Hong Kong. Within South China, if United Front forces advanced northwards from Guangzhou to unite China, professional British troops could attack them from the rear. The British government also sent money to aid Sun's main rivals in Guangzhou, the city's wealthy merchants, who opposed the introduction of any left-wing regime there and wished to restore good relations with Hong Kong, their traditional trading partner. The only sea route along which the Soviet Union could assist the United Front government with supplies ran from Soviet-controlled Vladivostok to Guangzhou. Without such help the KMT army could not begin advancing toward North China to unite the country.

The Soviet Civil War, although essentially over by 1921, had a fairly protracted impact, scattering the Russian Far East Fleet, both military and civilian, to bases and ports around the region, almost halting the Soviet fishing industry. Only in 1923 did the Russian Far East Fleet resume operations. Although by 1924 the Fleet had only 14 ships and five freighters, it increased by June 1927 to 24 ships.[12] Hong Kong, however, posed the main obstacle to Soviet maritime deliveries of war matériel to Guangzhou. The British, who believed Communists dominated the United Front, did not encourage China's unification under KMT auspices. The substantial British naval and military contingents in Hong Kong could and did stop and search any Soviet ships bound for Guangzhou. In April 1923, G. I. Safronov, Head of the Comintern Far East Section, warned his colleagues on the CPSU Politburo that the British obstructed Soviet shipments of arms to Guangzhou through Hong Kong.[13] Hong Kong courts imposed customs duties and enforced health quarantine provisions on Soviet imports, posing further barriers to Soviet commerce. All vessels required a passenger certificate to enter Hong Kong, and Soviet ships often did not meet the high standards required to gain permission to enter the port. Although the Soviets resented British behavior, they had few means of effective retaliation. British obstructionism prevented the Soviets from establishing a quick, easy, and direct trade route between Vladivostok and Guangzhou. Even so, numerous Soviet ships successfully traveled from Vladivostok to South China carrying arms, defying an international embargo on such traffic. The British government declared that "it was highly regrettable that the Soviet government, though not a party to the arms embargo, should permit such shipments." Steamers from the now Soviet-owned Russian Volunteer Fleet, such as the SS *Astrakhan*, brought in arms and ammunition, often concealed under timber, destined for the KMT.[14]

Orthodox Marxist-Leninist theory stated that only the urban working class possessed the ability to begin a revolution. China, however, was an overwhelmingly rural country with a vast peasantry, and only a few urban industrial centers, mostly coastal cities, such as Shanghai, Tianjin, and Hong Kong, containing a sizable working class. Superficially Hong Kong appeared a colonial backwater of about 500,000 inhabitants, almost all uneducated Chinese.[15] Since the new Bolshevik government sought to encourage international revolution spearheaded by the international proletariat, within a few years Hong Kong, at that time the largest industrial working-class city in China, with the most numerous and best-organized proletariat, attracted close Soviet scrutiny.

By the early 1920s, differences were emerging between the attitudes of the Comintern and the MID toward Hong Kong.[16] The Comintern tended to be far more aggressive, seeking to use Hong Kong and its relative freedom to foment revolution not just in Hong Kong but throughout China. The organization had numerous paid activists in Hong Kong, each of whom received 40 gold rubles a month, a substantial sum at that time. Members of Hong Kong's tiny Communist Party, closely affiliated to the Comintern, conducted propaganda, and planned to develop the colony as a Communist center in any forthcoming revolution in China.[17] The MID, by contrast, hesitated to foment violence in Hong Kong. By late 1923, the Soviet Union was close to establishing full diplomatic relations with Great Britain, a breakthrough the Soviet government did not wish to jeopardize.[18] The opening of diplomatic relations was likely to facilitate the expansion of Soviet political and economic activities in South China and Hong Kong. Grigory Chicherin, the Soviet People's Commissar of Foreign Affairs, restricted Comintern activities, warning that talks were already going on to establish relations, and for the time being any provocative actions against Britain were therefore undesirable. Ambassador Leonid M. Karakhan wrote Mikhail Borodin that, once diplomatic relations were established, "Soviet citizens would have the same rights as citizens of other countries that had diplomatic ties with the

United Kingdom. Specifically, Soviet citizens would not need a visa to enter Hong Kong, at least for transit."[19] Just as with numerous other countries, therefore, the Soviet Union took an ambivalent attitude toward Hong Kong. The differing policies of its two international organizations, the activist Comintern and more cautious MID, reflected their divergent objectives.

From its inception, Hong Kong granted far more personal freedom to its citizens than other Chinese cities, operated under a British-style rule of law, and was generally far more politically, economically, and financially stable. Hong Kong, therefore, offered many more opportunities to Comintern activists and Communist groups, to the point that Comintern activist and Soviet diplomat Adolf Ioffe described the city to Soviet Ambassador Karakhan as a weak link for the capitalist world.[20] Although these features facilitated political activism, the Soviet Union and the Comintern contemptuously denigrated "bourgeois" freedom and democratic institutions, stating: "In those few colonies where the Imperialists have established 'democratic' institutions modeled on the home country, power still really rested in the hands of the governors. The 'democratic' form was just a 'plaything' in the hands of the governor."[21] Simultaneously, however, the Comintern urged local Communists and Comintern agents to form a Hong Kong Communist Party composed of "members of the workers and intelligentsia, and organize trade unions in Hong Kong."[22] The earliest overtly Communist presence in Hong Kong was represented by a Socialist Youth League, rather than a formal Communist Party, and at the time of its formation in 1923 that group had a mere handful of members. According to the seminal work of Chan Lau Kit-ching on the Communist Party in Hong Kong, from its very inception the Hong Kong Communist Party, formally organized in late 1923 and possessing only a few members, was heavily dependent on outside forces, namely, the Soviet Union and South Chinese radicals.[23]

Paradoxically, while Communist groups, strictly supervised by Comintern emissaries, began to operate and gain influence throughout China, they encountered great problems in doing so in Hong Kong, an elegant illustration of the existing contradictions between Marxist theory and practice. Major differences divided Hong Kong trade union policies from those of the contemporary KMT, and most Hong Kong trade unions had a low opinion of both Sun and the Communists. In fact,

Hong Kong trade unions were hardly unions in the modern sense. Most were poorly organized, resembled guilds and associations, and were frequently led by triad (secret society) bosses.[24] Soviet agents recognized that pro-Soviet Chinese Communists had virtually no influence among Hong Kong workers, who looked, if anywhere, to the indigenous KMT and did not wish to struggle for the interests of a Communist Party that was under Soviet external control. Hong Kong workers primarily sought neither revolution, nor even China's unification, but to satisfy their economic demands within Hong Kong, valuing stability and order if only as the means to increase their generally very low standard of living. In a 1924 report, Borodin stated that Hong Kong had over 200,000 well-organized Chinese workers, who were strong enough to shut Hong Kong down, and that the British feared Soviet influence on these workers. Borodin also noted, however, that Hong Kong workers were still independent-minded—he even characterized them as "arrogant"—and "accepted control from no one."[25] Making it even more difficult for Comintern and Communist agents to organize and propagandize was the fact that Hong Kong workers represented a highly transient element in an ever shifting population. All attempts by Sun himself, as well as by Soviet advisers in Guangzhou, to organize a political strike in Hong Kong to destabilize the territory eventually ended in complete failure.

In 1922, one Communist activist, Victor Chen Su Chao, wrote that a 1920 strike by Hong Kong metal workers marked the effective beginning of the Chinese labor movement.[26] Responding to a report that to date the only labor activism in China had been economic strikes by workers seeking higher wages, one Communist operative, the Dutch Communist Henk Sneevliet (under the pseudonym Maring), wrote: "This was wrong; the big sailors' strike at Hong Kong in January 1922 was a political move of the KMT against the Hong Kong government, as well as an economic strike."[27] Yet, even though Hong Kong's Chinese population occasionally made use of organized strikes and boycotts to protest against what appeared to them British injustices, in the early 1920s, the situation in the territory was not one where agitation and strikes were likely to precipitate revolution. In April 1920, high inflation, which greatly increased their cost of living, making simple economic survival difficult, led Hong Kong engineers to demand a 40 percent pay raise. When their request was rejected, the engineers left Hong Kong for neighboring Guangzhou. Their withdrawal brought life to a standstill in Hong Kong, now a modern industrial city dependent upon telecommunications, trams, electricity, and gas, to serve a growing industrial base. Soon the employers agreed to a 32 percent pay increase, nearly the strikers' original demand, whereupon the engineers returned and Hong Kong soon resumed normal life.[28]

In early 1922, the Chinese Seamen's Union demanded similar wage hikes. The British government permitted local companies to pay the ethnic Chinese among Hong Kong's 50,000 seamen a fraction of the wages their European counterparts received for the same work, as well as providing inferior living conditions.[29] Private dormitories, where most Chinese seamen lodged, took some 20 percent of their wages in rent. To combat the high World War I inflation, the Hong Kong government promised Chinese seamen an additional monthly insurance allowance, but the companies pocketed the money and never passed it on to their workers. Seamen who took the issue to the Hong Kong courts were rebuffed. With no other recourse, on January 22, 1922, 3,000 seamen went on strike, rejecting pleas from the Hong Kong government to resume work, and soon their numbers grew to over 10,000. Most Hong Kong grocery stores closed, due to exhausted stocks, forcing the government to dispatch ships manned by 500 soldiers to Guangzhou to obtain food supplies. As the situation snowballed, the number of strikers increased further, to 30,000; half Hong Kong's businesses and banks shut their doors; and transport workers joined, bringing the number of strikers to 60,000, at which point the government brought in strikebreakers from the Philippines and from the city of Shanghai. About 1,000 British troops patrolled Hong Kong's streets, but 20 warehouses were nonetheless set on fire, while other workers, including domestic servants, engineers, coolies, printers, mechanics, and even—despite their usual loyalty to the British—some civil servants, joined the strike. By March 3, an estimated 120,000 workers participated in what was approaching a full-scale general strike, which virtually closed the city down for three weeks.[30] In fact, the Seamen's strike was the most extensive strike in modern Chinese history up to that time. While Communists played no leadership role in the strike, some Communists in Hong Kong participated, and other Communists in neighboring Guangzhou made supporting speeches and published the strikers' manifesto.[31]

The Hong Kong government adopted a carrot-and-stick approach to these disturbances. It declared martial law, put more troops on the streets, banned the Chinese Seamen's Union, forbade Hong Kong people to leave the colony, and authorized forced labor. British Indian troops fired on the assembled crowds, killing five people. Declaring that local police and troops were overwhelmed, on March 11, Governor Sir Reginald Stubbs wrote to the Colonial Office requesting additional police and up to two more battalions of troops. He did, however, state that the Colonial Office's fear that up to 70,000 military and paramilitary forces from Guangzhou might attack Hong Kong was greatly exaggerated.[32] The Hong Kong government also declared that the hostile attitude of Nationalist Chinese president Sun Yat-sen toward British rule had contributed to these events and that Bolsheviks had assisted him in this, and therefore banned Sun and his purported Bolshevik supporters from Hong Kong.

Repressive measures proved ineffective and only provoked significant criticism. The Hong Kong government itself conceded that it had made mistakes, such as banning the Seamen's Union and underestimating the strength of the opposition. The government agreed to further negotiations with the strikers, and eventually conceded most of the large wage increases they demanded.[33] Hong Kong returned to normal and, despite their victory, inflation eroded the seamen's wage increases.[34] The Comintern believed the CCP should have given more active support to the strikers.[35] Certainly, many of their gains were illusory. In 1929, Albert Thomas, a representative of the League of Nations' affiliate the ILO, visited Guangzhou, where the International Seamen's Union informed him of their grievances against the Hong Kong government. When the Hong Kong Seamen's Strike ended in 1922, for example, the seamen were promised 300,000 Chinese dollars as partial compensation for lost wages, but over the next seven years the shipping companies had never paid the settlement money.[36]

The International Seamen's Union continued its work and even expanded to other cities. Under Comintern auspices, in June 1924, they held an organizing conference in Guangzhou, composed of delegates from China, the Philippines, the Dutch East Indies, British India, and Japan. An invitation issued to their Chinese comrades to attend a dinner on June 23 reveals that Hong Kong representatives were also present at this conference.[37] The delegates at the organizing conference, whose exact number the available documents failed to mention, agreed to unite forces to form a federation to centralize administration and leadership. This newly formed Transport Conference of the Orient agreed on a governing bureau, composed of one delegate from each of the five participating countries. With branches already established in Hong Kong and Guangzhou, the governing bureau initially decided to expand its organization to the ports of Manila and Batavia (Jakarta), and then coordinate common activities to foster mutual connections. In those four cities, the governing bureau's branches would "propagate and explain to seamen their trade and class needs, and the necessity of an international organization. Clubs would also have small libraries, as well as arrange entertainment for visiting sailors." The governing bureau agreed to publish a bulletin in English and Chinese.[38] The conference credited Hong Kong with being the largest port in the entire Pacific Ocean. The real significance of the Guangzhou conference was that it marked the first important attempt since the Baku Congress of 1920 to develop closer contacts among workers from different countries, cultures, and languages in East and Southeast Asia.

The Comintern and Revolution in South China, 1921–1927

The second half of the 1920s was a particularly turbulent period in both South China and Hong Kong, during which Soviet Communist influence peaked but was eventually savagely repressed after the KMT general, official, and politician, Chiang Kai-shek, consolidated his hold on power. British officials in Hong Kong likewise took measures, albeit somewhat less ferocious, to suppress both indigenous and Soviet radicals, though in 1927, they did provide brief temporary asylum for a party of fleeing Soviet diplomats who had survived brutal Nationalist assaults in Guangzhou.

In March 1925, Sun Yat-sen died, generating further instability in China, where Communist Party membership in all cities, including Hong Kong, was growing.[39] The British government sought to discourage Soviet Communists from entering Hong Kong. Between 1925 and 1927, only ten Soviet citizens were granted transit visas which allowed them to pass through Hong Kong on their way to Guangzhou. The British Legation in Beijing resented issuing even such visas, stating: "We are highly reluctant at a time when Soviet authorities were using every effort to foment anti-British feeling in China, that we should have to grant visas to persons who are taking part." The Legation therefore sought permission from Foreign Secretary Austen Chamberlain to deny Soviet officials and citizens transit visas to Hong Kong, though the official in question conceded that this might cause some difficulties. First, the number of transit visas granted to Soviet citizens to pass through Hong Kong had been minimal, and refusing these "would not impede their travels in China." Secondly, any blanket refusal to grant Hong Kong visas to Soviets "would be certain to evoke reprisals, which would definitely affect large numbers of British subjects (who wish to travel to the Soviet Union) as well as mail that went between Britain and the Soviet Union." Yet, except for the issue of extremely temporary transit visas, Hong Kong Governor Stubbs "did not wish visas to be granted unless definite recommendations could be given with the visa request."[40]

British resentment over Soviet efforts to foment unrest in Hong Kong increased after the 1925 May 30th Incident in Shanghai. In May 1925, Chinese and Indian police under British command killed 11 demonstrators in Shanghai's International Settlement, giving radical activists the excuse they sought to take action. A wave of nationalist indignation and demands to end all foreign privileges swept throughout China. On June 19, 1925, general strikes were proclaimed in Shanghai and Hong Kong.[41] Chinese workers in those cities and elsewhere refused to board or unload British ships, and Chinese refused to trade with or buy and sell from or to British firms and individuals. Four days later, on June 23, British-led troops fired into a crowd in the diplomatic quarter of Shamien in Guangzhou, killing 52 Chinese demonstrators and wounding over a hundred more, many of them students. Chinese particularly resented the existence of an armed foreign enclave in a Chinese city, and many Guangzhou people called for a war to drive out all foreigners. Tensions rose throughout numerous Chinese cities, as more and more Chinese cried out that harsh and discriminatory treatment in their own country had to end.

Violent anti-British sentiment swept throughout Hong Kong, intensifying the Hong Kong strike. In response, the Hong Kong government instituted a blockade of Guangzhou, which, with the rest of Guangdong province, depended on Hong Kong for rice and other foodstuffs. "The British attempted to starve and crush Guangzhou as a center of Nationalist activity."[42] Victor Chen, the leading Soviet Comintern agent in Hong Kong, became head of its strike committee. In fact, Hong Kong Communists, as a whole, played a significant leading role in the strike and the subsequent boycott. Communists saw these activities as a golden opportunity to recruit new members, and expand their influence. Authorities in Hong

Kong sponsored volunteers, who staffed essential services, and anti-Communists attacked strikers. 250,000 strikers and their families left for Guangzhou, where they were fed and housed by the well-funded Guangzhou strike committee, which had already organized the boycott of Hong Kong.[43] The Soviet Union undoubtedly played a major role in the General Strike, though the growth of CCP influence widened existing internal divisions between the leftists and the rightists within the KMT. Having received an intelligence report, Foreign Secretary Austen Chamberlain commented on December 6, 1925: "There can be no doubt as to the close connection between the Bolsheviks and the anti-foreign and labor movement in South China."[44] Seeking to counter Soviet propaganda and anti-British sentiment, the Hong Kong government spent HK$200,000 (£20,000) to mount a pro-British propaganda campaign against the Soviet Union. The government used its Publicity Bureau and the pro-British Chinese newspaper *Kung Sheung Yat Po* to present "the correct news, and fairly represent British aims and actions."[45]

Independent action by textile workers in Shanghai resulted in a 16-month long strike and boycott of foreign businesses in Guangzhou and Hong Kong. As the strike went on, commerce in Hong Kong fell by 80 percent.[46] Interestingly, Soviet trade benefited significantly from the boycott of British products in Guangzhou and Shanghai, and 66 Soviet ships in all sailed from Vladivostok to Guangzhou. The balance of trade heavily favored the Soviets, who sold far more goods to Guangzhou and other parts of Southern China than they shipped in return from China to Vladivostok. The most significant commodity the Soviets delivered to Guangzhou was kerosene.[47] Preoccupied with their own problems, the British authorities could take little action to stop Soviet shipments, and Soviet officials admitted that the boycott of the British fleet gave their own shipping a free field in South China.[48]

Both the AVP RF and PRO(CO) contain documents claiming that, between 1924 and 1927, besides relatively innocent items such as fish, oil, kerosene, or even arms, Soviet vessels carried cargoes of opium from Vladivostok to Guangzhou.[49] Two Chinese newspapers in Beijing, *Zhi Bao* and *Chen Bao*, reported on this trade, allegations which aroused great concern among Soviet officials. The MID in Moscow sent a telegram to its Beijing Consulate, stating that the Chinese Consulate in Moscow had passed on these accusations to them, and characterizing as "bizarre" the newspaper articles concerned.[50] In October 1927, Mr. Demidov, the MID representative in the Far Eastern city of Nikolaevsk-Ussurisk, had a personal conversation concerning these reports with Han Shu Tsin, the city's Chinese Consul. Demidov subsequently wrote the Consul angrily on the subject, demanding that the Chinese deny all such reports published in the Chinese press: "1. There is no direct evidence for these charges, just hearsay. 2. Did you, the Chinese Consul, give any information about opium to the Beijing newspapers? 3. Officially, you will also deny all the accusations. You promised me (in our earlier meeting) to make a written denial of these charges."[51] Han meekly complied with Soviet browbeating, replying to Demidov two weeks later: "I inform you that the Chinese government will deny all these accusations made against the Soviet Union."[52] Given the MID's indignant yet defensive attitude, it is likely that, at least for the 1920s, allegations that the cash-strapped Soviet Union took part in the international drug trade may well have had some foundation.

The Hong Kong government feared that, should the British policy of inaction continue, Hong Kong would be ruined and British trade with South China would disappear, perhaps permanently. On September 25, 1925, Governor Stubbs sent the Colonial Secretary a telegram reiterating these fears, urging Britain to provide financial assistance to the Beijing-based northern Chinese government's efforts to suppress the United Front regime in Guangzhou. He warned that Foreign Office functionaries had commented in meetings that the Hong Kong situation "almost certainly was getting desperate unless the credit stringency gripping Hong Kong is relieved." He also stated that Soviet arms shipments must be cut off.[53] The Colonial Secretary quickly cabled back, responding that the "present disastrous situation was fully realized by His Majesty's Government, especially in Hong Kong, whose losses and sufferings HMG deeply deplored."[54] The Hong Kong government urged the British government to grant permission to the Beijing government, a warlord regime that claimed jurisdiction over all China, to use Hong Kong's naval facilities. Governor Stubbs also proposed that the British government furnish the northern Chinese government with launches, to stop Soviet ships carrying arms at the mouth of the Pearl River, which runs from Hong Kong to Guangzhou. Hong Kong was prepared to contribute HK$100,000,000 to the cost of overthrowing the left-wing Guangzhou government.[55] Foreign Secretary Austen Chamberlain, however, "was unwilling to take a decision on a matter of such importance without full knowledge as to the probable effect of the proposed action on Canton and the rest of China."[56] Another Foreign Office official, S. P. Waterlow, agreed that the Hong Kong government had acted rashly in suggesting such action.[57]

Many on all sides feared that the situation was escalating dangerously. On September 10, 1925, in an *Izvestiya* interview, Soviet Ambassador Karakhan stated that "late events (the strike and boycott) have shown that Guangzhou's main danger is from Hong Kong. It was only the trade unions which have declared the boycott, and the Chinese government (in Guangzhou) could not be held responsible."[58] Britain feared that "unless steps were taken soon to arrest the Communist movement, the whole of South China would be under Bolshevik control by the end of the year."[59] The Hong Kong government declared that Russians fostered the situation by contributing arms and money to the left-wing Guangzhou government, and that Borodin himself played a major role in fostering these activities.[60] In 1925 British authorities in Shanghai granted M. Z. Dosser, a Soviet citizen, a visa to proceed to Guangzhou via Hong Kong on business for the Soviet Petroleum Syndicate. While in Hong Kong he aroused the suspicions of the police, who examined his personal effects and found inflammatory materials. The Hong Kong authorities determined that Dosser's real purpose in visiting Shanghai and Hong Kong was to organize strikes, so they sent him and his wife back to Shanghai, where local police arrested him. This incident constituted Hong Kong's first real proof of the Soviet government's complicity in the anti-foreign disorders, which until then had only rested on well-founded speculation.[61]

For various reasons of their own, all parties concerned—the Hong Kong government, Hong Kong workers, the Soviet Union, and the Shanghai-based KMT—believed that the General Strike should end before the situation got completely out of hand, and effectively cooperated to bring this about. On April 28, 1926, MID official Nikolai Rogachev wrote that his government believed the strike had lasted too long, though he gave no reasons for this.[62] On June 5, 1926, the Guangzhou KMT government wrote to the Hong Kong governor, stating that Chiang Kai-shek, the new KMT leader, sought to improve relations with the British and would facilitate negotiations to this end. This letter expressed readiness to open talks to reach a final settlement, and proposed that three representatives from each side meet and work together.[63] During these talks, those Hong Kong workers who still remained in Guangzhou agreed to return to their old jobs in Hong Kong, though their demands that they should receive back pay totaling HK$1,000,000 for the period they were on strike were unsuccessful.[64] Bellicose Governor Stubbs left the territory, to be replaced by the far quieter Sir Cecil Clementi, a scholar from the Colonial Service, who—even though the British still hoped it would eventually be overthrown—reestablished relations with the KMT government in Guangzhou, albeit on a chilly basis.

On all sides, the consequences of the Hong Kong General Strike were substantial. The Soviet Union successfully reestablished a direct route from Vladivostok to Guangzhou to ship arms, petroleum, and other products, supplies that would be critical to the KMT's forthcoming military campaign against North China's warlords.[65] Soon after the British reestablished order in Hong Kong, however, British warships once again began to intercept Soviet vessels passing near Hong Kong on their way to Guangzhou. On March 19, 1927, for example, the British navy seized the Soviet ship *Grigori* near the Hong Kong island of Tan Shan and took it to Hong Kong. There the vessel was searched and the crew arrested; though 24 hours later both ship and crew were released and allowed to proceed to Guangzhou. On April 12, Soviet chargé d'affaires M. Rosengol'ts protested formally to the British government, stating that between 1925 and that date, the *Grigori* had traveled the same route nine times without encountering any problems. The Soviet government politely requested that no further actions of this nature should be taken, warning that otherwise, "the Soviet government would reserve to itself the right to ask compensation for any material loss, sustained in connection with such action of the British authorities."[66] In response to this and other incidents, the Soviet government urged the Guangzhou government to construct a new deep-water port. Reporting to Ambassador Karakhan, Soviet Consul-General Boris Pokhvalinsky noted that, because Guangzhou's port was not deep enough, 80 percent of large ships had to use Hong Kong. "A new port is important to free Guangzhou from dependence on Hong Kong."[67] The British government naturally enough opposed building such a facility. The United States government, by contrast, supported the left-wing Guangzhou government on the issue, reaffirming its support for Chinese independence and territorial integrity, and perhaps also demonstrating its own commercial rivalries with Britain and disinclination to depend on Hong Kong's facilities.

The strike and boycott severely damaged Hong Kong's economy, inflicting substantial and protracted damage on Hong Kong commerce. It was estimated that the territory lost £100,000,000. The British underestimated the power of Chinese nationalism among ordinary Hong Kong people, and the strike likewise increased the influence of the CCP and its backers, the Comintern and the Soviet Union. It also contributed to the severance of relations between the Soviet Union and Great Britain in May 1927.[68] The British government believed the Soviet Union had directly interfered in the internal affairs of one of its colonies, Hong Kong, through alleged contributions of funds and advice to the strikers.[69] In British eyes, the Soviet Union was very willing, despite disclaimers, to use its precious financial resources to try and destabilize a British colony with the ultimate goal of destroying the British Empire. Britain questioned the value of relations with a state, which was fully controlled by a political party "whose objective was the world-wide triumph of an alien and hostile ideology."[70] While neither the Comintern nor the MID files contain a "smoking gun" of orders relayed from the headquarters of the Comintern, the Soviet Union was certainly pleased with its results, which weakened British rule in Hong Kong, and heightened anti-British feelings throughout the territory.[71]

One final result of the Hong Kong General Strike was a strengthening of the Guangzhou KMT government, which then decided to launch its Northern Expedition to unify all China under its control. As originally conceived by Sun Yat-sen, the Northern Expedition had a clear purpose, to wipe out the warlords and frustrate their Western "imperialist" supporters. Sun's death aborted the first planned expedition. Chiang Kai-shek, head of the Huangpu Military Academy near Guangzhou, who replaced Sun as KMT leader, developed a powerful officer corps around a nucleus of Huangpu cadets, to staff a new party-directed army of 85,000 troops which could reestablish central authority. Within six months, Chiang established authoritarian rule over both the KMT and South China. On July 1, 1925, he established a Nationalist government in Guangzhou, which rivaled the warlord government in Beijing in claiming sovereignty over all China.[72]

Initially, a KMT-CCP split over the issue of dual membership threatened to wreck the Communist Party and interrupt the Northern Expedition. Whereas the KMT expected Communists to accept KMT leadership and obey its orders, the CCP demanded that its members take orders from the Communist Party and form a secret internal bloc within the KMT. In August 1925, right-wing KMT leaders demanded the ouster of Communists from the United Front, and the deportation of all Soviet advisers, including Borodin, from China. Left-wing KMT members declared this August meeting invalid and called their own conference, precipitating a complete split between left and right. Despite well-founded Communist anxieties, Stalin continued to support Chiang.[73]

For different reasons, both Soviet and British officials were apprehensive over the potential impact of Chiang's military plans on the Japanese position in North China. After the August meeting, Fedor F. Roskolnikov wrote to Voitinsky, who was still in China, declaring that "we should not interfere with Japan's interests in North China. The Chinese government in the north should be a coalition. We should make the Japanese understand that any anti-Japanese activities in the north were not our doing, but were intended to worsen Soviet-Japanese relations."[74] Stalin likewise opposed any advance of southern forces into North China, believing that they were too weak to undertake such a campaign, and that Chiang should focus on the internal strengthening of the KMT, which was threatened by splits. Stalin believed any future northern government must be a coalition, declaring: "There is no possibility of forming a total KMT government." The Soviet Union feared any increase of Japanese military influence in North China, and at a crucial December 1925 Politburo meeting, Stalin warned that any drive north by Chiang might provoke Japanese military intervention, which he thought would be disastrous.[75] Writing to Commissar Chicherin in May 1926, a Soviet diplomat in Shanghai characterized Chiang's plans to lead his army north as complete lunacy, a view in which his colleagues in Shanghai concurred.[76] British officials, by contrast, regarded Japan as a relatively reliable bulwark against both China and the Soviet Union. A December 1926 Foreign Office memorandum declared that the Soviet Union pursued the same expansionist aims in East Asia as had Tsarist Russia, but more effectively and less scrupulously. Urging that Britain cooperate with Japan to counter Soviet activities, the report stated that British policy in the region should be based upon the assumption that Russia, not Japan, was the enemy. It concluded that all Britain need fear from Japan was commercial competition, rather than any military threat.[77] British officials were unlikely to endorse any move by Chiang that might, in their opinion, enhance Russian influence at Japan's expense.

The British were, by contrast, unlikely to quarrel with Chiang's increasingly anti-Soviet bias, even when they distrusted other aspects of

Chiang's nationalist and anti-colonialist outlook. Reverberations from Chiang's anti-Communist and anti-Soviet measures in Guangzhou would ultimately reach Hong Kong. In spring 1926, Chiang launched his campaign against the Communists and his Soviet advisers. In March, he ordered the arrest of Communist political commissars attached to all military units under his command, confined his Soviet advisers to the Tun Shan district outside Guangzhou, and disarmed the strike committees that had actively conducted the General Strike in Hong Kong, Guangzhou, and Shanghai. On March 20, Chiang arrested Li Chi Lun, commander of the Nationalist Fleet and a CCP member. The KMT Politburo later freed many of those arrested, whereupon Chiang, isolated within his Politburo and realizing that at least for the moment he had gone too far, apologized and tried to shift the blame to others. The Comintern accepted his apology, ignored his actions, and refused to retaliate against Chiang.

In Guangzhou, the increasingly apprehensive local CCP realized that Chiang would take further action once he felt politically stronger, and therefore urged immediate action against him.[78] Reinforcing CCP fears, in March 1926 Chinese troops surrounded the Guangzhou street where most Russians lived. When Razgon, a Soviet official from the Consulate, protested, Chiang feigned outrage. Razgon feared that both the Comintern and Soviet leaders were naïve in dealing with Chiang.[79] In May 1926, Chiang ordered the expulsion of Communists from all senior posts. Even then, Stalin, Bukharin, and Borodin, all of whom still believed the KMT must be the main instrument to unify China, reacted cautiously, and Borodin still refused to arm Communist units with Soviet weapons. In a speech reported in the Guangzhou newspaper *Kwok Man San Man* on February 17, 1926, Borodin identified himself completely with the Nationalist government and urged the establishment of a united KMT government representing all China.[80] The response of other Comintern officials was fragmented and inconsistent. The opposition of Leon Trotsky and Grigory Zinoviev, Stalin's main rivals in the bitter Soviet internal power struggle, to the ever less united Chinese United Front only intensified Stalin's support for Chiang, regardless of the counsels of both CCP leaders and several of his own Soviet advisers.[81]

Mikhail Borodin, the chief Soviet adviser in Guangzhou, remained a staunch supporter of the Northern Expedition. In late 1925 he urged that Hong Kong workers should strike once again to paralyze British rule in the city, which would allow a United Front army to march northwards without any British opposition, and advance on Shanghai and Nanjing as the first step to uniting China. Fedor F. Roskolnikov disagreed, labeling Borodin "a Napoleon" for promoting himself as a leader in the Northern Expedition.[82] Kisanok, another KMT Soviet adviser, simultaneously begged Moscow to remove Borodin from his post, terming him a troublemaker and accusing him of practicing "cheap diplomacy" by making promises he could not fulfill, and of conducting personal diplomacy with KMT generals instead of a "systematic (regular) diplomacy."[83] The Soviet Consul-General in Guangzhou urged the government to recall Borodin, complaining to Ambassador Karakhan that Borodin acted like a dictator, and he himself always had to go through Borodin's wife.[84] In early 1926, these complaints impelled Borodin's superior to send Valerian V. Kuibyshev, a Politburo member, to China to supervise his activities.[85] After six months, Kuibyshev finally decided that Borodin must leave. A much relieved Kisanok wrote Moscow: "Borodin is leaving, a good thing because he is causing more harm than good." Needing a replacement forthwith, he begged: "[S]end me someone, but not Borodin."[86] A German Communist, Heinz Neumann, replaced Borodin in South China.[87] It took a while, however, for Borodin to actually leave China. On October 1, 1927, *Izvestiya* reported that Borodin had arrived at the Siberian town of Verkhneudink en route to Moscow. The news report claimed, misleadingly, that his departure was voluntary.[88]

Bolstered by Soviet supplies, in July 1926, Chiang launched a lightning campaign from Guangzhou through central China, capturing Wuhan in September, Nanchang in November, Fuzhou in December, and—assisted by Communist-organized strikes in both—the major cities of Shanghai and Nanjing in March 1927. In January 1927, the KMT moved its capital to Wuhan, and Chiang rapidly consolidated his power base in Eastern and Southeastern China, successfully winning control of China's southern half. Large-scale Soviet assistance to Chiang's forces led Governor Clementi of Hong Kong to question continuing British adherence to the China Arms Embargo Agreement and urge the Colonial Office that British firms be allowed to supply arms and ammunition to the Northern warlords, a proposal his superiors rejected. The Colonial Office only allowed Clementi to provide non-military assistance to such recipients, rebuking him with a reminder that the Hong Kong government was not empowered to act unilaterally on such matters, but must follow London's direction.[89]

The Soviet Union, Hong Kong, and the Guangzhou Uprising, 1927

1927 was a disastrous year for the Soviet Union, the Comintern, and the CCP, marking a debacle for "progressive" forces in China. By the time it ended Stalin's China policy lay in shambles; tens of thousands of Chinese Communist activists and their working-class supporters in several key cities lay dead; the CCP itself was divided and greatly weakened; and Chiang firmly controlled the KMT, which became a fiercely anti-Communist force. In city after city, beginning with Shanghai in April and culminating with Guangzhou in December, the Communists resisted, but unsuccessfully. Battered and shocked Soviet refugees from Guangzhou finally rather dramatically sought temporary sanctuary in Hong Kong, which even antagonistic British officials were not prepared to deny them.

When 1927 began two distinct KMT armies existed: one, under leftist control, was based in Guangzhou; the other, campaigning in the field under Chiang, sought to take Shanghai. As Chiang's forces approached the city in February 1927, Communist-dominated trade unions called a general strike, ensuring that Chiang's army encountered no serious opposition when it entered Shanghai in April. At that juncture the cunning Chiang, supported by merchants and other businessmen, turned decisively against his Communist supporters in Shanghai, massacring thousands of workers and their intellectual leaders.[90] At the same time, the Hong Kong government feared that, in order to demonstrate solidarity with their persecuted Shanghai comrades, Hong Kong Communists would lead another general strike in the colony, which was only just recovering from that of 1925–1926. To prevent this, on April 7, 1927, Governor Clementi outlawed the General Labour Union of Hong Kong, which was trying to foment another general strike. In response, the Hong Kong government reported that the left-wing Guangzhou government had sent a four-man squad to Hong Kong to assassinate Governor Clementi and several other leading political figures in the hope of sparking off an uprising.[91] The CCP dilemma was whether to continue to preserve the United Front in compliance with Comintern directives, or dissolve the alliance with the KMT and invite Comintern censure. Stalin recognized that his China policies lay in total ruins. Leon Trotsky, his still powerful and popular opponent, correctly accused him of following a flawed policy, which had caused the deaths of so many Chinese supporters and wrecked the CCP.

Stalin had no real choice but finally to swing to the left and agree to dissolve the United Front and establish Chinese Soviets.

In mid-November 1927, CCP activists and Comintern agents under Neumann's direction decided to launch an uprising in Guangzhou, which would begin one month later. "Red Guangzhou," since the mid-1920s a leading Chinese revolutionary center, was an obvious choice. For several years, until Li Jishen, an anti-Communist landowner, overthrew it in 1926, Guangzhou had a radical government. Its trade unions, especially its seamen, printers, and rickshaw drivers, had very actively assisted Hong Kong's workers in their 1925–1926 General Strike. The Hong Kong press claimed that the Soviet Union had controlled the former Guangzhou government, even alleging that all major decisions were made in the Soviet Consulate, located in the city's Tun Shan suburb.[92] The city government, trade unions, and the Strike Committee sheltered and financially aided the destitute Hong Kong strikers, who retreated to Guangzhou. Furthermore, workers and Communists were greatly angered when merchants and anti-Communists took control of the city government in October 1926, after the Hong Kong General Strike ended. Once conservatives regained control of the Guangzhou government, Soviet activities in the city declined. On February 19, 1927, a British observer reported that a mere 25 Russians remained in the Tun Shan district, once swarming with them. No new Soviet advisers arrived in the city to train Chinese soldiers, and only three Soviet officers were still based at the Huangpu Military Academy.[93]

After the April 1927 Shanghai massacre, around 2,000 to 3,000 labor activists were arrested in Guangzhou, of whom 200 were executed. For the next few months arrests and executions continued. This purge threw the entire Communist Party within Guangzhou, the center for the Party in South China, into disarray. The Comintern assisted survivors in their flight to Hong Kong, where they attempted to reconstitute a Communist Party cell, hampered by a hostile British government and a general lack of funds, in absolute secrecy.[94] In May an American teacher living in Guangzhou wrote in his diary: "This clearing out of Communists has gone on for about a month now. Several thousand have been arrested and it is believed that about two thousand have been executed. These executions are at night and no public report is made of them. They are simply taken to the East Parade ground and shot."[95]

Guangzhou leftists resisted fiercely, through strikes, demonstrations, and other actions. In an atmosphere of betrayal and despair, anger and desperation, CCP activists and their worker allies decided on November 17, 1927, to rise up against the forces of reaction. Although the Soviet Union was directly involved through its consulate and the Comintern in this decision and in the uprising itself, most operations were the result of local Chinese initiative.[96] The Guangzhou CCP branch, located in Hong Kong, ordered the uprising. On December 11, 1927, over 20,000 men from military units as well as working-class Red Guard forces launched their uprising.[97] Within a few hours, they took control over much of the city. The CCP then announced the formation of a Guangzhou *Soviet*, modeled on the 1871 Paris Commune, to govern the city. However, within two days, on December 13, warlord armies recaptured Guangzhou. Over the next five days they instituted a "White Terror," killing nearly 6,000 men, women, and children. The leftist forces, badly armed and led, stood no chance against professional KMT and warlord troops. Harold Isaacs described that defeat as one more betrayal of the Chinese working class by the Comintern, the Soviet Union, and the CCP. A scholar of the Chinese revolutions, Arif Dirlik, believed the workers were fighting impossible odds, and did the best they could. These massacres repelled even the anti-Communist British, who reported that "anti-Red Nationalists who wrested the city from a Bolshevik reign of terror are themselves indulging in an orgy of execution of all Communists, Russians, and their Chinese dupes."[98]

The MID conceded that most foreigners and Chinese believed the Soviet Union was involved in the uprising. The Conservative British newspaper, the *Daily Telegraph*, flatly declared that Consul-General Boris Pokhvalinsky started the uprising. The *Lausanne Gazette*, a Swiss daily, claimed that a Russian identified only as one Mr. Kolachev, later killed during the uprising, took the decision to establish a Communist regime in Guangzhou on orders from Moscow. The newspaper further claimed that, when the KMT authorities learned of this, they sent a telegram to the anti-Communist Guangzhou government, ordering it to close the Soviet Consulate, and that in response the Consulate moved the dates of the uprising forward.[99] Other foreign and some Chinese newspapers claimed that two Communist generals and alleged Soviet agents, Van Sing-Vi and Chan Fa Gui, who had been appointed to lead the Guangzhou Commune, started the uprising. Unfortunately, all those documents which might have resolved these questions were destroyed when the Consulate was sacked after the uprising failed, and no documents the author has seen in the Russian archives either confirm or disprove whether there was any Soviet direct role. The Soviet news agency *Tass* characterized as lies allegations that the commanders were Soviet agents, even claiming, though far from credibly, that Van Sing-Vi, who led the uprising, was a KMT rather than a Communist agent.[100]

From the day the uprising began, the Consulate was in an exposed position. From its start the Soviets also believed that the uprising would fail, and feared that they would face repercussions once anti-Communist forces regained control of the city. They therefore prepared to leave the city, destroying all secret documents. Although all work in the Consulate ceased, its Soviet staff, fearing to expose their precarious position, nonetheless tried to give the outside world the impression that all was normal.[101] Distant from the city center where the uprising occurred, the Consulate was cut off from the city and the uprising. No police offered to protect its staff. Many thieves and other criminals appeared on the streets near the Consulate. Armed only with revolvers, the Russian staff prepared to defend themselves as they helplessly watched fires spreading throughout Guangzhou. Far from directing and controlling the uprising, as the KMT and British alleged, Soviet diplomats unsuccessfully sought to learn what had transpired in the city and the uprising.

On December 13, two days after the uprising began, and facing certain defeat, revolutionary forces began to flee Guangzhou. On that day, police and KMT troops surrounded the Consulate, preventing anyone either entering or leaving its grounds. Meanwhile, soldiers and paramilitary forces began hunting down and killing Chinese Communists and their working-class allies. KMT officers ordered Consul Pokhvalinsky to open the gates to the Consulate's grounds, which he did. Soldiers then entered the Consulate, taking prisoner the Consul and all other Russians, including women and children, tying them up, and threatening to line them up against the Consulate wall and shoot them all. That threat was not carried out, but more soldiers entered the compound and took all the Russians to a nearby square, where they were roughly handled and once more threatened with shooting. Eventually, their hands still tied, they were moved to a jail, where, the Consul recollected, in considerable pain, their bound hands aching, they waited through the night, fearing for their lives.[102]

At around ten the next morning, a group of Chinese KMT officers, led by a colonel, visited the prisoners, apologized for their rough treatment of the diplomats, and untied them. At that point, Pokhvalinsky protested. The Chinese collected the names of all prisoners, both Russians and Chinese. Some individuals, all adults, both Russians and Chinese citizens, were then taken outside, and placed on the street. Each Russian carried a sign stating: "This person is a Russian Communist, and anyone can do what he wants to him." Passersby stopped and beat, spat on, and even knifed them. Afterwards they were led to the nearest police station and shot. 14 Chinese women had their hair cut off, like common prostitutes, before being shot. Among the Russians killed in Guangzhou were Moisei Mikhailovich Volatsky, a student from Vladivostok who acted as an interpreter; Kirishev and his wife, formerly Borodin's secretary; and Kolachev, the uprising's supposed director. Only those four Russian bodies were recovered, and it is still uncertain just how many others were killed. The German Consul-General reported that on the night of December other Russian staff from the Consulate were arrested, spent the night in jail, and at lunch time the next day were taken away and never returned. The Germans and Soviets believed that all were executed. Those Soviet diplomats missing and presumed dead included Vice Consul Khassiz, Makarov, Vakulov, Ivanov, and Popov, as well as seven Chinese employees of the Consulate.[103] Other Soviet citizens that the Germans reported as killed during the Guangzhou "White Terror" included Gogol, Kornivalov, Tseletsky, Psegelov, Lylov, Zavitsky, Trozol, and Antonov, making a total of 17 Soviets murdered in Guangzhou, together with untold thousands of Chinese men, women, and children.

At that point all the remaining prisoners, who included not just Russian diplomats, but also Boris Volin, a Communist Party Secretary and reporter for *Tass*, certain their turn was next and convinced they would be shot, were taken out to the street. Instead, the prisoners were placed in the Consulate's car and moved to KMT Headquarters. Of the Consulate staff only seven Russians remained, who were all placed in a tiny room where, hungry and cold, they spent five days. Finally, on December 16, KMT Foreign Minister Chu Chao Sin visited the Russians, giving them the less than reassuring message: "Sorry, but I can do nothing because the military is controlling things in Guangzhou." Two days later the seven survivors, including the Consul-General and his wife, were transferred to another room, leading the Consul to comment that the accommodation was better but the food worse. On December 21, two unidentified Chinese and two

Americans visited the prisoners and, without offering any explanation, the Americans took photographs of the Russian prisoners.

Finally, on December 24, a benefactor appeared, German Consul Wilhelm Crull, accompanied by Foreign Minister Chu Chao Sin. The Soviet government had already asked the Germans to help defend the survivors, and their KMT captors now assured the Germans that the Consul-General and his wife would not be harmed. Consul Crull asked if they needed anything, and told the Soviet diplomats that on Christmas day, December 25, the next day, they would receive better quarters. For the intervening 24 hours, however, the Russians were moved to a tiny, dirty, rat-infested room in a police station, though, as the Germans had promised, the following day they were given a larger and better room, as well as decent food. At that point the diplomats were informed they would all be deported to the Soviet Union, though not told when. On December 27, a Japanese reporter arrived and wrote a story describing the Russian diplomats' travails to the world. Consul-General Pokhvalinsky took this opportunity to give his interviewer a message to relay through Hong Kong to Moscow, that he had not been harmed. "The following people: the Consul-General, Vice Consul Khassiz, Makarov, Vakulov, Ivanov, Popov and seven women were arrested on the evening of 13 December at the Consulate. All of us were held in a prison. However soon we will all be deported from China."[104] On December 28, Crull informed the survivors that on December 30, they would be deported via Hong Kong to Kobe, Japan.

Still under guard, on December 30 some Russians were escorted to the British ship *Kinshan* in Guangzhou harbor. In all, 38 Russians, including 17 adult males, 13 adult females, and eight children, only seven of them from the Consulate-General, left Guangzhou.[105] Since the Russians were now destitute, the Germans provided them with food, clothing, and money. A German banker, for example, gave them HK$5,874 (then worth almost US$3,000), enough to tide them over while in transit in Hong Kong. No further Russian survivors remained behind in Guangzhou. Reports gave a total of ten Russians as murdered, often brutally through beatings and stabbings, in the KMT "White Terror." The Chinese closed the Soviet Trade Mission and all other Soviet organizations in Guangzhou, including the Far Eastern Bank.

In spring 1927, the British had broken diplomatic relations with the Soviet Union, and they had also opposed Soviet activities in Guangzhou, which they held largely to blame for the December uprising. To land in Hong Kong the Soviet refugees therefore needed a special transit visa. According to a Foreign Office directive of September 23, 1927, "all applications for visas to Hong Kong made by holders of Soviet passports must be forwarded to London for decision, which will be decided by the Colonial Office. The Governor himself might be consulted regarding recommendations. However, given the fact that the Chinese authorities in Canton no longer wanted Soviet citizens to arrive in Canton, it was decided in late August to refuse all future transit visas."[106] Even so, the White Terror, which sent thousands of Chinese refugees pouring into Hong Kong, horrified the British and Hong Kong governments.[107] On humanitarian grounds, the British government therefore granted special transit visas to the Consul-General and the other Russians, even though their movements while in Hong Kong were closely monitored, and only if accompanied by an English policeman could they walk around the city.[108]

After spending two days in the territory, the Russians embarked for Shanghai on a British-owned vessel, *Soo Yan*, where they arrived on January 5, 1928, but were not allowed to leave the ship. On January 8, the Russian party received Japanese visas and were promptly taken to a Japanese ship, the *Nagasaki Naru*, which sailed for Kobe, arriving there the same day. Reaching Tokyo on January 10, Consul-General Pokhvalinsky briefed the Soviet Ambassador in Japan on the events in Guangzhou. On January 16, the entire party left for Vladivostok on the *Tsurug*, arriving there three days later. MID officials met them at the Soviet port, and the entire party took the Trans-Siberian Railroad to Moscow, arriving in the capital on February 1, the end of a horrific six weeks, during which their fate had often seemed precarious.[109]

Only after the Soviet diplomats left Guangzhou did they learn the fate of the Consulate and its contents, responsibility for which was transferred to the Germans. During and after the uprising, Chinese sacked the Consulate, looting most of its valuables. Pokhvalinsky compiled for the MID a list of goods, including furniture and automobiles, destroyed or stolen, estimating that property valued at HK$27,000 was lost, and almost HK$5,000 in cash stolen from the Consulate and its staff. The *Times* correspondent in Hong Kong reported Soviet losses in Guangzhou of around £10,000, that is about US$50,000.[110] Since Chinese officials considered all Soviet consulates and commercial agencies centers of subversion and rebellion, anti-Russian Chinese mobs, encouraged by

KMT agents, also inflicted serious damage on the Soviet Consulate in Shanghai and the Embassy in Beijing.[111] Not just the Soviet Consulates, but the entire Soviet policy in China, including Hong Kong and Guangzhou, lay in ruins. The Comintern had not recognized the strength of Chinese nationalism, which the KMT skillfully played upon in its anti-Communist campaign, and the weakness of China's urban working class, which was defeated in city after city, not just Guangzhou.

The sudden and swift failure of the uprising left Guangzhou severely shaken. Most Communist survivors went to Hong Kong, where they hoped eventually to reconsolidate themselves. Within months, "Red Canton" became "British Canton." In March 1928, Hong Kong Governor Cecil Clementi visited Guangzhou at the invitation of the city's warlord strongman, Li Jishen, a trip that reflected the new alignment in the region.[112]

Hong Kong provided an environment only slightly more hospitable to Chinese Communists than did Guangzhou. The Royal Hong Kong Police raided a number of Communist hideouts and offices, arresting numerous Communists and deporting them to China, and almost certain torture and death at the hands of the Chinese authorities. Furthermore, the Communist Party lacked money and manpower, and remained isolated.[113] Nevertheless, despite the 1927 debacle and subsequent repression, the Comintern was anxious to show that the Communist organization still existed in China and Hong Kong. They held Communist demonstrations in several cities, including Hong Kong, on August 1, 1929. That day was selected because it was International Red Day.[114] Only a tiny group could be mustered for a demonstration in the center of Hong Kong, out of whom the police detained some eight people. Governor Clementi correctly wrote: "This fiasco would seem to justify the belief the Communist movement (in Hong Kong) has little significance."[115] The Hong Kong Communist Party would never recover its former size and influence, small as that may have been.

Conclusions

Many parallels existed between Soviet policy toward Hong Kong, and that of the former Russian Empire. For both, trade with this fast growing international port was essential to facilitate their commerce with China. Secondly, although both Russian regimes claimed to be friends of the then

Chinese government, Britain trusted neither Tsarist nor Soviet intentions toward China, considering them mere disguises for attempted imperialist political and economic control, a potential threat to existing British interests in China. Thirdly, both Russia and its successor state, the Soviet Union, loathed British liberal capitalism in all its political and economic manifestations, while Britain detested both Russian authoritarianism and the Soviet version that succeeded it. The Marxist-Leninist doctrine of irreconcilable confrontation, the belief that war was inevitable between Britain and the Soviet Union, further distorted such ideological antagonism.

The Soviet Union frequently pursued a divided and often contradictory foreign policy toward both Hong Kong and China. Two organizations directed Soviet foreign policy in the region: the regular MID, through its Far East Department in Moscow and Consulates in several Chinese cities, including Guangzhou, Shanghai, Nanjing, and Beijing; and the Comintern, a group of international Communist parties, led and directed by the Soviet Communist Party. The Comintern believed socialist world revolution was inevitable, not only in the developed West, but also in Asian and African colonial and semi-colonial territories, including China. Since the October 1917 Bolshevik Revolution provided the model for that revolution, throughout the 1920s, the Soviet Union set the parameters of overseas Comintern activities everywhere, including China. The MID was generally more cautious and pragmatic, and the Comintern more activist, generating conflicts between the two. In practice, Soviet needs increasingly took priority over Comintern undertakings and foreign activities, a pattern that solidified after 1927, when Chiang Kai-shek moved against the Communists and forcibly expelled all Soviet advisers from China. At the same time, the Soviet Union faced the challenges of industrialization at home, and the rise of strong, often fascist opponents abroad, two important reasons why Soviet policies toward British Hong Kong during the 1930s became more accommodating and conciliatory.

1. Cartoon showing British forces firing on Chinese in Guangzhou (RGASPI, f. 532, op. 5, d. 13)

2. Vice Consul Khassiz being led to execution by KMT forces during the Guangzhou Uprising, December 1927 (RGASPI, f. 532, op. 5, d. 29)

3. Consul-General Boris Pokhvalinsky, his wife, his children, and some other survivors from the Guangzhou Uprising arriving at Vladivostok, January 1928 (RGASPI, f. 532, op. 5, d. 79)

4. Mikhail Borodin, Soviet Comintern agent in South China, 1923–1927 (RGASPI, f. 495, op. 261, d. 1969)

5. Portrait of Vice Consul Popov
(RGASPI, f. 532, op. 5, d. 29)

6. Portrait of Vice Consul Ivanov
(RGASPI, f. 532, op. 5, d. 29)

7. Chinese Communists being led off to execution during the Guangzhou Uprising, December 1927 (RGASPI, f. 532, op. 5, d. 30)

8. Chinese Communists being tortured in wooden cages (RGASPI, f. 532, op. 5, d. 33)

9. Destruction in the aftermath of the Guangzhou Uprising, December 1927 (RGASPI, f. 532, op. 5, d. 28)

4

The Gathering Storm: The Soviet Union and Hong Kong, 1930–1945

Introduction

By 1930, Hong Kong had become one of Asia's principal business centers and among the world's most important ports, as it still is today. Trade remained its most important source of income because Hong Kong served as an entrepôt for goods entering and leaving China. Especially after the Sino-Japanese War began in earnest after 1937, the territory turned to other sources of income, notably industrial development. After the Japanese conquered Shanghai and other major coastal cities, Chinese merchants and industrialists fled to Hong Kong, where they set up textile, sugar refining, cement manufacturing, and munitions plants. This development would prove a crucial precursor of Hong Kong's industrial revolution, which gained full momentum after World War II.

The Japanese capture of virtually all other major Chinese coastal cities diverted the flow of food, fuel, and war matériel for the Chinese armies fighting the Japanese through Hong Kong. While highly beneficial to the Hong Kong economy, this trade caused tensions between the British and the Japanese governments. Simultaneously, the 1930s were among the great eras of ocean-going vessels, both cargo and passenger liners, a decade that arguably saw the real beginning of mass tourism, with Hong Kong a port of call for every major ship crossing the Pacific Ocean. Foreign exchange from tourism began to flow into Hong Kong, sparking off the building of hotels, restaurants, and shops, all designed for visitors. Despite the effects of the Great Depression, which left Europe and North America economically crippled, Hong Kong's economy continued to grow.[1]

At this time and later, Hong Kong was a modernizing city rather paradoxically saddled with an increasingly archaic social and political structure. Although 98 percent of Hong Kong's population was Chinese, white British people monopolized nearly all positions of political power, with the civil service and even the police force almost entirely British. Chinese people were still banned from residing, except as servants, in several districts in the territory. Social and racial discrimination were much resented features of daily life. The British government rejected all proposals for democratic reform, since it believed this would mean the end of British rule in Hong Kong. More positively, as an indication that Hong Kong was joining the wider world, the British introduced needed social reforms, such as banning or regulating bonded labor, opium smoking, and prostitution. British colonial arrogance and snobbery would remain rampant until shattered by World War II and the rapid surrender of Hong Kong on Christmas Day in 1941.[2]

As the 1930s began, the Soviet Union turned inward. Stalin had clearly and decisively won the struggle for political power, removing all opponents from any positions where they might challenge him, leaving him at least temporarily accountable to no one for his actions. Political supremacy allowed Stalin to implement radical economic changes, notably the forced collectivization of agriculture and the first Five-Year Plan for the rapid industrialization and modernization of the Soviet economy. These, in turn, precipitated huge social changes as throngs of displaced people flooded into the cities seeking jobs. Thanks to these massive developments, often termed the "Stalin Revolution," ideological factors, so important in driving Soviet policy toward Hong Kong and the rest of China during the 1920s, became secondary. At least until the mid-1930s, economic factors became primary, until German and Japanese militarism forced a new direction in Soviet policy. Whereas during the 1920s, the Soviet Union sought to destabilize and even end British rule over Hong Kong, during the 1930s, Japanese expansionism brought a complete reversal of this policy. Soviet foreign policy transmuted into support not just for the existing British presence in Hong Kong, but even for still stronger British control and military assertiveness.

As before, for much of this period the Soviet Union frequently followed a divided and often contradictory foreign policy. On the one hand, the Comintern still pursued a course of world revolution, especially during the early 1930s, even characterizing European Social Democrats as "social fascists." Comintern-backed Asian Communists, not just Chinese but also Vietnamese, still found that Hong Kong, despite its largely antagonistic British government and the presence of substantial numbers of White Russians in the Royal Hong Kong Police Force, in some ways provided more hospitable revolutionary base facilities than were available in most other Asian cities. On the other hand, the MID favored diplomatic measures designed to promote Soviet industrialization and modernization, as the country introduced huge and tumultuous changes, the collectivization of agriculture and the rapid expansion of Soviet heavy industry, that transformed the Soviet Union. Both Commissar Grigory Chicherin and his successor Maxim Litvinov acted entirely in Soviet interests, naturally as defined by Stalin. They did all in their power to encourage trade, to obtain the imports from advanced states the Soviet Union needed for its industrialization and collectivization campaigns, and also to find markets for Soviet exports. The sole objective of Soviet foreign policy became the promotion of Soviet national interests, which meant the success of the Five-Year Plan. The gap between a cautious MID and a revolutionary Comintern, already apparent in the 1920s, widened. As the danger of a major war loomed larger on the horizon, the power of the Comintern to shape Soviet policy declined with every passing year. Furthermore, by the mid- and late 1930s, the Comintern effectively submerged its policies to allow them to coincide with those of MID policy makers. In 1943, the Comintern, by then only a shadow of its original self, was abolished.

This chapter investigates the new importance of economic factors in driving Soviet foreign policy, and their influence in changing and shaping Soviet relations with Hong Kong; the continuing roles of Hong Kong as both a haven for Asian Communist activists and a sanctuary for fiercely anti-Communist White Russians; how and why Soviet foreign policy changed by the mid-1930s, and the consequent impact on Soviet–Hong Kong relations; the manner in which the new Soviet policy of "collective security" caused a reversal of Soviet policy toward British control of Hong Kong; and Soviet policies and attitudes toward the Japanese conquest and occupation of Hong Kong during the period from December 1941 to September 1945. These factors and issues are crucial to any understanding of Soviet policy toward Hong Kong not just during the 1930s, but also in the early post–World War II period.

Soviet Foreign Policy Turns from Ideology to Trade

After the success of Chiang Kai-shek's Northern Expedition and the failure of the Guangzhou Uprising, Hong Kong declined greatly in significance in Comintern and Soviet policy in South China. For the next ten years, ideology lost much of its former importance as trade and economic ties became preeminent in shaping relations between Hong Kong and the Soviet Union. Even so, the threat of war increasingly preoccupied Soviet officials dealing with Hong Kong, China, and Japan, a concern that had an increasing impact upon Soviet–Hong Kong trade, and which was demonstrated in Soviet intelligence reports and clippings on British defenses in the colony the Soviets gathered from regional newspapers.

Despite or perhaps because of its 1927 debacle, the Comintern sought to prove that Communist organizations still existed in China and Hong Kong. On International Red Day, August 1, 1929, Communist demonstrations took place in several cities, including Hong Kong.[3] The Communists could only muster a tiny group to demonstrate in central Hong Kong. The Hong Kong Communist Party had fewer than 1,000 members, most of them young, between 16 and 20 years old, and inexperienced. Even so, their links to triad gangs, control of over 20 trade unions, and their semi-legal newspaper, *Xianggang Xiaozhibao*, that appeared three times a week, left Hong Kong Communists some residual influence.[4] The Hong Kong government's continuing intolerance of Communist organizations helped to weaken their position, but also indicated that the authorities considered them a more than negligible threat. In response to the December 1927 Guangzhou Uprising, the International Seamen's Union was banned, a position Governor Clementi justified, when the ILO inquired why, on the grounds of "its open advocacy of Communism and subversion of the existing authority." Furthermore, he added, since the organization had played a leading role in anti-British strikes during 1925 and 1926, he considered it a "menace to orderly government." Clementi told the ILO that during the Guangzhou Uprising in December 1927 the Seamen's Union had been involved in a plot to overthrow that city's government. He also assured the ILO that, while the Seamen's Union was illegal, Hong Kong seamen had two other acceptable unions to represent them.[5] For several decades, the International Seamen's Union remained a banned organization, though according to the reports of the Hong Kong Special

Branch, it remained active until at least the early 1960s.[6] British authorities generally maintained a very hostile attitude toward the labor movement in Hong Kong, regarding most trade unions as either Communist or potentially destabilizing elements in Hong Kong's economic and social structure. Strong links between British colonial authorities and leaders or tycoons of the big business community remained in place until British rule ended in 1997.

As the freest territory within East and Southeast Asia during the early twentieth century, Hong Kong provided a refuge and asylum for numerous Chinese and foreign revolutionary leaders, including first Sun Yat-sen and then, in the late 1920s and 1930s, his widow Soong Ching-ling, the Vietnamese Communist Ho Chi Minh, who could not live freely in French-controlled Indochina, and other leading Chinese and Asian Communists. The Comintern utilized Hong Kong as a base to host meetings, write and distribute revolutionary pamphlets, collect funds, and plan revolutionary activities against governments in Malaya, Siam (present-day Thailand), Indonesia, and Indochina. Following the severe anti-Communist repression during and after the crushing of the Guangzhou Uprising in December 1927, tens of thousands of Communist rank-and-file members and activists, as well as leaders from China and elsewhere, fled to Hong Kong. While the British authorities frowned upon their activities, so long as such Communists and other leftists did not interfere with British rule in Hong Kong, they were not breaking British Hong Kong law. The presence of thousands of Communist activists gave rise to alarm, and in 1930 the Hong Kong government established the Anti-Communist Squad of the Royal Hong Kong Police, the forerunner of the Special Branch, to monitor these revolutionaries and their activities as closely as possible.[7]

The strong British reaction reflected the fact that the Comintern had by no means abandoned interest in Hong Kong. At the end of the 1920s, the Comintern dispatched Jean Cremet, a French Communist going under the pseudonym "Thibault," to Hong Kong and other cities in Southeast Asia to survey the various Communist movements. With Comintern backing, moreover, in December 1929, the veteran Vietnamese Communist leader Ho Chi Minh arrived in Hong Kong. Ho, who had helped found the French Communist Party in 1924, had spent several years in China in the mid-1920s, serving as an interpreter to one of the Soviet missions in South China, before fleeting to Moscow in the aftermath of 1927. Ho Chi

Minh arrived in Hong Kong in December 1929 as a representative of the Comintern, and in February 1930, Vietnamese Communist revolutionaries held their founding National Congress in Hong Kong, where they agreed to establish a Communist Party modeled on the Bolsheviks, and to end all ties with the Chinese KMT and other "notables, landowners and capitalists." The first Central Committee meeting of a unified Vietnamese Communist Party was held in Hong Kong in October 1930. Ho used Hong Kong as a base to travel to Shanghai, Bangkok, and other cities seeking to unify the various Asian Communist movements. While Ho and other Vietnamese revolutionaries held themselves aloof from Hong Kong politics, they plotted actively against French rule in Indochina, and were implicated in a fall 1930 popular uprising in Indochina, which the French Foreign Legion suppressed with considerable bloodshed. The French government condemned Ho to death in absentia and requested that the British government extradite him for trial. British treatment of Ho Chi Minh demonstrated that, while British officials in Hong Kong were constrained to respect the rule of law, they were by no means particularly sympathetic toward the presence of radical Soviet-backed revolutionaries. Arrested by the Royal Hong Kong Police in 1931, Ho spent six months in a Hong Kong prison, before the workings of British justice blocked French intentions. Since under Hong Kong law Ho had committed no offence, the only grounds for deporting him were his Communist sympathies, not an extraditable crime in Hong Kong. The Comintern hired him an excellent defense team, led by an able young British lawyer, Frank Loseby, indirectly assisted by the King's Counsel and Labour politician Sir Stafford Cripps, who was personally sympathetic to Ho's plight, even though the Hong Kong government had retained Cripps to handle the appeal.[8] Loseby and Cripps reached an out-of-court settlement in June 1932, which maintained the deportation order, but allowed Ho to remove himself to a place of his choosing. Cripps defended his action on the grounds that a successful appeal only would have made Ho a martyr and would have caused a public outcry.[9] Ho was in no hurry to leave the comfort of Hong Kong, but realizing at last that Hong Kong no longer furnished an amenable refuge, Ho departed Hong Kong for the British colony, Singapore, on December 28, 1932, only to be rearrested there and promptly returned to Hong Kong, where Loseby once more obtained his release. Since the political climate had improved in China, on January 25, 1933, Ho left the territory for China by boat, disguised as a Chinese merchant, and made contact with the Chinese Communist underground, who spirited him to Moscow, where he spent much of the following seven years before returning to China in 1938 as an adviser to the Communist armed forces.[10]

By no means all Russian or Russian-backed activities in Hong Kong were pro-Communist. Throughout the 1930s a small Russian community still existed in Hong Kong. After the 1917 Bolshevik Revolution, hundreds of thousands of mostly middle- and upper-class Russians fled the country, and many took refuge in Chinese cities in the interior and all along the China coast, including Hong Kong. In tribute to their anti-Communist views, these refugees were called "White Russians," to distinguish them from Communist "Red Russians." While most "White Russians" came from upper and middle-class backgrounds, virtually all left Russia with little more than they could carry. Gold, jewels, antiques, and other valuables were usually seized during their journeys out of war-torn Russia. The White Russian community in Hong Kong remained small, scarcely more than a hundred in number. Its members ran several restaurants, tailor shops, and small food stores. The center of the community was the Russian Orthodox Church, and its vicar, Archpriest Dmitry Uspensky, who served as its head from 1934 until his death in 1970.[11] Over time most White Russians either died or emigrated to the United States, Canada, or Australia, so that today no remnant of their community is left in Hong Kong.

If only through necessity, most White Russians became hardworking and, despite their background, largely non-political. While the MID showed great interest in and collected reports on the activities of such White Russians, there is no extant evidence of any anti-Soviet plotting amongst the White Russian community scattered along the China coast. White Russian émigrés were mostly too concerned with simple survival to have the time and energy for anti-Soviet conspiracies. Even so, during the 1930s at least one notable White Russian self-styled fascist *Führer* made repeated visits to Hong Kong. Count Anastase Andreivitch Vonsiatsky, a former Tsarist military officer, born in Warsaw, who fought in World War I and the Russian Civil War and then became a naturalized American citizen and founder of the Russian National Fascist Revolutionary Party, stopped in Hong Kong and other Asian ports three times, in 1934, 1936, and 1939 respectively, on round-the-world cruises intended to rally White Russians to an anti-Soviet crusade to overthrow Josef Stalin's government and replace it with a fascist regime headed by himself.[12]

Quite possibly Vonsiatsky's repeated stopovers in Hong Kong were not merely dictated by the schedules of the cruise liner companies, but were also encouraged and facilitated by the fact that by the 1930s former White Russian officers represented a significant component of the Royal Hong Kong Police Force. Due to an upsurge of crime, violence, and strikes within the colony during the 1920s, the Hong Kong government decided to enlarge the police force by 15 percent, or some 300 officers. Many of the White Russian refugees who had fled south to Hong Kong were combat veterans of the White Armies, who had fought the Communists in Central and East Asia during the Russian Civil War of 1918–1921. Not only were they experienced and accurate marksmen, but they were disciplined and physically strong—in other words natural recruits for the Royal Hong Kong Police. Sufficient numbers of these poverty-stricken stateless refugees joined to warrant their own separate contingent, whose badge bore the letter "E."[13] These White Russian policemen became a prized addition to the Royal Hong Kong Police Force, and proved an effective deterrent to violent criminals.

White Russians were particularly well represented in the marine police. After World War I, piracy became a serious problem throughout East and South East Asia, causing severe cargo losses, and even attacks on liners' passengers and crews. Ten ships were attacked between 1922 and 1926. Pirates, disguised as passengers, hijacked entire ships, robbing passengers and crew, before fleeing to waiting fast moving boats. To prevent such piratical attacks, for several years the British coast guard patrolled the China coast. However, due to lack of funds, in 1930 the military authorities announced they could no longer provide anti-piracy guards for ships operating out of Hong Kong.[14] Responsibility for protecting shipping from piracy and maintaining Hong Kong as a safe destination passed to the Royal Hong Kong Police, who hired 104 assorted guards, including some 30 Russians, together with British, northern Chinese, and Indians. The White Russians and others, described as of "good physique, keen, reliable, efficient, and disciplined in their services," were sworn in as Hong Kong Police Constables, but assigned only to anti-piracy duties on the Hong Kong–Singapore and Hong Kong–Shanghai routes, where they remained for much of the 1930s, until Japanese military activity curtailed ocean traffic. On average each ship had some four to eight guards, who were paid around HK$1,000 a year, a reasonable income for these mostly impoverished individuals.[15] Like their counterparts in the regular police force, these White Russians, well-armed with machine guns, shot guns, rifles, and pistols, proved an effective deterrent force, preventing attacks along the entire coast.

Ironically, some of these White Russian guards may well have helped to protect Soviet trading ventures. As the Soviet Union launched its first Five-Year Plan in 1929, it badly needed certain products to propel industrial development. Obtaining those products became a primary motive driving Soviet foreign policy, and shaped Soviet relations with Hong Kong and China. Soviet officials considered Hong Kong, together with Shanghai, one of the two most important ports they used in China.[16] During the 1920s, the Soviet Union sent a variety of products to Hong Kong, including salt, neftalin, soda, lumber, canned fish, and the mineral water with the brand name *Narzan*, produced in the North Caucasus and even today considered very healthy by many Russians. Canned fish from the Soviet Union, imported by the Rangoon-Singapore Trading Company, was very popular among Chinese people in Hong Kong.[17] These products retained their popularity during the 1930s. Because the British would not allow the establishment of a permanent Soviet trading company in the territory, the General Credit Company, HK, handled all direct Soviet exports to Hong Kong.[18] In return, the Soviets continued fishing in waters near Hong Kong. As the Sino-Japanese War intensified during the 1930s and North China increasingly became a war zone and hazardous to commercial shipping, the Soviet Union sent ever more goods through Hong Kong and other southern ports.[19]

In 1932 and the subsequent year, Union Petroleum Trust, a Soviet oil firm whose parent company, *Soiuzneft,* had been active in the import and sale of petroleum products in the Soviet Union, sought British permission to build an oil tank in Hong Kong. Previously, the Soviet Union had sought to destroy Hong Kong. Now it wanted to invest in the colony, which would contribute to Hong Kong's stability, as well as aid the Soviet Union's industrial drive. In September 1932, two Soviet citizens, Piotr Libanov and G. A. Ravue, applied at the British Consulate in Shanghai for one-week visas to visit Hong Kong to ascertain the feasibility of building the oil tank. Traditional British suspicions, however, remained strong as the Admiralty, Foreign Office, and War Office requested the rejection of this visa request and the Hong Kong government duly complied.[20] The Colonial Office noted that the British Asiatic Petroleum Company, a division of Royal Dutch-Shell, would be negatively impacted by such Soviet competition and also urged rejection.[21] Erroneously or not, the British government had failed to observe the sharp change in Soviet attitudes.

British policy was modified once more when in February 1933 the Hong Kong government stated it had no objection to the oil tank. "A large import trade in Russian kerosene had already been built up, and attempts were now being made to expand trade in benzene (gasoline) and fuel oils." British documents never quite explained the reasons for these oscillations in British policy. Even so, the Governor expressed reservations over permitting a Soviet company or Russian employees to base themselves in Hong Kong, enabling them to establish a permanent Soviet presence there. He wrote rather intemperately on February 4: "There will be difficulty of control if a Soviet oil company is allowed to establish its own agency here with Russian employees, and I am prepared to refuse such a company permission to own land here."[22] The War Office expressed opposition even earlier, writing on December 24, 1932: "It is considered that if the application is granted, an opportunity will be created for the installation of a center for Soviet propaganda and possibly espionage." On January 3, the Admiralty added: "[T]he establishment of a Soviet oil organization at Hong Kong would involve a danger of political propaganda and Communistic activity in the colony."[23] Shortly afterwards, in early March 1933, diplomatic relations between the Soviet Union and Great Britain were once again severed.[24] On March 29, therefore, the Colonial Office informed the Hong Kong Governor: "In view of changed circumstances concerning relations with the Soviet Union, the granting of facilities for the erection in Hong Kong of an installation for the storage and marketing of Soviet oil should be suspended." In a letter dated the same day, the Foreign Secretary concurred.[25] British diplomacy had therefore failed to recognize that the Soviet attitude toward Hong Kong had changed, and that the Soviets now regarded Hong Kong as a place where they could conduct business rather than a focal point for revolution. Once relations were broken, the whole issue became moot in any case, as all talk of Soviet investment in Hong Kong temporarily ceased.

The War Clouds Thicken

Although Japanese behavior increasingly alarmed British officials, during the 1930s, Hong Kong remained a quiet and stable oasis of tranquility in an increasingly turbulent region. Fighting erupted between China and

Japan on September 18, 1931, when Japanese troops took Manchuria and installed a puppet government there. During the 1930s, Japanese control gradually spread through North China, including Beijing, down to Central China and its cities, including Shanghai and Nanjing. As the war moved south and China became ever more chaotic internally, refugees flocked into the territory, roughly doubling Hong Kong's population, to over one million in 1938, and another half million had poured into Hong Kong by the time the Japanese invaded the territory in December 1941.

Within the Soviet Union, as Stalin gained political supremacy, virtually all independent voices within the Comintern were purged. Nevertheless, Comintern policy continued to espouse world revolution. In fact, Comintern activists believed the intensifying and spreading economic depression would increase the potential for a world revolution. Once again, uprisings during the fall of 1930 in several Chinese cities failed disastrously. The KMT, which by now controlled most of China, once more arrested and executed numerous Communists. The leader of the CCP, Li Lisan, left China in 1931 for Moscow in disgrace.[26] A new CCP leadership centralized and purged the Party of all non-Stalinists. Meanwhile, the Comintern adopted a unilateral policy, in which there would be no more discussion of united fronts, or working with non-Communists to overthrow the old order. European Social Democrats were labeled "social fascists." In German and other European cities Communists and Social Democrats engaged in street warfare, actions which only weakened the political left, facilitating the rise to power of the German National Socialists (Nazis), fascists, and other extreme right-wing political parties.[27]

In China, following the Japanese invasion of Manchuria in 1931, the Comintern became increasingly concerned over Japanese expansion. In the summer of 1935, both the MID and the Comintern espoused the Popular Front policy, an updating of the previous decade's United Front policy, adopted as Communist policy worldwide out of necessity, due to fear of German, Italian, and Japanese military expansionism. In 1937, the Soviet Union signed a non-aggression treaty with the Chinese KMT-controlled government, committing the Soviet Union to support the KMT, even at the expense of the CCP. Under its terms Stalin would send increasing quantities of war matériel to Chiang Kai-shek's armies, while still subsidizing the CCP. In many respects, it was almost as if the clock had been turned back some 15 years. Increasingly, the Comintern became an arm of the MID, following the instructions of Stalin and his Foreign Minister, Maxim Litvinov.

Following the Japanese invasion of Manchuria in 1931 and subsequently of China itself in 1937, Communists and other leftists based in Hong Kong—some, undoubtedly, receiving financial and other backing from Moscow—engaged very actively in a variety of efforts to combat the Japanese occupation and military operations. Most notably, from June 1938, Soong Ching-ling, widow of Sun Yat-sen, who spent substantial periods of time in Moscow after her husband's death in 1925 and had close ties to leading Chinese leftists, headed the Defend China League in Hong Kong. Based on Seymour Road and operating quite openly, the League collected money, medical supplies, and arms, conducted propaganda activities, and even recruited young local Hong Kong people to fight in China as Communist guerrillas. Chinese Communists were also using Hong Kong as a sanctuary from which to wage anti-Japanese operations.[28] Despite protests from Japan, the British government tolerated these activities. Thus the Comintern and foreign and Chinese Communists all took advantage of Hong Kong's strategic location and, equally as important, relative personal and political freedom to foment both anti-colonial and eventually anti-Japanese activities.

During the 1930s, such anti-Japanese endeavors aside, Soviet policy toward Hong Kong was largely restricted to trade and observation, with little if any attempt to play an appreciably active role in the colony's own affairs. As Japanese activities loomed ever larger, over time strategic factors came to outweigh economic considerations. Soviet diplomats in China frequently collected and sent to Moscow clippings from regional English-language newspapers on Japanese military activities. Together with clippings from *Tass*, these materials kept Soviet officials in touch with East Asian developments as war embroiled the region. Their selection of these clippings, plus their underlinings and annotations, indicate which issues and developments in Hong Kong and South China most interested MID officials. Clippings came from a variety of newspapers and magazines, such as *The Economist* (Great Britain), the *Peking and Tientsin Times*, the *North China Herald* (Beijing), the *Canton Daily Sun*, the *South China Morning Post*, the *Shanghai Evening Post*, the Chinese-language *Sin Wan Pao*, and others. Except for the Hong Kong–based *South China Morning Post*, virtually all these Asian newspapers ceased publication during World War II. During the war itself, the

Soviets relied almost entirely on *Tass* clippings and intelligence reports from Tokyo for information on Japanese-occupied Hong Kong and South China.[29] The following pages, which are based on these clippings, provide some insight into the information Soviet officials drew on during the 1930s to help them shape their policy toward Hong Kong and South China. Trade apart, in the case of Hong Kong that policy was for the most part one of more or less hopeful observation rather than active involvement, as the threat of war and outside attack increasingly came to preoccupy the Soviet leadership.

As early as 1934, Britain strengthened Hong Kong's defenses, secretly building numerous fortresses in the harbor areas, another 24 on Hong Kong Island, and several in the northern New Territories.[30] Though quite prepared to welcome this development and jettison any ideological hostility to Britain in the face of a common threat, the MID feared these fortifications would be too little and too late, neither sufficient to repel a Japanese attack nor completed soon enough.[31]

In 1935, *Tass* reported that the Hong Kong economy continued to deteriorate. The overvalued Hong Kong dollar had caused most domestic industry to disappear, since Hong Kong–produced goods could not compete with Japanese imports. Much of Hong Kong's exports to Japan consisted of scrap metal. Japanese imports to Hong Kong were reported as being 90 percent higher than those from the United Kingdom and the United States, making Japan Hong Kong's largest trading partner, and included products as varied as silk, textiles, and tea. That same year *The Economist* reported that Sir Frederick Leith-Ross, a British banking expert who visited the territory to advise on its economic crisis, had stated that Hong Kong needed to resolve its financial relationship with China, since currency differences between the two adversely affected Hong Kong trade.[32] Unfortunately, none of these numerous clippings mentioned Soviet trade with Hong Kong during the relevant period.

The Seventh Comintern Congress, held in August 1935, called for the formation of Popular Fronts, alliances of Communists with socialists and liberals to combat fascism, just as the Soviet Union was prepared to work with non-Communist powers against shared foes. Once again, therefore, the CCP, now controlled by Mao Zedong, uneasily agreed to ally itself with the KMT in the common battle against Japan. The *Peking and Tientsin Times* commented rather wryly on the CCP's resilience, implying that the Communists would be more effective than the KMT in opposing

Japan: "The only serious alternative regime to the Nationalist KMT is one that would favor an alignment with Russia. Nobody would welcome that in Japan."[33] From the mid-1930s onward, the Soviet Union no longer regarded Great Britain, but rather Japan, as its major enemy in Asia. The Soviet desire that the British augment their defenses reflected the altered emphasis in Soviet policy, which was a direct product of the new embrace of collective security.

After Germany and Japan concluded an Anti-Communist Pact (also known as the Anti-Comintern Pact) on March 12, 1937, an agreement the Soviets considered an effort to disguise the two powers' drive for territorial expansion as an anti-Communist crusade, the Soviet Union feared its signatories would develop a close military relationship. In summer 1937, when low-level Sino-Japanese conflicts expanded into full-scale war, Soviet journalists warned that the Japanese had become increasingly overconfident and even arrogant in believing that it would be easy to march through China, declaring they should learn from history. "If the Japanese incautiously attempted to penetrate into the very heart of China, they would risk a debacle compared with which Napoleon's flight from Moscow might seem mild."[34]

Such concerns focused Soviet attention on the weakness of Hong Kong's defenses, which Soviet officials feared made it vulnerable to Japanese attack and seizure. Not long afterwards, a *Tass* report noted that the British were finally constructing some fortifications in the Hong Kong hills in the New Territories near the Chinese frontier, and also in Tolo Harbor. "Britain decided to speed up the fortification of Hong Kong. Britain sought to convert Hong Kong into a military bastion of South China."[35] One article optimistically but inaccurately predicted that within the next five years Hong Kong would become impregnable, as the British allocated US$120 million to build new forts and antiaircraft guns, and to increase its garrison to six battalions. *Tass* further reported that the Hong Kong government had also earmarked an additional one million US dollars to build bomb shelters and provide gas masks to protect government workers from chemical attacks.[36] Soviet officials also noted Hong Kong's potential to serve not just as a major naval base, but also as a military and civilian aviation center. A *Canton Daily Sun* clipping predicted Hong Kong would become a huge transit point for airmail. The article noted that in March 1937 Pan American World Airways announced the opening on April 27 of a new clipper service from the

United States to Asia via Hong Kong, which would become the gateway for American passengers bound for South East Asia, Australia, China, and Japan.[37]

The Soviets also observed that Hong Kong had become a significant hub for smuggling. Contraband, including kerosene, cement, and waste paper, entered Guangdong province illicitly across its New Territories border. The practice did not contravene Hong Kong law, but since many of the commodities transported were used in the anti-Japanese war effort, it quickly became an increasingly contentious issue between Britain and Japan.[38] Once the smugglers began to carry arms and munitions, Japanese complaints that the British authorities were taking unfair advantage of Hong Kong's immunity from the Japanese blockade of Chinese ports became fiercer and far more numerous. In retaliation, the Japanese began to bomb the Kowloon-Canton Railway line (KCR) running from Hong Kong to Guangzhou. Tensions between Britain and Japan increased in December 1937, when 15 Japanese planes flew over Hong Kong–controlled Lantau Island, returning 45 minutes later to pass over the strategically important Taikoo Dockyard, a center of Hong Kong's ship manufacture and repair. The British Ambassador in Tokyo delivered a strong protest to the Japanese government.[39] In response to the Japanese over-flights, the British increased Hong Kong's garrison, which now included one brigade of antiaircraft troops, and began a submarine training program. British officials noted that, in the early stages of the Sino-Japanese War, the Soviet Union assisted the Chinese Air Force against the Japanese and provided other military aid to KMT forces in Southern China. The fall of Hankow to Japanese forces in October 1938 convinced Soviet leaders that Chiang's troops could not defend China effectively, whereupon they switched much of their assistance to Chinese Communist forces in Northern China.[40]

By October 1938, Soviet officials were conscious of Hong Kong's increasing isolation from China. After Guangzhou fell to Japanese forces that month, trade between Hong Kong and South China, a leading customer, declined by 20 percent. The Soviets believed that British regional interests were dwindling to nothing and that, with Japanese troops not far distant, even continued British control of Hong Kong itself had become uncertain, since it was almost certainly an objective of the Japanese, who had become the dominant military force in East Asia. In response to increasing Japanese military activity in the surrounding area, and seeking a unified and centralized command, the British government appointed the Hong Kong Governor commander of all the colony's armed forces.[41] As trade continued to decline, in the first half of 1939, Hong Kong's already weak and depressed economy deteriorated, a development which further compromised Hong Kong's ability to resist the Japanese invasion a growing number of observers anticipated. The Soviet Union became increasingly preoccupied with Japan's drive to war as that country's forces marched further southward into South China and even Southeast Asia.

On July 29, 1939, only a month before World War II opened in Europe, one of the most significant yet least-known battles in military history took place, when Soviet and Japanese forces fought each other near Nomonhan, along the Soviet-Manchurian border. Each side claimed that the other's troops began the battle and its own forces merely reacted defensively. In either case, this large battle, involving substantial numbers of tanks on both sides, was a decisive Soviet victory. That outcome was one reason why in December 1941 Japanese forces moved south against United States and British possessions, including Pearl Harbor and Hong Kong, rather than north against Soviet forces in Eastern Siberia.[42]

An interesting mid-June 1941 *Tass* article, written just before Germany invaded the Soviet Union, accurately predicted that Hong Kong would be an early target of any Japanese operation, but less correctly prophesied that Japanese troops would face major difficulties in mounting such an invasion. The Soviets thought the British were well-armed, with sufficient food to hold out for several months, which would allow British and American reinforcements enough time to arrive and help the British garrison repel the Japanese invaders. In reality, in just over two weeks in December 1941 the Japanese took Hong Kong, which surrendered on Christmas Day 1941.[43] Interestingly, by then the war-ravaged Soviet Union and Britain had become allies, and until the entry of the United States into the war earlier that month each had indeed since June 1941 been the other's only significant coalition partner in the struggle against Hitler's Germany. Their alliance did not, however, extend to Asia. In April 1941, Japan and the Soviet Union signed a non-aggression pact and for more than four years, until August 1945, while its energies were fully absorbed by the conflict in Europe, the Soviet Union continued to observe formal neutrality in the war against Japan.[44]

In mid-January 1942, *Tass* sent Moscow a report on conditions in recently defeated Hong Kong, a relatively optimistic account of the changes the first month of occupation had brought. *Tass* reported that a new Japanese occupation government had been established and, although foreign nationals from enemy countries, such as Britain and the United States, were interned, most people's lives had returned to normal, and shops and public transport had reopened. According to this report, few Chinese residents of Hong Kong, even among the police, had assisted the British in defending the territory. The *Tass* account did, however, mention the low disciplinary standards of the Japanese troops, and their frequent indulgence in looting and even rape against civilians.[45] Virtually all other non-Japanese accounts gave a very different picture of newly conquered Hong Kong, one of death, destruction, hunger, and widespread mistreatment of the Hong Kong Chinese population by the Japanese military. As the Soviet Union had no resident correspondents in Hong Kong at the time, *Tass* was heavily dependent on Japanese correspondents, who naturally reflected their government's propaganda line.

At this juncture, however, the Soviet Union was too preoccupied with the concurrent German invasion of its territory to generate any real policy toward or documents descriptive of the Japanese takeover of Hong Kong and its subsequent occupation. Officials collected few, if any, clippings from English-language newspapers, virtually all of which disappeared during the Japanese occupation. While maintaining full diplomatic relations with Japan, the Soviet Union was unable to assign correspondents or other observers to Hong Kong, and therefore remained heavily dependent on Japanese accounts of the occupation. *Tass* articles thus tended to be overly optimistic and largely fictional, reporting on an allegedly growing and flourishing Hong Kong economy, large-scale commercial activity by Koreans, the creation of new industries, and even the reopening of hundreds of Chinese factories in the colony.[46]

Actual conditions in the territory were appreciably different, with continued and pervasive hunger, poverty, and the persecution of ordinary Chinese citizens by Japanese occupation forces. Despite these horrendous conditions, Europeans from non-belligerent countries, such as the Soviet Union (not at war with Japan until 1945), tried to continue life as usual as best they could. For example, the Russian restaurant *Balalaika* offered floor shows in the Kowloon Hotel. A White Russian, George Goncharoff, was employed by the Japanese to teach ballroom dancing to numerous prominent Japanese officials.[47] While most White Russians were not interned, some of those in the Royal Hong Kong Police eventually fought the Japanese in the December 1941 Battle of Hong Kong, and for the duration of the war those White Russian policemen who survived were interned together with other British military and quasi-military fighting men. As with other European members of the Royal Hong Kong Police, the Japanese interned the White Russians in their camp at Stanley, on the southern end of Hong Kong Island. Having experienced severe hardships in Russia before fleeing south to Hong Kong, the White Russians proved the most adaptable and resourceful of all the Europeans, and consequently almost all survived the sometimes horrific rigors of Stanley.[48] One former White Russian policeman from the Anti-Piracy Squad, Victor Veriga, was even cited personally in the accounts of other detainees, and taught his fellow prisoners Russian.[49] Two White Russians carved the gravestones for those internees who passed away.[50] During the Japanese occupation, Chinese Communists continued to collect funds and volunteer recruits within poverty-stricken Hong Kong. In the first weeks of the occupation they successfully evacuated a number of Westerners.[51] In Hong Kong itself, the largely Communist Hong Kong Kowloon Independent Brigade was formed in March 1942 to sabotage Japanese positions in the colony, and when possible rescue prisoners of war from Japanese concentration camps, such as the one in Stanley.[52] Yet Russian archives show no evidence that the Soviet Union, preoccupied with its own invasion and occupation and eager to keep Japan neutral, gave any financial or other assistance to such activities during World War II.

As the war ended in 1945 and the future postwar world was under discussion, the question of Hong Kong came up again. The Chinese government sought the city's return, something Great Britain opposed so strongly that the Soviets observed the British did not even wish to discuss the question.[53] Although United States President Franklin D. Roosevelt supported Chiang Kai-shek on the matter, Britain was even prepared to break its 1943 Treaty of Friendship with China over Hong Kong. Despite his own promises to support Chiang's claims to Hong Kong, Stalin covertly supported British Prime Minister Winston Churchill. He himself planned to incorporate substantial additional territories, including parts of Northeastern China, into the Soviet Union, and so was reluctant to support Chinese demands for the reunification of all Chinese lands. The Soviets therefore made only halfhearted protests when the British successfully reoccupied Hong Kong in September 1945.[54]

Conclusions

During the 1920s, the Soviet Union viewed Hong Kong as a potential center for a future Chinese revolution. The Comintern had been the major vehicle for this future Hong Kong and all-China revolution. During the 1930s, that idea was largely shelved, though Hong Kong continued to provide safe haven for Chinese and other Asian Communist revolutionaries, some of whom eventually used it as a base for anti-Japanese efforts. But by then, instead of working to destabilize and destroy British Hong Kong, the Soviet Union sought and encouraged the reverse. The Soviets recognized that they needed Hong Kong as a source of essential goods and services, with one of Asia's and indeed the world's best ports, through which salt, sugar, oil, fish, and numerous other crucial products flowed. In 1933, the Soviets even attempted to invest in Hong Kong by building an oil refinery, a request rejected by British policy makers, who never recognized the fundamental reversal in Soviet policy toward Hong Kong. While the British retained the mentality of the previous decade, regarding any potential Soviet investment as an effort at subversion, they had considerable justification for this belief given the numerous Communist attempts at strikes and political demonstrations, most recently in 1930.

By the mid-1930s, increasing Soviet fears of the expansion of Nazi Germany, Fascist Italy, and militaristic Japan, all marching evermore in unison, provoked growing Soviet interest in any Hong Kong developments or products that might help their own country to resist attack. No longer denouncing British imperialism, the Soviets bemoaned British military weakness in Hong Kong and viewed benignly attempts to bolster the British garrison and navy in the territory. Instead of desiring a British withdrawal from Hong Kong and China, the Soviets sought the opposite, bringing another fundamental reversal in Soviet policy. The new Soviet Collective Security policy urged Britain and other major capitalist powers to work together economically and militarily to combat expansionist Germany, Italy, and Japan, overtures Britain once again rejected, considering them simply tricks to enhance Soviet potential for subversion in Britain and her colonies, including Hong Kong. By the time Britain finally reversed course in 1939 and explored the possibility of a Soviet alliance, Stalin had adopted another tack. In August 1939, the Soviets signed a non-aggression pact with Germany, which meant that Adolf Hitler faced little real opposition when he invaded Poland in September

1939, the opening move of World War II in Europe. After Germany invaded the Soviet Union in June 1941, the Soviets had little attention to spare for Hong Kong or South China. In December 1941, the Japanese easily took Hong Kong, transforming the territory the Soviet Union had once considered a promising seedbed of Chinese revolution into an occupied urban wasteland. Despite public protestations to the contrary, in September 1945, after the Japanese surrender, the Soviet Union acquiesced in British reoccupation of Hong Kong. Once again Hong Kong was a British colony, and the Soviet Union still an outsider looking in.

5

The Soviet Union, Hong Kong, and the Cold War: Years of Sino-Soviet Alliance, 1945–1960

Introduction

The former British crown colony of Hong Kong played a role in the Cold War disproportionate to its tiny size. It was a crucial Western listening post to study developments in huge, neighboring China. The scale of American and British intelligence-gathering efforts in Hong Kong was comparable to similar efforts in West Berlin.[1] Located on the South China coast, Hong Kong was roughly equidistant from two East Asian countries where the Cold War became "hot": Korea and Vietnam. Furthermore, after World War II Hong Kong became one of the world's greatest ports, a financial and trading center, and even an industrial power in its own right.

Historians and political scientists have scrutinized the Cold War in Hong Kong itself, as well as Chinese, Taiwanese, British, and American activities in Hong Kong during the first 35 years of the Cold War, from 1945 through the late 1970s.[2] No one, however, has examined the Soviet Union, one of the most crucial actors in the Cold War, and its activities in and around Hong Kong, an omission due in part to the myth that there simply was no Soviet policy toward Hong Kong. Hong Kong, it is argued, was considered too small and too distant, and it lacked any permanent Soviet personnel after 1948, when all remaining Soviet officials on the island were asked to leave. Hence the territory was deemed too insignificant to merit a specific policy. As a British colony in the shadow of China, Hong Kong, both Western specialists and Russian academics contended, was merely a side show in Soviet policy toward China and Britain.[3]

Recently opened Soviet archives, notably the AVP RF, reveal that this perception is inaccurate, or at least incomplete. Throughout the 15 years covered in this chapter, Soviet policy on Hong Kong was informed and affected by the conflicting pressures of Marxist-Leninist hostility toward British colonial rule; constant Soviet strategic rivalries with Great Britain and the West; and a certain Soviet desire to profit from Hong Kong's economic potential. After 1945 and specifically because of the Cold War, the Soviet Union maintained a strong interest in Hong Kong and conducted numerous activities—political, economic, and cultural—in the region, activities targeted specifically at Hong Kong. Before the split between Moscow and Beijing emerged in the late 1950s, Marxist-Leninist ideology was the paramount feature governing Soviet policy toward Hong Kong. In accord with Marxist-Leninist distaste for Western imperialism and colonialism, the Soviet Union adopted the Chinese position that Hong Kong was an integral part of China, and should be returned forthwith. Concurrently, the Soviet Union deferred to the PRC decision to acquiesce in continued British rule in Hong Kong, a triumph of economic pragmatism over ideological and anti-colonial imperatives. The Soviet Union attempted no activities independent of the Chinese, particularly after the Chinese Communists triumphed in 1949.

This chapter examines the following issues: Russian activities in and around Hong Kong from 1945 to 1960, focusing particularly on the economic and strategic, but also including political and cultural activities; the significance of Hong Kong as a security and intelligence asset to both Western and Soviet policy makers; and the impact of Soviet activities and factors on the Sino-Soviet relationship. A subsequent chapter will explore the ramifications of the Sino-Soviet split for Soviet policies toward Hong Kong.

The Formative Years of the Cold War, 1945–1948

Soviet Organizations in Hong Kong, 1945–1948

As World War II drew to a close, a small Soviet presence did exist in Hong Kong. In the fluid situation between Japan's defeat in August 1945 and Communism's 1949 triumph in China, when the swiftly developing Cold War was still in its infancy, the Soviet Union maintained economic and propaganda bureaus in Hong Kong. Although the British colonial government regarded them with some suspicion, until 1948 it tolerated them. There was no Soviet Consulate in Hong Kong after 1920, and by mid-1948 only two Soviet organizations still functioned there: the VOKS and *Exportkhleb*. Only *Exportkhleb*, which handled trade for the Soviet Union, had Russian personnel, and the British government closed it down at the end of the year. VOKS was manned completely by Chinese, both local and mainland. The Soviet presence in Hong Kong was very small. Only 27 Soviet nationals were registered in Hong Kong. Another 65 people were from Eastern Europe, mostly Czechs and Poles, and they were not necessarily pro-Soviet.[4] There were, however, 224 stateless people, mostly Russians, about half of whom had permanent residency. Hong Kong had a very small foreign presence, much smaller than today when foreigners comprise about 5 percent of the total population of over six million. While most of the stateless people were ethnic Russians, many were émigrés, or children of émigrés, who had fled Russia following the Bolshevik Revolution of 1917, and whose sympathies were unlikely to be pro-Soviet.

While the permanent Soviet presence was very small, often Soviet citizens, officials, business people, and newspaper correspondents sought visas to come to Hong Kong. As had been the case ever since the 1920s, the British government habitually made this very difficult for them. The Soviet Embassy in China, supported by the Soviet Embassy in London, made repeated efforts to obtain entry visas, but the British government almost routinely denied all such requests, and the only visas Soviet citizens could obtain were transit visas. A British Foreign Office report stated: "They [Russians] all represent a security threat and in the present state of world affairs it is not proposed to be liberal in giving visas to such persons."[5] Yet Soviet citizens often simply overstayed the very limited time they were granted for transit visas. The reaction of the British government was to demand their immediate departure.

Some Soviet government representatives resented how their citizens were routinely denied entry into Hong Kong when citizens of virtually all non-Communist countries, many needing no visa at all, had no problems entering Hong Kong. One Soviet consular official in Guangzhou, Alexei Roshin, proposed to the MID that the Soviet government should refuse to grant visas to British subjects who wished to travel to the Soviet Union. He further suggested that the MID should make clear that the reason for those refusals was the British government's policy of refusing to grant Hong Kong visas to Soviet citizens. Had this policy been implemented it would have heightened tensions between the United Kingdom and the Soviet Union, and would have ended virtually all travel to the Soviet Union by British subjects. Fortunately moderation prevailed within the MID, which refused to utilize "tit for tat" measures. The MID thought the matter not worth pursuing. "The point of view of the Far East Department [of the MID] is that Soviet citizens in Guangzhou who want to go to Hong Kong, about which Roshin speaks in his telegram, are not numerous enough to make it a major issue."[6] Right up through the collapse of the Soviet Union in 1991, it remained virtually impossible for Soviet citizens to obtain visas to enter Hong Kong. Furthermore, Special Branch agents of the Royal Hong Kong Police routinely followed Soviet citizens wherever they went in the territory. The United States Department of State instructed its Consulate in Hong Kong to report the arrivals and departures, as well as the movements, of all visitors from the Soviet Union and Eastern Europe.[7]

Despite very tight control over the movements of Soviet citizens to and within Hong Kong, both the British and American governments believed it harbored numerous ethnic Chinese Soviet agents. Most were journalists or editors from left-wing Hong Kong newspapers and magazines. Some distributed pamphlets claiming the United States was trying to revive German and Japanese military power, for use in a war against the Soviet Union. Others gathered information on Hong Kong politics, economy, and society, and then conveyed it to the Soviet Consulate in Guangzhou. American and British officials claimed these agents' activities were financially subsidized by the Soviet government. On September 22, 1946, the American Consulate sent a list of some ten Soviet agents to Washington. Most were well educated, often at universities in the United Kingdom, and spoke English. None had studied in the Soviet Union, and the list included no individuals who had even paid a short visit to the Soviet Union. There was, however, one agent, Wang Yau Min, nicknamed "Stalin Say" because he habitually approved or disapproved whatever Stalin supported or opposed. Several people were rich; a few were millionaires. None had any military or police training, which one might expect of agents.[8] None of the archives examined for this study contains any evidence whatever of any Soviet agents in Hong Kong, but this is by no means conclusive, since references to such agents were most likely to occur in the TsA FSB *Rossii*, to which access was flatly denied.

Exportkhleb, an official Soviet trading firm, had offices in Hong Kong as well as in South China, in the city of Guangzhou. Its Hong Kong director was Piotr Sizov. *Exportkhleb* had operated in Hong Kong before and during World War II, suspending work only during the few months of 1945 when Japan was at war with the Soviet Union. Deteriorating Soviet-British relations caused the British and Hong Kong governments to force Sizov out of Hong Kong at the end of 1947, leaving the *Exportkleb* office under the directorship of a stateless Russian, Nikolai Ivanchenko. The Hong Kong government then asked the British government in 1948 for permission to shut *Exportkhleb* altogether. Permission was granted, and *Exportkleb* closed its doors by the end of 1948.[9]

The other major Soviet organization in Hong Kong during these early postwar years was the VOKS. VOKS, the main tool of Soviet propaganda, was often used to gather information on foreign countries. Another objective of the China branch of VOKS was to build links between the Soviet Union and Chinese intellectuals and students. As China became less stable, Soviet Vice Foreign Minister Yakov Malik proposed that all Chinese offices of VOKS be moved to Hong Kong.[10] Malik believed the British would permit this because the "British try to present the picture that Hong Kong is a 'bastion of freedom in China,' and do sanction some democratic [meaning Communist] newspapers, magazines and organizations."[11] The Soviets also wanted to remove the Chinese head of VOKS, Sun Fo, whom they considered anti-Soviet. One way to accomplish this was to persuade members of the newly established Hong Kong organization to send an open letter highly critical of Sun to be published in "progressive" newspapers in Hong Kong.[12] While Soviet Foreign Minister Vyacheslav Molotov agreed to the transfer of the Chinese VOKS headquarters to Hong Kong, he did not endorse Nikolai Fedorenko's idea of ceasing all activities in China. By early May 1948, the organization had moved to Hong Kong from Nanjing and Shanghai.[13]

VOKS published and distributed Chinese language magazines describing cultural and economic life in the USSR. For example, VOKS published 100,000 copies of a 100-page magazine, *Svobodnaya kul'tura*, which featured articles such as "Freedom of Literature in the USSR" by Mao Dun, and "Study of Shakespeare in the USSR" and a "New Path of Soviet Linguistic Science" by Lin Chiu. The magazine also published translations of recent Soviet literature, listed bookstores in Hong Kong where Soviet books could be purchased, and provided information on Russian museums for any Chinese able to travel there. The Soviet authorities concluded that Hong Kong allowed Soviet materials to be published much more freely than in China itself, particularly articles of a political character.[14] VOKS and *Exportkhleb* both imported Soviet books and records into Hong Kong. Books in English and Chinese included materials on Lenin, Stalin, Marx, Gorky, and Soviet history. VOKS also held a photo exhibition in 1948 entitled "Soviet Sculpture and Graphics," although the Soviet report noted that they encountered problems transporting exhibition materials to Hong Kong.[15] VOKS also showed several Soviet movies. However, few books or movies were brought in. For example, in 1946 only two Soviet movies, both World War II documentaries, were exhibited, at a very low rental fee to encourage cinema owners to show them.[16] The British government kept abreast of these activities. A report written, somewhat ironically, by the Soviet spy Guy Burgess indicated that it would be informative to know the titles of Soviet movies shown in the working-class districts of Hong Kong, commenting, "The Russians continued to take an interest in Hong Kong from the commercial and propaganda angle. They are anxious to obtain a foothold in the colony."[17]

The Soviets admitted they encountered problems conducting cultural activities in Hong Kong. For example, due to a Hong Kong law banning mass meetings, they could not hold these very often. Articles on life in the Soviet Union could only be published in the Communist press, which had a more limited circulation than pro-Western newspapers. Because few people in Hong Kong could read Russian, translators were difficult to find.[18] Finally, in market-oriented Hong Kong, the Soviets admitted that few people wanted to read Soviet books or watch Soviet movies.

While the Soviet Union had a poor image of Hong Kong as a poverty-stricken land "infested with prostitutes, thieves and ex-warlords," it also realized Hong Kong's potential, given its strategic location and good port.[19] Soviet observers recognized that in the changed post–World War II international system, the United States would play the major role among the Western allies, and that American activities, in particular, would have to be closely monitored.[20] As the United States emerged as the Soviet Union's most significant adversary in the Cold War, increasing

American activities in Hong Kong would only cause the Soviet Union to accord the territory closer attention.

The Soviet Union took a decided and ideologically driven position on Hong Kong's status, one which may also have owed much to a desire to weaken Britain strategically. As World War II drew to a close in 1945, the question of whether the British or the Chinese would control Hong Kong after the Japanese surrender remained undecided. British troops had been humiliated in December 1941 when Japanese forces swiftly captured Hong Kong after a two-week campaign. The KMT Chinese government, led by Chiang Kai-shek, demanded "the recovery of all territories, including Hong Kong, lost in the preceding century of 'humiliation' through a series of 'unequal treaties' to restore China's rightful place in the world."[21] United States President Franklin D. Roosevelt also firmly supported Chinese aspirations to recover Hong Kong, in part because of his aversion to British colonialism. Yet military events did not develop in China's favor, while British armies won a number of battles, mostly in Southeast Asia. After Roosevelt's death in April 1945, his successor, Harry Truman, had little patience with Chiang and his government, and viewed British imperialism far less negatively. Finally, Chiang himself, learning of the dispatch of a British fleet to retake Hong Kong and to receive the Japanese surrender, declined to order his nearby armies to hurry and retake Hong Kong for China. Chiang refused because he sought British support in his impending struggle against Communist forces, and did not wish to risk a possible Communist takeover of Hong Kong by guerrilla forces operating nearby Hong Kong.

Once reinstalled, the British reneged on their wartime promise to the Chinese government to negotiate the future of Hong Kong. The Chinese government was in no position to force the British either to negotiate or to relinquish Hong Kong. Chiang Kai-shek faced a multitude of problems: a brewing civil war with the Communists, raging inflation, an ineffective army, and war-torn cities and countryside. He needed British goodwill to enable his forces to use Hong Kong port facilities for transportation to North China to fight the Communists and attempt to regain control of that area. The American government demanded that Chiang fight and defeat the Communists, rather than become embroiled with the British over Hong Kong.

At that time, the Soviet Union, whose relations with Chiang were reasonably friendly, demanded the return of Hong Kong to China. An article in *Pravda* on February 16, 1946 noted China's "just desire to recover a sovereign territory and to abolish unjust treaties." Hong Kong was an "outpost of British economic aggression and a memorial for the unjust Opium Wars." Furthermore, the *Pravda* article noted that Britain's continued possession of Hong Kong impeded the development of friendly relations between China and the United Kingdom.[22] A subsequent article in *Pravda* on May 15 noted that Chinese people in both China and Hong Kong favored the return of Hong Kong to China. Furthermore, as almost all Hong Kong's population was Chinese, *Pravda* declared that Britain's continued possession of Hong Kong violated the principles of the Atlantic Charter, which supported the right of all peoples to self-determination.[23] The Soviet Union criticized the Chinese government's passive position on Hong Kong, essentially one of just waiting and hoping for its return. China, it contended, needed a plan, which should be quickly prepared. According to *Pravda*, China had the historical right to regain Hong Kong and should familiarize the world with its case.[24] The demand for Hong Kong's immediate and unconditional return to China formed the bedrock of the Soviet Union's ideological stance during the entire period 1945–1980, embodying its fundamental opposition to all manifestations of Western imperialism and colonialism.

This Soviet stance represented something of a modification of the position it had taken during World War II, when Stalin offered only half-hearted opposition to the return of Hong Kong to Britain. At that time Stalin sought British support for Soviet gains in Eastern Europe, and therefore had no desire to antagonize Churchill over an issue that was not of critical importance to the Soviet Union. Overmuch insistence on the territorial integrity of China might also have undercut Stalin's intention of winning substantial territorial and political concessions from Chiang Kai-shek in Northeast China, a continuation of the policies followed by the Tsarist government before 1905. From late 1945 onward, the advent of the Cold War hardened attitudes on both the Soviet and Western sides. Stalin now thought it advisable to take a firm anti-imperialist position on all areas, including Hong Kong. Most interestingly, the Soviet refusal to recognize Hong Kong's colonial status remained a constant, even at the height of the Sino-Soviet split during the mid- and late 1960s.

Despite a firm hard-line ideological position, Soviet officials nonetheless understood that any return of Hong Kong to China would not be simple. In a report to the MID following a visit to Hong Kong in late

October 1946, Nikolai Fedorenko of the Soviet Embassy in China commented that China could not raise the question of recovering Hong Kong without American support. The return of Hong Kong to China "is no longer a near-term issue," because British control was so firm. Furthermore, Fedorenko warned that if Hong Kong were returned to China, it would "go into chaos," as had much of China by late 1946.[25] Thus, from the very start the ideological thrust of Soviet policy was tinged by pragmatism.

At the close of the war, the city and people of Hong Kong had suffered greatly during almost four years of Japanese occupation.[26] The Soviet Union had a low opinion of Hong Kong at that time, regarding it as a "place of opium, prostitutes and displaced warlord émigrés."[27] Yet, following his visit to Hong Kong, Fedorenko recognized its potential as a regional communications and trade center. He noted with something approaching amusement brewing economic competition between Britain and the United States in Hong Kong, a struggle Britain was losing.[28] In his report, Fedorenko noted that already in 1946: "Hong Kong was a link in United States policy—economic and military—in the Far East."[29] Thus on the eve of the Cold War in Asia, Hong Kong was perceived as a source of friction between the United States and Great Britain, rather than between the Soviet Union and the capitalist bloc.

The Soviet Union also recognized Hong Kong's importance as a trading center facilitating the passage of goods from South China to the USSR, or to Communist-dominated Manchuria and Korea. A British intelligence report noted that "Soviet ships have been coming to Hong Kong on the average about one or two a month, trading from Vladivostok or from North Korean ports."[30] Soviet ships carried to Hong Kong such products as window glass, ammonia, soya beans, and Siberian deer antlers for Chinese medicine. In return the Soviets purchased minerals and metals, such as wolfram, tin, antimony, and tungsten. The Americans even claimed the Soviet Union smuggled "narcotics produced in the North, which were then shipped to Hong Kong in exchange for tungsten."[31] From 1946 to 1948 total exports from Hong Kong to the Soviet Union amounted to hundreds of thousands of US dollars per year.[32] The level of Soviet exports to Hong Kong was much lower, leaving the Soviet Union with a huge trade deficit.[33] Even so, the Soviet Union found Hong Kong a useful and reliable source for products from South China, as that region drifted deeper into civil war and anarchy.

The Years of Close Sino-Soviet Relations, 1949–1956

From 1949 onward, the Cold War came to Asia in general and to Hong Kong in particular. Furthermore, it became "hot" in Asia. Three events transformed the situation in Asia: the Chinese Revolution, which culminated in the proclamation of the PRC in October 1949; the Korean War, which began in June 1950 and within six months would see North Korean and Chinese Communist troops fighting British, American, South Korean, and other forces; and an anti-colonial struggle by the Vietnamese against the French, which metamorphosed into a war of Communism versus the West. These three developments caused a change in American and Soviet views on Hong Kong. Rather than being seen simply as a sleepy colonial outpost, Hong Kong was viewed increasingly as a very useful crossroads for gathering intelligence about the other side. Both sides valued its port for naval as well as commercial reasons, as a base and a repair depot for warships, supplying ships with food and fuel, and providing sailors with rest and relaxation. The Soviet Union noted Hong Kong's potential to serve as an entrepôt for trade between China and the rest of the world. In the face of a severe American embargo, Hong Kong could save the new Communist government from economic collapse. Conversely, the Soviet Union recognized that Hong Kong also served as a hub for propaganda and even terrorism against the PRC. The Soviet Union had to reconcile these contradictions when shaping its relationship with Hong Kong. The preferred Soviet solution was that China should "liberate" Hong Kong from British rule and take over the colony itself, a recommendation which, for pragmatic reasons, the new PRC rejected, leaving the Soviet Union little alternative but to acquiesce in China's restraint.

As early as 1947 there were reports that, due to the colony's relative freedom and its strategic location, the Soviet Union had secretly opened an office of the Cominform (the successor to the Comintern) in Hong Kong. In 1950 both the British newspaper *The Guardian* and the French newspaper *Le Figaro* stated this as a fact. The *Guardian* article was headlined, "Communist Network in Far East: Headquarters in Hong Kong."[34] British and American officials differed over the accuracy of the reports submitted to them. The US Consulate in Shanghai considered reports that Hong Kong housed at least a sub-office of the Cominform as "fairly reliable, but truth can not be judged." The Consul-General even wrote that the head of this reputed Hong Kong Cominform office was a man named Chiao Cu, and that the main office for the Cominform in East Asia was in Khabarovsk.[35] The British government, however, was very skeptical that any Cominform office existed in Hong Kong. A report in 1950 described it as an "old story," for which no real evidence existed. If there were any Cominform offices in East Asia, which the British Foreign Office doubted, they would logically be located in China, which had recently come under complete Communist control.[36] None of the four Russian archives consulted for this study makes any reference to any Hong Kong office of the Cominform. Furthermore, the *Guardian* article stated that the Kremlin strongly opposed China's desire to absorb Hong Kong, whereas documents obtained from the AVP RF show that the opposite was the case. The Soviet Union sought the annexation of Hong Kong by China, which the new Communist government refused to do.[37] This suggests that reports of a Cominform Hong Kong office were unfounded, simply another example of Cold War hysteria.

As Communist victory approached in the Chinese Civil War, in 1949 the British increased their land and sea garrison significantly. Military exercises by the British and American fleets were conducted in or near Hong Kong waters. Tensions increased in Hong Kong itself following a large increase in population due to a huge influx of refugees from China, which gave rise to higher inflation and unemployment. In response, Great Britain increased its garrison yet further, curbed civil liberties, and closed its border with China. The Soviet Union scrutinized these developments closely. Twice a month the Chinese Military-Control Commission in Guangzhou, a section of the Ministry of Foreign Affairs of the PRC, wrote extensive 14- to 18-page reports describing political, economic, and social developments in Hong Kong during the preceding two weeks. Repressive police and military measures by the British were also outlined in these reports. Activities by US officials or KMT agents, particularly anti-Communist propaganda, espionage, and terrorist activities, which included bombings and assassinations within the PRC, were detailed. Strikes, particularly those conducted by the Communist controlled trade unions, were also described, but hardly objectively since they always laid the blame on the Hong Kong government or the employers, but never the workers. These reports in Chinese were then given to the Soviet Consulate in Guangzhou, where they were translated into Russian. Both the Russian translation and the original Chinese-language reports were forwarded to the Far East Department of the MID. Since no questions were raised about the validity of these reports, apparently the Russians either accepted all the information supplied by the Chinese as accurate, or they did not care enough to query this.

Once the Korean War ended in 1953, the reports became less frequent, initially once a month, later once every six to eight weeks. When Sino-Soviet relations began to deteriorate in 1956, Chinese intelligence reports to the Soviet Consulate ceased completely. Thereafter, the Soviet Union had to write its own reports based on its own sources. This led the Soviets to attempt to reestablish a presence again in Hong Kong, the first in nearly a decade. The Soviets obtained much of their information on Hong Kong from Hong Kong Chinese- and English-language newspapers. They could obtain no assistance from the secret and illegal Hong Kong Communist Party, a virtual appendage of the CCP, since the "pro-Soviet" agents noted by the British and American governments had switched their allegiance completely to the Chinese. Thus, at a time of worsening relations between the two Communist powers in the late 1950s and early 1960s, when the Soviet Union most needed accurate information about Hong Kong, Moscow found most sources closed to it.

The Chinese Revolution of 1949 and Hong Kong

During 1949, the KMT-led Chinese government crumbled. In the fall Communist forces captured the city of Guangzhou, located only a few hours from Hong Kong. On October 1, Mao Zedong proclaimed the establishment of the PRC, with its capital in Beijing. As Mao's armies neared the Hong Kong border, observers asked if they would stop at the border, or would those armies cross the frontier, and retake Hong Kong militarily? To prepare for the worst, the British greatly augmented their garrison to some 40,000 troops, supported by tanks, heavy artillery, ships, and planes. Nervous about a possible invasion, the British publicly claimed they had 60,000 troops there.[38]

In that crucial fall, the Soviet Union urged a Chinese takeover of Hong Kong. The Soviets believed that a British-controlled Hong Kong would play a purely negative role. Great Britain did not have the forces, they argued, to stave off a Chinese attack. Their defenses would crumble quickly, as they had against the Japanese in 1941. The Soviets further did not believe the United States would help the British defend an anachronistic colony, an "outpost of British imperialism."[39] Thus, the Chinese had little to fear militarily from attacking Hong Kong. Ideologically, the Soviet Union believed the taking of Hong Kong by the Chinese would represent the simultaneous triumph of Communism over capitalism and Western imperialism. Furthermore, the Soviets recognized that once Communism was victorious in China, the nature of Hong Kong would change. Stalin habitually tried to persuade his allies to take serious risks to advance Soviet interests. In a long report on Hong Kong, M. Safronov, stationed at the Soviet Embassy in Beijing, stated that Hong Kong was extremely useful to the British. It was a base for English capital in China and a "place for the expansion of British imperialism in South China. Britain hoped to use the defeat of Japan and its position in Hong Kong to take a preeminent economic position in East Asia." Hong Kong was already one of the world's major centers for the export and import of goods. By the end of the 1940s Hong Kong stood at eighth place in the world in trade turnover for a port. More importantly, at a time of growing tensions between the Soviet Union and the West, Hong Kong was the British navy's base for the Western Pacific, posing a threat to the Soviet fleet. Even at this early stage, the Soviet Union recognized that the United States, its paramount enemy, would become more active in Hong Kong, and "would use Hong Kong as a naval base and a base for intelligence activities against China."[40]

Self-interest and ideology alike led the Soviets to argue that the Chinese had little to fear militarily from Great Britain and the United States, while morally and ideologically the Chinese were in the right and should stamp out this potential base of subversion before it could be established. Perhaps reflecting the influence of advice received from Soviet diplomats on the spot in South China, Stalin's position on Hong Kong gradually hardened. At first Stalin perceived Hong Kong primarily as a British hostage to Communist policies. When Mao Zedong visited Moscow in December 1949, Stalin initially suggested to him that, should he wish at any time to exert pressure on Great Britain, all that would be needed was to create tension between Hong Kong and neighboring Guangdong province, giving Mao the opportunity to step in and play a mediating role in any such conflict.[41] From January 1950 onward, however, Stalin—possibly emboldened, too, by secret intelligence that in National Security Council policy papers and meetings the United States government had decided to abandon Taiwan to Chinese rule—encouraged Mao not just to plan to take Taiwan, but also to mount an attack on Hong Kong.[42] It seems that Stalin hoped that such policies might drive a permanent wedge between the United States and the new PRC. In 1951 Soviet officials once more repeated their suggestion that China take back Hong Kong, urging that the treaties under which Hong Kong had been ceded to Britain had no validity in international law, and the UN would therefore take no action should China regain the territory.[43] The Chinese, by now embroiled in the Korean War, rejected the Soviet advice, stating that, while they agreed "the liberation of Hong Kong militarily was not a problem. However, military liberation would not be profitable because of the international situation."[44] The Soviets correctly believed that while the Chinese used tough rhetoric on Hong Kong's need and desire to return to China, in reality they found it convenient to leave Hong Kong British, to serve as a trading entrepôt and a source of needed hard currency. "Hong Kong was a place where it was easy to buy and sell hard currency."[45]

From the very birth of the PRC, therefore, the Soviet Union and China had different attitudes toward British control of Hong Kong. Both countries regarded Hong Kong as an occupied territory and did not recognize its colonial status. However, the Soviet Union, perceiving only negative aspects to British control, favored its military liberation. The Chinese, on the other hand, recognized a number of positive advantages in maintaining British-controlled Hong Kong. Among them Hong Kong would serve as a trade outlet for Chinese goods due to its excellent harbor and status as a free port, as well as a financial source of hard currency badly needed for the reconstruction of war-devastated China. In Chinese policy, pragmatism prevailed over ideological anti-colonialism. Also, while the Hong Kong outlet may have been advantageous to China, this was not the case for the Soviet Union which, to further its own interests, was anxious to weaken Anglo-American capitalism. Neither nation's analysis was entirely without merit. Many of the Soviet fears as to Hong Kong's use as a base for subversion against China and, to a lesser extent, against the Soviet Union and other Communist states would prove correct. Nevertheless, despite Hong Kong's annoying prominence in Western naval and espionage activities, the Soviet Union acquiesced in China's pragmatic decision to leave it under British rule.

The Korean and Indochinese Wars and Hong Kong

The Korean War at least temporarily reinforced the Sino-Soviet alliance, even as it simultaneously increased Hong Kong's strategic significance and generated Anglo-American tensions over the degree to which the colony should subordinate its economic interests to the United States anti-China embargo. In June 1950, North Korea invaded South Korea, swiftly overrunning most of the peninsula. Soon the United States, heading a UN coalition of states, sent forces to the South to assist that beleaguered nation. As American troops neared the Chinese-Korean border in the fall, the PRC dispatched volunteer forces to fight on the side of Communist North Korea. While the war was mostly localized on the Korean Peninsula, Hong Kong played a major role. The Korean War initially benefited Hong Kong's economy, which prospered due to increased trade. That caused Hong Kong to attract more Soviet attention. Furthermore, Hong Kong became a center for the transport of armies and soldiers, mostly but not exclusively British. For example, according to information supplied to the Soviet Union by Chinese intelligence, "4,000 cases of weapons, as well as large quantities of artillery shells were sent from Hong Kong bound for Korea."[46] Further frequent reports sent to Moscow noted more troops and weapons passing through Hong Kong en route to Korea. At the height of the Korean War such reports arrived almost weekly. British and American troops came to Hong Kong, mostly for "rest and relaxation." "In 1952 during the Korean War, 130 American warships called on Hong Kong. 130,000 American servicemen visited Hong Kong in 1953. Frequently top American military officers came to Hong Kong as well."[47] As the Soviets feared earlier on, Hong Kong therefore actively supported the anti-Communist side during the Korean War.

Throughout the Korean War, Soviet diplomats sent the MID detailed reports on the state of Hong Kong, many remarkably accurate, on which this section draws. Angered by "the fall of China" to the Communists, and then infuriated by the new Communist government's intervention in the Korean War, in 1951, the United States imposed an embargo on China, closing its huge market to all goods made in the PRC and also refusing to allow any "strategic" American-made goods to enter China. Soviet observers paid close attention to this policy's effects. This embargo had a huge immediate impact on Hong Kong, as most of Hong Kong's trade depended on funneling goods in and out of China. Trade almost immediately fell by 20 percent. Unemployment rose in the colony.[48] Great Britain compiled a list of more than 200 items normally exported to China that were forbidden under the US embargo. The

American Consulate directed the embargo and supervised its implementation by Hong Kong authorities. The US Consul-General himself warned Hong Kong businessmen to observe the embargo. "If they don't they will be placed on a black list and have their assets frozen."[49]

Fortunately for the Hong Kong economy, the embargo was less than complete. The British feared that if Hong Kong was too severely affected, this would cause increased social and political unrest which, naturally enough, they wished to avoid. Trade in forbidden goods continued. While officials at the American Consulate instructed both the Hong Kong Ministry of Trade and Industry and the British authorities to help them enforce the embargo, others within the ministry helped the Chinese avoid controls. Chinese employees in various trading companies also assisted in evading the embargo on metals and rubber.[50] Yet even a limited embargo had a significant negative impact on Hong Kong, its economy, and its standard of living. The embargo also forced Hong Kong to reorient its economy away from acting as an entrepôt for China to developing a manufacturing industry in textiles, toys, and other inexpensive consumer goods. The embargo also caused problems in Anglo-American relations, because the British-administered Hong Kong government did not appreciate American meddling. Unintentionally, the embargo affected the Soviet Union positively, as China increased its trade with the Soviet Union, where it could obtain certain otherwise unavailable products. The embargo proved an example of one of the many ways in which the Korean War brought China even closer to its northern neighbor.[51] The Chinese decision to leave Hong Kong undisturbed reflected not only China's pragmatism, but also Britain's readiness to accommodate the PRC's interests at the expense of other Cold War priorities.

The Soviets also recognized that, increasingly, the United States publicly viewed Hong Kong as an East Asian military bastion in the battle against Soviet military expansion. Hong Kong served as a springboard for covert military operations against the PRC, staged by anti-Communist groups, usually under American and Taiwanese direction. These raids were intended at a minimum to create chaos for Beijing and, at best, to overthrow the Communist government, but lacking support from the local population, virtually all were unsuccessful. The British government nonetheless grew increasingly concerned that these operations might destabilize the entire region, including Hong Kong, and even provoke a

Chinese military invasion of Hong Kong. British Prime Minister Clement Attlee viewed these raids as needless and risky, and tried to end entirely their being launched from Hong Kong soil. While the Americans did not cease all such covert operations, realizing that Hong Kong depended on Chinese goodwill for its survival, from then onward they kept their activities in Hong Kong very discreet.[52]

To reaffirm Hong Kong's strategic value to the United States, in fall 1953 Vice President Richard Nixon visited the colony and declared that Hong Kong played a major role in fighting Communism in South Korea, Japan, Taiwan, and throughout the Far East.[53] In 1954, as the Korean War wound down, the Battle of Dien Bien Phu marked the end of French rule in Indochina. In an attempt to warn the Soviet Union and China to relax their perceived offensive against "free, democratic countries," especially Taiwan and Hong Kong, in February 1954, the American, British, and French fleets held a huge naval exercise, "Sonata," in the South China Sea. Up to 10,000 personnel and numerous warships and airplanes participated in the exercise, in whose preparation Hong Kong played a major role. On January 14, the American naval commander, the Vice Commander of the British General Staff, the Chief of Staff of the French Army, the American Secretary of Defense, and the commanders of the fleets who would participate in the exercises all gathered in Hong Kong. One of their aims, according to Soviet observers, was to train the Western naval forces involved for antisubmarine activity against Soviet submarines. Western leaders believed that the Soviet Union had stationed about one-third of its submarines in the South China Sea. At the Hong Kong meetings Western leaders also discussed mounting a potential blockade of Chinese and Vietnamese ports, or implementing a landing by Western troops on the South China coast. In response, Chinese troops and Soviet ships and submarines in the area heightened their alert status. Orders were given to Chinese aircraft and defenses to shoot down any airplanes which strayed into Chinese air space.[54] Great Britain conducted further land, sea, and air exercises in and around Hong Kong in November 1954. The next month yet more joint American-British naval exercises were held off the Hong Kong coast, the biggest such operations in the region since World War II. In response, the Soviet Union and China held major joint naval maneuvers north of Shanghai in Yan Yuan Bay in late August 1955, in which air squadrons from the Soviet naval fleet at Vladivostok also participated. Two Soviet submarines were placed on permanent patrol off the Chinese coast.[55] These repeated military efforts by both sides heightened tensions in the region and involved Hong Kong directly in the Cold War.

The continued imposition of the American embargo against China was a further irritant in Anglo-American relations, because Britain rightly viewed the embargo as threatening Hong Kong's economy, and consequently its own control of the colony. A tightly enforced ban would greatly restrict trade with Hong Kong's large neighbor, increasing unemployment and depressing living standards, all of which might generate large-scale social unrest among average Hong Kong people. In 1956, the Soviets observed: "The embargo caused problems in relations between the United States and Britain as the local Hong Kong government does not appreciate American meddling in Hong Kong affairs."[56] Thus, Britain quietly allowed various Chinese trading firms and even its own Hong Kong ministries to evade the restrictions. Finally, the Soviets noted that the Americans were trying to control the local Hong Kong government because they viewed Hong Kong as a "military base against the PRC." While the United States hoped KMT agents would once again become more active, the British wanted to cut back on such enterprises and were infuriated by this American attempt to militarize Hong Kong.[57] The British were highly embarrassed when in April 1955 Taiwan's secret service placed a bomb on an Air India flight that originated in Hong Kong, killing all passengers and crew on board. What made matters even worse in China's eyes was the fact that their Premier and second ranking official, Zhou Enlai, was supposed to have been on board, but prior engagements forced him, fortunately, to postpone his departure from the Chinese capital. Exacerbating matters even more, the British colonial government failed to prosecute anyone for this state-sponsored act of terrorism, confirming in Beijing's eyes that Hong Kong was a nest of KMT spies and saboteurs.[58] Then, too, the quick and heated American response to PRC shellings of the offshore islands, Jinmen and Mazu, in 1954 and 1958, when the United States stationed its troops, airplanes, ships, and missiles close to Hong Kong, refocused international attention on the adjacent area, and might have caused China to take military action against Hong Kong.[59] Once again in British eyes, the Americans were needlessly provoking difficulties between Hong Kong and the PRC. Hong Kong was thus a source of alliance tension on both sides of the Cold War, generating both Anglo-American and ultimately, as shown in a subsequent chapter, Sino-Soviet discord.

The Zenith of the Sino-Soviet Alliance: The 1950s

From 1949 through 1955, the alliance between the Soviet Union and PRC was at its closest. The PRC and the Soviet Union signed a Treaty of Friendship and Alliance in February 1950. The two countries shared intelligence information. The Soviet Embassy in Beijing and the Consulate in Guangzhou regularly received intelligence reports from the Chinese military and police on Hong Kong and other matters. For its part, the Soviet Union did not deviate from the Chinese position that Hong Kong was an occupied territory, and never recognized its status as a British colony. While conducting assorted activities in Hong Kong, the Soviet Union never undertook these independently of the Chinese, but subordinated its actions to the Chinese.

The takeover of China by the Communists, the Korean War, and the United States embargo all led the British authorities in Hong Kong to adopt coercive measures: tightening the border between Hong Kong and China, curbing civil liberties, and heightening military readiness. Prior treaties between China and Britain provided for the free movement of people across the border. Fearing the territory might be overwhelmed by refugees fleeing the new Communist order as well as by Communist spies pretending to be refugees, the British for the first time imposed controls at the border. As Soviet observers noted, on May 9, 1950, free access to Hong Kong ended when the British instituted formal checkpoints and cut direct rail links. On February 1951, the Chinese closed their side of the border. Except for business purposes the border between Hong Kong and China was sealed, and would remain closed for more than two decades.[60] Besides boosting the size of the British garrison, the size, powers, and budget of the Royal Hong Kong Police were also increased. For example, in December 1951, the Hong Kong government declared that the police could arrest people without the sanction of the courts. 2,000 individuals were arrested. Press censorship was introduced. All foreign affiliated organizations had to register with the police. In May 1950, the Hong Kong government instituted a set of emergency laws, which gave it greater authority to ban strikes and demonstrations. All Hong Kong people were registered. Border defenses were strengthened.[61]

Despite these border controls, a flood of refugees continued to pour into Hong Kong. By May 1951, an estimated half million people of all ages and occupations had arrived, raising Hong Kong's total population to nearly 2.4 million people.[62] These refugees greatly exacerbated an already severe housing shortage, as most were forced into shantytowns on the side of hills, near the sea, or wherever there was any available space. Most of these "homes" lacked running water, electricity, and basic toilets or kitchens as entire families were crowded into one room. Disease and fire were constant scourges. The British government became very concerned that refugees living in such abysmal circumstances would become susceptible to Communist propaganda. Maintaining stability among the local population was one of the major goals of British policy in Hong Kong. The Soviet government viewed these refugees very negatively, alleging these "reactionary elements and criminals" fled China to save themselves from revolution and well-deserved punishment. Furthermore, many had left as a result of American as well as KMT sabotage activities.[63] In a meeting between Shu Ming, a Counselor at the Chinese Embassy in East Berlin, and representatives of the Ministry of Foreign Affairs of the GDR in September 1957, Shu told the East Germans: "In the PRC, there is an exodus of certain parts of the population to Hong Kong. The number of refugees to Hong Kong increased after the sharpening of the fight against the rightist classes. The refugees belong mostly to the bourgeoisie or large landowning classes."[64] Until the construction of the Berlin Wall in 1961, the GDR was likewise hemorrhaging people to capitalist West Germany. Soviet documents naturally never mentioned the real reason most people fled, leaving behind their homes and occupations, namely the fear of Communism and the new order that would follow. In Soviet eyes, Hong Kong provided "asylum for KMT reactionaries who wanted to use Hong Kong to launch sabotage raids against South China."[65]

While the great majority of these refugees were ethnic Chinese, thousands of Europeans also fled China through Hong Kong, on average about 300 individuals per month. In 1953, for example, 3,266 such refugees went on from Hong Kong to Brazil, Turkey, Australia, Israel, and Paraguay, and a few to the United States. Most came from North China, especially from Manchuria. They were often initially stateless, lacking passports from any nation, and of varying ages and occupations, and some suffered from tuberculosis. Many were ethnic Russians, descendants of formerly upper and middle-class émigrés who had fled following Bolshevik successes in Eastern Siberia after 1917. The Soviet Consulate in Harbin, Manchuria, only gave assistance or offered exit visas to the Soviet Union to a few. The Hong Kong government feared that large numbers of Russians could end up permanently in the already seriously overcrowded territory. Consequently, it announced that not unless it could be ensured that the Russian presence in Hong Kong would only be temporary would it permit arrangements for the evacuation of such refugees through the territory. None but those who already had a definite onward final destination organized and promised to them would be allowed into the colony. The Hong Kong authorities did, however, note rather more sympathetically that many of these Russian émigrés were old, sick, and demoralized, with nowhere else to go, and naturally feared maltreatment if they returned to the Soviet Union.[66] Despite such humanitarian sentiments, British authorities in Hong Kong feared the territory's limited space might become "dumping grounds" for thousands of ethnic Russians. Consequently, the Hong Kong government went so far as to send back to China several Russians who lacked papers indicating a final destination elsewhere, as a warning to Beijing not to send more Russians without papers to Hong Kong. The tough British policy was intended to prevent additional financial and political problems in the territory.[67]

The frequent survey reports submitted at least annually by officials at the Soviet Consulate in Guangzhou commented on the plight of the Hong Kong working class and labor movement. Most of these reports were quite factual, detailing political, economic, and social conditions in Hong Kong almost encyclopedically. Their accounts of the territory's historical background and even events in Hong Kong during the preceding six to 12 months also tended to be objective. When describing the Hong Kong working class, trade unions, and their conditions, they tended to be far less objective and more ideological. Hong Kong was correctly characterized as a highly stratified society, racially and economically. However the reports contended that the Chinese population was treated the same way it had been a century earlier, which was untrue. They correctly described the workers as a large group (about a half million), and badly paid, but inaccurately added that because many workers were unemployed or underemployed, large numbers died of hunger or committed suicide.[68] About one third of Hong Kong's workers were organized into trade unions. There were three groups of trade unions: Communist, Nationalist or KMT, and Independent. The pro-Beijing Communist trade unions were described as "democratic," while the Nationalist unions were all "reactionary, unpopular, and represented the interests only of the capitalists."[69] In the same document, Soviet Vice-Consul in Guangzhou V. Kapralov wrongly stated that Hong Kong had no future as a manufacturing city, and Hong Kong's economic situation would not improve.[70] His report was written on the eve of Hong Kong's industrial revolution, when rapid manufacturing growth would cause Hong Kong to enter a boom period.

Arguably the most significant labor event in Hong Kong during this entire period occurred in the latter half of 1955, a strike by Hong Kong's tram workers. To cut costs, a number of tram employees were fired on July 1, and those remaining had to work harder, exhausting themselves. Consequently, on August 31, tram workers conducted a two-hour warning strike. On October 10, a one-day strike began. Many other workers supported the strike, signing petitions and contributing assistance, money and food. In particular, the pro-Beijing Federation of Trade Unions collected HK$250,000. The fired workers were rehired, and the strike ended successfully. In other industries, many factories had to recognize trade unions. Kapralov's report to the MID detailed these events. He contended that the tram workers represented the "vanguard of the Hong Kong working class." The report also contended that pro-Nationalist trade unions tried to sabotage the strike, while pro-Beijing trade unions only employed "moderate methods to conduct the strike."[71] The tram strike was the largest such action in Hong Kong up to that point, and Soviet officials clearly showed great interest in its development, but no document ever mentioned any Soviet assistance or financial support for the strikers. Had the Soviets helped the tram workers, the British and Americans would have mentioned this, so it seems that outside support came only from Beijing. During the mid-1950s, the Soviet Union did not wish to risk antagonizing its close relations and alliance with the PRC, as any independent Soviet assistance to the strikers would almost certainly have done.

Soviet deference to Chinese sensitivities may have owed something to Soviet consciousness that from the late 1940s the United States, and to a lesser extent Great Britain, hoped that the Sino-Soviet alliance would fracture. The Americans noted, for example, historical ties dating back to the 1920s between the KMT and the Soviet Union, which predated any Soviet-Chinese Communist links. Many of Chiang Kai-shek's aides, including his son and heir apparent, Chiang Ching-kuo, were educated and trained in the Soviet Union. The Americans and British believed that, as China became more powerful and self-confident, a split between China and the Soviet Union would become increasingly likely. In a report filed from the Soviet Embassy in Beijing, N. Shesterikov stated: "They believe that China will be a new Yugoslavia, and that Mao will be a new Tito."[72] Soviet officials also noted numerous articles in the Hong Kong press that repeatedly predicted a split between the two countries. Often the Guangzhou Consulate translated verbatim articles from both the Chinese and English language press and sent both translations and the originals to the MID. An article in the Hong Kong–based *Far Eastern Economic Review* of March 12, 1953 speculated, for example, on the effect the recent death of Stalin would have on the alliance. "Despite pronouncements of great friendship, the reality was quite different." The Soviets believed these articles were simply provocations designed to create a rift. These articles tended to extol Mao as a great revolutionary, while "spreading lies about Soviet political life."[73] As relations between China and the Soviet Union genuinely deteriorated during the mid- to late 1950s, such articles proliferated but were increasingly based on fact.

The Russians soon discovered that anti-Soviet propaganda was quite pervasive in Hong Kong. The USIS distributed widely throughout Hong Kong a booklet called "Little Moe" in March 1953, showing in pictures and in Chinese language how dreadful daily life was in the Soviet Union. The USIS requested there be no publicity as to its origins. Another booklet, "Facts about Communism," described the complete absence of workers' rights in the Soviet Union and was distributed among Hong Kong workers, who were viewed as particularly susceptible to Communism.[74] A telegram from the State Department to the Hong Kong USIS office urged that the agency use a "Soviet Exploitation of Labor" address delivered by Secretary of State John Foster Dulles, in which he stressed that Soviet workers were regimented and had no rights, and that the entire history of the Soviet Union had proved a total failure. The telegram stated that this speech should be directed to labor and to intellectual audiences.[75] Soviet officials repeatedly noted that the Hong Kong radio, newspapers, and brochures carried anti-Soviet propaganda and also spread anti-Soviet rumors, and accused the Hong Kong press of publishing frightening headlines concerning an alleged "Communist Menace," directed against the Soviet Union and China. The Soviet Guangzhou Consulate claimed that most of the Hong Kong press was "reactionary," launching campaigns of hatred against the Soviet Union and exaggerating the lack of personal rights there, while the Hong Kong media diverted people "through pornography and Hollywood movies."[76]

Few Soviet books, journals, and brochures were distributed in Hong Kong after 1949, simply because, once the Communists controlled the mainland, they could publish books in Chinese much more easily and cheaply than the Soviets. Few materials were written in English because the target audience was Chinese. The Hong Kong USIS sent examples of pro-Communist reading matter to the State Department. In a report the USIS even commented on how minor the Soviet role was. "There is little or no evidence of direct Soviet participation in Communist propaganda activities in Hong Kong since the Soviets prefer that local parties do the work for them." Furthermore, USIS noted that "where Soviet materials are found in Hong Kong, they are not noted to be especially anti-American."[77] Viewed overall, Soviet activities in Hong Kong during the alliance period, 1949 through 1955, had no great intrinsic significance. Despite all the heavy propaganda from each side, British intelligence and the Hong Kong government concluded that most Hong Kong people were not deeply committed to either the political left or right, with only a vocal "hard core" on either side strongly ideological.[78]

While the Soviet Union subordinated its activities in Hong Kong to those of China, it did not abandon them completely. Even at the Cold War's height, the Soviet Union maintained a small presence in Hong Kong, despite the British authorities' somewhat inhospitable attitude. The most significant Soviet representation was in trade. Frequently, Soviet ships docked in Hong Kong loaded with petroleum bound for Guangzhou, returning later to the Soviet Union laden with wolfram and cassia oil. Vessels from Vladivostok loaded with fish bound for European Soviet Black Sea or Baltic Sea ports stopped in Hong Kong to refuel and take on food and water. All available information on each ship that docked in Hong Kong was noted by the US Consulate, and reported immediately to the State Department.[79] British intelligence reports provided the name and type of every ship from either Eastern Europe or the Soviet Union, its cargo, and whether and for what purpose it stopped in Hong Kong. Such reports also stated that many more Polish or Czech than Soviet ships docked in Hong Kong. Ships generally stopped in Hong Kong for refueling and repairs en route to their final destination, Guangzhou.[80] Rather sketchy Soviet figures reveal that trade between the Soviet Union and Hong Kong itself declined during the Korean War, when tensions rose very high between the Communist and anti-Communist blocs. During the first two months of 1950, the Soviet Union imported US$108,771 worth of goods from Hong Kong, whereas in the first two months of 1951, after China entered the Korean War, the Soviet Union's imports from Hong Kong were only valued at US$40,468, about 40 percent of the previous year's level. No figures were given for 1952. For all 1953, while the Korean War continued and the war in Indochina assumed greater international importance, the Soviets quoted trade figures of only US$2,807, an amount that would barely pay for one automobile. During 1954, trade began to recover, and the Soviets reported a figure of US$36,315. Soviet commerce was nonetheless insignificant to Hong Kong, whose trade in 1954 totaled nearly US$60 million, and remained much smaller than before 1949. Soviet exports to Hong Kong remained minuscule. Only for 1954 did the Soviets even bother to supply figures. The archives never mentioned which specific products Hong Kong supplied to the Soviet Union.[81]

Apart from trade, Soviet activities in Hong Kong focused mainly on cinema. According to a USIS report, those movies "ranged from blatant Communist propaganda to subtle anti-Western themes." Some pleased the Hong Kong audience. For example, the Russian movie *The Circus* was the most popular one in Hong Kong during its 1954 run.[82] In 1955, four movies based on either ballets or operas were shown: Tchaikovsky's *Swan Lake*, Puskhin's *Bakhchisaraiskii fontan* and *Plamia Parisha*, and the *Sadko* opera. The Soviet Consulate in Guangzhou noted that advertising in the pro-British newspaper *South China Morning Post* mentioned these movies were from the Soviet Union, while pro-Nationalist Chinese newspapers listed them, but ignored their origins. The Soviets believed that they were seriously disadvantaged in penetrating the Hong Kong movie market. Most cinema houses were American- or British-owned, and tended to show Hollywood productions, not the more serious Soviet ones. For example, during all 1954 and early 1955, 380 American movies were shown, in contrast to only ten mainland Chinese movies and four Soviet ones.[83] This meant that, virtually from the establishment of the PRC in late 1949, Hong Kong gave rise to problems over cultural diplomacy between the two great Communist powers. The Soviet Union wished, for example, to increase the numbers of its movies screened in Chinese cinemas. Yet the Soviets often found mainland China almost equally inhospitable to their cinematic offerings. When the Guangzhou

Consulate urged that Soviet movies replace Hong Kong ones in Guangzhou theaters, the Chinese refused, or censored the Soviet movies. The Chinese authorities claimed: "Sometimes we have nothing else to show, so we must [only show American and Hong Kong movies]." The Soviets complained the Chinese were unnecessarily nationalistic.[84] Yet such incidents were not enough to disturb the relatively smooth course of Soviet-Chinese relations up to and during the mid-1950s.

For much of the Cold War, Soviet officials would undoubtedly have welcomed a more substantial stake in Hong Kong. In the later 1950s, growing links with and increased interest in Hong Kong led the Soviet Union once again to seek some kind of permanent representation in the territory, which it had lacked since 1948. The presence of Soviet representatives in Hong Kong, in whatever formal capacity, would also enable them to gather intelligence and information on events and trends in both Hong Kong and China. On May 29, 1956, the Soviet Union first requested the British government to allow them to establish a trading office in Hong Kong. For over a year the British government delayed any formal response. This was not due to any hesitancy as to the British reply. All British departments involved, the Foreign Office, the Colonial Office, the Board of Trade, and the Hong Kong government, agreed their response should be negative, but they could not decide which department would issue the denial to the Soviets and on what stated grounds, economic or political. The Hong Kong government suggested the request be turned down for economic reasons, stating that there was insufficient trade between the two states to warrant a permanent Soviet office. At the time Hong Kong only exported about HK$3 million annually to the USSR, while imports from the Soviet Union to Hong Kong were minimal. The Board of Trade disagreed mildly, since trade might increase in the near future. The Foreign Office categorically opposed any Russian presence in Hong Kong. Ultimately, the British government decided on May 1, 1957 to send the Soviets a formal letter refusing their request, and on May 21 this was delivered officially to Mr. V. A. Kamensky, the Soviet Trade Representative in London. On September 6, Kamensky responded by letter that he considered the British refusal unjustified, but the British replied in their turn that they found his protest unconvincing, stating that nothing in their commercial agreements with the Soviet Union required Britain to open her colonies to Soviet trade. At a diplomatic reception, Mr. C. Brimlow of the Foreign Office told Kamensky that the GRU often conducted "undesirable" activities overseas under the cover of commercial offices. Although Kamensky repudiated the British charge, the trade office was not opened.[85] As had been the case ever since the 1920s, in the early Cold War, British officials, strongly anti-Soviet in outlook, sought to discourage any prospective enhancement of the limited Soviet presence and personnel in Hong Kong.

British hostility toward any new Soviet representation in Hong Kong may have reflected the fact that, although until 1958 the Soviet Union took no specific stand itself on Hong Kong's status, when necessary it simply reiterated and endorsed the Chinese position as its own. When China was weak in the nineteenth century, the argument went, the British forcibly took Hong Kong from the Chinese following the infamous Opium War, subsequently imposing various unequal treaties, which the Soviets believed were invalid under international law. Thus, neither the UN nor anyone else could oppose China taking back what was rightfully Chinese territory.[86] Soviet officials consistently argued that "without doubt Hong Kong belongs to China. To prove its colonial legitimacy, Britain had invented a theory that its Hong Kong colony had existed before the foundation of a united China. That theory was disproved by Chinese historical documents."[87]

Some Soviet offices and even sections of the MID were nonetheless hazy as to the status of Hong Kong. This lack of clarity could not last indefinitely. Matters came to a climax in 1957 when the Soviet journal, *Fizikul'tura i sport*, printed in its pages the colonial flag of Hong Kong, which had the British Union Jack in its upper left corner. When some Chinese officials noted the flag, which implied recognition of Hong Kong's colonial status, they naturally complained to the Soviet Embassy in Beijing. In response, the Beijing Embassy wrote to Soviet Foreign Minister Andrei Gromyko on March 22, 1958, specifically requesting guidance on the Soviet stance as to the status of Hong Kong. Copies of the letter were sent to all MID offices in Moscow and overseas, which would probably force the MID to respond more quickly to the request.[88] Within two months, Gromyko replied:

> As there is some vagueness regarding Soviet attitudes toward the status of Hong Kong, MID has decided to give the following information. Hong Kong is historically and naturally a Chinese territory, which was occupied in the nineteenth century by the English according to unequal treaties. The government of the PRC considers Hong Kong a Chinese territory and

> believes it should be united with China. However, China does not openly and forcibly demand its return. The PRC does not want to worsen its relations with Britain in light of the current world political situation.... Taking into account the appearance of any wrong ideas about Hong Kong as a territory, which belongs to Britain, Soviet offices and organizations, which have any questions regarding the status of Hong Kong, should bear in mind the position of the Chinese government.[89]

There was a postwar movement in Hong Kong to grant the colony self-rule and make Hong Kong a self-governing territory within the British Commonwealth, essentially giving it dominion status. China vigorously opposed this because self-rule would cement the notion that Hong Kong was a state separate from China, a status which, if accepted, would delay if not suspend its return to China. Self-rule would also have removed Hong Kong's anachronistic colonial status, and would probably have kept it in the Western orbit. Whatever the tensions between itself and the PRC, the Soviet Union fully supported China in rejecting moves toward self-rule for Hong Kong as a Western trick.[90] From a cynical viewpoint, it was advantageous to Soviet and Chinese propaganda for Hong Kong to remain a colony under direct "imperialist" control. Both powers preferred that the existing colonial system of government, under which Hong Kong had a strong executive-led administration whose head, the governor, was directly appointed by London, should continue until Hong Kong was returned to China. Throughout the Cold War, both China and the Soviet Union staunchly opposed any movements for political reform as diversions designed to maintain Western dominance in Hong Kong. Their stance was symptomatic of the manner in which, at least until the Sino-Soviet split became intense, Cold War Chinese and Soviet policies on Hong Kong marched in virtual lockstep.

Conclusions

Throughout the entire postwar period, Hong Kong's economic significance to the Soviet Union was small, although strategically it provided the Western powers with useful naval and intelligence facilities which the Soviets clearly found irritating. Ideologically the Soviet Union held to the Marxist-Leninist precept that all Western colonies should be released from the grip of their European masters and granted independence. Hong Kong, however, did not rate colonial status. It was simply an occupied territory, an integral part of China, whose independent existence separate and different from China was therefore unacceptable to Soviet foreign policy makers. Yet economic realities and to some extent, particularly from the late 1950s, geopolitical factors meant those same policy makers could not ignore Hong Kong. Soviet policy toward Hong Kong from 1945 onward was a perfect illustration of the triangular tension that existed among ideology, geopolitics, and economics. At all times, however, the ideological and strategic rivalry between the Soviet Union and the Western bloc in the Cold War era placed serious constraints upon Soviet room for maneuver and the effectiveness of Soviet Hong Kong policies.

During the Cold War's formative period in Asia, from 1945 to 1948, China itself was weak, divided, and in chaos. Hong Kong was also weak, poor, and in need of reconstruction following the wartime Japanese occupation. The Soviet Union strongly asserted that China should recover the territory at the earliest possible moment; yet the Nationalist Chinese government faced innumerable far more pressing issues, above all its own survival. Until the opportunity arose for China to retake Hong Kong, the Soviet Union remained quietly active in Hong Kong, where it still maintained a permanent presence and Hong Kong–based Soviet personnel.

In the course of 1949, Chinese Communist forces swiftly conquered China. As the Communist armies neared the frontier with Hong Kong, the Soviet Union urged them to cross the border and retake Hong Kong by force of arms. The Chinese refused. One wonders what the consequences would have been for international affairs, in fact for world peace, had the Chinese Communists taken Soviet advice and attempted to seize Hong Kong. That might well have precipitated a war, or at least open fighting between China and the United Kingdom, which had considerable land, naval, and air forces in the territory. Ironically, however, British alarm, generated not only by the intensifying Cold War in Europe, but also by the increasing probability of a Communist victory in China, may well have been the crucial factor, that impelled the Hong Kong authorities to close all Soviet offices in Hong Kong and expel all their personnel.

For most of the 1950s, the Soviet Union subordinated its policies to those of its close ally, the PRC, which normally placed its own self-interest well ahead of Soviet concerns. Despite some rhetoric to the contrary, China seemed to tolerate Hong Kong's status as a British colony, knowing that it could make great profits in Hong Kong precisely because it was not part of China. Even when Hong Kong was used as a base for

American-supported KMT espionage and terrorist raids into South China, the PRC only protested perfunctorily to the British. The Soviet Union maintained a strong interest in Hong Kong, evidenced by the large number of reports included in the AVP RF, but the USSR itself played a very small direct role in the colony. Its intelligence and information on developments in Hong Kong were completely dependent on Chinese sources. Frequently the Chinese military forwarded lengthy reports about Hong Kong to the Soviet Consulate in Guangzhou, which were then translated into Russian and sent on to the MID. Those reports were never queried, but simply accepted as accurate, perhaps an indication of Hong Kong's relative insignificance in Soviet foreign policy. As the Cold War intensified in Asia, with military contests between Communist and anti-Communist forces in Korea and Indochina, the Soviet Union feared Hong Kong would become an American base, which would limit the freedom of action of the Soviet Pacific Fleet. Despite some evidence of Soviet interest in reestablishing a permanent presence in Hong Kong, during the 1950s ideological distaste for "outposts of Western imperialism" remained supreme in Soviet thinking toward the colony and ostentatious support for the Chinese line toward the territory characterized all Soviet pronouncements and policies on Hong Kong.

6

The Soviet Union, Hong Kong, and the Cold War: The Sino-Soviet Split, 1960–1980

During the 1960s and 1970s, the rivalries consequent on the Sino-Soviet split featured prominently in the relations between the Soviet Union and China, and also had a major impact on Soviet dealings with Hong Kong. While still maintaining their hostile view, perhaps sometimes moderated, of British colonial rule, and engaged in perennial strategic competition with Great Britain and the West, especially where Vietnam was concerned, during these decades Soviet officials also viewed Hong Kong as a potential source of scarce intelligence on China itself. Soviet business interests also demonstrated a certain desire to profit from the economic opportunities Hong Kong offered them. Soviet inability to win British trust in Hong Kong was indicative not just of the Hong Kong administration's longstanding commitment to maintaining Anglo-Soviet Cold War policies, but of the well-established though tacit Sino-British understanding that Britain would not allow Hong Kong to serve as a significant base for anti-PRC forces.

New archival evidence illuminates related divisions among the individuals and agencies formulating Soviet policy toward Hong Kong. As one would expect, the central apparatus of the CPSU tended to be ideological, whereas the MID tended to be more pragmatic. Within the MID itself, policy making was divided between China hands and British experts. Until 1956 most Soviet reports on Hong Kong came from the Soviet Consulate in Guangzhou (Canton), and the remainder came from the Soviet Embassy in Beijing. However, as relations between the Soviet Union and China deteriorated, valuable sources of information from the Chinese Military-Control Commission, a section of the Ministry of Foreign Affairs of the PRC, ceased to be available. Furthermore, the Soviet Consulate in Guangzhou was closed in the early 1960s. All subsequent reports relating to Hong Kong came from the Soviet Embassy in London and, to a far lesser degree, from the Soviet embassies in Bangkok, Manila, and Rangoon. Soviet experts on Britain tended to view British control of Hong Kong more favorably, and to seek at least some relationship with the territory. They also recognized Hong Kong's growing economic and financial power. For the Soviet Union to benefit thereby demanded reaching an accommodation with Hong Kong's British colonial masters, an objective which was never really accomplished. Divisions between the MID officials and specialists at the International Department of the Central Committee, as well as a split between Chinese and British experts within the MID, helped to thwart efforts to develop an advantageous and consistent policy toward Hong Kong. The success of any endeavors would in any case probably have been undercut by the longstanding Anglo-Soviet Cold War antagonism.

Once the split between Moscow and Beijing widened in the 1960s and 1970s, economic factors bulked larger in Soviet dealings with Hong Kong. Recognizing the city's growing significance as a major port and financial and trading center, the Soviet Union sought its own offices in Hong Kong to increase its trade with and involvement in the territory, notwithstanding its continuing British colonial status. Soviet intelligence operatives also unavailingly hankered after obtaining a toehold in Hong Kong as a means of gathering scarce information on Hong Kong and China. Even so, ideological anti-colonialism still informed Soviet policy throughout this period, as did its broader Cold War geopolitical rivalry with Britain and the West, who controlled Hong Kong. While the Sino-Soviet split might at first glance have seemed to free the Soviet Union to exploit Hong Kong's economic possibilities with a clear conscience, in practice this was not so. Rather, it functioned as yet another constraint on Soviet hopes of utilizing either the economic or the informational potential of Hong Kong, where it was tacitly understood that the British would discourage activities by third countries which China might see as undesirable. Ultimately the three-way tug-of-war between ideology, Cold War *realpolitik,* and economics caused Soviet Cold War policies toward

Hong Kong to be both inconsistent and effectively fruitless, an indication of Moscow's inability to disturb the implicit Sino-British consensus on Hong Kong.

The Years of the Sino-Soviet Split, 1960–1980

In the two decades after the Sino-Soviet split emerged, where Soviet policies toward Hong Kong were concerned, tensions between the ideological constraints of anti-colonialism, the anti-Chinese thrust of its geopolitical strategy, and the demands of economics sharpened. For the first time, the Soviet Union defined its stance toward British rule in Hong Kong, and determined the precise parameters of acceptable behavior for Soviet citizens and firms on Hong Kong. The Soviet Union increasingly recognized the value of Hong Kong as a locale in which to do business, yet it refused to deviate from its ideologically driven anti-colonial and implicitly pro-PRC policy, even as Sino-Soviet relations deteriorated dramatically. In this instance, Marxist-Leninist solidarity with even a deviant Communist state clearly still took priority over any attempt to improve economic, let alone political, relations with British-ruled Hong Kong.

The collapse of the Sino-Soviet alliance and the subsequent split had a dual impact on Soviet policy toward Hong Kong. First, the Soviet Union lost its best source of information on Hong Kong, namely the Chinese Military-Control Commission, which had relayed intelligence materials to the Soviet Consulate in Guangzhou. The last available file from the Guangzhou Consulate that the author consulted in the various Russian archives was dated 1956. A Soviet official in Beijing subsequently noted: "Due to a significant reduction in work for Soviet advisers in China, the Soviet Union told the Chinese it would close its Consulate in Guangzhou in 1958."[1] The Soviet Union then had to obtain its information about Hong Kong from other sources, such as Soviet embassies in London, Bangkok, Rangoon, and Manila. One unusual additional source of information on Hong Kong was Russian students who studied the Chinese language in Singapore, and who traveled from Russia to Singapore via Japan and Hong Kong, though their stays in the territory were necessarily brief.[2] The power of the China experts within the MID declined in favor of British specialists, who were readier to accept British rule in Hong Kong. The other major change was that the Soviet Union actively sought to reestablish a permanent presence in Hong Kong through a Consulate, a trade office, a branch of the Moscow *Narodny* Bank, an office for *Tass*, the Soviet news agency, or contracts with Hong Kong firms. A permanent presence would allow the Soviet Union to obtain independent information on Hong Kong, rather than rely on outside "friendly sources." Moscow also hoped to use Hong Kong as a listening post on China, something the Western powers had been doing for years.

Such ambitions in no way affected the Soviet Union's by now well-established existing stance on what it considered to be Hong Kong's illegitimate colonial status. Soviet officials elaborated on this during a 1962 debate at the UNGA over the issue of Chinese refugees in Hong Kong. The Soviet delegation stated that the issue could not even be discussed since, as Hong Kong was an integral part of China, any discussion would constitute interference in the PRC's internal affairs. Furthermore, as the PRC was not yet a member of the UN (at that time Taiwan still held China's seat), the question could not be raised without the participation of the PRC. Then the Soviet delegation stated that differences existed among colonial territories and made an interesting comparison. "Of course, the conditions of the various small colonial territories are different. There are territories nowadays which are in the condition of colonial occupation, but which are part of another independent state. Hong Kong and Macao are examples of the former situation. Such territories, separated from the motherland, must be given back as others have been given back. For example, India was given back its native land."[3] This last statement compared Hong Kong to Goa, the Portuguese colony forcibly annexed by India in 1962. Like Hong Kong, Goa was situated on a coast and was never recognized by the mother country as a separate territory. The Soviet Union believed there was a significant difference between those territories, which belonged to currently sovereign states such as India and China, and those such as Indochina, which had possessed independent sovereignty before colonization. The latter should be granted independence, while the former should simply be returned to the mother country, which alone had the right to determine the government of the former colony. When Hong Kong should be returned to China was a matter for China alone to decide. The Soviet Union flatly stated: "We the Soviet Union will not press China. But the time will come when China will tell the colonials to get out. We will salute this step. But when to do it is the decision of our Chinese friends. We will not hurry them."[4]

By 1962, China and the Soviet Union were far from friends, as relations between them had plummeted to a state of virtual enmity. The British government concluded that the Sino-Soviet dispute was advantageous to Hong Kong. "A protracted Sino-Soviet dispute at about the present level (1969) would be to the colony's advantage. Any change, though, would be for the worse. In a war between the PRC and the USSR, the PRC would most likely lose. The PRC might then look for an easy face saving victory elsewhere, such as in Hong Kong."[5] Even so, the Soviet position on Hong Kong remained unchanged, scarcely altering from the 1940s onward. Essentially the Soviets refused to recognize the legitimacy of British rule in Hong Kong, and consequently argued that Hong Kong should be returned to China as soon as possible. China's failure to bring this about did, however, provide the Soviet Union with valuable propaganda opportunities in the two countries' ongoing public relations battle.

Hong Kong soon featured in the increasingly bitter disputes between China and the Soviet Union, serving as a rhetorical weapon which one country used to level charges against the other. The British government in Hong Kong carefully monitored Soviet thinking on Hong Kong, collecting Soviet newspaper and magazine articles dealing with Hong Kong, many of which were highly critical of Chinese policy toward the colony. At least twice during 1962, Soviet Premier Nikita Khrushchev denounced China's policy on Hong Kong and Macao. First, to his Kremlin colleagues at a rump meeting of the Presidium on January 8, Khrushchev attacked China's toleration of British rule in Hong Kong and Portuguese control of Macao, reminding his audience that the Chinese had time and again resisted using force to eliminate their own West Berlins (a reference to strident Chinese criticisms of Khrushchev's refusal to occupy West Berlin).[6] Then, at the close of the year, during a speech to the Supreme Soviet on December 12, 1962, he defended his policy in the Cuban missile crisis against criticisms leveled by the Chinese and Albanians.[7] Furious at China's criticism that he had succumbed to American pressure on Cuba, Khrushchev noted that the Chinese seemed in no hurry to evict British and Portuguese imperialists from Hong Kong and Macao.[8] The April 30, 1964 issue of *Izvestiya* contained another provocative article on Hong Kong, which charged: "Foreign investors were not concerned about

Hong Kong's future since they see nobody threatening the existence of this sore of colonialism on ancient soil. Conditions were so bad in China that a million Chinese left their country to escape into 'the hell of Hong Kong.'" It also noted that the Chinese "get not less than half of their yearly currency receipts" from Hong Kong.[9] The official Soviet press also complained strongly about alleged Chinese anti-Soviet activities in Hong Kong. A few weeks later, on May 22, 1964, *Pravda* went further and declared that "the colony was being used by the Chinese as a center of propaganda and subversion against the Soviet Union and the international Communist movement."[10]

Such Soviet criticisms continued. In 1967 a published Soviet article on Hong Kong and Macao sardonically noted that it seemed paradoxical that by the late 1960s most remaining colonies, namely Hong Kong and Macao, should exist on the territory of China, a socialist state, whose leadership seemed indifferent to Hong Kong's recovery.[11] The Soviets charged the Chinese with insincerity, since they continually claimed Hong Kong was a part of China, yet did nothing to regain it. The Soviets inaccurately contended that the colonial regime in Hong Kong had changed little in the past 150 years, and accused the Chinese of outright hypocrisy in their policy toward Hong Kong. According to this Soviet report, the British had been most surprised when the Chinese army failed to attack Hong Kong in late 1949.[12] (This was not true, since the Chinese informed the British in advance that they did not intend to take Hong Kong.[13]) Furthermore, the Soviets charged, Beijing was only interested in maintaining the status quo in Hong Kong. "The Chinese government actively assists in the exploitation of the Chinese population of Hong Kong. The reason for this policy is so China can keep economic profits for itself."[14] While China certainly benefited from Hong Kong's separate status, as a source of valuable hard currency, a venue for trade and contacts with other countries, and a base for numerous Chinese companies and banks, there is no evidence that China ever condoned any British exploitation of the local Hong Kong population. The 1967 Soviet newspaper report was more accurate in characterizing Hong Kong as a locale where China could maintain unofficial contacts with other countries with whom she had no diplomatic relations: Japan, the United States, South Africa, and even Taiwan. Finally, it complained, to add insult to injury, China even used Hong Kong as a base for anti-Soviet activities. The Chinese government sold and distributed "anti-socialist," that is, anti-Soviet, materials in bookstores they controlled, and from Hong Kong these were circulated to countries around the world. Soviet journalists charged: "This Beijing literature was aimed at the destruction of the International and workers' movement." The Soviets even asserted that pro-Beijing Hong Kong people distributed anti-Soviet propaganda to foreign tourists in Hong Kong. In 1966, moreover, Chinese pressure led the British to close the only bookstore in Hong Kong selling Soviet literature.[15]

The mid- and late 1960s were also a period of growing American involvement in the Vietnam War. Both China and the Soviet Union resented the degree to which Hong Kong provided support for American activities in Vietnam. Twice, on September 1, 1965 and again on February 1, 1966, China delivered notes of protest to the British government, demanding the British government take expeditious action to prohibit American military use of Hong Kong. During 1965, for example, 300 American warships, some nuclear-armed, docked in Hong Kong en route to or from Vietnam.[16] Hong Kong's value as the American watchtower on China grew during the 1960s as US involvement in Vietnam expanded. The CIA also used Hong Kong as a black market exchange service to provide currency to cover its operations throughout East Asia.[17] In late 1967, the Soviet Union again commented on Hong Kong's assistance to the American war effort. "Hong Kong supplies water and food to the American Seventh Fleet which mans the Taiwan Strait and is active in the Vietnam War." Hong Kong also served as a major locale for "rest and relaxation" for American military personnel serving in Vietnam, a factor which benefited the local economy substantially.[18] According to Stephen Dorril's work on MI6, the British military intelligence organization, during the Vietnam War Hong Kong also covertly served as a staging post for arms and a source of intelligence information for the United States, since:

> Secret air flights also took place from Hong Kong—the center of Britain's contribution to the Vietnam War—with clandestine deliveries of British arms, particularly napalm and five-hundred-pound bombs. In the end, the most significant British contribution came from the GCHQ [Government Communication Headquarters] monitoring station at Little Sai Wan in Hong Kong. Working overtime to provide the US with intelligence, its intercepts of North Vietnamese military traffic were used by the American military command to target bombing strikes over the North. Together with NSA [National Security Agency] stations in Thailand and the Philippines, the British also monitored diplomatic traffic and North Vietnamese

> surface-to-air missile sites, enabling early warnings to be relayed to bomber crews in mid-flight. British help was explained away by referring to it as an Australian operation.[19]

Even so, Hong Kong's role in the Vietnam War was extremely minor and it only provided the United States with assorted useful but by no means essential backup facilities. Indeed, British concerns for Chinese sensibilities were such that it was highly unlikely that Hong Kong's colonial masters would have permitted it to assume any larger part in the conflict.

Events in Hong Kong during the 1960s

Soviet reporting of specific developments affecting Hong Kong during the 1960s differed from the way similar events were portrayed in the 1940s and 1950s. Largely due to the Sino-Soviet split, descriptions became far more objective, as the Soviets no longer believed they must simply repeat Chinese views, however inaccurate these might be. Three examples were the famine that devastated China, especially its countryside, in 1961 and 1962, the subsequent flood of refugees into Hong Kong, and the large-scale riots that erupted in 1967.

The main cause of the famine was economic problems in China: a lack of fertilizers, a drought, together with deliberate government policies, which forced people to leave the cities for an already overcrowded countryside, as well as grossly excessively allocations of grain from the peasantry to the state, which left the newly collectivized peasants with no food. Factories in Guangdong province near Hong Kong were forced to close due to lack of raw materials, causing much unemployment. In both rural and urban areas throughout China, tens of millions perished and some 300,000 people fled China for Hong Kong.[20] Earlier Soviet reports of Chinese famines and the resulting flood of refugees into Hong Kong had been very different, blaming these upon external factors but never on misguided Chinese government policies. Famines in the early 1950s, for example, were the result of "sabotage and espionage activities directed against the PRC by KMT and American agents."[21] Soviet reporting on refugees in 1962 was not entirely objective. For example, a report claimed that the Hong Kong press highlighted refugees' difficulties mainly to embarrass the Chinese authorities over their "internal difficulties," using refugees as an excuse for anti-Communist propaganda.[22] As in the 1950s, the Soviets never depicted refugees as ordinary people fleeing intense poverty and government-induced crises, but as "reactionary Chinese criminals fleeing the victory of Communism to avoid their just punishment."[23] Even so, the Soviets admitted factors within China, both natural and government-induced, had caused refugees to flee to Hong Kong.

During 1967, large-scale riots erupted in Hong Kong. While some of the causes were internal, such as the lack of jobs, decent housing, and educational opportunities, particularly for young men, the most significant cause was the Cultural Revolution's transmigration to Hong Kong. Factories, businesses, schools, and public transport all closed down. Several times during the spring, summer, and fall, Hong Kong ground to a virtual halt for days at a time. Tourism evaporated and many foreigners fled in fear of their lives. The British bolstered their garrison with Gurkha troops and hired more police. Tens of people were killed and hundreds wounded in street battles in which demonstrators confronted the police and army. As a result of the 1967 riots, over 1,800 people were convicted and imprisoned.[24]

Like most other major powers, the Soviet Union closely scrutinized the riots, and in the second half of 1967, the MID received four detailed reports describing and analyzing the riots, one from the Bangkok Embassy, the others from its London counterpart. The report from Bangkok, based on the views of both local (Bangkok) informed sources and academic specialists on Chinese affairs, was by far the most hostile toward the PRC, perhaps due to Thailand's proximity to events. The report's anti-Chinese bias may have reflected the strongly negative views of the PRC and its policies then prevalent throughout Southeast Asia in 1967, at the height of the Vietnam War. Many states in the region believed that China, through its alleged proxy, North Vietnam, was striving to conquer all Southeast Asia for Communism. The Bangkok report specifically stated that Beijing instigated the riots in pursuit of Chinese political and especially propagandistic aims. In particular, the Chinese wanted to pressure the British over their support of the United States in Vietnam, reminding them that ultimately Chinese power in Hong Kong exceeded that of Britain. A final reason was to divert the Chinese population in the PRC from their internal problems, largely generated by the Cultural Revolution. The factors listed completely omitted the role of internal Hong Kong conditions in causing the riots.[25]

By contrast, a contemporaneous report from the Soviet Embassy in

London stated that while the impact of the Cultural Revolution was one contributory factor underlying the riots, poor living conditions for Hong Kong workers were another. The London report described how the riots began in April at two factories in Kowloon due to a dispute between factory managers and workers over their low wages and poor working conditions. Exacerbating the problem, management closed down the factories and fired the workers. May saw the beginning of fierce riots, which were only temporarily suppressed by British troops and the Royal Hong Kong Police, who used rubber truncheons and tear gas. At this stage, the London report criticized the Chinese for describing these events as a "fascist massacre against patriotic students, teachers and other co-patriots armed only with the ideas of Mao."[26] Emphasizing the crucial role played by China in provoking these riots, in a subsequent report, B. Chiudinov, a Third Secretary, stated that "any future riots would be determined by the Chinese government."[27] Both the Bangkok and London reports listed, with little comment, the same Chinese demands: Britain should cease all repressive measures against the rioters; the Hong Kong government must free all arrested people and apologize to all arrested and injured as well as to the families of those killed; and finally, Britain should pledge not to use repressive measures in Hong Kong again. Their silence was eloquent testimony to the degree to which the Soviets were hedging their bets on the Hong Kong situation.

The Chinese rioters, both local Hong Kong and mainland, failed, and by the fall the worst of the unrest had subsided. All Soviet reports mentioned that the British used force against the demonstrators until order had been restored, but only the Bangkok report stated the authorities had the support of most ordinary Hong Kong people, "who are oriented toward Taiwan and have pro-British and Taiwan views." It also noted that after this failure Beijing sought a face-saving explanation. Some organizers of the riots were recalled to Beijing. Premier Zhou Enlai created a commission to determine why the riots failed to "mobilize the masses." The Communist Party in Guangzhou sent representatives to Hong Kong, who sharply criticized leaders of the Hong Kong Communist Party for failing to secure mass support from the population. The Soviet report mentioned that "rather than using political aims, Hong Kong Communists used financial inducements (HK$10 to 15 per day). When the British authorities got really tough with the demonstrators, the Chinese payments increased to ￡3.26 a day (about US$10 to 15, about six times more)."[28]

The report stated that when the riots began, Hong Kong Communist leaders had assured Beijing that the demonstrations would have wide popular support. Accordingly, Beijing gave new instructions to Hong Kong Communists and their supporters. The clashes should stop, and demonstrators should revert to underground methods, such as small strikes and protests, as well as "educate the population to hate the British." As the Soviet report pointed out, these actions marked a clear retreat for China.[29]

The London reports also highlighted problems the riots caused for Britain, including a deterioration in Sino-British relations. China twice formally protested to Britain. Anti-British demonstrations erupted in several Chinese cities. The British Consulate in Shanghai was closed, while the Embassy in Beijing was sacked. "Britain was afraid."[30] Furthermore, Hong Kong itself needed the good graces of China to survive. The British were seriously worried that border clashes between Chinese and British troops could escalate. Moreover, to crush Hong Kong, China did not even really need to use its army. By the late 1960s, Hong Kong had become almost totally dependent on China for its water and food supplies. The reports mentioned that after the riots Britain actively sought to restore at least fair relations with China. Yet Britain recognized that the situation in China was far from stable. 1967 was still early in the Cultural Revolution, during its most deadly and unpredictable phase, and Hong Kong was only outwardly calm. "Below the surface, the British recognized that riots could erupt at any time the Chinese wanted."[31] The riots naturally had a negative impact on the Hong Kong economy, particularly on foreign investment and tourism. Britain recognized that a prosperous Hong Kong generally demanded a calm Hong Kong. Britain was determined to retain Hong Kong as long as possible for several reasons. Hong Kong was a financial center for East Asia for British banks, companies, and investors. Secondly, Hong Kong was an important communications and intelligence gathering center for developments in China. Thirdly, the British used Hong Kong as a major naval base. For those reasons, the British did not want to leave Hong Kong unless this became absolutely necessary.[32] The reports concluded that neither the PRC nor Britain nor Hong Kong had emerged victorious from the 1967 riots. Personnel in those embassies in London, Bangkok, Manila, and Rangoon, especially specialists on British affairs located in London, had thus become more important in determining Soviet policy toward Hong

Kong, at the expense of the "China hands" in Moscow or in the Soviet Embassy in Beijing who had formerly predominated.

The official Soviet press also covered the Hong Kong riots. The first Soviet newspaper article on the subject appeared on June 19, 1967. Initial Soviet reaction to the riots was very low key, emphasizing China's economic interests in Hong Kong. Over time, however, as the summer progressed, Soviet newspaper articles became increasingly hostile to and critical of the PRC government, claiming it had colluded with the British in suppressing the riots. Those articles culminated in a long piece, "The Story of a Betrayal," published in *Izvestiya* on September 18, 1967. It stated:

> The events in Hong Kong aroused anxiety and alarm in Beijing as well. Paradoxically enough Mao and his henchmen have resolved to preserve at all costs this miasmatic ulcer of British colonialism on the body of China. Working class action could throw their plans into disarray.... This [the alleged denunciation of the strike movement by Beijing] was nothing but a betrayal. The Mao group did not get the 30 pieces of silver anticipated for its betrayal.

Finally the article claimed that a "whole act [pretending to support the Hong Kong working class] has been played out in Beijing's betrayal of the Hong Kong proletariat."[33] To hammer home the point, on February 6, 1968, *Izvestiya* reprinted this article.

As a barometer of the depth of Sino-Soviet hostility at that time, during the riots the Soviets offered to exchange military intelligence on the Chinese with the British. The Soviet authorities apparently hoped the crisis might impel the British to move closer to themselves and upgrade the information available to them on China. On June 9, 1967, Colonel Nikolai Balakirev, the Russian military attaché in Phnom Penh, Cambodia, visited his British counterpart, who reported: "Balakirev said that things were serious for us in Hong Kong and could get worse. He said he knew that the 42nd Chinese Army Corps was in that part of China bordering on Hong Kong. He further remarked that the Soviet Union was most anxious to obtain military information on China. The USSR is most interested in any troop concentrations in the north opposite the Soviet border." The British Embassy relayed the Soviet request to the Foreign Office, who rejected it, a response Phnom Penh summarized in the words: "Foreign Secretary George Brown detested any proposed cooperation with the Soviets on military intelligence about China believing 'we should get little or nothing in return.'"[34] A second reason why the British turned the Soviets down was their fear of inflaming already tense relations with Beijing, where, at the height of the Cultural Revolution, Red Guards sacked and burned the British Embassy a few months later. Neither side made any further attempt to reopen the subject of potential exchanges of military intelligence.

Business Opportunities during the 1960s

The growing dominance of more economically-minded non-Chinese specialists may have been one reason why the sharpening contradiction between ideological anti-colonialism and anti-capitalism, the demands of geopolitics, and economic considerations heightened during the 1960s. The consistently hard-line Soviet ideological stance repeatedly undercut geopolitical and economic factors, which ascribed growing significance to Hong Kong precisely because the territory was separate from China. Soviet officials increasingly recognized that Hong Kong presented them with opportunities that would not have existed had Hong Kong been simply another Chinese city. Soviet perceptions of the economic potential of Hong Kong persisted even though, during the mid- to late 1960s, the territory provided ever growing backup services to American military undertakings in Vietnam.

Soviet views of Hong Kong unquestionably became more positive over time. By the 1960s, the MID reports could no longer ignore the huge changes Hong Kong was undergoing due to its industrial revolution, and its increasing prosperity and dynamism as "an open port and one of the world's leading trading centers. More than 700 foreign banks and companies are located there." Hong Kong housed the consulates not just of Western nations, whose main purpose in Soviet eyes was to conduct intelligence activities, but from countries all over the world, whose principal objective was to facilitate business. In 1966, Soviet reports argued that Hong Kong's impact on China was far from purely negative, but that it performed a major positive function as a "China trade counter-agent and liaison for trade for capitalist countries, as well as a source of hard currency for China. For example, each year more than US$500 million came into China from Hong Kong."[35] Another report the following year stated: "In 1964 exports from China to Hong Kong amounted to US$516 million, in 1965 these had grown to US$608 million, and by 1966, some US$730 million."[36] While the MID reports still mentioned poverty, they no longer gave it the same prominence as in the 1940s and 1950s. This positive impression of Hong Kong emphasized a new view of Hong Kong as a place offering opportunities to the Soviet Union resembling those available to China and Western countries. Trade, business cooperation and investment, travel, and shipping facilities became new foci of Soviet interest.

Soviet officials had to devise a formula that would permit greater Soviet economic activity in Hong Kong, while compromising neither commercial ideological purity nor Russian strategic interests in the Pacific. For the Soviet Union, Hong Kong had the potential to provide both valuable economic gains and much needed information on mainland China. Yet it remained under the colonial rule of Britain, simultaneously a firm strategic opponent with deep suspicions of the Soviet Union, and an exponent of imperialism. Thus the Soviet Union theoretically deplored and could not openly tolerate the political status quo in Hong Kong without losing the ideological high ground. For these reasons, while trade between Hong Kong and the Soviet Union increased during the late 1960s, it formed only a small percentage of the total trade for Hong Kong. Another interesting feature was that Hong Kong generally exported more to other countries than it imported. The reverse was the case with the Soviet Union, from which Hong Kong imported far more than it exported.[37] Except for sharp but temporary downturns during 1966 and 1967, when the Cultural Revolution was at its height, Hong Kong archives document a steady increase in trade between the Soviet Union and Hong Kong during the 1960s, as demonstrated by the figures below:

Year	Imports (HK$)[38]	Exports (HK$)
1962	$4,909,212	$11,807
1963	$9,889,230	$275,625
1965	$9,357,587	$182,108
1966	$16,294,461	$4,628
1967	$10,236,430	$535,796
1968	$28,500,000	$280,000
1969	$23,700,000	$2,600,000

Soviet imports from Hong Kong were no longer significant, a change from earlier decades, and the balance of trade heavily favored the Soviet Union, which sold ten times as much or even more in terms of Hong

Kong dollars to Hong Kong as it bought from the territory. By the end of the 1960s, the Soviet Union ranked only 35th on the list of countries to which Hong Kong exported. Imports from the Soviet Union covered a broad range of products: Siberian deer antlers and ginseng for medicinal use, other animal and vegetable products, newsprint, and pharmaceuticals. Exports shipped from Hong Kong to the Soviet Union included cotton fabric and clothing.[39] Given this advantageous ratio, it was entirely understandable that the Soviets sought to expand trade with the British colony, in which they succeeded. Indeed, during 1970 and 1971, imports from the Soviet Union soared by 156 percent, and included not just cotton, animal products, and ginseng, but also jewelry, semi-precious stones, watch movements, and cameras, all of which were much in demand because they were considered inexpensive and of high quality. On November 15, 1971, the *Hong Kong Standard* reported that imports from the Soviet Union had reached a significant HK$58,400,000, while exports to the Soviet Union amounted to only HK$300,000. This was a trade balance of over HK$58 million in the Soviet Union's favor, providing the USSR with much needed hard currency.[40]

Soviet business organizations, especially those concerned with travel, tourism, or foreign trade, also sought to establish representation or obtain partners in Hong Kong, and Hong Kong and foreign businesses expressed interest in working with them. All, of course, were ultimately under the control of the Soviet government. The MID tried to finesse an almost impossible situation and allow Soviet organizations to do business with companies under a government whose existence it did not even recognize.

In August 1964, the director of a travel firm, Herman Travel Center, with a Hong Kong office requested that his company be allowed to represent the interests of Aeroflot Airlines in Hong Kong. Herman Travel Center wished to sell Aeroflot tickets to Hong Kong people seeking to travel to the Soviet Union for tourism or business. While Aeroflot did not yet serve Hong Kong, Hong Kong people who wanted to go to the USSR could board Aeroflot airplanes in either Beijing or Bangkok, which then flew on to Moscow. While *Intourist*, the official Soviet tourist organization, recognized that Herman Travel was not a large company, it compensated for this by having branch offices in numerous countries and had dealt with *Intourist* many times in the past. "It knows the condition of tourism and transport in the Soviet Union, and <u>could send a lot of passengers to the Soviet Union</u>."[41] (original emphasis) Aeroflot asked the

MID for its advice on this matter. Accompanying the letter were supporting pamphlets giving added information on the company. One booklet mentioned: "The Director of Herman Travel has visited the USSR twice. The company has already sent 40 tourists to the Soviet Union. It has arranged for visas for people through the Soviet embassies in Tokyo, Delhi, and Karachi. The company has a bank account at the Soviet *Vneshtorgbank*, and puts advertisements in the local press to promote travel to the Soviet Union. The firm also helps stateless people—mostly Russians—to get Soviet visas." *Intourist* admitted two other companies larger than Herman Travel were also interested in promoting tourism to the Soviet Union.[42] While *Intourist* realized that Herman Travel was an American company with headquarters in California, it rightly believed this to be a friendly company, genuinely interested in promoting tourism and travel to the Soviet Union.

Two years later, in July 1966, the Soviet Ministry of Civil Aviation, still very eager to find agents to sell Aeroflot tickets, expanded the list of possible travel companies to three: CITA, World Travel Center, Inc., and the Hong Kong Travel Bureau. World Travel Center, Inc. was Herman Travel's parent company. In a letter to the Far East Department of the MID, V. Danil'chev, the Vice Chief of the International Department at the Ministry of Civil Aviation, commented that the Ministry was "interested in having agents of Aeroflot located in a busy center such as Hong Kong where there were numerous international companies." They sought advice from the MID on this question.[43] Six months later, the Ministry of Civil Aviation commented that the main offices of both companies, CITA and World Travel Center, Inc., were located in the United States. A. Besedin of the Ministry of Civil Aviation asked the MID: "In connection with this, could this influence your conclusion?"[44] While Aeroflot, *Intourist*, and the Ministry of Civil Aviation had no problems about awarding a potentially lucrative contract to an American company, they thought the tense relations between the Soviet Union and the United States might cause the MID to deny the contract.

The MID still made no decision on whether or to which company to award a contract to act as an Aeroflot agent. In the meantime a new Soviet air route, from Moscow to Tokyo, opened, presenting even greater possibilities for significant Hong Kong tourist and business traffic to the Soviet Union, because Hong Kong people could easily fly to Tokyo and then board direct Aeroflot flights to Moscow. In January 1967, A. Besedin, acting on behalf of Aeroflot, sent a letter to N. G. Sudarikov of the MID. Besedin reiterated that three travel agencies in Hong Kong, already working with *Intourist*, wished to act as agents: Compass Travel (formerly named Herman Travel Center), American Lloyd Travel Service, Ltd., and Mitravel International (Asia), Ltd. "All three named firms promise to attract in 1967 to Aeroflot more than 400 tourists from Hong Kong and other countries. The Ministry of Civil Aviation is considering an agreement with them regarding air transport on the basis of the approved typed agreement (enclosed with letter) with payments in commissions up to 7.5 percent in accounts in US dollars. I ask you for your opinion about the possibility of recommending such an agreement with the above named tourist firms in Hong Kong."[45] Given increased tourism from Hong Kong and the pointed request from the Ministry of Civil Aviation, the MID could not delay a decision much longer. Finally Sudarikov of the MID sent Besedin a short letter giving permission on the following conditions: "1. The agreement will not have formulations, which could be interpreted as recognition by us of Hong Kong's status as an English colony. 2. or recognition by us of the separate status of Hong Kong. 3. Any signed contracts with the firms could only remain as commercial activities."[46] The MID did not care which company or companies acted as Aeroflot's agent, but any agreement must remain only a commercial document and imply no recognition of Hong Kong as either a British colony or a territory separate from China. The Soviet Union's ideological position on Hong Kong's status thus would not interfere with increased business opportunities. These three conditions, which had to be included in all contracts, became Soviet policy when future business opportunities were presented, applying the position laid out by Foreign Minister Andrei Gromyko in 1958 to specific business propositions arising during the 1960s.

That same month, February 1967, a MID report on Hong Kong mentioned several Soviet foreign trade organizations, including *Raznoyeksport, Medeksport,* and some others, which had existing commercial contracts with Hong Kong firms. However, the amount of trade, according to this report, totaled only some US$2 million a year; while it noted that Aeroflot, *Intourist*, and other companies had contracts with Hong Kong firms governing air transport and tourism. It concluded that all Soviet organizations which established contracts "did so under the basis that Hong Kong is an 'occupied' Chinese territory, but not a 'colony,' or a 'self-ruled' territory. All contracts do not go beyond the commercial question."[47]

As other potential business deals between Hong Kong companies and Soviet trading firms were contemplated, each request was forwarded to the MID for approval. A Hong Kong mail order firm, "Shop-Buy-Mail," for example, sent a letter which stated: "We are interested in trade with the Soviet Union for antiquarian products, souvenirs, fake jewelry (costume jewelry), furs and leather, and Russian national costumes. We are interested in the import of these goods from your country."[48] Shortly afterwards Hong Kong's main air carrier, Cathay Pacific, requested Aeroflot that the two companies conclude "an agreement for commercial cooperation and land service for transit passengers who are changing planes." The Ministry of Civil Aviation, which handled the request for Aeroflot, recommended a positive response, in part because Cathay Pacific "has flights to 18 international airports, including Jakarta, Rangoon, and Tokyo, which Aeroflot also flies to." Once again, Besedin requested the MID grant him permission to conclude the agreement.[49] Within a few weeks, the MID responded affirmatively that Aeroflot could conclude an agreement with Cathay Pacific, subject to almost identical conditions. "The text of the agreement must not contain any statement that could be construed as recognition by us of Hong Kong's status as an English colony or any recognition of Hong Kong's possible independent status."[50] Although the MID was attempting to square the circle to allow Soviet businesses to establish branches in Hong Kong or cooperate with partners in the territory, naturally enough, these conditions hampered more extensive business and trade contacts. The MID statements also raised questions as to whether or not this policy could continue indefinitely, implicitly calling in question the very viability of the Soviet Union's policy toward Hong Kong.

Other problematic aspects in any expansion of Hong Kong–Soviet business dealings were British fears—not always groundless—that such enterprises might easily become a cover for Soviet espionage activities against both Britain and China, with the additional potential to destabilize relations between the two. In response to concerns raised in London over an alleged growing Soviet penetration of Hong Kong, the Hong Kong government noted in a report sent to the British government that these fears were largely unfounded. For example, for a while Soviet-built *Moskvich* cars were sold, but problems over spare parts caused their showroom to close. According to the report, the main Soviet export to Hong Kong was watch movements, regarded by Hong Kong people as cheap and reliable.[51]

The area of shipping, however, proved particularly volatile. Until the mid-1960s, when deteriorating Sino-Soviet relations led the Chinese to refuse admittance to any further such vessels, Soviet ships in the Far East had been able to use Chinese port facilities for repairs. In November 1966, M. Kutyrev, Soviet chargé d'affaires in Beijing, visited Hong Kong. There he met Mr. Leitch of the Hong Kong and Whampoa Docks Company, with whom he reached an agreement that in principle Soviet ships could be repaired at the company's docks, the details of this arrangement to be negotiated between Moscow and the Hong Kong government.[52] The two sides quickly came to an understanding whereby Hong Kong would allow Soviet ships to undergo repairs in its harbor facilities. Two Soviet engineers would be allowed to stay in Hong Kong a maximum of up to nine months, following which they would be replaced by two other Soviet nationals, who would receive the necessary resident visas. At any given time, it was expected, at least two ships and over 300 Soviet crewmen would be temporarily in the territory. Since it feared some of these sailors might be spies, the Hong Kong government insisted that they would have to be monitored. They would be permitted to walk around the territory, but only under escort, in groups of ten, and for no more than six hours a day during the hours of light.[53] In return, it was expected, the Soviet Union would spend on average some HK$180,000 per ship for repairs, which might take up to three months to complete.[54]

This arrangement brought much-needed income to the Hong Kong shipyards, and Soviet sailors spent money in Hong Kong. Rather predictably, however, incidents soon occurred, some of them serious enough to attract the attention of other foreign diplomats in Hong Kong. In late 1971, for example, Wilhelm Gunther von Heyden, the West German Consul-General in Hong Kong, sent a report to the German Ministry of Foreign Affairs discussing the ship repairs and the resulting problems. He characterized the repair facilities as excellent and relatively inexpensive, and stated that the number of ships undergoing repair had increased from 33 in 1966 to 73 in 1970. Less benign, however, in his view, were Soviet attempts to use the enterprise to distribute propaganda, even though he thought this had little impact, since the local population simply discarded most of it. According to von Heyden, some Soviet crewmen from the cruise liner *Sovetsky Soiuz* deposited Chinese-language materials on the docks for local workers to take away. Other crewmen had been seen actually distributing this propaganda, which gave the Soviet version of recent 1969 border clashes between Soviet and Chinese forces along the Amur River, to local Chinese workers in the area.[55] Soviet activities in Hong Kong aroused some German diplomatic concern. Consul-General von Heyden's report concluded that "the Soviets were trying to gain a foothold in Hong Kong, using trade and especially shipping to collect information on China." He reported to Bonn that two Soviet engineers had even visited him at the Consulate-General and asked him numerous questions about Hong Kong.[56]

Soon, the Soviet Union was accused of using sailors not just to distribute propaganda, but also to conduct espionage in the territory. In August 1972, Hong Kong Special Branch officers arrested two Soviet crewmen, Andrei Ivanovich Polikarov and Stepan Tsuanaev, together with Ho Hung Yan, a stateless Chinese. Special Branch charged them with spying, and British authorities claimed that the 50-year-old export-import merchant carried detailed plans to extend a Soviet spy ring around Southeast Asia at the time of his arrest. Furthermore, two Taiwanese businessmen were accused of helping them establish a spy ring in the territory. One of them was deported to Taiwan, and the other released due to insufficient evidence. The two Soviet crewmen were deported on Soviet ships that left Hong Kong shortly afterward, while Ho was likewise placed aboard the *Kavalerovo*, a Soviet ship bound for Vladivostok.[57] The episode soon sparked off a very touchy diplomatic and political imbroglio. Humiliated Soviet officials protested that all involved had been arrested and detained without any justification and in violation of international law. For ten days a stalemate reigned with the Hong Kong authorities refusing to allow Ho to debark, and the Soviet captain refusing to sail with Ho on board on the grounds that he had no papers to enter the Soviet Union. Finally, on November 23, 1972, the *Kavalerovo* sailed as its captain cited "humanitarian reasons," and Ho eventually debarked at Vladivostok. The British archives provided no information on Ho's subsequent travels after he arrived in the Soviet port.[58]

The *South China Morning Post* described alleged Soviet spies "flooding into Hong Kong," and published several further sensational articles on the topic that year. The PRC government, naturally very upset, protested to both the Hong Kong and British governments. In response, the Hong Kong authorities placed more restrictions on Soviet sailors, who were already tailed wherever they went. Henceforth, Soviet sailors were allowed on shore only in groups of five or more for a maximum of six hours a day. Tensions diminished somewhat thereafter, and if the *South China Morning Post* is to be believed, did so on the orders of the Soviet government, which recognized that it had gone too far. There were, however, further cases of alleged spying by Soviet sailors. Although reluctant to give up entirely the lucrative income from these repairs, the British government made it exceptionally clear that in future it would scrutinize all requests for such facilities extremely closely.[59]

Besides undergoing repairs, Soviet cargo ships, research vessels, and passenger liners all docked in Hong Kong. In 1968, the Hong Kong government noted that, during the past few years, Soviet cruise liners had called at Hong Kong on nine occasions. Two passenger vessels sailing from Vladivostok, the *Baikal* and the *Khabarovsk*, stopped regularly in Hong Kong.[60] In August 1971, the *South China Morning Post* reported that over 80 Soviet ships of varying types, carrying over 4,000 men, had put into Hong Kong during the prior year.[61] Most cruise liners came directly from Japan, carrying mostly Japanese nationals taking advantage of their inexpensive fares. Only those few Soviet nationals whose passports had valid visas arranged well in advance were allowed to debark. The British Embassy in Moscow urged that neither the British government nor the Hong Kong government should impose a complete ban on shore leave for Soviet crewmen on either cargo ships or passenger liners, because such restrictions on Soviet seamen would contravene international law. Furthermore, if Hong Kong did so, British seamen would face similar constraints in such Soviet ports as Leningrad. The Embassy also supported the Hong Kong government's view that business from these ships was valuable to the docks. Each ship spent an average of US$180,000 on repairs, and any attempt by the Hong Kong authorities to stop this practice would "entail a major row with the dockyards." On average, 15 Soviet ships docked annually in Hong Kong for repairs. The British government concluded that the level of Soviet activities was less important than their rate of increase, and that they should not be allowed to expand too rapidly.[62]

Desire for a Renewed Permanent Presence

During the 1960s, Soviet commercial interest in Hong Kong burgeoned, even though more often than not the British government was extremely wary of giving too much encouragement to Soviet officials. In its 1967 general report on Hong Kong, the Far East Department at the MID mentioned that the Soviet trade representative in China had visited Hong Kong three times, in May 1962, February 1964, and again once more in late 1966. On these occasions: "Entrance visas were granted by the United Kingdom."[63] In 1964, the issue of a permanent Soviet trade office came up again. In January 1964, several Soviet nationals made separate requests to the British government for Hong Kong visas. One was from the Soviet Commercial Minister attached to the Beijing Embassy, M. I. Sladkovsky, who claimed to want a visa simply to allow him to buy goods in Hong Kong on his country's behalf. The second request came from the leader of the Soviet delegation to the UNESCAP, V. B. Spandarian, who made the request unofficially in Bangkok to a Mr. William Dorward from the Hong Kong Commerce and Industry Department. To entice Dorward, Spandarian "referred to the possibility of substantial opportunities for Hong Kong consumer goods on the Soviet market," in the British view "holding out the bait of commercial advantages." The third request came from Tokyo, where Soviet Embassy officials pressed their British counterparts to reverse the decision to refuse a visa to a Soviet journalist, A. Ilyin, who wished to visit Hong Kong at the same time as Sladkovsky. The British skeptically remarked this would only be for "a holiday, which hardly seems consistent with these representations." A fourth request came from London, where Mr. Andrei Doubonossov, the manager of the Moscow *Narodny* Bank, requested a visa to come to Hong Kong.[64]

In the Hong Kong government's view: "The evidence is not conclusive, but it does suggest a deliberate Soviet intention to extend their influence here, and in the context of the Sino-Soviet quarrel this would be a logical step. Since there is no reason to believe that this would work to our advantage, and a distinct likelihood that it would add to our problems, the balance of local advantage seemed to us to keep the Russians out of Hong Kong from the outset."[65] Despite this plea by the Hong Kong government that all Soviet requests for visas be denied, such visas were generally granted. The Colonial Office declared that while no permanent Soviet office should be allowed in Hong Kong, "occasional visits should be allowed if genuine commercial reasons exist. On this occasion there are genuine commercial reasons." The Foreign Office itself was divided. The Head of the Northern Department, W. K. Slather, which handled the Soviet Union, wanted to deny the requests, believing their purpose was intelligence gathering, not commerce. His superior at the Foreign Office, A. B. Brunswick, supported the British Embassy in Beijing in urging that Sladkovsky's visa request be granted, fearing a British refusal would cause the Soviets to refuse British visa requests to enter the Soviet Union. Responding to fears raised by the Hong Kong government regarding Chinese sensitivities, he wrote that while the Chinese would strongly object to a permanent Soviet presence in Hong Kong, they had few objections to occasional visits by Soviet individuals.[66] Ultimately Sladkovsky, together with his commercial aide in Beijing, Katusov, were granted visas, but the journalist Ilyin was not. Spandarian's unofficial request in Bangkok never became official and he never came to Hong Kong. No decision was given to Doubovossov regarding his request for a visa to visit Hong Kong banks until both Sladkovsky and Katusov had left Hong Kong. On the understanding that Doubovossov did not intend to open a Hong Kong branch of the Moscow *Narodny* Bank, his visa was authorized on February 28.[67]

On March 14, Doubovossov arrived in Hong Kong. The British government accepted that he was now investigating the possibility of establishing a Hong Kong branch of his bank, but that prospect no longer seemed to concern them. Regarding Hong Kong as a lucrative prospect, the Russians wanted the bank to be used as an outlet for Soviet gold. Mr. J. A. H. G. Smith, a British employee of the Moscow *Narodny* Bank, accompanied Doubovossov. The British accepted that nothing in their visit seemed related to the trips by other Russians during the previous month, but characterized these visits as "a symptom of the same phenomenon of increasing Soviet interests in Hong Kong." Nevertheless, J. D. Higham at the Colonial Office conceded in April that "all told the evidence of Soviet activity in Hong Kong amounts to very little. Recent signs of Russian interest are straws in the wind." Higham proceeded, however, to state that both China and local Hong Kong Communists were very concerned over "the possible development of a Russian presence in the colony. Trading links could serve propaganda and intelligence purposes." He therefore concluded, "visits by Russians should be few and far between. The Special Branch [the organization responsible for internal security in Hong Kong], already overtaxed, viewed surveillance of all Russian visitors as necessary."[68]

During March 1967, E. G. Willan of the Hong Kong government wrote a report to the Colonial Office, detailing the recent visit by Sladkovsky and Katusov. Despite the fears expressed by both the Hong Kong and Chinese governments, their visit had passed uneventfully. "Most of their time was spent doing the things that most tourists here do, and they went back over the border with three extra heavily laden suitcases of purchases." They also met representatives of banks and companies that did business with the Soviet Union. The Hong Kong Section of Special Branch almost incessantly watched Sladkovsky and Katusov. The British surmised one reason for the innocuousness of the Soviets' behavior was that they were fully aware they were under constant surveillance. The Hong Kong government concluded its report: "We must therefore continue to mistrust Soviet intentions vis-à-vis Hong Kong."[69]

In April 1964, the Head of the *Tass* office in London, Mr. Egorov, requested that the news agency be allowed to open an office in Hong Kong. When the idea was floated before Murray MacLehose, then Head of the Far Eastern Division at the Foreign Office and later Governor of Hong Kong, he responded coolly, and Britain gently rebuffed the informal Soviet request.[70] On May 22, 1964, *Pravda* published an article, "Hong Kong's Ill Repute," by two Russian "special correspondents" who purported to demonstrate that Beijing was prepared to go to considerable lengths to prevent Soviet citizens visiting Hong Kong.[71] Three years later, E. Boland, a diplomat at the British Embassy in Beijing, sent London a memorandum describing how at a garden party in spring 1967 he had recently met a Mr. Mussin from the Soviet Embassy. Mussin asked Boland if his government would allow the Soviet Union to open an office of the *Tass* news agency in Hong Kong. According to Boland, in response he sharply asked Mussin how the Russians could expect the British to agree "when we saw the hostile articles they wrote about Hong Kong denigrating the British administration there." Mussin, taken aback, could offer no defense for the articles. This informal Soviet proposal never went any farther.[72] In 1970, Soviet Deputy Foreign Minister Nikolai Kozyrev met British officials, and during their meeting once again raised the question of the Soviets opening a consulate in Hong Kong, or at the very least, a shipping office. British officials told Kozyrev there was no prospect of either due to "Hong Kong's special position." The British government feared that the Soviets would use any permanent facility for intelligence purposes, as a locale to gather information about events in rapidly changing China.[73]

As the 1970s began, the British government continued to review very carefully all visa requests from Soviet citizens. Three Russian members of the UNESCO Secretariat, for example, asked to visit Hong Kong so that they could make flight connections back to Paris after attending a conference in Tokyo in July 1971. The British government, however, refused their request, concluding that the stopover in Hong Kong was not a matter of necessity, but one of pleasure and financial convenience. In October 1971, the British turned down another request for a visa for Hong Kong from Boris Boubnov, the *Tass* correspondent in Hanoi, Vietnam.[74] The Hong Kong and British governments nonetheless approved a few visa requests, especially for cultural activities. In November 1971, for example, when some 30 artistes from the Moscow Variety Theater came to Hong Kong to perform, Hong Kong Governor David Trench personally wrote to the Foreign and Colonial Office urging approval of these visas.[75] Despite such exceptions, from the late 1940s until the end of the Cold War, the British government refused numerous Soviet visa requests. Perhaps because it considered such difficulties routine and inevitable, the MID remained untroubled by such repeated refusals, and habitually adopted a very low-key approach toward visa denials, while diplomatic reports never even bothered to mention the problems Soviet citizens encountered when obtaining visas.

Such lengthy agonizing by assorted British government departments over whether or not to grant visas to a few Soviet nationals was symptomatic of several considerations. Firstly, the British were clearly wary and would not grant the Soviet Union any permanent office in Hong Kong. Secondly, even visa requests for visits to Hong Kong by individual Soviet citizens gave rise to protracted debates at the highest levels among several departments, and were only granted on an individual case-by-case basis. Thirdly, the reasons cited for denials were not simply British apprehensions, but also Chinese anxieties as to what such Soviet nationals might do in Hong Kong and Britain's desire to remain on reasonable terms with China. The British feared that admitting too many Soviets to Hong Kong might anger the Chinese government to the point that it would destabilize British rule in Hong Kong. By extension, all East Europeans, not just Russians, found it very difficult to obtain visas to come to Hong Kong. As a Foreign Office functionary wrote in 1970: "The Russians have been trying for several years to establish a permanent presence in Hong Kong, largely, no doubt, for intelligence purposes. We have every reason to believe that the Chinese would react most unfavorably to any such Soviet presence."[76] An incident a few years later seemed to confirm Russian intelligence interest in Hong Kong. As a young lecturer, Ronald Hill, currently Professor Emeritus of Geography at the University of Hong Kong, attended the 1976 International Geographical Congress in Moscow, where he met a number of Soviet professors. Several months later, an unidentified unaccompanied Soviet sailor on shore leave arrived at the University of Hong Kong campus inquiring as to the whereabouts of Professor Hill, then away from Hong Kong. Although Professor Hill was never contacted again, the episode left him convinced that this purported sailor was one of his Moscow acquaintances who sought to recruit him for intelligence gathering activities, and was probably especially interested in him since, as a geographer, Professor Hill traveled frequently in Asia, particularly in newly opened China.[77]

Fears that the Soviet Union might establish an intelligence base in Hong Kong were also controlling when, during the mid-1970s, the Hong Kong government learned that the Soviet Union might gain title to then undeveloped territory on one of its large outlying islands, Lantau, through the auspices of the Soviet Moscow *Narodny* Bank. In 1973 a Singapore businessman, Edward Wong Wing-cheung, proposed developing Discovery Bay into a holiday resort "of sandy beaches, cable car rides, golf courses, tennis courts, and luxury hotels," a pristine locale that would attract tourists and affluent Hong Kong residents.[78] Later that decade Wong went bankrupt, throwing the development into liquidation. All local investors withdrew, except for the Moscow *Narodny* Bank, which had loaned Wong US$200 million. In 1977, the Moscow *Narodny* Bank sued Wong for payment in bankruptcy proceedings before the Hong Kong High Court, claiming ownership over his company, Hong Kong Resorts.

Fearing that, at a very sensitive time when the post–Mao Zedong Beijing government was still in transition and the question of Hong Kong's future was becoming increasingly prominent in Sino-British relations, prime Hong Kong land would be owned and operated by the Soviet Union and could be turned into a listening post to gather intelligence on Hong Kong and China, the Hong Kong government intervened. Secretly and without the knowledge of Hong Kong's Executive Council,

Sir David Akers-Jones, then Secretary for the New Territories, where Lantau Island was located, allowed an extremely well-connected pro-Beijing tycoon, Cha Chi-ming, chairman of Thornleigh Limited and China Dyeing Works, to take over the project.[79] In return, Cha was allowed to change Discovery Bay from its original resort concept into a full-fledged residential property. Instead of low-rise hotels and housing units with parks and playgrounds for vacationers, 25 high-rise tower blocks designed for tens of thousands of commuters were built, all without any planning approval. In its determination to exclude the Soviets, moreover, the Hong Kong government sacrificed US$20 million in lost revenue opportunities from uncharged land premiums.[80] When this long-past Cold War drama surfaced some 30 years later, Sir David Akers-Jones, questioned before the Hong Kong Legislative Council, showed no regret for the secrecy with which the government had implemented this deal or his failure to inform those government bodies, such as the Executive Council, supposedly entitled to be consulted on such matters. In his memoirs, Sir David defended his action as necessary to prevent "Russia from becoming the extraordinary owners of a large tract of Hong Kong hillside," characterizing Cha Chi-ming, "a Hong Kong citizen renowned for his quiet business acumen," as a true Hong Kong and Chinese patriot.[81] The incident demonstrated the lengths to which the Hong Kong government would go to deny the Soviets access to Hong Kong at a delicate juncture when the eventual handover of Hong Kong to the PRC loomed increasingly large in Sino-British relations.

Conclusion

From the late 1950s onward, for two decades conflicting impulses affected Soviet policy toward Hong Kong. As Hong Kong became an ever more prosperous and important trading and business center, the Soviet Union recognized the necessity and desirability of doing business with the territory. The problem for the Soviet Union was how to deal economically with an entity whose legitimacy it did not even recognize. With British goodwill, the colony conceivably might have proved a source of valuable intelligence on China as well as a useful trading partner for the Soviet Union. Yet ideological considerations of two kinds constrained its ability to attain these benefits. Despite the Sino-Soviet split, the Soviet Union refused to abandon its commitment to anti-colonialism and its stated position that the British administration was illegitimate, and therefore Hong Kong should be returned to China. Caveats to this effect were included in all contracts.

Moreover, throughout the Cold War the British authorities themselves viewed with great suspicion any Soviet attempt to enhance its activities in Hong Kong, and only after 1989 would such apprehensions lose their force. Not until 1994, after the end of the Cold War and the collapse of the Soviet Union, would the Russians again be allowed to reestablish a permanent diplomatic and trade presence in the territory. Soviet prospects of gaining even a toehold in British Hong Kong were limited by their own anti-Western foreign policy, and also by British reluctance to irritate China during the Sino-Soviet split by allowing Soviet diplomats or other personnel easy access to Hong Kong. Moreover, as it had since 1950, Hong Kong provided the Western powers with useful though not vital naval facilities, which posed a continuing strategic threat to the Soviet position in the Pacific. Until 1980 and beyond, the dictates of Soviet policy and the international situation therefore left Soviet options and room for maneuver toward Hong Kong exceptionally limited.

7

Ideological Enmity and Non-Recognition: Russian and Soviet Relations with Taiwan to 1960

Introduction

To a far greater degree than Hong Kong, the island of Taiwan constituted a fortress on the Asian front in the West's Cold War struggle against Communism. Once only an outlying province, first of China and then of Japan, Taiwan became a refuge for the KMT Chinese government when it was driven out from the mainland in the summer of 1949. Taiwan then took on crucial political, geographical, and ideological importance for the West. However inaccurate the reality, on a symbolic level, politically, ideologically, and economically, Taiwan represented democracy, capitalism, and the free market in the world contest against totalitarian Communism. Geographically, Taiwan guarded the crucial sea routes leading from Northeast to Southeast Asia, and was roughly equidistant from Korea and Vietnam, two nations where the Cold War became hot. Taiwan often served as a base for covert military operations against the PRC just across the narrow Taiwan Strait, as well as against Communist forces in more distant Indonesia and Indochina. The United States used Taiwan as a major base to gather intelligence material on the PRC. Due to its symbolic and strategic importance, the United States was determined to deny Taiwan to the Soviet Union or any country allied with it.

Historians and political scientists—albeit hampered by rather restricted access to materials from the Taiwanese side—have thoroughly examined American policy and activities toward Taiwan, noting how the KMT Chinese government ably utilized the United States Cold War obsession with Communism to obtain American economic and military assistance worth billions of dollars and, in 1954, a defense treaty pledging American military protection against outright attack by the PRC.[1] Should American resolve appear to falter, a large and powerful "China lobby" swung into action. Yet in the early 1970s, the Nixon and Kissinger visits to China, the consequent Shanghai Communiqué of 1972, and the subsequent 1978 full normalization of relations between the United States and the PRC, surprised an ill-prepared Taiwan, which responded by continuing along the path to economic prosperity and democratization.[2]

Numerous studies of Soviet relations with the PRC exist, but very few have focused on Soviet dealings with Nationalist China, especially after 1949, and most of these are largely speculative, based on Soviet and Taiwanese newspaper accounts. To date there are no Russian-language studies of Soviet-Taiwan relations. Reinhard Drifte, stating that after 1949 trade between the Soviet Union and Taiwan ceased entirely, contends "all discussion of the Soviet perspective on Taiwan must be based on conjecture." All accounts agree that Soviet ties with Taiwan only developed in response to the growing rapprochement between the PRC and the United States in the early 1970s, when Soviet newspapers for the first time wrote favorably of Taiwan, while the Taiwanese likewise warmed toward the Soviets, differentiating, for example, between Soviet and Chinese Communism, and officials from each country visited the other. Taiwan hoped hints of closer Soviet-Taiwanese relations would discourage growing links between the PRC and the United States, while the Soviets believed better relations with Taiwan might prevent Sino-Soviet relations deteriorating still further. Yet both sides limited their involvement. Taiwan denied interest in any close association, insisting its national policy would always be staunchly anti-Communist. For the Soviets, closer ties with Taiwan might easily generate increased tensions and preclude any potential reconciliation with the PRC. Academic specialists therefore concluded that, while improved Soviet-Taiwan relations might have been mutually advantageous, ideological and strategic considerations prevented the development of significant ties.[3]

For the first time, newly available Russian and Soviet materials allow historians to assess with some confidence the accuracy of these earlier interpretations, and determine precisely what Soviet-Taiwan ties developed when, why, and how. This chapter examines Soviet-Taiwanese ties up to the early 1960s, focusing upon the issues of Soviet attitudes toward Japanese colonial policies; the role of the Comintern in Formosa's revolutionary movement during the 1920s and 1930s; UN membership; the "two Chinas" question; and the role of Taiwan in precipitating the Sino-Soviet split. The subsequent chapter examines the repercussions for Soviet-Taiwanese relations of the Sino-Soviet break and the reopening of Sino-American relations in the early 1970s.

Both chapters are based primarily upon documents from three Russian collections: materials from the two Central Committee of the Communist Party archives, the extensive Comintern collection at RGASPI, and documents from RGANI covering the mid-1950s through the early 1960s; and the AVP RF for the post–World War II period. For the interwar period, previously unexamined Comintern files include over a dozen well-researched reports, written and filed in Japan, China, or Formosa itself, in English, Russian, Japanese, or Chinese, that outline Japanese occupation policies, and broad Taiwanese resistance to that occupation, with particular stress on opposition by the CPF. From 1949 through 1955, the Soviet Embassy in Beijing sent the MID annual detailed reports on Taiwan's domestic and external situation, drawn mainly from press accounts, Chinese military intelligence assessments, and the opinions of diplomats. During this period, when the PRC and Soviet Union were close allies, the Soviets provided no editorial gloss to their information on Taiwan, which—like that on Hong Kong—Soviet diplomats in Beijing, Shanghai, and Guangzhou obtained directly from the Chinese. As Sino-Soviet relations deteriorated, the Soviets were driven to compile information on Taiwan—mostly only newspaper accounts—independently, from Soviet embassies in Japan, Thailand, Singapore, and elsewhere. Unfortunately, despite repeated requests, the author could not consult two other significant resources: Politburo records in the AP RF, and those of the TsA FSB *Rossii*. Documents from the NA and the PRO, and a limited selection from Taiwan's Foreign Ministry Archive, supplement these Soviet files. Together these materials provide a fairly complete picture of Soviet-Taiwanese relations during the past 75 years, illustrating the respective value of such ties to each state. These two chapters also illustrate the manner in which Cold War priorities constrained the room for maneuver not just of small, vulnerable clients, but even of such a superpower as the Soviet Union.

Russian and Soviet Interest in Formosa up to 1949

Formosa, meaning "beautiful island," the name which early Dutch navigators gave to the island known to the Chinese as Taiwan, is located 100 miles east of the central Chinese coast, with an area of 14,000 square miles. The original Taiwanese were the indigenous aboriginal Malay inhabitants of the island, who today number fewer than 250,000. While China was the nominal ruler of Formosa, and the Chinese had begun settling along the coast from 700AD onward, essentially the island remained an independent loosely-organized tribal society. During the early seventeenth century, Europeans became interested in Formosa, with the Dutch temporarily occupying the southern part of the island, and the Spanish the northern part. Yet their occupation during the 1620s and 1630s was not permanent. A generation later, in 1662, the last Ming dynasty ruler, Chung Chung Kung, was driven from the mainland and took refuge on Formosa.[4] His flight, reminiscent to later readers of that of a successor, Chiang Kai-shek who, with his KMT government, fled China almost 300 years later, initiated a series of successive waves of settlement on Formosa by Chinese migrants. The victorious Qing dynasty formally annexed Formosa in 1683, defeating Chung's grandson in battle.[5]

Tsarist Russia noted that throughout the entire eighteenth and most of the nineteenth century, the Chinese government showed little interest or concern over what transpired in Formosa, an island the Chinese government considered a "far away province on the periphery of China" and treated as part of the neighboring mainland province of Fujian (Fukien). Disputes between Chinese migrants and the indigenous aborigines reduced the island to chaos. This indifference makes a somewhat ironic counterpoint to the subsequent contentions of both mainland China and Nationalist China that Taiwan had always been closely tied to and an integral part of China. Official disinterest lasted until the beginning of the Sino-French War in 1884, when some fighting took place on Formosa, directing the Chinese government's attention to the offshore island. Chinese officials realized that if an enemy nation captured Formosa, it would provide a base for operations against the mainland. After the war ended, the Chinese government made Formosa a separate province with its own governor. About the same time, China experienced a border crisis with Russia in Central Asia over possession of its town Ili in Xinjiang.

That crisis likewise caused a heightening of Chinese interest along the country's entire periphery.[6] In further recognition of Taiwan's strategic importance, Liu Ming Chuan, a military general and hero of the Sino-French War, was appointed governor. He taxed the local population heavily in order to strengthen the island's infrastructure, developing roads and railways.[7]

In the late nineteenth century, Japan became interested in acquiring Formosa. After its defeat in the Sino-Japanese War of 1894–1895, under the 1895 Treaty of Shimonoseki China ceded Formosa to Japan, which made it into a colony. In the name of a "Formosa Republic" inhabitants led by Liu Ei Suk unsuccessfully resisted this takeover, but by June 1895, Japan had crushed the opposition. This uprising foreshadowed a series of eight military rebellions against Japanese rule during the next half century by Formosans, both Chinese and aborigines.[8] Seeking to promote continuity, Japan assured foreign states and nationals that they need feel no anxiety, since all prior treaties would remain in effect and foreigners could live and trade in certain designated ports. In 1896, Russia established a Consulate there and, on the recommendation of France, its ally, appointed Paul Shabert, a German national, as the first Russian Consul.[9]

Most Western and Japanese accounts portrayed Japanese colonial rule fairly positively. One broad survey of Taiwan summarized that "Japanese colonial policy may be described as beneficial and progressive. Some observers have described Japan's intent as expansionist and militaristic from the outset, but that claim is difficult to prove."[10] They stressed that Taiwan produced rice, sugar, bananas, tea, salt, tobacco, and sweet potatoes, and was economically important to Japan as a source particularly of the first two commodities. These accounts further mentioned that the Japanese built roads, railroads, harbors, hydroelectric generators, telephone and telegraph lines, and other infrastructure projects, responding quickly and effectively to the economic and social needs of the population, which made their occupation fairly popular with many locals.[11] The Japanese established the basis for a modern economy by standardizing currency, and founding banks and a banking system. Conditions for Taiwanese people improved. For example, the caloric content of their daily diet approached that of Japanese living in Japan itself, and certainly exceeded that in China. Public hygiene improved radically, eliminating plagues. The death rate dropped from 33 per 1,000 in 1906 to 19 by 1940 due to a better diet and modern medical services.[12]

Japan greatly improved the educational system, giving most people basic literacy, and establishing Formosa's first university. One historian even contended that Japanese colonial rule laid the basis for the emergence of Taiwan as one of Asia's "little tigers" after World War II.[13] Interwar Formosa had a population of roughly four million people, of whom Chinese were the largest single ethnic group by far at 3.5 million; the Japanese population numbered 200,000, mostly officials and businessmen; 130,000 were aborigines, from over 100 tribes; and the remainder were foreigners, again many from China.[14] One historian, John Franklin Copper, argues that most Chinese supported Japanese rule, or at least accommodated to it. "There were no meaningful protests against the Japanese War against China." He further contends that Formosa's population benefited from Japan's war preparation policies, especially the development of heavy industries in the island. Copper noted that Formosan Chinese served Japan loyally during World War II, even fighting Chinese people in China, including participating in the 1937 "Rape of Nanjing."[15] In sum, the Japanese recognized that the welfare and happiness of its colonial subjects were linked to Japan's reputation as a responsible colonial power, which sought to civilize its territories.

Previously unexamined Tsarist and Comintern files reveal, by contrast, a very different picture. As early as March 1897, the newly appointed Russian Consul reported that a number of local Chinese in Taiwan had requested Russian citizenship, seeking to benefit from Russian protection against what the Consul termed "Japanese misrule."[16] A significant uprising took place in 1915, when some 30,000 peasants died in the south.[17] For the interwar period over a dozen well-researched Comintern reports invariably portrayed a brutal and repressive Japanese occupation, bolstered by a harsh army and police force, who implemented draconian occupation policies, crushing all who opposed Japanese dominion. Overall, these reports described Formosa as suffering under a severe occupation regime, which in turn provoked further resistance to Japanese rule. According to these reports, while the Japanese invested in factories and developed Formosa's transportation and communications infrastructure extensively, Japan did so not to improve conditions for local inhabitants, but to militarize and control the island.[18] The Japanese monopolized and dominated major industries and all banks. Cheap Japanese products flooded into Formosa. Japanese businessmen and landowners received heavy government subsidies. To get a decent job, individuals had to be able to read, write, and speak Japanese. Often Japanese individuals received twice the salary of Formosan Chinese for the same work.[19]

Arguably, the largest uprising occurred in October 1930 when indigenous aborigines rather than the Chinese population rebelled against the Japanese. The aborigines, whom first the Chinese and then the Japanese forced onto ever less desirable land in the mountainous interior of Formosa, were of Malay origin. Much like the Native Americans or American Indians, the aborigines, numbering some 130,000, tended to be mostly hunters and gatherers. They were divided into nine major tribes, and their frequent inter-tribal warfare made them an easy prey. The aboriginal population suffered persistent discrimination, receiving wages half those of the Chinese, and was subjected to forced labor, high taxes, and the seizure of their crops. Almost no aboriginal children attended schools, in contrast to the Japanese and to a lesser extent Chinese populations. From the beginning of Japanese rule, the aborigines were subjugated and confined behind electrified barbed wire, which surrounded their lands. Reporting on the uprising, one Comintern agent estimated that 50,000 aborigines had died since the Japanese takeover in 1895.[20] As increasing amounts of their lands were seized, while the completion of a dam which would flood their lands was planned for 1930, the aboriginal population, facing virtual starvation, rose up against Japanese rule on October 27, 1930.[21] The Japanese brutally suppressed the rebellion in March 1931, employing cannons, machine guns, airplanes, bombs, poison gas, red-hot iron bars, mass shootings, and rape against aborigines armed with old rifles, spears, and swords. Even so, the Japanese, contending with rough terrain, inadequate local knowledge, and 19,000 opponents, including women and children, determined to fight to the death, found it difficult to crush the rebels, whose fierce resistance won them great sympathy from the previously indifferent, even hostile, Chinese population.[22] Ultimately, however, most rebels were killed, while the Japanese lost fewer than 200 police and troops. After they had suppressed the rebellion, the Japanese built large numbers of police stations, virtually at five-mile intervals, to supervise the restive population, whether Chinese or aboriginal, rural or urban. As they moved toward war against China, Japanese officials wanted no further resistance or uprisings from the restive Formosan population.

Most Formosans, especially the Chinese, were peasants, which meant land ownership was arguably the island's most contentious issue. 82 percent of the rural population possessed only 28 percent of the land, amounting to about two acres for each. The richest 2 percent of the rural population owned 36 percent of the land, 70 percent of peasants rented their land, and 40 percent had no land at all.[23] In this feudal-style economy, landowners tended to be either Japanese or Chinese, but the old Chinese feudal lords lost many of their old rights. The Japanese persistently purchased land at artificially low prices, which left most peasants poor or very poor. The Japanese promoted the cultivation of cash crops, diverting land that had been devoted to subsistence farming, growing rice and other staples, to the production on large estates of commodities such as sugar, which amounted to almost half of the total capital investment in the countryside, and tea.[24] Sugar magnates tended to be Japanese, and constituted the largest capitalists and landowners, as sugar companies were often subsidiaries of firms based in Japan.

Between 1910 and 1923 the rural population declined slightly, from 63 percent to 58 percent, as land rents rose by some 20 percent to 50 percent under Japanese rule. Comintern files listed numerous small uprisings by peasants against their landlords, as well as against the Japanese state monopolies over salt, opium, camphor, tobacco, opium, and vodka, which maintained artificially high prices peasants could ill afford. Prices for these commodities increased by 350 percent over the 25-year period from 1902 to 1928, further increasing the burden on the local population.[25] In 1914, according to subsequent Comintern archives, peasants in the south staged risings, in which thousands soon died thanks to repression by Japanese soldiers and police. A decade later, in 1924, Comintern agents reported widespread rural resistance, as peasants in Taichu formed a union, most of whose leaders the colonial government quickly arrested.[26] Peasants reacted again in 1927, demanding: "Give us our land."[27] When the worldwide economic depression hit Formosa in 1930, its effect was speedy and sharp. Sugar prices dropped by 30 percent, rice even more, by some 70 percent, while wages of farm laborers fell between 40 percent and 50 percent, all of which had a brutal impact on the rural economy and population. According to Comintern reports, the peasants could no longer earn a living, as prices for sugar and tea, their two largest crops, continued to decline, while their taxes continued to rise. When Japan began its war against China in the 1930s, the plight of the peasants deteriorated even further, as their taxes increased to pay for the war, crops were requisitioned at less than market rates, irrigation fees rose, and peasants continued to be forced off their lands. Any attempt at resistance was suppressed.

Except for the small Japanese industrial working class, which constituted some 8 percent of the total, the economic conditions of Formosa's urban working class were no better. The total urban proletariat of all kinds amounted to 300,000, of whom 100,000 were factory workers, who rarely received daily wages higher than one yen, their pay ranging roughly from ten US cents to one dollar per day for working 13 or more hours under harsh conditions. Many workers were unemployed; those workers who were employed had little job security.[28] Japanese products flooded into Taiwan, much to the detriment of weaker domestic industries. Under these circumstances, during the more liberal mid-1920s, Formosan workers predictably began to establish labor organizations, and during that period, printers, lumbermen, construction workers, textile workers, machinists, sugar refiners, and miners set up more than ten trade unions. By 1927, trade unions were divided into left and right factions. The right faction, affiliated with the conservative People's Party, established the Formosan Workers General Federation, concentrated among the more skilled artisans and handicraft workers; while the left faction consolidated into the General Federation of Labour. These divisions, together with an increasingly repressive political climate, severely weakened the trade union movement.[29]

In 1926, waves of strikes began in the Kuo-Hsuen Iron Factory and spread to other sectors of industry as workers protested against low wages, arbitrary dismissals, high taxes, and long hours.[30] Just as for the agricultural sector, the economic depression seriously affected Formosa's industrial workers, bringing wage cuts of up to 50 percent and higher taxes, as well as rising unemployment as factories closed. One Comintern agent reported wage reductions of some 60 percent, to 50 or 60 sen a day.[31] In December 1930, 1,000 workers at the Van Hwa Tin Paper Manufacturing Plant went on strike to protest against wage cuts of 20 percent, but the strike fizzled out when the conservative trade unions accepted a 5 percent wage cut. That same month, workers at a straw packing factory went on strike, again protesting wage cuts, and in January 1931, a similar strike took place at a lumber plant. Further strikes, generally spontaneous and unorganized, broke out that year among coal miners, who were suffering from hunger, communications workers, machinists, printing operatives, cement, rubber, and sugar cane workers, and even among unskilled Formosan coolies. Trade union leadership proved weak and divided. Harsh police repression crushed virtually all such strikes, as Japanese officials sought to keep industries working at full speed to prepare for the impending war against China. In reaction workers became very demoralized, some even leaving Formosa for either Japan or China.[32] As Japan readied for war against China, it raised taxes, requisitioned crops, and increased irrigation fees, all to help pay for the conflict. Those added expenses, coupled with lower wages, the effective closing of the China market, and the economic depression, all contributed to make the conditions of Formosa's workers and peasants ever harsher.

Through the Comintern the Soviet Union devoted considerable attention to the CPF, organized originally in the mid-1920s, largely by Chinese middle-class intellectuals, members of the CCP, and members of the CPJ in Shanghai. During the interwar years, Communist operatives and Comintern agents were on occasion extremely active in Hong Kong, using the British colony as a base for undertakings in China and Southeast Asia, but the same was not true of Formosa. A small political party whose membership, including individuals in China, never exceeded 1,000, in August 1928, the CPF began to have relations with the much larger and more powerful CPJ. The following spring, however, harsh government repression crushed the CPJ. From then on the CPF was isolated from the Comintern and world communism. Its predominantly middle class membership dropped precipitately, and its executive committee numbered only five individuals.[33] However, another agent's report mentioned that in 1931 CPF membership still amounted to 870, distributed in some 20 branches.[34]

Comintern agents showed little respect for the CPF, criticizing it from almost every aspect, including its absence of any real base in factories and on agricultural estates. One dispatch urged it to emulate the Soviet model, which allegedly had a strong working-class and peasant base. These instructions urged that the fundamental party unit should consist of factory cadres, followed by the formation of party fractions in trade unions, peasant committees, student organizations, and other non-Communist organizations. Comintern agents also exhorted the CPF to organize and centralize a peasant movement to mount strikes against increases in rents and land taxes. The Comintern believed that only through a socialist revolution could Formosa achieve independence from Japanese rule. It argued that Japanese imperialism exploited Formosa in a colonial relationship resembling that Western countries employed to take advantage of their colonies in Africa and Asia. The Comintern hoped that, in Formosa as in other colonies, by "sharpening the antagonisms of international imperialism," the global economic depression that began in 1929 would hasten the coming of the inevitable revolution.[35] The Comintern urged the CPF to form a Communist Trade Union, and also to work with the unemployed, requests that went unheeded, causing a Comintern agent in 1931 to bemoan the CPF on the grounds that it "worked badly, lacked initiative, [and] a working class membership, [was] passive, and generally did not work with workers and peasants." He went on to declare that the party needed to be more active.[36] The same dispatch castigated the CPF as a party full of "passive opportunists" whose numerous shortcomings included poor work, undue timidity, a lack of initiative, and a failure to assist striking workers and peasants. In conclusion, its author warned: "If the party does not overcome its passivity, the revolutionary movement will be stopped for a long time."[37]

Some three months later another Comintern dispatch listed ten objectives the party should strive for. It recommended that the CPF should conduct agitation and propaganda among disaffected groups in the population, including peasants, workers, students, and aboriginal minorities. It urged the CPF to establish a daily party newspaper and trade union, organize the unemployed, and set up schools, clubs, and public kitchens for workers and the unemployed. The agent believed the party had to become more active in the peasant movement, and should work particularly with young workers, peasants, and women.[38] Specifically, the Comintern urged that the CPF advocate lower taxes, lower prices for necessities, such as salt, an eight-hour work day for all urban and rural workers, a five-day work week, unemployment insurance, and equal wages for all, as well as a living minimum wage, the banning of child slavery, which was then widespread, autonomy for the university, and basic civil liberties, such as freedom of speech and the press.[39] Drawing on the Soviet example, and reflecting Stalin's views that the peasantry could not play a leadership role in developing a revolutionary movement, a 1932 Comintern dispatch recommended that the CPF should create an alliance of workers and poor peasants under the hegemony of the working class. This ignored the fact that Formosa was predominantly rural, with only a tiny industrial working class. These instructions also urged the CPF to found a party newspaper, even though 70 percent of Formosa's population was illiterate, so would never read it.[40]

In terms of Formosa's political future, the CPF and Comintern were never clear whether or not Formosa should remain within the Japanese Empire, as a self-governing territory; whether it should become a province of China; or whether the island should become an independent republic. Reports varied, with some Comintern agents favoring one and others a different course. Some Comintern reports advocated political, economic, and social reforms within the Japanese Empire. Other reports favored full independence for Formosa. Nevertheless, two scholars contend that Chinese Communist leaders from 1928 up to the Cairo Conference in 1943 consistently recognized the Formosans were a distinct nation or a nationality, a *minzu*, accepting that they had the right to self-determination, including full independence from Japan and from China. The CCP grouped the Formosans with other non-Han minority groups, such as Mongols, Uighurs, and Tibetans. However, their article does not differentiate between the Taiwanese aborigines, who were definitely non-Chinese, or the descendants of Han Chinese, who settled in Formosa during the past two centuries, and constituted the bulk of the Formosan population. Despite the claims of this article, given the evidence provided, it is by no means certain that the CCP clearly favored an independent Taiwan.[41] Such differences regarding Taiwan's future were somewhat academic, since Comintern agents noted that by the early 1930s party work had come to a standstill. The CPF supported peasant uprisings, including the large aboriginal rebellion of October 1930. By then, however, the CPF was such a spent and insignificant force that its views hardly mattered.

By 1931, Comintern agents recognized Formosa's crucial importance to Japan, as its richest colony and, more importantly, a strategic location which could serve as a launching pad for a Japanese invasion of South China, as eventually transpired in 1937. Comintern agents noted its increasing militarization, for example, the construction of airfields, military roads, and new railway lines throughout the island. Japanese officials directly controlled all communications and transportation facilities, and factories switched more and more to producing war-related goods.[42] Once Japan launched its war against China in 1931, the Comintern urged the CPF to oppose the war by organizing strikes and demonstrations, and even to sabotage defense plants, to support their

Chinese brothers in this struggle against Japanese aggression. Comintern agents further urged party members to conduct anti-war agitation among Japanese troops, declaring that "all oppressed groups must unite against Japanese imperialism, capitalism and militarism."[43] By this time, however, the party's scope was minimal, as Japanese officials ensured that all opposition, however small and powerless, was crushed as they moved toward war. Paradoxically, though, Soviet diplomats noted, during the 1930s, Taiwan increasingly functioned as a base for smuggling goods, including sugar, rayon, kerosene, and cement, across into Fujian province on the mainland, activities of which the Japanese overlords were not only aware but for which they sometimes corruptly and opportunistically contributed their own ships.[44]

During the 1930s, Soviet officials watched the growth of Japanese power in Asia with growing apprehension, which became stronger as Japan seized Manchuria in 1931, and then embarked on full-scale war with China six years later. Right up to Pearl Harbor in December 1941, Soviet leaders feared that Japan, which still contemplated further military operations in Asia, would follow a northern strategy and move against Russia, as opposed to a southern strategy targeted at Southeast Asia. Until July 1945, the Soviet Union was officially neutral toward Japan, which precluded any overt Russian involvement in military operations against Japan. Even so, in the early years of the Sino-Japanese War, the Soviet Union gave very substantial military aid to Chiang Kai-shek's Nationalist Chinese government. In response to a Soviet proposal, in August 1937, China and the Soviet Union signed a non-aggression treaty with the KMT government, with which the CCP had recently, under some Soviet pressure, formed a united anti-Japanese front. Over the next four years, the Soviet government dispatched massive quantities of aid to China, granting somewhere between US$300 and US$450 million in credits and almost 1,000 Russian-made airplanes, 86 T-82 tanks, over 2,000 motor vehicles, more than 1,000 artillery pieces, 2,000,000 artillery shells, almost 10,000 machine guns, 50,000 rifles, 180 million rounds of ammunition, and 31,600 aerial bombs. The bulk of this assistance was delivered before the Soviet Union signed the August 1939 Non-Aggression Pact with Germany, but appreciable amounts continued to arrive until the June 1941 German invasion of Russia dictated that Stalin devote all his country's resources to homeland defense. About 1,500 high-level Soviet military advisers also served in China, giving technical advice on artillery, armor, transportation, engineering, communications, intelligence, and antiaircraft and aviation operations.[45]

One particularly significant component of Soviet military aid during this period was in aviation, since the Japanese swiftly destroyed most of the existing Chinese air force. In the two years from November 1937, a total of 2,000 Soviet pilots, plus support crews, served in rotation in China, with between 200 and 300 pilots there at any one time, usually on six-month tours of duty. Nominally these fliers, who were selected from the most highly skilled Soviet aviators, were volunteers, who wore civilian clothes but retained their military rank and won an automatic promotion when they returned to Russia. While some trained Chinese pilots, most flew combat missions in the modern SB-2 bombers and I-16 fighters their country had sent to China. In the first two years of the war, they shot down 986 Japanese airplanes, attacked Japanese airbases, transport facilities, and communications lines, and had a major impact in terms of boosting Chinese morale. The American aviator Colonel—later Lieutenant-General—Claire Lee Chennault admired them, describing them as "tough and determined with a tremendous vitality," adding: "They could combine twelve-hour alerts, bitter air combat and all-night carousing to a degree I have never seen remotely approached by other breeds."[46] One of their more spectacular operations was a daring February 1938 raid to mark Red Army Day (February 23) launched from Nanchang in Guangxi province against a Japanese air base on Taiwan, in which 12 Soviet bombers destroyed about 40 airplanes on the ground near Taipei, together with a three-year stock of fuel, and sank or damaged several ships. The raid was widely publicized in the press, and the returning air crew were feted at a banquet attended by Chiang Kai-shek's wife, Soong May-ling, China's Finance Minister, her brother T. V. Soong, and assorted Chinese generals.[47]

Publicly, the Chinese government merely stated that a "foreign volunteer" had led this raid, ironically enough leading many to suppose that an American flier had been responsible. The episode was, however, a precursor of subsequent operational raids against Japanese air bases in Taiwan by the United States–backed American Volunteer Group or "Flying Tigers," a somewhat comparable American government-funded "volunteer" air force established in 1940, that eventually in 1942 became an official US unit, the China Air Task Force. Headed by the charismatic Chennault, a retired American aviator who initially came to China in 1937 to train Chinese pilots but was eventually reenrolled as a US brigadier general, the new air force took up some of the slack after Soviet pilots were withdrawn. Between 1942 and January 1945, the Flying Tigers targeted several major raids on Japanese air bases in Taiwan, as these facilities not only expedited attacks by Japanese airplanes on China, but also enabled Japan to intercept and destroy shipping carrying supplies to the Chinese mainland. Chennault himself became a good friend of both Chiang and his wife, eventually founding the "Flying Tigers" Chinese civil aviation company, accompanying the couple to Taiwan in 1949, and relocating his business activities, which often had close links with the CIA, on the island.[48]

Japanese use of Taiwan as a military and aviation asset during World War II indicated that the island could be strategically valuable, and for that and other reasons its future was therefore of interest to the Allied powers. During World War II, the Allies considered Taiwan an occupied territory. In 1943, the Soviet Embassy in Washington obtained and forwarded to Moscow a copy of a United States Department of State secret study paper on Taiwan's postwar fate, which the MID translated into Russian. It gave seven possible options for Taiwan, of which the first, its return to Chinese sovereignty, was the preferred American solution. The first option would deprive Japan of a strategic asset, and also satisfy Chinese governmental demands to regain sovereignty over its alienated territories, which the "predominantly Chinese character of its population" justified. At the same time Taiwan could provide China with needed rice.[49] The Americans also expressed interest in negotiating an agreement whereby the Chinese government would permit either the United States or the UN to establish air and naval bases on Taiwan. The Soviets noted that, while the Chinese would accept no formal restrictions on their sovereignty, unofficially they might well allow the Americans to establish such bases. Given "the predominantly Chinese composition of the population" and its identification with China, the report argued that, even though the island might theoretically support a viable separate economy, "there is little likelihood of an independence movement developing."[50] Nor, since the Chinese population and government opposed this, was the internationalization of Taiwan as a UN trustee territory seriously considered. Six weeks later, when a much shorter revised version of this report was released, its preferred solution likewise favored Taiwan's return to full Chinese sovereignty, entirely ignoring both the independence and internationalization options. It assumed the Chinese would grant the Americans naval and air bases, but eschewed any prior formal treaty agreement thereon, since China would not sanction a "return to the old policy of unequal treaties."[51] Although Soviet officials did not comment on either document, their action in copying and translating both documents in full indicated some interest in American thinking on Taiwan's future. No great power opposed the return of Taiwan to the KMT Chinese government, on which Franklin D. Roosevelt, Winston Churchill, and Chiang Kai-shek agreed at the December 1943 Cairo Conference.[52] The CCP also accepted the Cairo Provisions that Taiwan was an integral part of China, effectively denying the island the right of self-determination it had once been willing to grant. After 1949 for the CCP to claim otherwise would indeed have added legitimacy to the KMT occupation of Taiwan.[53] At Teheran shortly afterwards, Stalin accepted their decision, which was reconfirmed at Potsdam in July 1945.

In September 1945, Chinese forces assumed administrative control of Taiwan. As the civil war against the Chinese Communists intensified, Chiang Kai-shek's KMT government soon demonstrated its suspicions of any Russian involvement in the island. In 1948, the British Consulate outside Taipei noted how "a steady influx of Soviet and White Russian holiday makers into Formosa continued throughout the summer. Police tightened up their regulations to prevent an infiltration of Communists, and often stopped foreigners on the streets for their identification cards."[54] In fact, Formosan authorities decreed that all Soviet citizens and White Russians had to leave Formosa no later than June 25, or they would be forcibly deported to unnamed third countries. No specific figures on the actual numbers of Russians, Soviet citizens, or stateless people involved were supplied.[55] Soviet merchant ships visited Taiwan to load such cargoes as tea and rice. In June 1949, Chiang Kai-shek, the leader of the KMT, arrived in Taiwan, and on August 18, 1949, a *Tass* report first mentioned Taiwan as a possible asylum for KMT armies.[56]

Mainland Ambitions toward Taiwan after 1949

During the Chinese Civil War, Stalin hesitated over whether to support the Communists or Chiang's Nationalists. In fact, as late as early 1949, the Soviets advised the Communists not to cross the Yangtze River, which divides North and South China, and to leave the South under the control of the KMT. Still believing the Communists would not take full control of China, almost incredibly, the Soviet Ambassador at the time, Nikolai Roshchin, was the only member of the diplomatic corps to follow the KMT south to Guangzhou.[57] The CCP disregarded Soviet advice, crossed the Yangtze in May 1949, and soon took over the rest of China. Attempting to make up for lost time, on October 1, 1949, the Soviet Union became the first country to recognize the new PRC. All contacts between the KMT and the Soviet Union ceased after the Nationalists fled to Taiwan, and on October 3, 1949, the Nationalist Chinese government formally severed diplomatic relations with the Soviet Union.[58] From then onward, the Soviet Union never officially recognized Taiwan's independence from the mainland.

The initial expectation was that some time in the near future mainland China would probably gain Taiwan. After the PRC was established in autumn 1949, the British Consul in Taiwan noted that as a refuge for the Nationalist Chinese, Taiwan had little strategic importance to the Americans. However the Consul noted that, "Formosa might well provide an excellent base for Russia to exercise control over the coast of China and threaten the strategic positions of Great Britain and the United States in Hong Kong, the Philippines, Okinawa, and Japan. The island is ideally suited for this purpose. Therefore every effort should be made to prevent Formosa from falling into Communist hands."[59] Even so, contemporary American military and intelligence assessments argued that, without massive American military support, Taiwan would inevitably fall to the Communists. In January 1950, Secretary of State Dean Acheson placed Taiwan outside the United States defense perimeter, though stating that it might rely on the UN for its defense.[60]

After some initial misgivings, the Soviets supported Chinese Communist efforts to take the island of Taiwan. When Mao Zedong met Stalin in Moscow in December 1949, he asked Stalin if the Soviet Union could supply "volunteer" pilots and even Soviet detachments for this purpose. Specifically, Mao asked if the Soviet Union could train 1,000 pilots, and deliver up to 200 fighters and 80 bombers.[61] Mao realized that the very complicated amphibious operation could only be successful if the Soviets gave large-scale air and naval support.[62] Stalin, who feared a military attack on Taiwan might provoke outright war with the United States, initially demurred, promising only to consider such assistance, and instead urged Mao to concentrate on encouraging an uprising on the island, rather than focusing on an invasion. Stalin promised only to help the Chinese build up their own air force and navy, which might take years. By early 1950, however, Stalin believed—possibly relying on intelligence sources—that the United States would not fight to maintain Taiwan under non-Communist rule and, as with Hong Kong, began to encourage Mao's government to take Taiwan in the foreseeable future. At this stage he allowed the PRC to use half of its US$300 million credit recently granted by the Soviet Union to purchase Soviet arms, with the intention that many of these would be used to liberate Taiwan. It seems, however, that the ever cautious Stalin, reluctant to engage in direct military hostilities with the United States, never pledged Soviet air and naval support for any such operation.[63] During 1949 and 1950, the Soviets nonetheless stationed military advisers and specialists, who manned antiaircraft defenses, opposite Taiwan on the mainland Fujian province.[64] The Soviets helped to establish an office of the Taiwan League for Democratic Self-Rule, a Communist front organization pledged to recapture Taiwan, at their naval base in Port Arthur, Manchuria.[65] In practice, without direct Soviet military support, the Chinese Communists still probably lacked the naval capability to launch the necessary amphibious expedition to capture Taiwan. Furthermore, in January 1950, the PLA suffered two unexpected and crushing defeats when attempting to take the two offshore islands of Jinmen and Dengbu.[66] Nevertheless, when PRC military forces captured Hainan Island off the coast of Southeast China on April 23, 1950, morale in Taiwan plummeted, as most people there believed their island would be the next prize of mainland forces.[67]

The North Korean invasion of South Korea, which Stalin authorized in spring 1950, a decision of which Mao was informed, though he did not learn the specific date, had major implications for the future status of Taiwan. Prior to the North Korean invasion of South Korea, the United States intended to let Mao invade Taiwan to finish the Chinese Civil War. The outbreak of the Korean War on June 25, 1950, however, enhanced Taiwan's strategic significance to both sides. North Korean leader Kim Il-sung and Mao had both, wrongly, assumed that the United States would not send military forces to fight for South Korea, and had convinced Stalin of this. Within a few days, the United States ordered its Seventh Fleet to patrol the Taiwan Strait to prevent any Communist attack. Mao was shocked by the swift American reaction, and also by the successes of American troops in Korea from mid-September 1950 onward. These developments forced the Chinese to reconsider any amphibious action, and defer any further action against Taiwan. China, moreover, believed that the safety of its vital industrial Northeast (Manchuria) depended on maintaining a friendly power on its border, and in October 1950, as UN forces drove up into North Korea, ever closer to the North Korean border with China, Mao took the decision to send major Chinese forces to intervene in the Korean War. Preoccupied with the Korean War, and blocked by the Seventh Fleet, Beijing was forced to put its Taiwan operation on hold at least until after the Korean War, and in practice the invasion was deferred indefinitely.[68]

During the Korean War, Soviet officials verbally supported mainland Chinese claims to Taiwan, but did little more than make such rhetorical gestures. In September 1950, Yakov Malik, the Soviet delegate to the UN, unsuccessfully demanded that Taiwan's status be included on the UNSC agenda, and that a PRC representative be invited to participate in these discussions. During the debate, he formally proposed that, since "Taiwan is part of China," all American military forces stationed in and around Taiwan be withdrawn immediately. He asked why Taiwan had not reverted to China, in accordance with the joint Soviet, British, and American Potsdam Conference declaration.[69] The historian Nancy Bernkopf Tucker argues, though she offers no corroborating evidence, that the Soviets did not genuinely support PRC inclusion in this debate, as they sought to keep the PRC dependent on Moscow.[70] Later in September, the Soviet Union again used the UN forum to condemn American actions in sending United States military and naval forces to Taiwan, alleging this constituted American aggression against the PRC.

Superficially, during the next four decades Soviet policy changed little, recognizing only "one China," the PRC, but—at least after the Korean War—almost invariably favoring a political rather than military solution to the "Taiwan question." The Soviets habitually used such pejorative terms as "lying," "KMT remnants," and "terrorists" to characterize the Taiwan government.[71] All the Eastern European Communist governments supported PRC control over Taiwan, the East Germans with particular fervor, since they believed that the Chinese were in a similar situation to themselves, with "imperialists" maintaining control over "their" respective territories in West Berlin and Taiwan. Both wanted to expel the "imperialists" from their territories, if necessary employing military force and with Soviet help to that end.[72] Both governments, too, were almost certainly more dedicated to the goal of reunification than were their Soviet patrons.

The chilly state of Soviet-Taiwanese relations made for occasional hostile diplomatic incidents. Soon after the Korean War ended, Taiwan seized a Soviet oil tanker, the *Tuapsi*, crossing the South China Sea from Vladivostok to Guangzhou, and detained all its 49 crew members. During the vessel's confused capture, four crew members eluded the Taiwan authorities and eventually returned to the Soviet Union, where, during a news conference in Moscow, on June 18, 1954, they charged that Taiwan had subjected the Soviet sailors to unspecified atrocities. One year later, 29 crewmen were returned to the Soviet Union, while the remainder chose to remain temporarily in Taiwan, nine of them subsequently settling in the United States and several others in West Germany. Even in 1958, seven crew members were still detained in Taiwan.[73] Unfortunately, all Taiwanese Foreign Ministry files on this episode remain closed, while the former Soviet archives have yet to release any files relating to it. Peter Ivanov's recent work on Russian-Taiwanese relations revealed that in August 1988 three of the four remaining Soviet ex-crewmen returned to the Soviet Union via Singapore. The final crewman chose to remain in Taiwan, and applied for ROC citizenship.[74]

On December 2, 1954, 18 months after the Korean War ended, the United States and Nationalist China signed a Treaty of Mutual Defense, formally committing the US to defend Taiwan against a mainland attack. The Treaty did not explicitly include the several groupings of offshore islands Nationalist forces still controlled. The PRC would use that ambiguity to test American resolve over the next several years in the three Taiwan Strait Crises, episodes which also had an impact of Sino-Soviet relations. Marshal Kliment Voroshilov, Chairman of the Presidium of the Supreme Soviet of the USSR, vehemently denounced this treaty as an outdated American attempt to regain its dominance over all China. He concluded by declaring that, in order to restore peace and security in the Far East, all Chinese territory must be liberated (reunified).[75] In December 1954, the MID publicly supported PRC demands for the withdrawal of American forces from Taiwan and the Taiwan Strait. The MID further castigated the "so-called" mutual security treaty as a "crude violation of international agreements and the sovereignty and territorial integrity of the PRC and therefore a violation of the United Nations Charter."[76]

The end of the Korean War allowed Mao to shift his attention back to

Taiwan. The KMT had used the Zhoushan Islands off the coast of Zhejiang province to harass PRC shipping to nearby Shanghai. Mao believed that those islands would be easier to take compared with the two clusters of Nationalist controlled offshore islands further south opposite Fujian province, Jinmen and Mazu. Hoping to dissuade the United States from implementing the Mutual Defense Treaty, and to create a diversionary feint, in September 1954, the PRC began shelling Jinmen and Mazu. The United States continued its firm support for the Nationalists, only accelerating the negotiations for the proposed treaty. The PRC did, however, partially attain its goals in launching the bombardment by liberating the Zhoushan Islands in January 1955, freeing up maritime traffic in and out of Shanghai, an action to which, PRC officials complacently noted, the Americans responded only by assisting with the evacuation of the islands. Having taken those islands, and realizing further actions only bolstered American support for Taiwan, the PRC ended the crisis.[77]

Publicly, the Soviet Union staunchly endorsed the Chinese action. Premier Nikita Khrushchev told several prominent American journalists: "The declaration that Taiwan and other islands were not Chinese territory contradicted existing international agreements and historical facts. Chiang Kai-shek was nothing more than a puppet ruler of the United States." Simultaneously, however, Soviet Foreign Minister Vyacheslav M. Molotov, while blaming the Americans for the shelling, expressed concern that these incidents might escalate into a greater war. Privately, Soviet UN Ambassador Valerian Zorin suggested that the Chinese were inclined "to be too trigger happy."[78] The Soviet press was extremely cautious in its coverage throughout the crisis. On the whole, the Soviets were uneasy over China's campaign in the Taiwan Strait. Soviet political leaders were focused on the succession to power which followed the death of Stalin in 1953, a struggle not settled until 1955. Neither American President Dwight Eisenhower nor his Secretary of State John Foster Dulles believed the Soviets had a major role in the crisis or wanted war.[79] Eisenhower believed the Soviet line was less violent, and discounted the likelihood of Soviet involvement if war broke out between the United States and China. Dulles further concluded the Soviets were overextended, and could not meet the demands of the Chinese government, even if they so wished. Dulles openly played upon the emergent differences between the Soviets and the Chinese, making conciliatory gestures to more moderate elements within the Soviet leadership. Ultimately, the Soviets regarded the Strait Crisis as a local matter, and sought to reduce tensions with the United States, not the reverse. Thus, while the years 1954 to 1956 may be considered a "golden age" for Sino-Soviet ties, the relationship, nonetheless, was an uneasy one.[80]

The islands remained a continuing irritant in international relations. Perhaps in retaliation for the shelling, in April 1955, Taiwan's secret service placed a bomb on an Air India flight, as it flew from Hong Kong to Indonesia carrying several Chinese Communists to the Bandung Conference of non-aligned nations, killing all passengers and crew on board. The Chinese government was infuriated when the Hong Kong government failed to prosecute anyone for this terrorist action, thereby confirming their existing belief that Hong Kong was full of KMT agents.[81] Although most military specialists considered the offshore islands, Jinmen and Mazu, indefensible, Chiang Kai-shek refused to abandon them but, regarding them as potential stepping-stones for a future invasion of the mainland, stationed over 100,000 troops there. The United States introduced nuclear-capable Matador missiles in the area.[82] Furthermore, the KMT continued to use the islands as launching pads for sporadic blockades of Chinese ports, for espionage, and to conduct propaganda.

In January 1958, Yuri Andropov, the Central Committee member responsible for CPSU relations with foreign Communist parties, prepared a detailed report on Taiwan, based on information from the PRC Ministry of Foreign Affairs. This document discussed problems in United States relations with the Nationalist Chinese, contending that the United States supported the most bellicose KMT elements, who like the Americans feared any possibility of negotiations between Taiwan and the PRC. It alleged that the United States, hoping to promote a tougher KMT stance, was secretly assisting Chen Cheng, a staunchly anti-Chiang Nationalist Chinese leader who had lived in exile in Hong Kong since 1949, a policy that led Chiang and his supporters to criticize American intervention in Taiwan's internal affairs. Soviet and Chinese Communist officials alike expected a future deterioration in Taiwanese-American relations. After the aging Chiang's death the Soviets anticipated a power struggle between his son, Chiang Ching-kuo, and Chen Cheng. They also noted that Taiwan's heavy military expenditures generated major economic problems, arguing that only massive infusions of American aid enabled Taiwan to survive.[83]

Two weeks later the Soviet Embassy in Beijing filed a more detailed follow-up report, which likewise suggested that Chiang's control over Taiwan was slipping and that, to prop up his regime, the United States had sent additional troops, ships, and missiles to Taiwan. The Soviets also noted how the Americans moderated Chiang's behavior, opposing his desire to invade the mainland so strongly, for example, that they reduced their aid to him and, by forcing Chiang to increase still further his excessive defense budget, exacerbated the island's economic crisis.[84]

Soviet diplomats also studied the press, clipping relevant Taiwanese and Hong Kong newspaper articles, including a Taiwanese report in January 1958 that Vice Admiral A. K. Doyle, Commander of US Forces in Taiwan, had assured a local audience that the United States possessed and was always ready to use nuclear-tipped missiles with a range of 600 miles to defend Taiwan against Communist attack.[85] Even so, both the PRC and the Soviet Union doubted whether the Americans would staunchly defend Taiwan should a PRC-Taiwan confrontation arise. On April 5, 1958, Soviet Ambassador Pavel Yudin met Premier Zhou Enlai at the Beijing airport, where they discussed the recent visit of American Secretary of State John Foster Dulles to Taiwan and his meetings with Chiang. Both noted that Dulles had spent less than two hours in Taiwan, which they thought too short for substantive talks. They observed that Chiang had appeared nervous during the meeting, and concluded that this was because he believed American support for Taiwan was diminishing.[86] On July 31, Nikita Khrushchev made a hurried trip to Beijing to discuss with Mao Chinese objections to Soviet proposals for a joint-submarine fleet and radio station. Following a cold airport reception, their four meetings over four days broke down in acrimony, with Mao characterizing the Soviet proposals as "great power chauvinism." During his meetings with Khrushchev and other Soviet leaders, Mao said nothing about his future plans regarding Taiwan, and specifically a major military operation to capture the disputed offshore islands, an omission Khrushchev subsequently resented.[87] Soviet leaders did not forget this lapse, which they believed was indicative of the worsening relationship between the Soviet Union and the PRC. At a meeting in Moscow in July 1963, Yuri Andropov told Deng Xiaoping, who led a high ranking Chinese delegation: "Long ago you ceased any sort of consultation with us. In 1958, the Chinese side did not inform us in a timely fashion about its intentions to carry out the shelling of the coastal islands in the Taiwan

Strait carried out soon after Khrushchev left Beijing." Andropov further noted that Mao Zedong admitted that the Chinese had already decided on the operation and had prepared for it, but "did not consider it necessary to inform the Soviet government about it."[88] At least one Russian scholar, Constantine Pleshakov, contended however that some evidence existed that Khrushchev knew in advance of the attack, but was given no details. He conceded, though, that the Soviet Embassy in Beijing was caught completely by surprise when the shelling in Jinmen began within weeks of Khrushchev's departure from Beijing, and the Soviets had absolutely no idea what China's goals were in mounting the operation.[89] Another Russian scholar, Viktor Usov, was also skeptical that Khrushchev did not know about the impending Chinese artillery shelling.[90] Nevertheless, they were the exceptions to those who believed this episode to be a probably deliberate omission by Mao, which impacted on subsequent Sino-Soviet relations.

Seeking to distract the Chinese population from domestic problems caused by the Great Leap Forward policy and the political crackdown following the Hundred Flowers Campaign, on August 23, 1958, the PRC again began shelling Jinmen and Mazu, inaugurating the Second Taiwan Strait Crisis, which the Soviets followed very closely. Chinese scholar Chen Jian noted: "The tension over the strait could legitimize the unprecedented mass mobilization in China to support the Great Leap Forward."[91] Scholars have cited additional reasons for the PRC action, including a desire to weaken the KMT government on Taiwan by demonstrating its inability to defend itself; a wish to take advantage of American and British preoccupation with the Middle East, where both nations had already intervened militarily in Lebanon and Jordan; and the quest to shore up Mao's credentials in the world Communist movement.[92] William Taubman, in his biography of Khrushchev, suggested that one reason Mao provoked the crisis was to sabotage Khrushchev's policy of peaceful coexistence with the West, specifically with the United States.[93] Whatever Mao's precise motivations, the incident quickly accelerated into a major international imbroglio, characterized by one academic as one of the "most dangerous international crises in Cold War history."[94] The United States rushed naval and military units to Taiwan and the Strait. On August 27, it declared that the defense of the shelled offshore islands was vital to the defense of Taiwan itself. On September 4, the PRC announced its territorial waters included the offshore islands. In response, Secretary of State John Foster Dulles declared that the United States would escort Taiwanese supply ships to Jinmen and Mazu, essentially daring the PRC to hit American vessels.[95] Meanwhile, shells rained daily on the islands, destroying ships, airfields, and buildings and killing and wounding numerous individuals, both civilian and military.

The American response was, however, unexpectedly forceful. After the PLA launched its first heavy artillery bombardment of Jinmen, and patrol boats were sent to blockade the islands, within a few days the United States dispatched a huge naval contingent to the Taiwan Strait. President Eisenhower and Secretary of State John Foster Dulles staunchly reaffirmed their commitment to protect Taiwan. American ships escorted Taiwanese resupply vessels and US jets provided air cover. Faced with the real threat of American military retaliation, Mao abandoned any hopes of seizing the islands or attacking Taiwan and, despite his harsh rhetoric, in practice his actions were very cautious. China refrained, for example, from firing on any American escort ships.

Despite strained Sino-Soviet relations, and the failure of the Chinese to inform him in advance of their plans during his recent visit, on the whole, Khrushchev initially welcomed the confrontation. Khrushchev pledged his backing and sent the Chinese Soviet long-range artillery, antiaircraft missiles, amphibious equipment, and aircraft.[96] On September 5, the Soviet newspaper *Pravda* sternly warned the United States: "Those who risk war will meet with disaster. The Soviet Union will help the Chinese people in every way."[97] Behind the scenes, the Soviets were far less confident about their Chinese "brothers." Secretly Khrushchev dispatched his Foreign Minister Andrei Gromyko to Beijing on September 6 to inquire as to China's goals in this operation. Premier Zhou Enlai assured Gromyko that the PRC had no intention of invading the islands, let alone Taiwan itself. For his part, Gromyko told the Chinese leader that Khrushchev would address an urgent letter to Eisenhower, supporting Beijing's position of September 8.[98] In subsequent meetings with Soviet Embassy officials, Mao promised no war over Taiwan. On September 19, Khrushchev sent another note to Eisenhower, reiterating his September 8 statement that an attack on China was an attack on the Soviet Union, which would respond accordingly. On September 22, Gromyko stated at the UNGA meeting in New York that "China was and still is one China, while the island of Taiwan with coastal islands was an integral part of Chinese territory illegally captured by the United States and awaiting its liberation."[99] These actions alarmed Western officials. A United States intelligence report concluded: "There would be a better than even chance that the Soviets would give the Chinese atomic weapons if the United States attacked targets in the mainland beyond coastal areas with nuclear weapons. Further if the United States nuclear attacks threatened the survival of the PRC, the Soviets might accept the risk of a general World War III."[100] Discountenancing rumors that during his recent visit to China Soviet Premier Nikita Khrushchev had attempted to moderate Chinese behavior, in mid-September British diplomats in Moscow noted that recent *Pravda* and other Soviet press articles took a much stiffer tone, emphasizing that the Soviets would regard any attack on China as equivalent to an attack on themselves, and characterizing Chinese efforts to regain the islands as "lawful measures of self-defense provided by the United Nations Charter."[101]

In October, the immediate crisis eased greatly as it became clear that the PLA would not land on the islands, while the shelling had already accomplished its domestic purpose of rallying support behind the regime, as well as focusing international attention on Mao. Beijing thereupon decided to bring the crisis to an end. On October 6, Zhou told Soviet chargé d'affaires S. F. Antonov that the PRC had decided to leave Jinmen in Taiwan's hands, in order to, in Zhou's words, "let the islands become a defense burden for Washington."[102] Beginning that day, shelling was suspended for two weeks. Then the Chinese decided shelling would take place only on odd-numbered calendar days, allowing resupply of the islands on even days. After two months, all shelling stopped. Throughout the Chinese were very careful to avoid a direct confrontation with the US.[103]

On October 12, 1958, Liu Xiao, the PRC Ambassador to the Soviet Union, met Marshal Grigory Zhukov, Head of the Soviet State Committee for Cultural Ties, and thanked him for Soviet support during the recent crisis. Zhukov reiterated to Liu that the Soviet Union believed there was only one China, the PRC, whose government must decide itself whether to use peaceful or military means to liberate Taiwan, and that American opposition to this constituted intervention in internal Chinese affairs. Zhukov urged that the Chinese publicize their position to mobilize world support, especially from third world countries. Liu, largely ignorant of American politics, asked Zhukov whether prominent Democratic opposition politicians, such as Adlai Stevenson and Lyndon Baines

Johnson, or the influential journalist Walter Lippmann, supported American recognition of the PRC.[104]

In practice, however, the crisis had wreaked considerable damage on Sino-Soviet relations. Throughout the crisis, the Soviet Embassy in Beijing sent almost daily reports to both the MID and the International Department of the CPSU Central Committee, and unlike earlier dispatches, which simply translated Chinese statements into Russian, these contained substantial editorial comment and analysis. This was perhaps an indication of growing Soviet skepticism regarding Chinese policies. In September 1958, for instance, Acting Ambassador S. F. Antonov sent Moscow a detailed report describing the situation.[105] Even so, during this crisis some Soviet officials, fearing an invasion could precipitate a major regional war, tried to moderate Chairman Mao Zedong's behavior, with several Soviet diplomats even questioning Mao's sanity. Speaking to the New Zealand Ambassador in Moscow in the early 1970s, Mikhail Kapitsa, a China specialist and Director of the Far East Department of the MID, recalled:

> The Chinese were then our allies, and had an obligation both as allies and as fellow Communists to keep us informed of their intentions. The American Pacific Fleet was steaming before Taiwan. Yet the Chinese rashly went ahead with their shelling attack without any consultation. [Foreign Minister Andrei] Gromyko and I went to Beijing on the 7 September, 1958 to learn what was behind the Chinese action. Mao was completely unconcerned, and said Russia will drop its atomic bombs on America and America will drop its atomic bombs on the Soviet Union. You may both be wiped out. China too will suffer, but will have 400 million people left over.[106]

Perhaps most significantly, Mao eventually succeeded in alienating Khrushchev, a major factor in precipitating the Sino-Soviet split. When Khrushchev, for example, learned that Mao planned to shell the islands only on alternate days, he declared that this was not a normal course of action, and suggested the Chinese leader might be insane.[107] While the Soviet leader continued his public support for China's actions, behind the scenes Mao's inconsistent policies infuriated Khrushchev, who forthrightly told Mao at a meeting in Beijing in October 1959, a year after these events: "As for the firing at the offshore islands, if you shoot, then you ought to capture these islands. If you do not consider it necessary to capture them, then there is no use in firing. I do not understand this policy of yours."[108] Khrushchev thought Mao might be surreptitiously trying to embroil the Soviets in a war, without their prior knowledge or agreement.[109] Despite his ally's strange and inconsistent methods, Khrushchev still officially supported the PRC and Mao's brinkmanship policies. When Khrushchev met President Eisenhower and his Secretary of State Christian Herter in Washington during an official visit in September 1959, Khrushchev held to a hard-line policy. Khrushchev reiterated that Taiwan was a province of China, and what went on there was part of the process of the Chinese Revolution. Interestingly and originally, Khrushchev compared Chiang Kai-shek to former Russian Premier Alexander Kerensky, overthrown by the Bolsheviks in October 1917. He also told Eisenhower that if an American general should take an American island, and declare it his territory, the United States would immediately suppress that rebellion. Eisenhower replied that those were not valid analogies, and that "their views were so divergent on this subject, there was really no point in discussing the question further." Khrushchev had the final word when he replied that "there could not be two legal governments in Taiwan, and the only possible answer was Beijing."[110]

Privately, however, Khrushchev viewed the liberation of Taiwan as politically significant but militarily unattainable, believing that, lacking an adequate navy, it was impossible for the PRC to initiate an amphibious invasion of the island. He made it clear to the Chinese that the Soviet Pacific Fleet would not help the Chinese to seize Taiwan by force, and that any military action would provoke a world war with the United States.[111]

The Two Chinas Question

Policy differences over Taiwan during the 1958 Strait Crisis and to some extent even during its predecessor in 1954, contributed to the breakdown of Sino-Soviet relations in 1958, after which many subterranean changes took place. By the late 1950s, the interlinked question of whether or not to recognize the island's government also became a divisive subject in Sino-Soviet relations, helping to drive the two Communist great powers further apart.

Officially, the Soviet Union unfailingly accepted the PRC position that it was the only legitimate Chinese government, which should represent all China, while the Nationalist government on Taiwan was an usurper, to be expelled from all international organizations, including the

UN. The idea that there were two distinct Chinese national governments originated from the British, who recognized the PRC as early as 1950, while stating that the question of who enjoyed sovereignty over Taiwan remained undecided. As a close American ally, Britain did not wish to cross the United States over Taiwan. Recognizing reality, until November 1971, Britain maintained a Consulate in Taiwan, while simultaneously acknowledging this provoked "complaint and suspicions by the PRC government."[112]

By the late 1950s, American officials recognized that PRC control of the mainland was well-established, and began to believe that, to maintain East Asian stability, the PRC and ROC must learn to live with each other. The major obstacle was that neither Taiwan nor the PRC would accept a de facto two Chinas policy, and both greatly resented American moves in this direction. British and American proposals to place Taiwan under UN trusteeship or organize a plebiscite under UN auspices to allow the people of Taiwan to determine whether they would join the PRC or become an independent nation, first appeared publicly in 1957. The doyen of American sinologists, Harvard University Professor John King Fairbank, questioned the logic of accepting only one China. He suggested instead that the United States should recognize "the independent Chinese government in Taiwan," while simultaneously "increasing contacts with the PRC," and making the latter's admission to the UN conditional on its renunciation of "the use of force to regain Taiwan."[113] While many influential American policy makers shared Fairbank's views, these never became official government policy, since American and British leaders realized that KMT leaders would never consider any plan envisaging self-determination.[114] Soviet officials nonetheless believed that the United States considered destabilizing Chiang's regime and replacing it with a government led by pro-independence Taiwanese nationalists.[115] During the 1958 Strait Crisis, Soviet officials noted the new American inclination toward a two Chinas policy, which they criticized because this would facilitate the continued presence of American servicemen in Taiwan.[116]

Since most countries recognized the ROC on Taiwan as the only legitimate government of all China, ROC representatives generally attended international conferences and other gatherings. That forced Soviet ministries and organizations to confront the question of which Chinese government should participate in international conferences held on Soviet or Eastern European soil, and whether Soviet and East

European delegates should attend international gatherings where the ROC represented China. On April 18, 1958, the MID directed relevant Soviet ministries and organizations that, when hosting international meetings, they should "echo" the PRC line that the ROC was "illegitimate" and, regardless of "which name is used for Taiwan: ROC, Formosa, Taiwan,... [w]e must ensure that no ROC people will be granted visas to any conferences held on Soviet territory, even if this would cause the Soviet Union to lose those conferences altogether." Indeed, in 1958, the Soviets had already denied prospective Taiwanese representatives visas for international conferences of epizootiologists and meteorologists.[117]

Despite opposition from the ROC, the PRC, and the Soviet Union, the issue of two Chinas arose frequently in connection with various international forums. Before a spring 1958 UNESCO meeting in Paris, Marshal Zhukov wrote to the CPSU Central Committee demanding that the PRC replace Taiwan in UNESCO. S. F. Antonov replied to Zhukov on the Central Committee's behalf that the Soviet Union should not even participate in the forthcoming UNESCO conference in Paris unless the PRC was admitted in place of Taiwan. Any other course "would only risk the implementation of a 'two Chinas' policy which both the USSR and PRC oppose."[118] Reluctant, however, to exclude themselves, the Soviets eventually decided not to boycott the meeting, but to propose at its first session that China's representation be switched from Taiwan to the PRC.

These issues came up again in July 1958, in a Beijing meeting between K. A. Chrugikov, the Communist Party's Vice Chief of International Organizations, and Gong Pu Shen of the Ministry of Foreign Affairs of the PRC, who discussed PRC and Taiwan representation at sporting events.[119] The PRC intended to withdraw from all organizations where Taiwan was also represented. The Ministry of Foreign Affairs of the PRC sought Soviet assistance in organizing a meeting of all Communist states to discuss the "two Chinas" question; in determining to which specific international organizations Taiwan belonged; and in persuading UN organizations to cease publishing Taiwan-generated materials. Thanking the Soviets for their past hard line on the "two Chinas" issue and hoping this would continue, Gong indirectly implied that the Chinese found the Soviet position slightly less uncompromising than was desirable, something which conceivably contributed to the deterioration in Sino-Soviet relations. In a note to Soviet diplomats, China contended that it would not serve in any international organization where Taiwan was also represented, such as the UN and any of its affiliated organizations. China would only cooperate with those organizations which did not recognize Taiwan, appreciated Soviet understanding of China's position, and trusted that Soviet policies discountenancing "two Chinas" would continue.[120]

Despite Chinese hopes, by 1958 the Soviet Union, like the United States and Britain, was gingerly exploring the possibility of "two Chinas," as the United States encouraged Taiwan to join several organizations to which the PRC already belonged, while the PRC position became steadily more intransigent. At two international meetings early that year, the 19th Congress of the Red Cross and Red Crescent, and the Worldwide Hydrometeorological Commission Congress, PRC representatives demanded that Taiwan delegates be expelled and refused to participate if they also attended. At the PRC's urging, Soviet and other Eastern Bloc states protested verbally, but none was prepared to boycott or walk out from these meetings, even though such measures, especially the latter, would have generated much valuable international publicity on the matter.[121]

Bolstering Chinese fears that the Soviets would allow the membership of both the PRC and the ROC in the UN, China noted, with grave concern, that the Soviet Union in 1957 urged the admission of both Koreas and Vietnams to the UN. In January 1957, in response to a western proposal to admit South Korea and South Vietnam as members of the UN, the Soviets "proposed instead that the [UNSC] consider the simultaneous admission of the Democratic Republic of (North) Korea, South Korea, the Democratic Republic of (North) Vietnam and South Vietnam." The Soviet proposal mentioned the "states" of Vietnam and Korea, which implied a sovereign status for both Koreas and Vietnams. The Soviets made this proposal without consulting either of their two allies, North Korea and North Vietnam, which greatly upset both governments.[122] As the Soviet Union had already recognized and established full relations with West Germany, the Chinese had good reason to fear Soviet intentions. In his carefully researched book based on Soviet archives, Ilya V. Gaiduk believed the Soviets were even prepared to grant full recognition to South Vietnam should the North Vietnamese not vehemently oppose the proposition, which they did. Thus, the Chinese government believed that a Soviet de facto recognition of two Koreas and Vietnams would foreshadow an imminent "two Chinas" policy on the part of the Soviet Union.

Open Sino-Soviet dissension on the subject occurred in summer 1958, when a UN-sponsored International Geology Conference, attended by Taiwanese representatives, was held in Moscow. The PRC decided to boycott the meeting, even though Dr. Dmitri Pushkov, who headed the Soviet delegation, wrote to the Chinese suggesting that they might unite with their Nationalist colleagues in one joint, cooperative delegation, a request the Chinese speedily rejected, castigating Soviet "duplicity." Pushkov again urged this solution, begging the Chinese to be reasonable; whereupon the Chinese asked the CPSU Central Committee whether he was violating official Soviet policy, or whether the Soviets now supported a "two Chinas" position.[123] Reprimanded by the Committee for taking a personal position on the Chinese issue, Pushkov apologized that he was a scientist rather than a politician, who had failed to appreciate his actions' broader implications. In mitigation he claimed that neither the CPSU nor the MID had responded to his earlier requests for guidance on the matter. After receiving Pushkov's apology, the Soviets assured the Chinese that no similar mistakes would occur in future, and the Chinese praised the Soviet resolution of the matter. The MID subsequently released a formal "Memorandum on the Two Chinas Question," reiterating the official line that the PRC was the only legitimate Chinese state and represented all of China.[124]

Chinese participation in sporting events likewise soon became contentious. The IOC recognized the COC, founded in Shanghai in 1924, as China's amateur athletic organization. After World War II, the COC moved to Nanjing, with Professor Tong Shui-Ye, arguably China's leading sports figure, as its general secretary and China's IOC representative. He remained in the mainland after 1949, when the COC split into a pro-Communist faction, soon rechristened the All-China Athletic Federation, while its pro-Nationalist counterpart fled to Taiwan with the COC archives. Each claimed to be China's sole athletic organization, confronting the supposedly apolitical IOC with a difficult dilemma, as it sought for a decade, ultimately unsuccessfully, to retain both organizations as participants in the Olympic movement and events.

Despite vehement PRC protests at Taiwan's presence, which it claimed violated the organization's own rule that only one association could represent each member country, in August 1954, representatives of both Chinese athletic associations attended the 19th Congress of the IAAF in Berne, Switzerland.[125] Four years later, the issue of Taiwan's participation in the international Olympic movement generated a lengthy, bitter dispute between the PRC and the IOC, on which the PRC demanded Soviet support. The PRC sent the MID officials copies of the lengthy, initially polite but increasingly acrimonious correspondence with the IOC over Taiwanese representation. The American nationality of Avery Brundage, the President of the IOC, gave added force to PRC claims that the IOC was merely a United States puppet. In January 1958, Brundage apologized to Tong for listing China's name inaccurately in an earlier publicity brochure, stating that this would not happen again. Tong and other Chinese nonetheless found infuriating Brundage's statement that "on Taiwan there is a separate government, recognized by the United Nations and most governments in the world." Brundage further warned Tong that PRC membership in the IOC was conditional on its good behavior. "Sports and politics do not mix. We [the IOC] don't appreciate representatives from your country raising political issues in our meetings."[126] On April 25, Tong responded with a lengthy exposition of the official PRC interpretation of Taiwan's status, denouncing the Nationalist government as an unrepresentative puppet regime, dependent on United States military and economic aid for its survival. Its UN membership, he argued, meant nothing, since that organization was only "an American machine, American dominated and controlled." The IOC should recognize only the PRC, not Taiwan, a mere PRC province. Accusing Brundage of taking "a hostile position to China," Tong attacked him for "rais[ing] a political issue" in the supposedly nonpolitical IOC.[127]

On June 1, Brundage declared he was only acting on behalf of the entire IOC and merely enforcing IOC rules. He warned Tong that the IOC was simply interested in playing sports, not in conducting politics, and that the PRC should resign from the IOC if it continued to violate the "Olympic standards and rules" it had promised to observe on joining the organization.[128] On August 19, Tong responded both to Brundage and to the entire IOC, enclosing declarations from both the PRC's Athletic Association and Olympic Committee that they were withdrawing, with immediate effect, from the IOC and all its federated associations. Claiming that Brundage had refused to answer his questions, Tong attacked him personally, charging: "You [Brundage] are a tool of the Americans. You have no right to be President of the IOC. The [entire] Olympic movement is controlled by the [American] imperialists."[129] Besides giving lengthy historical expositions of the PRC-IOC dispute over Taiwan's continued membership and setting out the Chinese view on Taiwan's status, the two enclosed declarations by the PRC Athletic Association and Olympic Committee contained similar accusations that the IAAF and IOC had become "tool[s] of American imperialism," and stated that PRC representatives would not return until Taiwan was entirely excluded from them.[130]

In July 1958, a four-day meeting of representatives of sports organizations from socialist countries, attended by all Soviet Bloc countries, including the USSR, was held in Beijing. Before it opened, several Chinese Politburo members hosted a reception for the delegates, attended by Foreign Minister and Deputy Prime Minister Chen Yi. The head of the PRC's Physical, Cultural, and Sports Committee told delegates the "two Chinas" strategy was an American plot to maintain control of Taiwan. He further declared that even though the PRC valued highly its participation in such international sporting events as the Olympics, it would not compromise its principles to this end, but would withdraw from all events where Taiwan was represented. The PRC decided to protest the IOC's effective recognition of two Chinas, and to leave the IOC movement altogether should this continue, as well as those seven international sports federations, including basketball, swimming, track and field, shooting, bicycling, and table tennis, that recognized Taiwan. Contending that its hard-line position "would only hurt the American imperialists," the PRC declared that, to avoid any tacit acceptance of two Chinas, even if Taiwan athletes were not participating, it would boycott sports events hosted by groups to which Taiwan belonged.[131] All the Soviet and other delegates present fully endorsed this position, promising to publicize the PRC demands, and to lobby their various organizations to force Taiwanese athletes to withdraw.[132]

None, however, considered emulating the PRC, which admitted that its athletic programs were still weak, in leaving the IOC, actions which might have had a major propaganda impact, but which would have jeopardized their own international sporting prestige. At an International Football Federation Congress in Stockholm, Sweden, representatives of more liberal Poland and Hungary did not even vote to exclude ROC representatives. In September 1958, Communist Bloc sports organizations met in East Berlin, their main goal to increase the number of medals their athletes won in such international sports fixtures as the Olympics. When the question of Taiwan's representation arose, the delegates affirmed their support for the PRC position and urged the IOC's "democratization," meaning the reduction of American influence. Far from withdrawing in solidarity, however, these organizations sought greater involvement in the IOC and its federated associations.[133]

Explaining its position in a press release to all sporting organizations, the IOC gave a factual account of the Chinese decision to withdraw. The IOC claimed that, while the organization always sought to remain above politics, "the PRC sent political agents, not sports figures to the meetings," who ignored repeated warnings, and "stubbornly tried to involve the IOC in their political interests." The IOC argued that the ROC's athletic committee was older and better established. The statement also defended Brundage as playing a "strictly neutral role in the Olympic movement." It concluded by hoping for the PRC's eventual return to international sports.[134] An unsigned MID response, possibly drafted for the Soviet Olympic Committee, expressed complete support for the PRC, denounced IOC actions as mistaken, and urged that this "abnormal position" be rectified and the PRC sports association recognized as the sole one for all China.[135] On reading this draft, Mikhail Zimyanin, a MID official, criticized it for bolstering the idea that two Chinas existed by even mentioning the Taiwanese sports association, albeit in a quotation from the IOC statement, and demanded greater precision in the document's concluding section. Ultimately, the statement was neither delivered nor published, perhaps indicating that Soviet officials considered it insufficiently strong, or maybe that they were fundamentally indifferent toward the matter.[136]

The acrimonious IOC-PRC relationship soon improved when, meeting in Munich on May 27, 1959, the IOC withdrew recognition from the Taiwanese Olympic Committee, "on the grounds it no longer represents sports for all China." The action enraged the Taiwan government, which like its PRC counterpart could not conceive of American citizens acting independently on the international stage and was, the British reported, "puzzled and annoyed by the apparent failure of the United States government to exercise adequate control over Brundage." Brundage stated that the "decision was based on a simple commonsense view of the situation, and was not motivated by political considerations." Although fearing that the IOC decision had ominous portents for its claim to represent all China, the ROC successfully applied to rejoin under the title of Taiwan, China.[137] Moderating its original position, shortly afterwards the PRC rejoined the IOC, subsequently becoming one of its most prominent members.

In October 1959, Khrushchev once again went to Beijing, this time to inform Mao of the results of his recent meetings with President Eisenhower in the United States, when Eisenhower had asked the Soviets why they did not take the same position on Taiwan as the Soviets already did on Germany. The Soviet Union established full diplomatic relations with the FRG in 1955, while maintaining full relations with its ally, the GDR. Eisenhower queried this apparent inconsistency of supporting a two Germanys policy, but still only recognizing one China. Khrushchev replied that China could not be compared with Germany, since China was one of the victors of World War II. Khrushchev pointed out to Eisenhower that both Korea and Vietnam, the remaining two states divided by the Cold War, had been partitioned as a result of war, and subsequently along a cease-fire line agreed upon by both sides at international conferences. Khrushchev assured Mao that Taiwan was an inalienable part, indeed a province, of China.[138] Thus, the Soviets argued there was no inconsistency in their policy of having full diplomatic relations with West Germany, and recognizing at least the de facto divisions of Korea and Vietnam, but maintaining there was no such thing as two Chinas.

As Sino-Soviet relations deteriorated rapidly in the late 1950s and early 1960s, the Soviets became far readier to contemplate an unapologetic "two Chinas" policy. In 1961 two Soviet diplomats in Beijing, political adviser F. Mochulski and third secretary G. Kireev, reported to Moscow that the PRC would only accept UN membership after Taiwan had been expelled from that body, and from all associated UN organizations, and only after all US troops had left Taiwan. Both diplomats believed that the PRC policy was unrealistic since 49 nations recognized Taiwan and only 39 the PRC, a balance that would never facilitate Chinese admission to the UN. They recommended that the Soviet government advise the PRC to this effect. They also believed that immediate PRC admission to the UN would enhance the international position of the Communist Bloc in its competition with capitalism. Escalating Sino-Soviet disputes notwithstanding, the diplomats noted that China could be a valuable Cold War partner, and on pragmatic grounds these Soviet officials therefore openly considered the idea of "two Chinas," favoring PRC admission to the UN without removing Taiwan.[139] Yet, whatever its problems with mainland China, publicly the Soviet

Union still maintained that only the PRC government was entitled to represent any part of China. In August 1963, the ROC, together with many other nations, affixed its signature to an international treaty banning nuclear testing in the atmosphere, under water, and in outer space. Three weeks later the Soviet Union refused to recognize this signature, protesting to the United States Department of State that "the Chiang Kai-shek clique does not represent anyone" and "had no right to act in the name of China," and "affirm[ing] there is only one Chinese state in the world, the PRC."[140] In terms of according China international recognition and status, even as Sino-Soviet relations steadily degenerated, for Soviet leaders ideological solidarity was still controlling when approaching Taiwan.

Conclusion

Before 1949, Russian and Soviet involvement in Taiwan was limited. Tsarist officials might have coveted the island as a potential colony, but any such designs were preempted by Japan's 1895 annexation of Formosa. To the Comintern's frustration, between the wars, firm Japanese control of the island kept the CPF a negligible political force, and Formosa became a strategic and industrial asset to Japan in intensifying hostilities against China. The island's wartime role and its impermeability to Communist penetration were major reasons why Stalin supported its postwar return to China. New archival evidence reveals that during the Chinese Civil War Stalin hesitated, uncertain whether to support the Communists or Chiang Kai-shek's Nationalists. By 1950, all such reservations had disappeared, and the Soviet Union was the first country to recognize the PRC, on October 1, 1949. From that date onward, the Soviet Union never officially recognized Taiwan's independence from the mainland. Superficially, over the next four decades, there was little change in Soviet policy, which recognized the existence of only "one China," the PRC, and from 1949 until the present Taiwan and the Soviet Union had no diplomatic relations. Although encouraging the Chinese to take Taiwan in early 1950, for the most part the Soviets did, however, favor a political rather than military solution of the "Taiwan Question," a bias that became apparent after the Korean War and an attitude they shared with the Americans. Interestingly, policy differences over Taiwan, which became apparent during the 1958 Strait Crisis and even, to some degree, the First Strait Crisis in 1954, contributed to the breakdown of relations between the two Communist giants in 1958. Beneath the surface many changes occurred after 1958, and somewhat contradictory attitudes emerged at different levels of the Soviet government. The principle of "one China," for example, was less strictly maintained at lower unofficial levels than at the highest official ones. Such practices also contributed to the dramatic deterioration of Sino-Soviet relations from the late 1950s onward. Over subsequent decades this, in turn, would pave the way for a cautious and limited Soviet-Taiwanese rapprochement.

8

The Limits of Friendship: Soviet and Russian Relations with Taiwan, 1960 to the Present

The Sino-Soviet split and, even more, the normalization of relations between the PRC and the United States in the 1970s, significantly altered the prevailing climate of Soviet-Taiwanese relations. Somewhat surprisingly, as was the case for Hong Kong and Macao, the accelerating deterioration of Sino-Soviet relations from the late 1950s through the 1960s scarcely affected the official Soviet attitude toward Taiwan. Soviet officials noted with some interest the existence of independence groups in Taiwan, but made no moves to support these. From the late 1960s, growing ties between the PRC and the United States nonetheless caused some individuals in both Taiwan and the Soviet Union to believe they could establish, if not full-scale diplomatic relations, at least some dealings between the two states. The first contacts between Taiwan and the Soviet Union took place, mostly in third countries, in 1968, and were perceived as mutually beneficial. Taiwanese leaders invariably showed themselves more flexible than their Soviet counterparts, since Nationalist Chinese politicians essentially had nothing to lose once their ties with the United States weakened. As relations between the Soviet Union and the PRC deteriorated, intelligence and diplomatic contacts between Taiwanese and Soviet officials made the island itself into a useful source of information for Moscow on such mainland developments as the Cultural Revolution.

A proposal in 1972 for economic cooperation, made by a Taiwanese company to the MID, might have been a first step toward closer and more direct Taiwanese-Soviet links, had the Soviet authorities correctly understood its implications and responded favorably, instead of rejecting it. Soviet-Taiwanese trade nonetheless developed, but for several decades was always conducted through third countries, such as Hong Kong or Japan. Growing and extensive commerce also took place between the Taiwanese and the Soviet Union's Eastern European allies, whom the Soviets themselves used as conduits for trade with Taiwan; they also worked through several private companies in Western Europe, in the FRG, for example. When the Soviet Union began its economic reforms in the 1980s, it came to view Taiwan as a successful example of the market economy, one of East Asia's "little dragons." Despite the absence of official diplomatic relations between Taiwan and the Soviet Union, unofficially there were significant and growing economic, political, military, and even cultural relations.

The Sixties: Exceedingly Cautious Changes

The 1960s saw tentative movement toward change on the part of both Taiwan and the Soviet Union, as both began to recognize that, as the international situation altered, neither should allow ideological differences entirely to dominate its relations with the other. Soviet officials in Beijing and elsewhere habitually scrutinized quite closely developments in Taiwan and ROC relations with other countries, especially with the United States, noting growing differences between Taiwan and the United States over particular policy issues and changes in their relationship. In its annual report to Moscow for 1961, the Soviet Embassy in Beijing stated that Taiwan officials viewed deteriorating Soviet-Chinese relations as advantageous to themselves. The same document also mentioned a conference held in October 1960 in Hong Kong between representatives of the PRC and Nationalist China, where the PRC delegates informed the latter that, should Taiwan agree to recognize Beijing's ultimate authority, it could keep its own government and maintain significant autonomy, a proposal effectively foreshadowing the "one country, two systems" policy implemented in Hong Kong and Macao in the late 1990s.[1]

In its frequent reports to Moscow in the early 1960s, the Beijing Embassy noted that American troops in Taiwan had dropped to only 4,500, fewer than the Americans had stationed in any other country. They recognized that, even though the Democratic presidential administrations of the 1960s never proposed recognizing the PRC, they were less close than their Republican predecessors to Chiang Kai-shek. During the 1960 election campaign, for example, Richard Nixon, the Republican presidential candidate, strongly supported continuing Taiwanese control of the offshore islands, whereas the Democrats, who considered them indefensible, preferred restricting American security commitments to defending merely the island of Taiwan itself. The Soviets noted, however, that up to the early 1960s, American economic and military aid to Taiwan still remained enormous. In fact, during the 1950s, Taiwan was the second greatest recipient of US foreign aid, as the United States financed and trained Taiwan's military, giving the island planes, ships, and artillery worth US$1.8 billion.[2]

In spring 1962, Soviet officials noted a significantly increased number of prominent Americans visiting the island-state and, in many cases, traveling on to America's increasingly jeopardized ally, South Vietnam. Among them were Attorney General Robert F. Kennedy, the Commander of the Pacific Fleet, Admiral Harry D. Felt, Assistant Secretary of State W. Averell Harriman, General Lyman L. Lemnitzer, Chairman of the Joint Chiefs of Staff, and the former Director of the CIA, Allen W. Dulles. All discussed issues relating to Southeast Asian security with various Taiwanese military and political leaders, including President Chiang Kai-shek, who was assured by Harriman that the United States still opposed PRC admission to the UN and its position that the ROC was the only Chinese state remained unchanged. Yet even the tightly controlled Taiwanese press reported some differences between the US and Taiwan. Whereas Taiwan sought to exploit political and economic difficulties in the PRC, which might enable Taiwan to invade the mainland, the United States urged restraint. When Taiwan sought to revise the 1954 Mutual Security Treaty to include offensive action against the PRC, Harriman—who privately favored American recognition of the PRC—and other visitors emphasized to Chiang that the treaty would remain strictly defensive. American officials also opposed provocative actions by Taiwan, such as reconnaissance flights over offshore PRC islands, whereas during the Eisenhower administration the US had sponsored covert Taiwanese military operations—occasionally launched from Hong Kong—against both the PRC mainland and its offshore islands.[3]

From September 6 to 17, 1963, Chiang Ching-kuo, Minister of Defense and Chiang Kai-shek's son and heir, visited the United States. There he met President John F. Kennedy, Secretary of State Dean Rusk, Averell Harriman, Admiral Harry Felt, Assistant Secretary of State Michael Forrestal, General Maxwell D. Taylor, Kennedy's White House military adviser, and Secretary of Defense Robert McNamara. Soviet diplomats in Beijing and Washington sent Moscow detailed reports on his visit, which coincided with escalating Sino-Soviet tensions. The reports described changes in American policy toward Taiwan, notably a continuing reduction and anticipated forthcoming total discontinuation of all non-military American economic aid to Taiwan, indicating both the declining priority American policy makers accorded Taiwan, and also the island's growing economic strength.[4] American officials themselves thought the Soviets favored the younger Chiang. In October 1963, several American embassy personnel attended a seminar in Moscow on the escalating Sino-Soviet crisis. Political Affairs Officer Malcolm Toon reported to Washington that while Chiang Kai-shek always talked of returning to the mainland, he knew he could never succeed. The Soviets, Toon claimed, recognized that the aged Chiang was by then a mere figurehead, and real power, they believed, rested in the hands of Chiang Ching-kuo, whom the Soviets suspected hated the United States and was favorably disposed to the USSR.[5]

During the 1960s, official Soviet support for the position that only the PRC represented China, that Taiwan should return to mainland China, and the Nationalist government was illegitimate, remained unchanged, even though the Soviets occasionally sent some contradictory signals. In 1965, Taiwan declared that, like most states, it adhered to the international Metric Convention, which France, the metric system's originator, accepted. Bulgaria, which often acted as a Soviet surrogate, formally protested against France's action, stating that, as the sole country legally entitled to represent the Chinese, only the PRC should be admitted into the Legal Convention.[6] Even in 1967, Soviet support for the PRC still remained overtly firm. When Taiwan joined the Swiss-administered Universal Postal Union, the Soviet Union, Ukraine, and Belorussia all sent the Swiss government identical protest notes.[7]

Yet as Sino-Soviet relations degenerated during the 1960s, the Soviet Union for the first time acknowledged the possibility that Taiwanese alternatives to Chiang Kai-shek's hard-line regime existed. In September

1962, Soviet Ambassador in Japan V. Vinogradov forwarded to the Far East Department of the MID without any comment a letter and a document that the Head of the Taiwan Overseas Organization, an independence opposition group, had sent him. The document pleaded for Soviet "support for the independence of Taiwanese from the perspective of defending peace and justice," proclaiming:

> Taiwan is still under the rule of a foreign government, the ROC. In 1945 China was ordered to occupy Taiwan, then a Japanese territory, disarm Japanese troops and seize administrative power. Nothing in the Peace Treaty with Japan of 1953 said it should be turned over to the Nationalists. Taiwan is still under colonial rule 17 years after World War II ended. Taiwan and its people are under military occupation by a foreign government. The Chiang regime has turned Taiwan into a war base causing great suffering to the Taiwan people—violating their human and economic rights. The Atlantic Charter of 1941 and the United Nations Charter both reject this situation. Taiwan is separate from the mainland historically and geographically and legally belongs to the Taiwanese. While numerous states in Asia and Africa are gaining independence, only Taiwan remains under colonial occupation. We demand our independence under the right of self-determination.[8]

No further information on either this organization or Moscow's reaction is available, and no archival evidence suggests that the Soviets either supported or opposed the Taiwanese struggle for independence, even though they contemporaneously assisted Uighur separatist groups in China's northwestern Xinjiang province, which bordered the Soviet Union. Yet the very fact that a Soviet Ambassador transmitted these materials to Moscow suggests a certain Soviet interest in the possibility of abandoning the one China policy and utilizing alternative groups in Taiwan.

Three years later the issue of Taiwanese self-determination came up again, in connection with the question of Chinese representation at the forthcoming 20th UN session. Richard Koo, President of the Formosan Association, a different independence group, told the Soviet Ambassador in Tokyo that a Taiwanese observer should attend the UN debate, "so that the will of the Formosan people need not be ignored," arguing that Chiang's "control is illegitimate and contrary to the wishes of the Taiwanese people." He demanded Taiwanese self-determination, stating that "Formosa belongs to neither Chinese regime—Communist or Nationalist," and claiming that "[t]he rights of the Formosan people were mercilessly tramped over by decisions of the US," whereas "[t]he UN is supposed to support the ideals of the Taiwanese." Arguing that "[i]t is not [their] issue" whether the Communists or Nationalists officially represented China, the association sought Soviet support in the forthcoming debate for its position.[9] Again, the Soviet ambassador forwarded this appeal without comment to Moscow, yet its very dispatch demonstrated some Soviet interest. Clearly, by the mid- to late 1960s, the Soviet Union knew of the existence of independence movements organized by native Taiwanese, who supported neither Chinese government, and whose claims for self-determination conceivably might provide useful ammunition in the entrenched ideological conflict with China.[10]

As Sino-Soviet relations deteriorated in the mid-1960s, Moscow and Taipei made tentative gestures in each other's direction. Soviet officials began to regard contacts with Taiwan as potential sources of valuable information on such mainland developments as the Cultural Revolution. In 1965, Soviet diplomats invited ROC representatives to a Soviet embassy reception in Tokyo. At the UNGA in New York, Soviet officials no longer sponsored or fervently advocated PRC admission to the UN.[11] Almost simultaneously, in 1967, the Taiwanese Foreign Ministry instructed its overseas embassies and consulates to permit ROC diplomats to talk and socialize with Soviet diplomats under certain, albeit unspecified, conditions, after which such meetings occurred increasingly frequently in Asian and Western capitals. Meanwhile a local Taiwanese newspaper editorial demanded changes in ROC attitudes toward Communist countries.[12]

Increasing Contacts, 1968–1977

Throughout the later 1960s and early 1970s Sino-Soviet relations continued to deteriorate, due to ideological, political, and cultural differences, Far Eastern border disputes, and Chinese fears of Czech-style Soviet intervention.[13] As the Nixon administration gradually moved toward rapprochement with mainland China, US-Taiwan political and military relations likewise declined commensurately. To convince the PRC the United States was no longer militarily hostile, in November 1969 the US ended its Seventh Fleet operations in the Taiwan Strait.[14] Watching their onetime closest partners draw ever nearer to each other, the Soviet Union and Taiwan alike began to reassess their own past antagonism and even, it seems, to collaborate in the sphere of intelligence on mainland China. In October 1968, Chiang Kai-shek directed KMT party and government officials to exercise restraint in public statements and articles on the Soviet Union, and openly urged international anti-Mao forces, including the Soviet Union, to unite.[15] That same month the *Washington Post* stringer Fox Butterfield reported that Ku Yu-Hsiu, a member of both the ROC National Assembly and the prestigious Academia Sinica, who taught at the University of Pennsylvania, had attended an International Scientific Conference in Moscow. While traveling on a United States passport, Ku had the approval of the Taiwanese authorities. Taiwan officials refused to confirm Ku's visit, the first by a Nationalist Chinese official to Soviet territory since 1949.[16]

One month later, in November 1968, Victor Louis, a Soviet citizen also known as both Viktor E. Lui and Vitali Yevgen'yevich, visited Taiwan, meeting Chiang Ching-kuo, with whom he reportedly discussed the poor state of PRC-Soviet relations, before spending four days touring Taiwan.[17] According to Ivanov, Louis promised Chiang that if Taiwan went to war against the PRC, the Soviet Union would maintain a friendly neutrality, even possibly limited cooperation.[18] A recent article, drawing on the memoirs of an official involved, suggests that the Soviet Union sought an alliance with Taiwan with the intent to overthrow the PRC.[19] Relations between the Soviet Union and China deteriorated to such an extent, that "Beijing became increasingly concerned that the strategic western border region of Xinjiang may become the focal point of conflict between the two countries."[20] It seems likely that the Soviets were sounding out the ROC over a possible two-front invasion of the PRC, the Soviets driving from Central Asia into China's northwest, while Taiwan invaded from the East. The younger Chiang, who spoke fluent Russian, had lived in the Soviet Union from 1925 to 1937, attending a military academy and marrying a Russian wife, which had already provoked American suspicions that he might be a Communist agent, fears that Louis' visit intensified.[21] Louis, the first Soviet visitor to Nationalist China in 19 years, was officially a journalist, married to a British woman, who worked for the *London Evening News*. It was well-known, however, that he was a KGB or secret police agent who frequently undertook highly sensitive Soviet missions, acting, for example, as an intermediary in the sale of the memoirs of Stalin's daughter, Svetlana Alliliuyeva. The MID's sole source of information on this visit was a news clipping from the English-language *Bangkok Post*, itself derived from a *Washington*

Post article, which the Soviet Embassy in Thailand copied, translated into Russian, and sent to Moscow. This suggests that Louis may have visited Taiwan at the behest, not of the MID, but of the CPSU's International Department, then headed by future General Secretary Yuri Andropov. Conceivably, this might indicate that the CPSU was taking a larger and more innovative role than the more cautious MID in directing international policy.[22] Taiwan never officially announced this visit, but the news was leaked to Stanley Karnow of the *Washington Post*, who reported it.[23] Although neither Taiwan nor the Soviets released any official statement on Louis' visit, the *Bangkok Post* article speculated that his objective was to establish some Soviet contacts, and perhaps even diplomatic and trade relations, with Taiwan. The *Bangkok Post* argued: "If the island of Taiwan does remain independent of the Chinese mainland, then the Russians have an interest in establishing relations and trade with it as one of the most influential smaller countries of the region."[24]

On returning to Moscow, Louis published several articles favorable to Taiwan in the Soviet press.[25] Writing in the *Washington Post*, moreover, he stated that he had found that he and Taiwanese officials, diplomats, and economists shared a common language. Louis praised the island's economic development, its agricultural policies, and "its traditional respect for the elderly for which the Chinese are famous." Those features, according to Louis, contrasted sharply with the mainland situation. He also noted that the Taiwanese took pride in no longer requiring American economic aid, and "maintaining an independent foreign policy." Although Louis was less complimentary toward Taiwan's political system, drawing parallels with the mainland, such as the "cult of personality and glorification of Chiang Kai-shek," he wrote much more positively of the latter's son and heir apparent, the younger Chiang, then Minister of Defense. Taiwan, he concluded, would welcome Soviet investment and opportunities to export products to the Soviet Union and Eastern Europe.[26] Both Taiwanese and Soviets used this visit to warn their former partners that they too could turn elsewhere. Chiang Ching-kuo even hinted he would consider reestablishing diplomatic relations with the Soviet Union, while allowing the Soviets to maintain formal relations with the PRC. Nevertheless, Chiang was highly skeptical, "suspecting that Louis' approach was another piece of Soviet psychological warfare against Beijing."[27] Western observers noted that anti-Soviet posters quietly disappeared from Taiwan's streets. Beijing declined to publicize Western reports of moves by Chiang Kai-shek toward a rapprochement with the Soviets. However, on March 10, the British Embassy in Beijing reported that the *People's Daily* had recently finally responded to Louis' visit under the headline: "Soviet revisionists step up counter-revolutionary collusion with the Chiang Kai-shek bandit gang."[28]

A few months later, in March 1969, Taiwan's Vice Minister of Education reciprocated with a semi-official visit to the Soviet Union.[29] On April 18, 1969, the *Washington Post* reported a possible return visit to Taiwan by Louis in May, but due to extensive press publicity he canceled his trip at the last moment. Interestingly, the Hong Kong and British governments decided that if Louis requested a visa to go to Hong Kong, it would be denied.[30] In May 1969, two Nationalist Chinese cabinet ministers, the Minister for Tourism and the Minister of Communications, attended a world conference on tourism in Bulgaria, an episode Beijing strongly denounced for violating the one China policy the Soviet Union and its Eastern Bloc allies had always endorsed. Beijing protested formally to Bulgaria, and on June 4, the *People's Daily* assailed their presence as "a crime committed by Bulgaria," characterizing the visit as part of a joint Soviet-US plot to create two Chinas, charges reiterated by the mainland Ministry of State Security.[31] Western diplomats in Moscow and Taipei noted that this incident marked a genuine thaw on both the Taiwan and Soviet sides.[32]

Some evidence suggests that, if only for a limited period in the late 1960s, Taiwan and the Soviet Union collaborated in the intelligence sphere. At the close of 1969, the British government noted a rumor that an influential Soviet general had secretly visited Taiwan, but the Foreign Office declared that it had found no supporting evidence of this. British diplomats agreed with "an editorial in the Taiwanese *China News* on December 26, 1969" that popular belief in "Soviet widespread penetration in East Asia is very exaggerated. According to the editorial," they stated, "the reality is very different; any penetration is very limited." The same newspaper also suggested that the August 1968 Russian invasion of Czechoslovakia had damaged Soviet moral standing and prestige in Taiwan.[33] According to Lo Chi, then Deputy Director of the Government Information Office, Taiwan's secret service agency, during 1968 and 1969, intensive exchanges of intelligence information on China nonetheless occurred between Taiwan and the Soviet Union, with over 30 contacts in all taking place.[34] In February 1970, Hsieh Jen-Chao, a member of the

Foreign and Overseas Compatriot Affairs Committee of Taiwan's parliament, the Legislative Yuan, published a series of articles in the *Independent Evening Press*, one of which stated: "At this time we should not regard the Soviet Union as our enemy."[35] Hsieh's statement represented the most outspoken public advocacy to date of a reversal of traditional ROC hostility toward the Soviet Union, indicating the extent to which, despite continuing caution and suspicion, ROC views of the Soviets had evolved over the previous decade.

In fall 1971, the UN voted to admit the PRC and expel Nationalist China.[36] In February 1972, President Richard Nixon visited mainland China, and as his trip ended the two powers released the Shanghai Communiqué, formally stating that the United States recognized there was only "one China," of which Taiwan was part. Privately, the United States also pledged not to support Taiwan's independence. These developments stunned both Taiwan and Soviet officials, giving them further reason to move toward each other. In New York, the Soviets had already made a noticeable but nuanced shift in their policy on PRC admission to the UN. In previous years, the Soviet Union had sponsored the annual resolution to admit the PRC as the representative of China. In 1971, the Soviet Union supported but no longer sponsored this resolution.[37] From late 1971 onward, Taiwan's Foreign Minister, Chou Siu-kai, publicly and privately discussed the possibility of relations with Eastern European countries and the Soviet Union. He told the KMT central committee in March 1972 that, while Taiwan remained anti-Communist, "so long as our basic national policy is not jeopardized, we may study the possibility of establishing trade, economic, and other relations with Communist countries which are in the interest of both sides."[38] Chou broke new ground by speaking specifically of the Soviets and even raising the possibility of secret talks with them, a veiled threat to the United States. Chou said, "We are anti-Communist. Without affecting our fundamental policy, our philosophy, we will have to try to explore what we could do with countries (such as the Soviet Union) which are not hostile to us."[39] Probably at his father's direction, the more cautious Chiang Ching-kuo effectively rebuffed Chou, stating that the press had misconstrued his remarks and taken some statements out of context, and reaffirming the ROC's continuing ties to the United States and other anti-Communist states.[40] In June, the State Department reported Chou's demotion to Minister without Portfolio "because of his outspoken position on the desirability of relations with Communist countries." Soon afterwards, Chou left the cabinet entirely, a temporary political exile. However, after Chiang Ching-kuo succeeded to the presidency in 1975, Chou reemerged as a foreign policy adviser.[41]

While Taiwanese policy retreated and moves toward more extensive relations with Communist states stalled, the ROC did not resume its earlier attitude of no dialogue and total hostility toward them. In March 1972, for example, Taiwanese newspapers reprinted in full an article from the Soviet journal *New Times*, supporting Chiang Kai-shek's renomination as ROC President. That same month four Taiwan journalists visited the Soviet Union, while Fei Hua, Taiwan's Commissioner for International Economic Cooperation, went to Moscow to discuss commercial ties with Soviet officials, trips neither Taiwanese nor Soviet officials would confirm.[42] Meanwhile, Soviet-Taiwanese trade through such third parties as Hong Kong and Japan expanded, as did extensive commerce between Taiwan and Soviet satellites in Eastern Europe, whom, together with several private companies in Western Europe, including one in the FRG, the Soviets used as intermediaries. A State Department intelligence assessment reported: "The ROC has embarked on a campaign of all out diplomacy. More than ever, Taipei is prepared to separate economics from politics, to the extent of being willing to trade with the USSR and Eastern Europe.... The new flexibility in Taipei's foreign policy reflects a determination to survive."[43]

Had the Soviet authorities been more receptive, a 1972 proposal for economic cooperation that a Taiwanese company submitted to the Soviet Foreign Trade Ministry and the MID, which rejected it, might have represented a first step toward deeper Taiwanese-Soviet relations. On January 7, 1972, "Consul Industrial Corporation, Ltd. requested commercial relations with the following Soviet firms that conduct international trade: *Stankoimport* [mechanical equipment], *Avtoexport* [air equipment], *Soiuznefteexport* [oil], *Soiuzximport* [chemical], *Medexport* [medical supplies], and *Exportkhleb* [grain]." Consul Industrial Corporation, Ltd. described itself as an export-import firm that had represented numerous foreign companies in Taiwan for over 28 years, and had established ties to large, solid European companies. The firm stated that it sought to import goods from the aforenamed companies and wished to send them catalogs and information on current markets for their products in Taiwan. In the absence of diplomatic relations, Consul sought "an agreement based on barter deals through mediators [third countries]," and "suggest[ed] as a mediator, the West German firm 'Kiling and Company,' located in Bremen, which had its own branches in Hamburg, Istanbul, and Zurich."[44] Signifying the importance of this letter, the Eastern Department of the Soviet Foreign Trade Ministry declared that this was the first occasion since 1950 any Soviet firms had received Nationalist Chinese proposals to establish commercial relations. The Ministry of Trade cautiously advised that any Soviet firm which received such enquiries "not respond because the USSR, as far as it is known, regards Taiwan as an integral part of the PRC, and does not have any relations with the Taiwanese regime."[45] In February 1972, the Far East Department of the MID likewise informed the Beijing Embassy that, at a forthcoming conference which Taiwan delegates would attend, the Soviets would announce: "The only representative of China is the PRC."[46] As with Hong Kong, Soviet bureaucrats' near reflexive continuing deference to the mainland position on Taiwan largely precluded the optimal development of economic opportunities.

Soviet officials nonetheless displayed considerable interest in political and economic developments in Taiwan. In Washington, two State Department East Asian specialists responded to questions on Taiwan from the Soviet Embassy's First Secretary, Viktor Krasheninnikov, by describing Taiwan's economic successes, especially the increases in its gross domestic product.[47] The American Embassy in Tokyo even reported unsubstantiated rumors of Soviet investments in Taiwan through Austria, inquiring whether such reports had surfaced in Taipei.[48] Soviet leaders were pleasantly surprised that Taiwan did not collapse after its expulsion from the UN. Soviet diplomats in neighboring countries sent Moscow detailed and accurate reports, noting that the island's literacy rates and personal per capita income far surpassed those of mainland China, and the huge expansion of exports from Taiwan, which every year enjoyed diplomatic relations with fewer nations but commercial ties with more. Soviet officials responded positively to the appointment of Chiang Ching-kuo as premier and his father's clear heir apparent, arguing that "he will regard Taiwan increasingly as an independent state in its own right."[49] The behavior of other nations did not necessarily bear out this prophecy. In the wake of Taiwan's expulsion from the UN, in March 1972, Britain closed the doors of its Consulate in Tamsui, outside the capital Taipei, converting the ancient and historic former Portuguese castle into a museum, and in return was allowed to raise its representation in Beijing to ambassadorial status. The United States took over the representation of British interests.[50]

While still eschewing official links, informally Taiwan and the Soviet Union moved closer. On May 12, 1973, three to five Soviet warships, including destroyers and submarines, passed through the Taiwan Strait between 20 and 40 miles from the mainland coast, the first such occasion since 1949, and then circumnavigated Taiwan, a voyage they would never have undertaken without the ROC government's knowledge and permission.[51] Taiwan defense officials stressed to their concerned American counterparts that their passage occurred on the high seas and was closely scrutinized by ROC units. Soviet officials denied that their government had notified Taiwan in advance of the warships' course.[52] Most Taiwanese believed the Soviets sought to demonstrate their naval strength to the mainland and test its defenses.

While flirting with Taiwan, the Soviet Union feared that formal official relations might further complicate its dealings with the mainland, making future reconciliation almost impossible, and damaging its international image as a leading Communist power. Taiwan, on its side, feared that moving too close to Russia might provoke the PRC into militant action, such as an invasion of Taiwan, while jeopardizing its American and anti-Communist support.[53] In June 1973, Chiang Ching-kuo reassured the American Ambassador there that the ROC held firmly to its anti-Communist policy and "would not consider establishing any understanding or relationship of any sort with the Soviet Union."[54] Even so, on two occasions, in late 1970 and again in July 1976, the ROC considered but rejected a Soviet request to use the Pescadores Islands as a naval refueling base. In November 1978, several Soviet freighters visited the Taiwanese port of Makung for repairs.[55] Such episodes sufficed to disturb other Western officials. In September 1974, J. E. Hoare, Head of the Far Eastern Department of the British Foreign Office, cautioned the Soviets that their attempts to improve ties with Taiwan were "fishing in troubled waters," and would ultimately prove unsuccessful.[56]

Soviet-Taiwanese Relations after US Withdrawal of Recognition, 1978–1990

For much of the 1970s, American and PRC relations stagnated, but on December 15, 1978, the two countries announced they would open full diplomatic relations on January 1, 1979. The United States withdrew recognition from Taiwan, even though arms sales and unofficial links continued. Shocked Taiwanese leaders, believing they carried little weight in American deliberations, began further to reorient Taiwan's diplomacy, cultivating broader connections and greater flexibility, while attempting to reduce Taiwanese dependence on the United States, an agenda which offered additional opportunities to the Soviet Union. While Taiwanese leaders were taken aback, Soviet officials had already predicted the full normalization of Chinese-American relations. In a report issued by the CPSU Central Committee on August 30, 1978, the Soviets contended that United States President Jimmy Carter had decided on the full normalization of relations by the end of the year, provided that the PRC permitted the United States to continue trade and military assistance to Taiwan, allowed it to maintain a "bureau" in Taipei to handle American-Taiwanese affairs and, most importantly, "indicated" that Beijing would refrain from using military force to recover Taiwan.[57]

Meanwhile, the MID asked its diplomats in various countries to submit assessments of the future of Taiwan.[58] The Soviet representatives at the UN Mission in New York believed that Taiwan would further expand its economic ties with the US and Japan, while developing some with the PRC. Taiwan would not, however, establish direct ties with Beijing, because Beijing wished Taiwan to recognize at least its own nominal suzerainty. The Soviets believed Taiwan's forcible recovery could not be considered a real possibility; and that, should relations between the PRC and Taiwan deteriorate, Taiwan would seek UN membership. If Taiwan moved toward independence, the United States would warn it that any declaration of independence would damage US-Taiwan relations. The Soviet Embassy in Uruguay noted that the Taiwanese believed the poor Sino-Soviet relationship precluded any PRC military invasion of Taiwan. In February 1979, the Soviet Embassy in Singapore submitted a report stating that the PRC displayed substantial distrust of Beijing's initiatives toward Taiwan. This dispatch placed quotation marks around all expressions mentioning "good will" and "peaceful initiatives," and argued that the PRC was acting more peaceably toward Taiwan only to conciliate the United States, whose power might offset that of the Soviets in East Asia. In early December, the Soviet Embassy in Japan commented on Taiwan's increasing economic prosperity, with annual growth rates of 8.5 percent, among the highest in Asia, which it contrasted with the PRC's prevalent poverty, noting, for example, that Taiwan's per capita income was tenfold that in the PRC. Soviet diplomats in Tokyo also described Taiwan's extensive and growing trade with various countries in Eastern Europe, including the Warsaw Pact members East Germany, Czechoslovakia, Poland, and Hungary, and how easily their businessmen obtained visas to Taiwan, perhaps implying the Soviets should follow suit. On receiving this dispatch, the MID asked the Ministry of Foreign Trade to submit by the end of the year a full report on the development of foreign commerce between Taiwan and other Communist countries, and in response received a detailed synopsis with statistics for 1970 through 1978.[59]

In 1980 and 1981, the Soviet Embassy in Japan sent the MID further detailed dispatches on Taiwan, based primarily upon Taiwan and Hong Kong newspaper sources. While conceding that Taiwan and the Soviet Union remained largely ignorant of each other, these argued that Taiwan officials no longer considered the Soviets threatening, but desired greater mutual trade and understanding.[60] Their January 13, 1982 report included the full text of an address by Chiang Ching-kuo to the Taiwan military, stating that allegations that Taiwan was "having contacts with the Soviet Union" were merely PRC propaganda, lies intended "to ruin our relations with the 'democratic states.'"[61] Later that year, the Soviets quoted Taiwan's Economic Minister, John Chang Kuan Shih, to the effect that Taiwan would establish no cultural, commercial, or tourist links with the Soviet Union.[62] Possibly these denials indicated that such contacts existed and at least some prominent Taiwan leaders supported them; alternatively, they may have been designed to restrain the US government's pro-mainland bias.

In 1982, China's paramount leader, Deng Xiaoping, announced his famed "one country, two systems" blueprint for Hong Kong and Macao. Upon their handover to China in 1997 and 1999 respectively, both Hong Kong and Macao would retain their own existing political, economic, and social systems, while China would have overall sovereignty and control over foreign affairs and defense. Though this declaration was primarily intended to reassure Hong Kong and Macao, both of which were very apprehensive as to their future under Chinese rule, another target was Taiwan. Chinese leaders hoped the island might be enticed and prodded into peaceful unification with the mainland after the return of Hong Kong and Macao. The Soviet Union recognized that despite these assurances, "one country, two systems" would be a very difficult proposition for

Taiwan to swallow. Taiwan labeled "one country, two systems" and all its assurances for Taiwan as "Communist propaganda," and even declared that instead of returning to the PRC, Macao and Hong Kong should revert to Taiwan, since it was the only legitimate government of all China. While Soviet diplomats reaffirmed that Taiwan was a part of China, they privately noted that Taiwan would never agree to reunite peacefully, and firmly believed that military force, war, and conquest would be needed to secure Taiwan's return to the PRC.[63]

The Soviet Union nonetheless hoped to finesse a difficult situation, seeking to improve its ties with Taiwan without still further alienating China. The Soviet Embassy in the Netherlands wrote a lengthy report favorably describing how the Dutch had handled their relations with both Taiwan and the PRC. The report noted that officially the Netherlands maintained that there was only one China, namely, the PRC. Several large multi-national Dutch companies, including Shell, Philips, and Unilever, all considered China a huge potential market for their exports, and the Dutch government wished to encourage the rapid conclusion of agreements between those companies and the PRC. Soviet diplomats also noted that in truth, however unofficially, the Netherlands recognized that two Chinas did exist, the second being in Taiwan, with which the Netherlands had few political but numerous economic ties. The Soviets commented that Taiwan, together with Hong Kong, Singapore, and South Korea, was one of the fastest growing economies in Asia, and might and ought to constitute a good trading partner not just for the capitalist but also for the socialist world. The report noted that Taiwan had very low labor costs but produced extremely high quality goods, which the Soviet Union, like the Netherlands, could use. The Netherlands, it pointed out, also understood that developing political ties with Taiwan would seriously and negatively impact its relations with the PRC, which were crucial for the long term future, because over time economic ties with the PRC would become more important than those with Taiwan. The Netherlands had therefore been able to maintain good relations with both the PRC and Taiwan.[64] The Soviet Embassy almost certainly produced this detailed report in order to explain to the MID how other countries successfully managed to finesse the "two Chinas" issue.

The Soviet Union and its successor state, the Russian Federation, themselves subsequently adopted similar policies, as they increased economic and cultural ties with Taiwan, but retained political ties only with China, a strategy the Chinese government understood and accepted without submitting any complaints to the Russian government. In 1988, the President of the Taiwanese Chamber of Commerce led a large delegation to Moscow to study the possibility of trade expansion. Interestingly, the Taiwanese cleared this high-powered mission in advance with the United States. Taiwan was concerned that the Americans would not approve of direct trade between Taiwan and the Soviet Union because it might involve high technology transfers to the USSR. This request for American approval illustrates how preoccupied Taiwan was to maintain good relations with the United States. While in Moscow, the trade mission received considerable favorable publicity in the Taiwanese press.[65] When the delegation returned to Taipei, however, conservatives in the Taiwanese Executive Yuan (or "the cabinet") challenged any trade expansion as a violation of Taiwan's laws, which banned direct trade with the Soviet Union. Soviet citizens were still denied entry visas, except for rare exceptions. Beijing was also furious, claiming Taiwan sought to do more than simply promote economic ties. To reassure the PRC, during Soviet President Mikhail Gorbachev's visit to Beijing in May 1989, he reiterated Soviet adherence to the one China principle. Finally, in March 1990, the Executive Yuan lifted the ban on direct trade between the Soviet Union and Taiwan, simultaneously greatly simplifying visa procedures to allow Soviet nationals to travel to Taiwan for business and pleasure.[66] Again, the Soviet Union nonetheless carefully reassured Beijing that it had no intention of allowing unofficial trade relations to develop into formal recognition. In April 1990, the following month, PRC Premier Li Peng visited Moscow. At the close of his visit, the PRC and the USSR issued a joint communiqué, reaffirming Moscow's complete support for Beijing's position on the Taiwan question. Once again, ideological constraints on each side precluded any further warming of ties between the Soviet Union and Taiwan, a microcosm of the situation that had characterized the entire relationship during the previous three decades.[67]

Post-Soviet Russian Ties with Taiwan, 1991–2006

Right up to dissolution of the Soviet Union on Christmas Day 1991, ties between Taiwan and the USSR remained limited and informal, as both parties continued to bear in mind potential reactions from the United States and the PRC toward any further warming. Even with the Soviet

Union no longer in being, official ties between the newly created Russian Federation and Taiwan remained exactly as they had been between the USSR and Taiwan—non-existent. Publicly, the formal Russian-Taiwan relationship was ostentatiously based on the principle of the Four Noes, namely: no recognition of Taiwanese independence; no recognition of the concept of two Chinas; no participation by Taiwan in any international organizations whose membership was restricted to sovereign states; and no arms sales to Taiwan.[68] Unofficial ties blossomed, however, especially in trade and cultural matters. Informal liaison offices, which acted as unofficial embassies, even issuing visas, opened in Moscow in 1993 and in Taipei in 1996. While much smaller than Sino-Russian commerce, trade between the Russian Federation and Taiwan grew steadily, reaching an annual US$2 billion by the mid-2000s. Increasing numbers of Taiwanese universities opened Russian Studies programs, offering courses in areas such as history, language, and culture at both undergraduate and postgraduate levels, with growing numbers of Russian academics staffing those programs. Significant numbers of Russian tourists and businessmen visited Taiwan, and in the reverse direction growing numbers of Taiwanese traveled to Russia, especially to Moscow and the Far Eastern port of Vladivostok. As late as the mid-2000s, however, political sensitivities made direct air travel between Moscow and Taipei still impossible, forcing transit through Hong Kong, Seoul, or Tokyo.

At the state level, moreover, increasingly warm Sino-Russian ties somewhat darkened this rosy picture. Russian trade with China mushroomed to an estimated US$30 billion in 2005, a substantial 37 percent increase over the prior year.[69] More distressing to Taiwan than this huge trade figure was the fact that a large percentage of it, perhaps over US$2 billion, constituted sales of armaments—many of them ultimately targeted on Taiwan—to modernize China's army, navy, and air force. While urging a peaceful solution of the Taiwan question, at least in public the Russian government would never oppose a Chinese invasion of the island. Moreover, the growing Sino-Russian reconciliation of the 1990s facilitated a shifting of China's military priorities and troop deployments from its western and southern borders to its eastern periphery, where they were directed against Taiwan and, to a lesser extent, Japan. Increasingly, China and Russia viewed world affairs through similar lenses, leading what had been a cool Sino-Russian relationship in 1991 to become an informal alliance by 2005. Russia would not be prepared to jeopardize its new and lucrative strategic relationship with China for improved Russian-Taiwanese ties, meaning that the relationship between Russia and Taiwan operated under constraints as great as the ideological ones governing it during the Soviet period.

During the late 1980s, Mikhail Gorbachev, the last President of the Soviet Union, managed to normalize relations with the PRC, something that had eluded his predecessors. After the collapse of the Soviet Union in December 1991, relations between China and the new Russian Federation initially remained quite cool. The aging Chinese leadership perceived as nightmarish developments within the new Russian Federation. The Chinese were extremely unhappy when Gorbachev's successor, Boris Yeltsin, dismantled the Soviet Union and, still worse, disgraced the CPSU, excluding it from power for the first time since 1917. In the eyes of the Chinese, the CPSU might have been a revisionist Communist Party, but it remained a Communist Party. Yeltsin, by contrast, did not hide the fact that economic capitalism and Western-style democracy were his goals, an outlook highly disturbing to the CCP, which still felt very insecure in the aftermath of the June 4th Incident in 1989, and believed the anti-Communist and democratization movements in the former Soviet Union might spread across their long border and threaten CCP control. Furthermore, Yeltsin's Foreign Minister, Andrei Kozyrev, embarked on a Westward-oriented "Atlanticist" foreign policy, to the detriment of an Eastward "Eurasian" one.[70]

If only from mutual necessity, however, within a few years, Sino-Russian relations warmed significantly. China was internationally isolated after the June 4th Incident, and the United States and the European powers also imposed an arms embargo, refusing to sell China any weaponry. Kozyrev's pro-Western foreign policy was rewarded with great quantities of advice but little financial assistance, while, adding injury to insult, the Soviet arch-enemy NATO expanded eastward into its former Soviet Eastern European Empire. Yeltsin flew to Beijing in 1992, and the two nations signed a joint declaration calling each other "friends" and establishing a framework for Russian-Chinese relations, a friendship that became genuine and deep over the next decade. In the areas of military strategy, economic and military aid, and political ties, this deepening harmony had a profound impact on Taiwan.

Since the foundation of the PRC in 1949, China has relied on a huge army, deployed along its land borders in the north and west against the

Soviet Union, and along the south against India. Chinese military thinking relied on utilizing its huge reserves of manpower rather than on technology, favoring a massive but ill-equipped army over its navy and air force, which both remained weak. During the 1990s the changing world situation and better relations with India and Russia allowed China to shift to a new forward deployment strategy aimed at its eastern periphery: Taiwan, Japan, the East China Sea, and the South China Sea. To implement this new approach, the Chinese needed a tougher but leaner army, a deep-water navy, and a modern air force.[71] Excluded from buying armaments from either Europe or the United States, the Chinese increased their purchases of modern technologically advanced weaponry from Russia. Since 1991 almost all of China's overseas purchases of weapons have come from Russia, with one author estimating the figure at 97 percent.[72] The value of Russian arms sales to China has increased from US$1.2 billion in 1992 to an average of US$2 billion a year since 2000. While Russia sold weapons to numerous other countries, China became its foremost customer.[73] The types of armaments purchased by China were as significant as the amount. Highly advanced Russian *Sukhoi* fighters were intended to form the backbone of an overhauled Chinese air force, as Beijing planned to scrap its obsolete MiGs. As it converted from its existing coastal and riverine fleet to a deep-water navy, China purchased the latest Russian *Sovremenny*-class destroyers, missile systems, and diesel electric submarines.[74]

To China, increasingly dynamic economically and possessing huge foreign currency reserves, money was not the main concern. The Chinese were willing to pay premiums to have weapons, including missiles, delivered ahead of schedule. Many of these missiles could be very quickly and easily deployed against Taiwan, and in 2006, approximately 700 were based in Fujian province, across the strait just a hundred miles away from Taiwan, from where they could within hours quickly destroy most of Taiwan's military defenses and industrial and technological infrastructure.[75] This would enable the reequipped PRC navy to launch a successful amphibious operation to capture first the offshore islands, and then Taiwan itself. Taking Taiwan would still be very costly for Beijing, but for the first time in many years had become feasible. In August 2005, in a very real display of the new Sino-Russian strategic relationship, both countries engaged in their first ever bilateral war games, called Peace Mission 2005, consisting of sea, land, and air maneuvers—in other words a dress rehearsal for an invasion of Taiwan.[76]

On every significant issue, the Russian Federation firmly supported the PRC in its position that Taiwan was an integral part of China, and should revert back to the mainland. In 2004, MID representative Kirill M. Barsky wrote: "'Respect for sovereignty and territorial integrity' is one of the basic principles of the Russian-Chinese relationship, enshrined in Article 1 of the [2001 Neighborliness and Friendly Cooperation Sino-Russian] Treaty. Article 5 reflected Russia's official position on the Taiwan issue: 'The Russian side recognizes that in the world there is only one China. The government of the PRC is the only legitimate government representing the whole of China, and Taiwan is an inalienable part of China.'"[77] Reiterating that stance, the Russian government successively denounced the 2001 election and 2004 reelection of Chen Shui-bian, the leader of Taiwan's independence-minded Democratic Progressive Party, declaring that his accession to power was not in the best interests of ordinary Taiwanese men and women.[78] Russia repeatedly and publicly strongly condemned any form of Taiwanese independence. Speaking to the Chinese Ambassador to Russia, Liu Guchang, on March 29, 2004, the Russian Deputy Foreign Minister reiterated that consistent policy, declaring: "Taiwan is an integral part of China."[79] The Russian State Duma applauded China's controversial anti-secession law enacted in March 2005, stating that China had the right to safeguard its territorial integrity. The Duma declared: "Russia opposes 'Taiwan independence' in whatever form and rejects the concept of 'two Chinas' or 'one China, one Taiwan.'" [80] The Russian press also noted when, on October 24, 2005, China marked the 60th anniversary of Taiwan's liberation at the end of World War II, a celebration highlighting the island's historical connection to the Chinese mainland.[81] When, early in 2006, China bitterly denounced Taiwanese President Chen's symbolic action in scrapping the National Unification Council, a largely defunct agency but one dedicated to uniting the island with the Chinese mainland, Russia followed suit and fiercely criticized Taiwan, stating that this action would threaten regional stability.[82] Russia also gave favorable press coverage to recent visits to Taiwan by opposition leaders James Soong and Lien Chan, both of whom oppose Taiwan independence, and commented favorably on concurrent Chinese offers to support Taiwan membership in the World Health Organization in exchange for Taiwan's recognition of China's sovereignty.[83]

Not only did the Russian government clearly demonstrate that it sided firmly with the PRC on the question of Taiwan independence, it also squelched any attempts by individual Russian politicians to veer from that path by trying to establish some formal ties between Russia and Taiwan. In October 1997, for example, several members of the Duma, led by Deputy Alexei Mitrofonov, introduced a bill, modeled on the American Taiwan Relations Act, to formalize ties with Taiwan, which got nowhere.[84] In October 1998, Vladimir Zhirinovsky, the leader of the ultranationalist Liberal Democratic Party of Russia, accompanied by some 40 other Russian politicians, journalists, and businessmen, made a three-day visit to Taiwan, where he met President Lee Teng-hui and other Taiwanese leaders. Zhirinovsky, who had three times been a candidate for the Russian presidency, was by far the most influential Russian visitor to the island state. A furious Chinese government formally protested to the MID over his visit, characterizing the trip as "an action that might lead to the forming of 'two Chinas' or 'one China and one Taiwan,'" and so "runs counter to clear obligations Russia assumed on the matter of Taiwan."[85] Coincidentally, about the same time Gennady Seleznev, the Speaker of the Russian Duma, was in Beijing, where he met Li Peng, the Chairman of the Chinese National People's Congress, with whom he discussed Zhirinovsky's visit. Seleznev assured Li that the Duma would abide strictly by the "one China" principle; that Zhirinovsky did not represent the Duma and was only making a private visit; and that, even so, he himself had from its inception opposed Zhirinovsky's trip.[86]

Despite the Russian government's sedulous endorsement of China's position on Taiwan, throughout the 1990s and beyond, unofficial ties between Russia and Taiwan grew much warmer and continued to deepen by the year. In the words of Russian diplomat Kirill M. Barsky, writing in 2004:

> Today non-official Russian-Taiwanese ties should be regarded as an integral part of Russia's overall policy toward China, whose crux is to strengthen Russian-Chinese strategic partnership on the basis of the 2001 Treaty of Good-Neighborliness and Friendly Cooperation. Understandably, the MID keeps tight control over non-official contacts with Taiwan, which it coordinates. Soon after the normalization of intergovernmental relations in the early 1990s, Moscow and Beijing reached a mutual understanding on the modalities of non-official Russian-Taiwanese links, establishing what might be termed 'rules of the game' stipulating what is and is not forbidden in relations with Taiwan. Russia abides strictly by this code of conduct. On

> the one hand, Russia does not tolerate any ambiguity with regard to China's sovereignty and territorial integrity. On the other hand, by being absolutely sincere and transparent vis-à-vis Beijing, Moscow ensures firm guarantees for the smooth development of its mutually beneficial cooperation with the island.[87]

On September 15, 1992, the President of the Russian Federation issued decree no. 1072—"On the relationship between the Russian Federation and Taiwan." Besides reiterating the principles of Russia's position on the relationship between Taiwan and China, the decree envisaged possible cooperation with Taiwan on a non-official level. To facilitate the promotion of Russian-Taiwanese ties each side established a non-governmental organization: the Russian one, opened in Taipei in 1996, was named the Moscow-Taipei Coordination Commission on Economic and Cultural Cooperation, and its Taiwanese counterpart, which began operations in Moscow in 1993, the Taipei-Moscow Coordination Commission on Economic and Cultural Cooperation. It was perhaps indicative of the respective importance to each side of this relationship that Taiwan was swifter than Russia to open such an office. While these offices were unofficial and intended primarily to promote trade, they also had the power to issue visas to prospective visitors and handle other matters. Some years later, Taiwan's chamber of commerce, the International Trade Development Council, also set up a mission in Moscow, which has apparently proved successful. Other aspects of the relationship likewise flourished. In 2004, Soviet diplomat Kirill M. Barsky proclaimed: "On both sides, the untiring efforts of many enthusiasts for Russian-Taiwanese exchanges put flesh and blood on the bones of cooperation between Russia and the 'Beautiful Island,' so that today it encompasses such areas as trade, investment, banking, transportation, science and technology, education, and culture. These practical ties are supported by appropriate organizational and legal infrastructure."[88]

The steady growth of the physical parameters of exchanges and cooperation between Russia and Taiwan stemmed in part from Taiwanese willingness to reconsider the paradigms of their relationship with Russia. There were several reasons for this. During the late 1990s and early 2000s, Taiwan's economy endured difficult times. The world recession hit both the United States and Japan, two of Taiwan's main trading partners, very hard, leading Taiwan to diversify its economic links and seek out new trade partners, among whom Russia stood at the top of the list. Russia was geographically close to Taiwan, and the two economies complemented each other. Once the Russian economic and political situation stabilized, its economy began growing by 6 to 7 percent a year, generating increasing interest in the Russian market among the Taiwanese business community. Meanwhile, developments during the 1990s persuaded Taipei that, when dealing with Russia, its attempts to link economics with politics, and its hopes to win political dividends through economic pledges, were unrealistic. The Taiwanese authorities rightly concluded that only genuine trade and real investment opportunities could convince Russian business circles that economic cooperation between Russia and Taiwan had a bright future.

Taiwan, one of the Asian dragons, had a powerful and effective economy, making it a leading player in global trade, so that Russia's main interest in the island was economic. In the early 1990s, bilateral trade increased rapidly, progressing from US$119 million in 1990, to US$227 million in 1991, to US$680 million in 1992, to US$760 million in 1993, surpassing the US$1 billion mark in 1994, and reaching US $1.9 billion in 1995.[89] By 2004, Russian-Taiwanese trade was close to US$3 billion annually, perhaps still relatively small compared to Russian trade with China, but impressive given that until 1990 such trade was still almost non-existent. Taiwan became Russia's fourth largest trading partner in East Asia, after the PRC, Japan, and South Korea. Russia exported mostly steel, iron products, oil, and other chemicals, and imported from Taiwan cheap consumer goods, computers, and electronics products. Another interesting feature was that Russia enjoyed a huge positive balance in its trade with Taiwan, since Russia exported almost four times as much as it imported.

The new synergy of practical cooperation was graphically demonstrated during the September 2003 visit of a Taiwanese trade and economic delegation to Russia, a group headed by Mr. Chang Chung-hsiung, Chairman of the one-year-old Russia-Taiwan Association. A bilateral business forum organized in Moscow during the visit brought together over three dozen representatives of the biggest Taiwanese corporations and banks with their Russian counterparts, together with legislators and scholars from both sides. As a result five commercial agreements were signed, new contacts established, and new and fruitful ideas proposed.[90]

Though still small, in the mid-2000s the Taiwanese economic presence in Russia was growing. Increasing numbers of Taiwanese companies sent missions to Moscow, St. Petersburg, Siberia, and the Far East, where they opened representative offices. Initial investment projects were under discussion, while Russian and Taiwanese banking sectors were exploring avenues of cooperation. From 2002 onward, Taiwan's Eximbank implemented a program of low-interest-rate loans. Credit lines to finance imports of Taiwan-made equipment were opened to five Russian banks. Over 20 Taiwanese businessmen working in Moscow on a permanent basis joined hands and registered themselves as the Taiwan Trade and Industrial Association. Every year over ten thousand Taiwanese tourists visited Russia. By 2004, about 120 students from the island were studying in Moscow and in St. Petersburg. The absence of direct air links between Moscow and Taipei still impeded the expansion of Russian-Taiwanese ties, but both sides were working on this issue. The private Russian air carrier Transaero and the Taiwanese China Airlines negotiated on opening regular charter flights between the two capitals in the near future, with the intention that these would eventually be transformed into regular flights.[91]

Taiwan also developed a Russian community. By 2004, nearly 200 Russians lived on the island, including researchers invited to work in Taiwan's laboratories, businessmen, university professors, and both undergraduate and postgraduate students, some of whom quickly settled in and won broad acceptance in Taiwan. Professor Alexander Pisarev was Director of the Slavic Studies Institute and Dean of the Russian Language Faculty in Tamkang University. This university also boasted among its professors such noted Russian sinologists as Dr. Mikhail Kriukov and Dr. Vladimir Maliavin. Alexander Tsveriniashvili edited the *Taipei Panorama* magazine and Igor Zaitsev was an anchor on the popular channel TVBS. Within Russia, the Institute of Far East Studies, under Iu. M. Galenovich, Alexander Larin, and Vladimir Miasnikov, launched an active research program in Taiwan history, economics, and politics, publishing monographs and journal articles, and organizing conferences. After 1990, Taiwanese studies developed into a separate field of Russian Sinology. Dr. Peter Ivanov headed the Taiwan Studies Center at the Institute of Oriental Studies in Moscow. Due to scarce government funding, however, such Russian academics were dependent on money from Taiwanese authorities to attend international conferences.[92]

The Russian media devoted increasing attention to Taiwan developments. While almost always consistently hostile to any moves by Taiwan to assert its independence and sovereignty, the same Russian press also covered the growing affluence of Taiwanese, the increasing democratization of Taiwanese political life, and the vibrancy of daily life in Taiwan. Russian journals commented very positively on the quality of Taiwanese consumer goods by comparison with goods from mainland China, with one 2002 *Pravda* article going so far as to describe similar articles: "Made in China: bad...Made in Taiwan: good."[93] Other major news stories covered included earthquakes, the SARS epidemic, and most recently, bird flu, as well as occasional quirky human interest stories, such as one describing the birth of a two-headed chicken and a three-headed tortoise in Taiwan.[94] Undoubtedly, the Russian media gave their audience at home a much fuller and more accurate picture of developments in Taiwan than was available to them during the Soviet period.

While heavily constrained on the political, diplomatic, and official levels, in all other respects, Russian-Taiwan relations blossomed in the 15 years after the collapse of the Soviet Union. Bilateral trade, while much smaller than that between the PRC and Russia, grew almost 30-fold, from US$100 million to US$3 billion. After having only sporadic contacts during the Soviet period, the two states opened offices in each other's capitals, where discussions and dealings could readily be conducted on a daily basis. Educationally, scholars and students studied each other's countries' history, politics, economy, and other academic specialties, with books and journals devoted to Taiwan and Russia, giving each country a more accurate perception of the other. After the collapse of the Soviet Union, the old ideological barrier between Communism and anti-Communism no longer existed. Nevertheless, politically and militarily, Russia firmly supported the Beijing position that Taiwan is a part of China, and Taiwan should at the earliest possible time revert, preferably peacefully, to Beijing. Given the huge level of Sino-Russian trade, estimated by the mid-2000s at US$30 billion, and the dependence of the Russian arms industry on Chinese buyers, this hard-line position seemed unlikely to change in the foreseeable future.

Conclusion

Regardless of which government, the Soviet Union or its successor, held power in Moscow, from the 1960s onward the opening and development of Russian relations with Taiwan operated under severe constraints.

Despite tentative feelers from both sides, even at the height of the Sino-Soviet split the Soviet Union was not prepared to compromise its role as leader of the Communist ideological camp, or still further exacerbate relations with its Chinese rival, by making any move that might be seen as endorsing Taiwan's permanent independence from mainland China. While perceiving the island as a useful source of intelligence information and even, in the 1970s, of potential naval facilities, Soviet officials made only half-hearted and rather unsystematic efforts to develop such opportunities. One reason why, as in Hong Kong, such endeavors to make Taiwan an intelligence or strategic asset bore little fruit, was that Taiwan officials were likewise wary of moving too close to the Soviet Union, for fear of alienating their usually conservative political backers in the United States, whose government still afforded the island considerable protection. In theory, the collapse of the Soviet Union in 1991 might be thought to have opened the road for closer Taiwanese-Russian relations. As with most other international states, however, mainland China bore a greater importance in post-Communist Russian priorities than did Taiwan. Russian businessmen and leaders welcomed burgeoning trade and cultural exchanges with Taiwan, but did not consider these worth the cost of alienating Beijing. This was even more the case after Mikhail Gorbachev reached agreements settling the vexed Sino-Russian border disputes, and China became not just the biggest customer for Russian armaments merchants but a potential strategic ally against the growing and increasingly resented international dominance of the world's one remaining hyperpower, the ever stronger United States. As had been the case ever since 1949, official Russian policy toward Taiwan largely reflected the position of the PRC.

9

The Permanent Afterthought: Russian and Soviet Relations with Macao

From the late nineteenth century until the handover of Macao to Chinese rule about a hundred years later, Russia and the Soviet Union demonstrated discernible, though far from overwhelming, interest in the tiny Portuguese territory of Macao. Their activities and involvement in the enclave served as an interesting contrast and coda to their more extensive dealings with the larger entities of British Hong Kong and even more problematic Taiwan. Both Tsarist Russia and the Soviet Union had definite policies toward both Hong Kong and Taiwan, and though policy emphases altered dramatically over time, especially toward Hong Kong, Russian officials sought to expand their trade with and activities in those territories. Soviet and Russian policies toward Macao were in some ways less consistent, circumscribed by the relative insignificance of the territory, and also for several decades from the 1920s onward by the implacable long-term hostility of the fascist Portuguese government toward Soviet Communism. Even so, the fact that first Russian and then Soviet foreign policy makers assigned some importance to Macao is amply demonstrated by the AVP RF, which contains nearly 30 files of varying size spanning the period from 1910 to 1987.

For over a century, the formerly Portuguese colony of Macao has been much overshadowed by its neighbor, the quondam British colony of Hong Kong, always far larger in both area and population. Today Macao consists of some 15 square kilometers and a half million people, whereas Hong Kong, though still very small in absolute terms, has nearly 1,000 square kilometers and almost seven million people. Hong Kong is also far richer, the eighth largest economy in Asia and a financial center with an average per capita income over US$20,000 per year. For the past 150 years until recent times, Macao has survived largely on sufferance, its economy heavily based on income from the often seedy trades of gambling, human trafficking in female prostitutes and male coolies, opium sales, and tourism, without which Macao might have collapsed entirely. Today, investment and tourism from China and Hong Kong, especially in its gambling industry, largely account for its current prosperity.[1]

Yet this was not always the case. 300 years before the British took Hong Kong, Portuguese explorers, missionaries, and merchants, then a common combination, first established an official presence and European settlement there in 1557, almost 450 years ago. Between 1550 and 1650, Macao enjoyed a golden age. Through Macao China found potatoes, the West discovered tea, and liberal ideas penetrated China. At the height of its prosperity, Macao was a city of wealth and splendor, the West's richest depot in Asia, an entrepôt for trade with Japan, the Philippines, China, Southeast Asia, and even Latin America. Macao supplied wealthy Japanese with Chinese silk in return for gold and silver. For over a century, Macao was the Venice of the East, the most important trading port in the world.[2] Since the tiny territory served the Roman Catholic Church as the fulcrum for penetration of China and Japan, Macao was also described as the Rome of the East. The powerful Jesuit Order or Society of Jesus used Macao as a base to conduct missionary activities throughout China, establishing the first Western-style university in Asia there in 1594, and soon afterwards the first seminary for training priests.[3] Thus, by the close of the sixteenth century, Macao had become a center for trade, religious activities, education, science, and culture.

By the mid-seventeenth century, however, Macao had lost its leading role. In 1602, 1603, 1622, and finally in 1627, the Dutch, major trading competitors of the Portuguese, launched several attacks on the largely undefended territory. Soon afterwards, during the 1630s, the Tokugawa Japanese shogun Iemitsu savagely persecuted and killed Christians and eventually forbade all Japanese contact with the outside world. Within a few years, Portugal lost all her other Asian trading cities—Guangzhou (Canton), Manila, and Melaka—except Goa. With the ending of the Japan trade, Macao embarked on a long economic decline, entering a lengthy dark period when the city became very impoverished and even faced the danger of total extinction. From around 1700, when regular British trade with China began, the situation in Macao improved somewhat, since virtually all foreign merchants were forbidden to live in China and were therefore forced to base themselves in Macao. The emerging British trade with China tempted the British to try to exploit Portugal's military weakness and political instability by taking over the territory themselves, but these attempts failed and Macao remained under Portuguese control, though at China's insistence, her precise borders and exact status both remained ill-defined. After the British founded Hong Kong in 1842, Macao sank once more into obscurity. Its shallow harbor, which frequently silted up, could never compete with Hong Kong's great deep-water port, that could accommodate the largest vessels in the world. The city differed little from that Joseph Kessel described a century later, during the mid-1950s: "a discreet city in white, languid, and drowsy even in its Chinese district, possessing a bewitching charm."[4]

Imperial Russia and Macao

Interestingly, it was during this time of decline that Russia first displayed some interest in the territory. Macao was, moreover, an early port of call for Russia in South China. In November 1805, the Russian ship *Nadezhda*, commanded by Admiral Ivan Kruzenshtern, followed two weeks later by the *Neva*, under Captain-Lieutenant Yuri Lisiansky, dropped anchor in the Bay of Aomen. The two vessels were on a lengthy around-the-world voyage, the plans for which the Russian Tsar Alexander I had approved as early as 1802, an exploration originally proposed during the reign of Catherine the Great which effectively constituted part of Russia's Far Eastern imperial project. Among this expedition's numerous strategic and scientific objectives was the very practical goal of exploring the possibilities of building up seaborne trade with China, especially in furs from Siberia and Russian America (Alaska). Kruzenshtern, who had spent several years during the 1790s serving in the British navy, had been particularly impressed when, during a stay in Guangzhou in 1798–1799, he watched a small 100-ton vessel outfitted in Macao five months earlier return from northwest America with a cargo of furs that were sold for 60,000 piastres. He hoped that his countrymen in Alaska might be able to develop comparable trading relationships, and also sought to enable Russian vessels to enter the lucrative carrying trade between South and Southeast Asia and Europe.[5]

Chinese chronicles testify that the Russians behaved very courteously and won the sympathy of local officials. Notwithstanding the Qing Empire's ban on contacts with foreigners, in December 1805 the two ships were allowed to proceed to Guangzhou, where they unloaded and sold their cargo of Russian goods.[6] During the two weeks he spent in Macao, Kruzenshtern carefully flew only the flag of a Russian merchantman, rather than that of the imperial navy, a distinction he suspected Chinese officials were incapable of appreciating, since when no other vessels were available foreign warships habitually transported merchant cargoes up to Guangzhou. Both Russian officers found the weakness of the Portuguese authorities disturbing. Lisiansky, who spent only one day in Macao, later wrote that:

> while the Portuguese are the professed masters, the Chinese in reality hold the sway; for nothing of any consequence can be done without their permission. Though the governor may attempt occasionally to defend his rights against the encroachment of the insolent mandarins, his garrison is too small for him to be able to enforce respect. I was told that there were as many monks and priests as soldiers, the number of which was about 200. It appears to me that the Portuguese are themselves principally in fault in this subjection. Being badly provided with necessaries, they are continually dependent on the Chinese, who, on the smallest dissatisfaction, threaten to stop the supplies, and thus govern the town.[7]

Kruzenshtern was likewise decidedly alarmed by the weakness of the Portuguese Governor when dealing with the Chinese authorities, and wished that the territory were administered by a stronger European power, commenting that: "If Macao were in the hands of the English, or even of the Spaniards, the dependence of this possession on the Chinese would soon fall to the ground; and, with the assistance of their important possessions in the vicinity of China, either of these nations established in Macao might bid defiance to the whole empire." According to Kruzenshtern, the British had recently attempted but failed to take over Macao, a bid he clearly wished had been successful. "Macao," he wrote later, "is a perfect sample of fallen greatness." He noted the existence of "[m]any fine buildings ranged in large squares, surrounded by courtyards and gardens; but most of them uninhabited, the number of Portuguese resident there having greatly decreased." Kruzenshtern was somewhat shocked that most of Macao's 12,000 to 15,000 residents were Chinese, with very few Portuguese or other Europeans to be seen on the streets, except for nuns and priests, who allegedly outnumbered Portugal's soldiers, "a piece of raillery that was literally true."[8] Macao's military weakness alarmed Kruzenshtern, who observed that:

> the number of soldiers amount[ed] only to 150, not one of whom is a European, the whole being mulattos of Macao and Goa. Even the officers are not all Europeans. With so small a garrison it is difficult to defend four large fortresses; and the natural insolence of the Chinese finds a sufficient motive in this weakness of the military, to heap insult upon insult. It is much to be wished, the existence of Portugal as an independent state being now very precarious, that some European power would take possession of Macao before the Portuguese themselves abandon it to the Chinese; an event which can scarcely fail of taking place, as Portugal is not able to maintain her possessions in the East Indies, and Macao is entirely supported by Goa.[9]

Kruzenshtern's rather dismal assessment of Portuguese rule and the situation in the territory may have been one reason why a protracted hiatus then ensued in Russian relations with Macao, as the mid-nineteenth century Tsarist Empire's attention switched to the rapidly developing and more dynamic British colony of Hong Kong. Occasionally, however, Macao still beckoned. Half a century later, in 1855, the Russian captain of the ship which had recently carried a mission headed by the naval expansionist Admiral Evfim Putyatin to Japan, to conclude a treaty opening diplomatic relations between Japan and Russia, expressed a desire to travel onward further into the Pacific and visit Macao, Manila, New Guinea, and the New Hebrides. Writing in a monthly magazine published in Moscow, he proclaimed the potential of both the China market and Australian gold mines, which in his view promised great riches that would "practically fall by themselves into the mouth" of enterprising mariners such as himself. The claims of naval expansion and commerce alike motivated this officer, who was, he said, "attracted there not by simple curiosity, not by an ambitious hunger for discovery, but rather by the desire to acquaint myself and our naval public with those places which, it seems to me, can with time become very suitable for our future ships on the Pacific."[10]

A further 25 years elapsed before Macao once again attracted the attention of Russian naval men. In 1880, a Russian admiral asked whether the warship he commanded might stop over in Macao, a request Portugal denied, evidence, perhaps, that the Portuguese authorities shared British fears that Russia coveted their own colonial territories in South China. Under the Treaty of Livadia that China and Russia concluded in 1879, China ceded to Russia the province of Kuldja in Central Asia, including the strategic Tian Shan mountain pass. The next year China disavowed its envoy and refused to ratify the treaty, actions which Portuguese officials noted caused a sharp deterioration in relations between Russia and China. On several occasions in 1880, both the Portuguese Consulate in Hong Kong and the Governor's Office in Macao sent dispatches to Lisbon warning that they and representatives of other European states believed the two countries were moving inexorably toward war.[11] This prompted the Russian frigate *Morge*, which belonged to the Far East Fleet, to visit several ports in South China to try to assess the effectiveness of China's defenses in case war broke out. In the course of this voyage, *Morge* spent a few hours in both Macao and Guangzhou. Believing armed conflict between Russia and China to be inevitable, as a precautionary measure several other European nations dispatched warships to the region.[12] The Portuguese government, for example, sent its warship *Tezo* to Shanghai, to protect its citizens in case of war.

Portuguese officials further believed that, if war did erupt between Russia and China, they should take advantage of the situation to gain formal sovereignty over Macao.[13] At one stage Portuguese officials fully expected there would be a war, on the grounds that Russia faced internal difficulties, and many within the Russian government thought a war could unite "all agitated spirits." Portugal believed that, in the event of such a conflict, no other European state would become militarily involved, but all neutral European nations would take advantage of China's weaknesses to force more concessions from the declining Qing Empire. As a consequence no European state would take any great pains to prevent the outbreak of war.[14] Fortunately for China, in August 1881, the Treaty of St. Petersburg settled the dispute between Russia and China. The treaty awarded Russia a smaller slice of Kuldja than she had secured in 1879, together with an indemnity of 9 million rubles (then worth about US$5 million), and new trade privileges in China and in Central Asia. At that time Portugal also took advantage of China's military weakness to pressure the Qing Empire to sign a treaty with Portugal to regularize and define the status of Macao. In December 1887, the Sino-Portuguese

Treaty of Tianjin (Tientsin) finally granted Portugal sovereignty and control over Macao.[15]

In April 1891, Portuguese officials in Macao prepared for the forthcoming visit in early April of Grand Duke Nicholas, soon to become Tsar Nicholas II. The Russian royal yacht bore the Grand Duke, accompanied by a large party, including Prince George, the future King of Greece, on a grand state tour around South and East Asia. As the royal party passed by Macao on April 5, Prince Esper Ukhtomskii, one of Nicholas's entourage, reflected on Macao's past history, noting that the Portuguese legally possessed "no territorial rights" in Macao, and occupied it "only by the permission of the Chinese government." The early Portuguese settlers of Macao he characterized as "no better than a crew of blackguards sent abroad from out of the prisons of their native land; while their descendants by marriages with Malay, Chinese, and Japanese women, who were, in all probability, of the worst kind also, were distinguished for similar qualities." Ukhtomskii, a romantic expansionist who hoped China and other Asian nations and peoples would eventually rise up against European imperialism and expel what he viewed as their colonial oppressors, and that Russia would ultimately become the ally and protector of the Chinese and other Asian peoples, commented that, given the past history of Portuguese and European exploitation, "one really cannot judge the Chinese harshly for their so-called 'barbarity' and 'stagnation.' When Europeans themselves have brought, and continue to bring, discord into the life of Asiatic states, it becomes impossible to judge the latter from a purely Western and progressive point of view."[16] Despite Ukhtomskii's unflattering opinions, the Portuguese authorities, hoping to improve their country's relations with Russia, prepared for a full state visit, including an official reception, a stay by the royal party at Macao's Government House, banquets, and other events. Anticlimactically, at the last moment Macao officials received a telegram from Prince Alexander Baryatinsky of the royal household. He regretted that, while they appreciated Macao's kind offer of hospitality, they had limited time, which meant the Grand Duke could only spend a few hours in Macao while en route from Hong Kong to Guangzhou. The humiliated Portuguese authorities were forced to rearrange and curtail their entire program.[17] The episode neatly encapsulated the entire Russian relationship with Macao: great expectations on the part of Macanese officials matched by Russian promises, but with little ultimate substantive Russian interest or involvement in Macao.

When the Russo-Japanese War began in February 1904, the Governor of Macao declared absolute neutrality between the two belligerents, a policy Macao observed much more strictly than did Hong Kong, which showed far greater partiality to the Japanese than the Russian side.[18] Whereas the Japanese received supplies and arms from vessels that had docked in Hong Kong, Macao, by contrast, banned all vessels that carried either Russian or Japanese troops or munitions from entering its harbor. The Portuguese colonial government also forbade all Portuguese and Macao citizens and all foreign residents in Macao from assisting either side, on penalty of arrest.[19]

The first mention of Macao in the Russian archives occurred during the 1910 Portuguese Revolution. On October 3, 1910, significant units of the Lisbon garrison, supported by armed civilians and naval warships, rebelled and, after eight centuries of monarchical rule, declared Portugal a republic. King Manuel II abdicated and retired to exile in England, leaving the rest of Portugal and its far-flung empire, including Macao, to accept, albeit rather unenthusiastically, a republican form of government modeled on the French Third Republic.[20] Eduardo Marques, for example, the royalist Governor of Macao, only reluctantly supported the revolution. An early decree of the strongly anticlerical new republican government in Lisbon demanded that religious orders in the tiny territory be closed, and all monks and nuns were ordered to leave Macao. Since religious orders ran most schools, orphanages, and hospitals, this move enraged many individuals in Macao, where people rightly asked who would assume the operation of these much-needed facilities, which catered particularly to Macao's mostly poverty-stricken population.

Piotr Tiedemann, the Tsarist Consul in Hong Kong, sent the Russian Mission in Beijing and the MID in St. Petersburg detailed and largely hostile reports on the impact of the Portuguese Revolution on Macao. Tiedemann noted that the Portuguese garrison in Macao had forced Governor Marques to expel numerous religious personnel, including all Jesuits, from the colony. The Russian Consul professed himself unable to understand why the Jesuits should be expelled, since in his opinion they had done many good things, and characterized Governor Marques as impolitic for closing the charity hospitals and schools. On November 16, radical soldiers held a meeting in the center of Macao, where some suggested that they kill the nuns and other female missionaries. While the governor managed to save the women's lives, they were ordered not to wear their clerical garb, fined an appreciable sum of money, and deported to Hong Kong. Even the Portuguese Consul in Hong Kong, who supported the revolution, deplored this antireligious action. The Consul indicated his disapproval when he met the nuns and missionaries as their ship arrived in Hong Kong. The Russian Consul, who possessed long-standing family ties and interests in Macao, hoped the situation would remedy itself, a process he believed would be protracted, calling for strong leadership from Lisbon. The Consul noted, however, that the situation in Macao was already improving, and clerical women still remaining there no longer needed to fear for their lives, but could safely stay in Macao.[21]

After this incident, Governor Marques resigned and left the colony, to be succeeded by Macao's Chief Justice, who only held the post for a few weeks before returning to Lisbon himself. During his short term, he closed the radical anticlerical newspaper *A Verde* (Truth). Alvaro Cardoso de Mello Machado, a young man who had been secretary to former Governor Marques, became the new governor. He relied heavily for advice upon the Portuguese Consul in Hong Kong, and both men acted quite conservatively. Russia recognized Governor Machado, who made a short trip to Hong Kong on November 1, 1911. While in Hong Kong he met Consul Tiedemann, who requested permission to visit Macao himself, which was granted on November 14, 1911.[22]

Macao and the Soviet Union

Following World War I and the Russian Revolution of 1917, during the interwar period, much of which coincided with a fascist regime in Portugal, such limited Russian activities in Macao as had existed in the Tsarist period shrank to virtually nothing. Foreigners of every political outlook found it far easier to seek political asylum and shelter in Macao than in more efficient Hong Kong. Those who settled in Macao included not just foreign Communists but, in the wake of the 1917 Bolshevik Revolution, numerous anti-Communist White Russians. While an émigré Russian community existed in the enclave, virtually all its members were strong anti-Communists who were, in any case, far too preoccupied with making money or their own sheer survival to take much interest in politics, let alone become recruits to the Communist cause. Despite the significant White Russian presence in Macao, to date no material has been as yet unearthed in either the Russian or Macanese archives suggesting that such individuals undertook any anti-Communist activities.

The years following the Republican Revolution in Portugal were marked by political instability. In 1926, a military coup overthrew the republic, whereupon General Antonio Salazar created a fascist dictatorship which remained in power for nearly five decades. Given the right-wing outlook of the new regime, the Macao authorities kept constant watch for Communist agitators. In October 1931, Police Chief Jose Guerreiro de Andrade ordered measures be taken against Communist or "Communist-leaning" teachers and students. Numerous people were arrested in Macao for being Communists. The Macao government sought to isolate and "exterminate" Communist activities, and from then onward the Macao authorities banned all trade with Russia and excluded all Soviet citizens from the colony.[23] However, the Macao archives never specified what Communist activities took place, nor how many people were arrested, nor whether any Russians were involved in those activities. In practice those foreign Communists, largely Chinese, Vietnamese, and Koreans, who took shelter in Macao rarely targeted the Portuguese, and usually preferred to intrigue against the ruling regimes in their home countries.[24] The Soviets were even less successful in penetrating Macao to make it a bastion of Communism, than they were in Hong Kong. While the Macao government expressed great concern over Communist propaganda in schools, there was no evidence that the Soviet Union instigated any such activities. Although the Soviet Union sponsored and supported strikes in Hong Kong through its Comintern organization, there was no sign of Soviet support for comparable labor unrest in Macao. The Soviet government tried, though unsuccessfully, to establish a permanent presence in Hong Kong, which Soviet officials several times considered making the Far Eastern Headquarters of the Comintern. No evidence whatever suggested that they regarded Macao as offering them any such potential. In neither Soviet nor Macao archives was there any mention of Soviet activities within the enclave.

Twenty years after the Russian Revolution, in March 1937, the Colonial Minister in Lisbon sent governors of all Portuguese colonies a circular prohibiting any additional Russians from entering any Portuguese colony, including Macao. This policy remained in effect throughout the entire period of the Salazar dictatorship, which lasted until 1974. From this point on, Macao had to ask Lisbon for the final decision before any

Russian was permitted to enter the territory. Such requests were carefully reviewed and, even in cases when a Russian sought to marry a Macao resident, in practice most were rejected. After 1937, the entry of a Russian into Macao became a complicated multistep process, demanding, first, a personal request from the individual concerned; and second, the approval of the civil administration in Macao, the Governor himself, and then the police. Once all the appropriate Macao authorities had given their consent, the request was forwarded to Lisbon for decision. The Macao authorities normally only admitted Russians who were in genuine danger or in transit to a third country. Even Archpriest Dmitry Mikhailovich Uspensky, Patriarch of the Russian Orthodox Church in South China and an obvious anti-Communist, was subjected to this laborious and time-consuming process before he was allowed to visit Macao for the few days of Holy Week 1938.[25] In spring 1940, as World War II approached, these rules were tightened further. In a memorandum which stated—without giving exact figures—that significant numbers of Russians already resided in Macao, Luis de Menezes Alves, the Macao Head of Immigration, requested the Portuguese Consulate in Hong Kong, for example, to be even stricter in granting visas. The existing Russian community in Macao was then sufficiently large to require an Orthodox priest to visit Macao some half-dozen times between 1939 and 1941.[26]

Because Portugal remained neutral during World War II, the Japanese occupied Hong Kong but left the tiny Portuguese territory unmolested even though, due to their control of the surrounding territories, they largely regulated the movement of people, food, and water into Macao. Hundreds of thousands of Chinese and tens of thousands of foreigners, including White Russians, among them Georgy Vitailovich Smirnov, a noted watercolor painter of Hong Kong and Macao, took refuge in relatively secure Macao, where they were safer than in occupied Hong Kong or South China.[27] Overcrowding nonetheless meant that disease, hunger, and suffering were rampant, making it very difficult for White Russian refugees to survive. Spies and intelligence agents, including Communists (never identified by nationality), Nationalists, Portuguese, British, and Japanese, all used Macao as an operational base. For some individuals, especially smugglers and middlemen, the war offered economic opportunities. Remarkably, civilian life in Macao—its newspapers, cultural life, gambling, casinos, cinemas, and even cabarets—continued undisturbed. Some observers even labeled the enclave the "most depraved city in the world."[28] Toward the end of World War II, on several occasions American planes accidentally dropped bombs on Macao. When the war ended, living conditions eased, as most refugees, including many White Russians, left.[29]

In spite of its strong anti-colonialist ideology, the issue of the return of Macao and Hong Kong to China was not at first a high priority for either the Nationalist KMT government, or for the Communist rulers which won control of China in 1949. Unlike Great Britain, after the Communist Revolution Portugal continued to recognize the ROC on Taiwan as the legitimate government of all China. Not until after the Portuguese Revolution of January 1975 did Portugal reverse its position and recognize the PRC as the only legitimate government of China, to which Portugal now considered Taiwan to belong. Even so, in 1949 Mao's armies stopped at the Macao boundary, the Barrier Gate, just as they halted at the Hong Kong border. In 1949, the Soviets urged the Chinese to annex Hong Kong, believing that the British would not be able to put up any great resistance, and that Britain's ally, the United States, would not oppose this liberation of a colonial territory that clearly was a part of China.[30] In discussions with Chinese Premier Zhou Enlai in Moscow in September 1952, Stalin claimed to be unaware that the PLA had not taken Macao, and expressed disappointment when Zhou informed him that the enclave was still in Portuguese hands. Upon learning that, Stalin urged the Chinese to end this situation, declaring that "this scum that has situated itself on the very entrance of China must be driven out."[31] For several decades thereafter, Soviet officials, at least rhetorically, would demonstrate greater eagerness to retake Macao and Hong Kong than would the PRC leadership.

After the creation of the PRC, Soviet officials also carefully scrutinized events in both Macao and Hong Kong. The first AVP RF record to mention Macao was a general background report written in 1950, describing the situation in Macao during and after World War II. The author noted, for example, that in 1939, 511 soldiers and 21 officers constituted Macao's total defense force.[32] During the height of the Cold War, the MID received reports on Macao and Hong Kong almost annually, and during the early and mid-1950s even more frequently, often several times a year. These dispatches, which gave a fascinating picture of developments in minuscule Macao during the Cold War, covered political developments in the enclave, including KMT agitation and intrigues, and provided analyses of Macao's finances, especially the military budget, and information on Macao's trade. Most such reports were originally written by Chinese Military Intelligence authorities in South China, and like those on Hong Kong were usually translated word for word into Russian without any commentary. Indicating the closeness of the alliance between Beijing and Moscow at that time, Soviet officials never queried the Chinese reports, nor offered a different interpretation of them.

During this period, Soviet reports noted, defense spending consistently increased, as did the Portuguese police and military presence, expanding substantially from the tiny forces stationed there on the eve of World War II. In 1950, Macao's population was only 187,000, of whom fewer than 3,000 were Portuguese and another 1,800 Eurasian Macanese, figures about half those during World War II. The United States government pressured the Portuguese authorities to enforce the American embargo forbidding trade with the PRC imposed after China's October 1950 intervention in the Korean War, sanctions in which the Portuguese acquiesced. As in Hong Kong, however, the ban was never very tightly imposed and numerous products flowed in and out of China. Nor could the embargo be strictly enforced, as the PRC virtually surrounded Macao on all sides, even maintaining a trade mission in the territory.[33] Many Nationalists took refuge in Macao, which like Hong Kong became a center for KMT agitation. Numerous acts of sabotage committed in South China originated in Macao, whose borders were far looser than Hong Kong's. Tension between Chinese factions quickly increased in Macao. In 1951, KMT terrorists exploded a bomb at the Chinese (PRC) Trade Mission Building, and set fires in several other Macao buildings. The Macao Electric Lighting Company laid off some workers regarded as Communists, replacing them with others whom Chinese reports characterized as KMT spies. Vatican pressure led some other companies to fire radical workers. The staunchly anti-Communist Macao government censored several "progressive" movies. At times, Macao became a battleground between pro-KMT and pro-PRC youth groups, and fighting even broke out in some schools. Despite all attempts at evasion, the coercive American embargo also had a strong negative impact on Macao's economy, contributing to political instability in the tiny and already impoverished territory. Fearing an influx of "outside agitators," Macao imposed visa requirements on all foreign visitors.[34] Thus the 1950s proved a decade of poverty, general bleakness, scarcity, and political repression on the part of the Portuguese dictatorship.

During the next three years through 1955, the MID continued to receive frequent detailed reports from the Guangzhou-based Chinese Military Intelligence, Fifth Bureau, Ministry of Foreign Affairs, Military Central Committee, bulletins that described the activities of Portuguese officials and examined the political, social, and military situation in the enclave. At the height of the Cold War, Soviet and Chinese reports emphasized the continuing deterioration of the economic situation in Macao, ascribing it accurately and primarily to the United States embargo, social and political instability caused largely by KMT terrorists, and political corruption by unaccountable and often incompetent Portuguese officials. They also depicted a militarized enclave, which conceivably might even threaten the economic and social stability of the huge neighboring PRC. The repressive Portuguese police broke up women's and trade union organizations' meetings. Arguments and clashes continued between KMT and Communist groups in Macao. KMT terrorists allegedly blew up several more buildings. Due to American pressure, despite perpetual poverty and instability, the Macanese authorities were forced to strengthen the embargo on trade with China, which naturally enough had previously been Macao's largest customer, only aggravating the situation in Macao.[35]

During 1953 and 1954, the Portuguese position in Macao apparently deteriorated, as corrupt Portuguese officials were sent back home, while desertions were reported among Chinese nationals within the Portuguese garrison in Macao.[36] Throughout, KMT agitators continued their subversive activities. Hong Kong traders protested new commercial regulations in Macao imposing tariffs on Hong Kong goods, which Hong Kong had imported into Macao duty free up to 1952. These rules were introduced after the American government convinced Macanese officials that many such goods had actually been produced in China, shipped unofficially to Hong Kong, and repackaged to evade the embargo. These measures inflicted further damage on an already depressed economy.[37] Soviet reports noted growing potential for an anti-colonial Communist revolution in Macao. Both Chinese intelligence and Soviet officials noted the damage the American embargo inflicted not just on Macao, but also on South China's economy. As a demonstration of its continuing authority, in 1955, the Portuguese government made plans to celebrate the 400th anniversary of its takeover of Macao, an event the Soviet Union pejoratively labeled an invasion. During this event, KMT activists bombed several restaurants and theaters owned by Chinese sympathetic to the PRC.[38]

From the late 1950s onward, the once close relations between the PRC and the Soviet Union deteriorated virtually by the year, as the Sino-Soviet alliance receded into the past. Although the outside world was still only dimly aware of the split between the two Communist giants, by the early 1960s, communication between the Soviet Union and the PRC was almost nonexistent. How did that deterioration affect Soviet activities in Macao? The Soviet Union could no longer rely on mainland Chinese sources for significant intelligence information on Hong Kong and Macao. From then onward, the Soviets were forced to gather all such data directly through Soviet sources, from its own embassies and consulates in China or those in such neighboring countries as Japan. Ironically, as China entered a very unstable period, enduring first the Great Leap Forward policy and then the Great Proletarian Cultural Revolution, the Soviets found themselves in greater need of reliable information on China, but with fewer means to gather it. Increasingly, this led the Soviet Union to view Hong Kong and Macao in a new light. Soviet officials noted that Macao, and even more so, larger and richer Hong Kong, functioned as major bases where Western intelligence agents could glean information on developments in neighboring China. As their intelligence sources within the PRC dried up, the Soviets recognized that Hong Kong and Macao might host their operatives. In fact, the author of one MID report, V. Kiuzmin, urged that the Soviet Union dispatch agents to Hong Kong and Macao to intercept communications inside China and observe British and American activities in the territories. However, to date, no documents have surfaced in the Russian archives indicating whether or not such secret operatives ever actually arrived in either colony.[39] While we may not be certain Russian secret agents were ever based in the enclave, the fact a MID official requested they be sent indicated the growing importance of Macao in Soviet eyes.

The status of Macao and Hong Kong now became a weapon in the Sino-Soviet split, as the Soviet Union taunted China for its ideological inconsistency. On the world stage and in domestic propaganda, China now portrayed itself as more radical than the Soviet Union and a better and more committed defender of the needs and interests of third world countries against the exploitative capitalist bloc. Two of the world's last few colonies were located on the China coast, and were clearly part of China's own territory. Officially, China itself charged that both Macao and Hong Kong had been invaded and then conquered by European powers, which took advantage of China's military weakness to impose unequal treaties, illegally granting sovereignty to the British and Portuguese.[40] Premier Nikita Khrushchev himself brought up the status of Macao as a weapon in his ongoing ideological battle with the PRC.[41] While China refused to recognize their colonial status, and in 1957 protested strongly against the 400th anniversary celebration in Macao, in practice on numerous occasions China refused to consider launching any military invasion of Macao or Hong Kong.[42] The Soviets noted that Macao served as a major trading center for China. Hong Kong and Macao were the two main nexuses for commerce between China and the bourgeois West.[43] In other words, radical China, while denouncing the Soviet Union for its policy of peaceful coexistence with the West, was itself ideologically inconsistent. As the Sino-Soviet split reached new heights in the late 1960s, the Soviet Union condemned such ideological inconstancy as an example of PRC hypocrisy. Thus Macao served as a weapon in the Soviet Union's arsenal in its propaganda war against the PRC as to which power was a better Communist. Even so, the Soviet Union never pushed relations with China over either Hong Kong or Macao to the breaking point.

Around the same time, political violence stirred up by those young Red Guards wracked Macao. During 1966, the Cultural Revolution in China crossed into the tiny territory and nearly brought about its collapse. Political tension between the Nationalist KMT and Communist forces grew ever fiercer. In March 1966, Ho Yin, leader of Macao's Communist Party, was almost killed in a bomb attack.[44] Due to the Portuguese administration's reluctance to provide any significant funding for education or other human services, most schools were affiliated with either the Roman Catholic Church or the PRC. The local pro-PRC schools inculcated their students with the ideals of the Cultural Revolution, radicalizing them with pithy sayings from Mao's "Little Red Book," and demonizing Europeans, especially the Portuguese. On November 25, 1966, a new Portuguese governor, Nobre de Carvalho, arrived in Macao. Five days after his arrival, Red Guard students and workers invaded and occupied Government House. The situation quickly spiraled out of control, as the masses became a mob, invading and looting government buildings. Two notable colonial buildings right in the center of the city, the *Leal Senada*, where the city council met, and the baroque *Misericordia* Cathedral, were severely damaged. Fearing anarchy and large-scale bloodshed, the injured Ho Yin unsuccessfully appealed to the Red Guards to remain calm. Clashes between Red Guards and Portuguese police and troops intensified, and eight people died, with hundreds of others arrested or injured. Increasing numbers of Chinese troops massed at the border, escalating tensions yet further.

Fearing a Chinese military invasion, most Portuguese fled to Hong Kong. At one point, the British government drew up an evacuation plan for the removal of British and Hong Kong subjects from Macao, and civilian transport was alerted to sail if need be to Macao, to rescue Portuguese civilians and troops alike should the Portuguese government request British assistance. While thinking a full-scale invasion of Macao unlikely, the British government believed that, should this occur, it would prove only a prelude to a similar operation against Hong Kong.[45] Tough negotiations followed between the Chinese and the Portuguese, who were quickly losing control of the enclave to Red Guard forces. The PRC negotiators demanded that all KMT associations must be closed and all KMT "agents" expelled. The final agreement gave China paramount authority in the territory, with the Portuguese government only retaining power at Chinese pleasure. To add insult to injury, Portugal had to accept full responsibility for the riots and free all those who had been arrested.[46] Hong Kong soon experienced similar riots, but there the far stronger and more effective British government restored order and emerged from 1967 in better shape than before the disorder. British Trade Commissioner T. W. Ashton conceded that "the Governor of Macao was in a much weaker position than the Governor of Hong Kong in dealing with local Communists and the PRC. The situation in Macao was not comparable to that of Hong Kong." Ashton queried whether Macao retained any mastery whatever over its own affairs. The British recognized that the fact that it brought China substantial foreign exchange earnings, some 30 million pounds sterling annually, was the only reason Macao had not been taken over entirely in 1966.[47]

For much of 1967, Soviet consulates and embassies in East and Southeast Asia filed numerous reports on the Hong Kong riots, giving details on virtually a weekly basis. While conceding that British rule had played some role in sparking the riots, such reports laid the major share of responsibility for them on the Chinese government in Beijing.[48] Interestingly, during 1966 and 1967, Soviet reports on Macao ignored the disorder in the Portuguese territory, indicating perhaps an absence of

Soviet concern, or the lower ranking of Macao in Soviet policy making, by contrast with Hong Kong, to which Soviet sinologists clearly devoted much attention. Soviet reports on Macao discussed Macao's emerging economy and American intelligence activities in the territory, but said nothing of the Red Guards, who at one point virtually controlled all Macao.

As they had earlier in the Cold War, in the 1970s, Soviet diplomats acquiesced in Chinese characterizations of the status of Macao. After two decades of attempts to join, in 1972 the PRC was finally admitted to the UN, replacing the ROC in the UNGA, with full veto power in the UNSC, and on all committees. This was a huge blow to Taiwan, though one that had been anticipated. Almost immediately the PRC's permanent representative presented a document entitled the "Memorandum of March 8" to the UN Special Committee on Decolonization, demanding that Hong Kong and Macao be taken off the list of territories under colonial rule. "Hong Kong and Macao are part of Chinese territory occupied by Britain and Portugal. To solve the question of Hong Kong and Macao is a question entirely within Chinese sovereignty."[49] In other words, China did not want Britain, the United States, or any other nations, including the Soviet Union, to use the forum of a UN committee to push for eventual independence for either territory. China's wishes were granted: Macao and Hong Kong were removed from the UN's list, and the UN would never discuss either territory's future. The Soviet Union conceded that China was well within her rights in treating Macao not as a colony of Portugal, but Chinese territory under Portuguese occupation.[50]

On April 25, 1974, the Portuguese army, dissatisfied for years after losing endless unsuccessful colonial wars in Africa, finally launched a coup, which overthrew the almost 50-year fascist dictatorship. Portugal quickly embarked on the road to democratization, one soon followed by its Spanish neighbor.[51] The new government's policy toward its colonies specified: "The right to self-determination and all inherent consequences, encompasses the intrinsic acceptance of independence for all overseas territories (including Macao)."[52] As early as September 1974, Portugal's Foreign Minister declared that Macao was simply a Portuguese trading port, not a colony.[53] At this time Portugal sought to return Macao to China and withdraw all its troops, a gift that China, still coping with the ravages of the Cultural Revolution and the impending demise of its supreme leader, Chairman Mao Zedong, refused. While China claimed the reason it declined the return of Macao was political uncertainties within China resulting from the ravages of the Cultural Revolution, the real motive, according to Soviet sinologists, was money. The PRC was not ready to accept Macao's restoration because keeping it a Portuguese-controlled territory was more lucrative for China. The Soviets believed that similar considerations governed the return of both Hong Kong and Macao to the PRC, that in each case the Chinese were unwilling to lose the financial benefits they gained from leaving each city under foreign administration.[54] Soviet officials mocked China for its hypocrisy, declaring that whenever the Portuguese government tried to have a discussion on Macao, China refused to talk, saying the present was not yet a good time. These events allowed the new Portuguese governor, G. Leander, to declare quite truthfully that Portuguese control over Macao had the full consent of all parties.[55] On January 6, 1975, the Portuguese Foreign Ministry recognized that Taiwan was an integral part of China, and that the PRC was the sole legitimate government of China. Simultaneously, Portugal sought to reassure the nervous Chinese residents of Macao by promising to safeguard their rights in all future talks with the PRC government.[56] One year later, on February 17, 1976, Portugal granted Macao wide autonomy. It was no longer considered an integral part of Portugal (literally a province of Portugal), but a Chinese territory under Portuguese administration. In other words, China regained full sovereignty over Macao, making its status very different from that of Hong Kong, which remained officially a British crown colony. On February 8, 1979, Portugal and the PRC established full diplomatic relations.

The Soviet reaction to these revolutionary events was restrained, even though China had—at least temporarily—rejected Portugal's offer to return Macao. Soviet officials believed the new government of Portugal genuinely wanted to give full freedom to Macao, and thought it quite natural that the Portuguese government was willing to open negotiations. Such decisions were to be expected of a country emerging from a long twilight of fascism and seeking to begin to rejoin the community of democratic European states. While considering China mistaken to refuse the return of Macao, the Soviet Union agreed that the future of Macao must remain a matter between China and Portugal. Soviet foreign policy represented a very delicate balancing act. On the one hand, the Soviet Union consistently declared Macao was an archaic colony, which must be returned forthwith to China. On the other hand, the Soviet Union had very close ties with the new Portuguese socialist provisional government. In fact, in "conversations between Portuguese and British colonial officials in Hong Kong on October 16, 1974, the Portuguese noted the strong Soviet influence in their new government." Even the newly appointed Minister of Overseas Territories, Dr. Antonio de Almeida Santos, conceded this in a visit to Macao at that time.[57]

The Soviet Union believed that China viewed the status of Macao as linked to the broader Hong Kong question. The major difference was that China had no conflict with Portugal over Macao, as it did with Britain over Hong Kong. The 1975 agreement between Portugal and the PRC declared that Macao was part of China, but governed by Portugal, which granted the territory considerable autonomy. The Chinese Foreign Minister expressed pleasure that in Macao China did not face problems similar to those with Hong Kong, and that no such issues divided Portugal and the PRC as separated the latter and Britain. Portugal itself affirmed that Macao was not another Hong Kong, and that its officials would collaborate comfortably with China. Almost ten years later, in 1984, the Soviets observed that the Chinese were delighted that Macao was a wide open free port, part of the international capitalist system, and was therefore highly profitable to China. The Soviets further noted that the Chinese possessed considerable property in Macao, including hotels, banks, casinos, and even brothels. Substantial Chinese trade passed through Macao, including, the Soviets claimed, illegal contraband, such as opium, a business from which they believed China received $50 million annually. Sustaining this trade, and therefore keeping Macao a Portuguese-run territory, was very important to Southeast China. China could use Macao as a conduit to win closer relations with Western Europe. Maintaining the status quo in Macao was therefore very useful to China.[58]

In the late 1970s, China emerged from isolation, led by Deng Xiaoping, who proved far more pragmatic than his predecessor, the ideological autocrat Mao Zedong, and who formulated the concept of "one country, two systems" for Hong Kong and Macao. In 1987, Deng stated: "If Hong Kong and Taiwan are not assured that they could go on as before, capitalism, stability, and prosperity in those places would be jeopardized and peaceful settlement would be out of the question."[59] While Deng did not mention Macao in his speech, he soon reassured the tiny enclave that it would receive the same generous treatment as the two other and far larger territories of Hong Kong and Taiwan. After long and frequently tortuous talks, in 1984, Britain and China signed the Joint Declaration, setting out Hong Kong's future. Following the return of Hong Kong to China in 1997 as prescribed by earlier treaties, the territory would become a SAR, and would control its own affairs, except in foreign policy and defense.

In May 1985, Portuguese President Ramalho Eanes visited China, where he discussed the future of Macao with the then Communist Party head Zhao Ziyang, who was later put under house arrest for opposing the crushing of the demonstrators at Tiananmen Square in 1989. Whereas the Sino-British talks had taken two years, the Sino-Portuguese negotiations lasted a mere nine months, from June 1986 to March 1987, and progressed far more smoothly than those over Hong Kong. Portugal and China reached agreement on Macao after three rounds of talks. The process of returning Macao to China would be easy. Portugal was concerned to maintain the Portuguese language and culture there, and also to preserve the economic rights as well as political freedoms of Portuguese citizens in Macao. Soviet officials nonetheless commented that many Portuguese people in Macao were very skeptical, packing their bags and preparing to leave because they did not trust the Chinese government. The Soviet Union further noted that China was actively seeking foreign capital and would do so through Macao, which was why it had created a special trading zone in the nearby city of Zhuhai. Soviet specialists accurately predicted that over the next 20 years, the entire region—Hong Kong, Macao, and neighboring Guangdong province—would develop enormously and become an economic center for China and all Southeast Asia, an economic boom that subsequently materialized.[60]

The Joint Declaration between Portugal and China, originally initialed on March 26, 1987, was officially signed during the April 11–17, 1987 visit to China of Portuguese Prime Minister Cavaco Silva. The agreement was almost identical to the Sino-British Joint Declaration on Hong Kong. Portugal agreed to return Macao to China on December 20, 1999. Both Hong Kong and Macao would become Chinese SARs and would receive extensive autonomy in all matters except foreign affairs and defense. As with Hong Kong, Macao was assured that its economic system and laws would remain intact for 50 years, and it could continue to enjoy separate representation in various international organizations, including the World Trade Organization (WTO), the IOC, the Asian Development Bank, and numerous others. Like Hong Kong, Macao could permit the free movement of capital and retain its own currency, the *Pataca*.[61] After the signing of the Joint Declaration, Macao entered a transitional period, with Portugal still responsible for Macao's administration, while China gradually assumed ever-increasing predominance within the enclave. Before any major decisions were made, China was consulted. The handover of Macao to China on December 20, 1999, went very smoothly, and unlike Hong Kong the enclave subsequently remained very quiet and politically inactive. Russian Deputy Foreign Minister Grigory Karasin attended on behalf of the Russian Federation, a symbol of Russia's interest in promoting ties with the territory.

Only toward the end of Portuguese rule over Macao, did the Soviet Union and Macao sign a formal treaty to expand trade. During 1989, Governor Carlos Montez Melancia established contacts between the Soviet Union and Macao, which opened unprecedented opportunities for trade. On Macao's part, trade would mostly be in textiles and its economic agent would be the Sino-Macao Ltd.[62] On April 30, 1990, the Macao Economic Services (representing Macao) and the USSR Chamber of Commerce signed a formal seven-part Cooperation Agreement to promote trade and mutual investment.[63] There is no evidence to suggest that the agreement remained in effect after the collapse of the Soviet Union in December 1991 and the end of Portuguese rule over Macao in 1999.

Post-Soviet Russia and Macao

Russian underworld and criminal contacts with Macao nonetheless increased markedly during the 1990s, as Russian showgirls, bargirls, and prostitutes became new and exotic, if somewhat seedy, features of Macao's casinos and nightlife.[64] In the late 1990s, the Russian Interior Ministry reported to President Boris Yeltsin on the international connections of Russian mobsters and organized crime, highlighting gangsters' links to Macao, as well as the United States, Canada, and Israel.[65] During the 1990s, Russian mafia syndicates allegedly attempted to forge alliances with Chinese counterparts not just in Macao but also in Hong Kong, Shanghai, and Malaysia, though one study suggested that Chinese triads, especially those with links to the Chinese military and ruling political elites, proved too tough for the Russian would-be interlopers to work with, "effectively negat[ing] any real possibilities for close collaboration between the Russian and Chinese mafias, at least in the medium term."[66] In the mid- to late 1990s, intense gang warfare among the various Chinese groupings characterized Macao, and among the assorted weaponry employed were Russian-made grenades as well as AK-47 machine guns, evidence of at least some illicit Russian arms trading into Macao.[67] By 2002, Macao was nonetheless considered one of the hubs of the Russian international narcotics trade.[68] A 2003 research paper suggested that Vladivostok served as the base camp for Russian criminal penetration of Hong Kong and Macao, as well as North China.[69]

The role of Russian organized crime in trafficking women to both Macao and Hong Kong attracted particular international attention and condemnation. In 1997, an Associated Press report cited Macao as a destination for "trafficked women from Ukraine and Russia."[70] A 2000 CIA report suggested that criminal groups in the Russian Far East were supplying women to brothels and clubs in both territories.[71] Some of the women involved were perfectly willing; one study even suggested that on occasion they were among the "more enterprising" of their contemporaries, "risk takers" in search of opportunities unavailable to them at home. Even for these intrepid adventurers, however, their careers could end in tragedy, as demonstrated by the 1994 story of "an educated Vladivostok woman, trafficked to Macao, [who] returned home only to be killed by her boyfriend, a distinguished Hong Kong lawyer, who came to Vladivostok to buy her out of prostitution." Other accounts of this story, which eventually became the basis of a novel, *The Living Room of the Dead* (2005), by a Hong Kong journalist, were more sinister, suggesting that the woman, 20-year-old Natalia Samofalova, and New Zealander Gary Alderdice, a leading Queen's Counsel in Hong Kong, were both tortured, robbed, and shot in her flat in Vladivostok, presumably by the Russian mafia syndicate which employed her.[72]

Other women involved were equally vulnerable and perhaps had no choice as to their fate. Speaking to the UNCHR in April 1998 during a discussion on children's rights, a representative of the organization Human Rights Advocates claimed that "thousands of girls from the former Soviet Union were trafficked each year to Macao" and other destinations "as striptease dancers and prostitutes."[73] In many cases, Russian women were smuggled in illegally, with fake visas, and as elsewhere in Asia some who had been promised jobs of other kinds were allegedly forced into prostitution to pay the debts they had incurred when making the journey to Macao, with their passports confiscated by their employers.[74] The 2004 report of the US State Department on human rights in Macao, issued in February 2005, also claimed that, while most Russian and other prostitutes in the territory were voluntary participants, some at least had been trafficked against their will.[75] A 2005 State Department report on "Human Trafficking and Modern Day Slavery" likewise highlighted the misleading nature of advertisements urging young Russian women to take well-paid jobs in both Macao and Japan.[76] While suggesting that no children had been forced into prostitution in Macao, the report mentioned claims by Macao officials that Russian, Chinese, and Thai criminal syndicates were involved in the lucrative trade in women for sexual exploitation.[77]

While Russian police may have quietly cooperated with international agencies in efforts to interdict cross-border flows of women, narcotics, and armaments into Macao and Hong Kong, official Russian pronouncements stressed more salubrious aspects of collaborative Russian-Macanese relations. After the handover, in July 2002, Igor Ivanov, then Russian Foreign Minister, visited Macao, where he met the new Chief Executive Edmund Ho. The two leaders agreed to strengthen their bilateral trade and explore economic opportunities, especially in the tourism, hotel, and entertainment areas, which Macao knows very well. Both sides agreed to exploit their mutual expertise—Russia with its scientific and technical resources, and Macao with its management skills—to consider establishing a joint science park in the new SAR. Both sides have expressed interest in establishing interregional partnerships, and Russian officials have characterized recent developments as positive.[78]

Conclusion

The interest Russian and Soviet policy makers demonstrated in Macao gave striking evidence of the global reach of the international ambitions of first the Tsarist, and then the Communist regimes, and the manner in which these expanded after the Bolshevik Revolution in 1917. Although Tsarist Russia established significant consulates in both Hong Kong and Japanese-controlled Taiwan, then known as Formosa, it never sought to do so in Macao. Instead Russia relied on its Hong Kong representative to handle the smaller colony, and on its consulates in Hong Kong and

Guangzhou and the embassy in Lisbon to provide any information needed. Despite the stated Soviet commitment to international revolution, between the wars Soviet activities in Macao remained insignificant, certainly by comparison with the far more substantial though ultimately fruitless endeavors of the 1920s to make Hong Kong a leading Asian revolutionary base, while Portuguese officials made determined efforts to exclude all Communists from the territory. Soviet relations with Macao also provide an interesting case study of Soviet opposition toward Western colonialism, and of the manner in which, where nominally Chinese territories were concerned, during the Sino-Soviet split these attitudes became embroiled in—but never fundamentally altered by—the ideological warfare the two Communist giants were waging against each other. Interestingly, Stalin was himself aware of the existence of Macao, though he may have been somewhat unclear as to its exact status. Although its information was often rather patchy, notably on the 1967 riots, the Soviet Union virtually automatically approved all PRC efforts to destabilize Macao to the detriment of Portuguese rule.

At the height of the Sino-Soviet split, during the 1960s, the Soviet Union nonetheless also contemplated using Macao as a base for covert intelligence gathering on the PRC, though whether such plans ever came to fruition is still unclear. Paradoxically, Macao's somewhat incompetent and inefficient colonial administration made it a more hospitable site for such undertakings than its more tightly controlled neighbor, British Hong Kong. Whatever the provocations and however poor its relations with China, however, the Soviet Union never compromised its fundamental ideological principles and always denied the legitimacy of both Portuguese control of Macao and British rule in Hong Kong. As it became increasingly clear in the later twentieth century that Macao's future lay with the PRC, Soviet officials followed most attentively the Sino-Portuguese negotiations that in March 1987 resulted in an agreement providing for Macao's return to full Chinese control in December 1999. Once this event took place, Russian economic ties with Macao increased. Despite concerns over the links between Russian organized crime and Macao, for the first time since World War I Russian officials contemplated what they believed were bright future prospects for Russian-Macanese relations.

10

Transitions: British Hong Kong and the Soviet Union Sail away into the Sunset

In 1970, neither the Soviet Union nor British Hong Kong could have envisaged their future some 30 years later, as the new century began. Most observers, in the East and West alike, believed that the Soviet Union would retain indefinitely its then existing authoritarian nature, and found any other possibility unimaginable. Hong Kong, on the other hand, had only just begun to understand that by 2000 the territory might not survive in its existing state as a British crown colony.

In the 15 years before 1985, under the stewardship of General Secretary Leonid Brezhnev, the Soviet Union embarked successively on policies of consolidation, stability, growth, and finally stagnation. Mikhail Gorbachev, Brezhnev's successor as General Secretary and President, following the short terms of Yuri Andropov and Konstantin Chernenko, first launched a cautious policy of economic and political reform, which modulated into an attempt at rapid reform, bringing a descent into chaos for both country and Communist Party. By the Christmas Day of 1991, the Soviet Union had ceased to exist.

Hong Kong, by contrast, changed dramatically after 1970 to become a very prosperous city-state, a fundamentally well-educated and sophisticated middle-class society. Hong Kong Chinese felt increasing concern over what might transpire and sought to know what would be Hong Kong's future and, almost inseparably, their own. Meanwhile, from the early 1970s, the British rulers of Hong Kong, in both the territory and in

London, were coming to realize that as the end of their country's control over the crown colony approached, Hong Kong's political future was becoming an issue of crucial importance to Great Britain, the United States, and the PRC.

British control of Hong Kong rested on three treaties concluded with China during the mid- and late nineteenth century. On August 29, 1842, China, defeated by Britain during the First Opium War, signed the Treaty of Nanjing, surrendering to the victor the 35 square miles of Hong Kong Island. After losing the Second Opium War to Britain in 1860, by the Convention of Peking China ceded the even tinier Kowloon Peninsula. During the 1890s, Germany, Russia, France, and Japan all exploited the Chinese Empire's growing weakness to demand Chinese territory, and Britain followed suit. In 1898, the British and Chinese governments opened talks that led in June to the Convention of Peking, granting Britain approximately 365 square miles of additional lands adjacent to Hong Kong, known as the New Territories and comprising almost 80 percent of Hong Kong's current territory. Whereas Hong Kong Island and the Kowloon Peninsula were ceded in perpetuity, the New Territories were granted on a 99-year lease, due to expire in 1997.[1]

For several decades after 1949, both Britain and China had ample reason to evade the issue of Hong Kong's postcolonial future. By the 1970s, the Hong Kong government faced long-term infrastructural decisions, such as whether to build a new airport and container port, while local banks sought guidance whether or not to grant mortgages on the New Territories leases due to expire after 1997. Without the New Territories, a rump Hong Kong was not viable. Self-determination was never a feasible option for the territory, since China, its huge neighbor, would never permit its independence, while the Soviet Union, at least nominally China's ideological ally, would use its veto in the UNSC to block any move in this direction. Should Britain even attempt to retain control of Hong Kong against China's wishes, the PRC could simply cut off Hong Kong's food and water supplies, starving the colony into submission at no military risk. By the late 1970s, Britain therefore chose to broach the hitherto ignored subject of post-1997 Hong Kong. The moment seemed relatively propitious. The Cultural Revolution was over, and the pragmatic Deng Xiaoping clearly controlled the PRC's government. China was modernizing and opening to the outside world, planning to create low tax Special Economic Zones near Hong Kong and

Portuguese-controlled Macao. In 1979, the PRC and the United States established full diplomatic relations, while overall Sino-British relations were comparatively good.[2]

Early and preliminary talks between the British and the Chinese on Hong Kong were supposedly conducted in secret, but as early as 1975, the Soviet Union got wind of such negotiations. In a note to Moscow, the Soviet Mission at the UN mentioned that its officials had learnt that discussions on the subject of Hong Kong's future had taken place between the United Kingdom and the PRC in New York. The note stated that it was believed China would not demand the immediate return of Hong Kong, but would let Britain retain continued political control of Hong Kong, at least until 1997. Previously, hundreds of thousands of people had fled the cripplingly repressive political atmosphere of the Cultural Revolution and famines in the PRC, to take shelter in Hong Kong. In a concession to China, the British had promised not to grant such refugees political asylum, unless an applicant had a genuine and strong case. The Soviet government was therefore very much aware that Britain was increasingly concerned over its future in Hong Kong, and followed the situation closely.[3]

In 1979, the PRC invited Hong Kong Governor Sir Murray MacLehose to become the first sitting governor to visit Beijing. The British government determined that it was essential to reach a clear resolution of the 1997 question. Although many advisers urged him to say and do nothing, MacLehose decided his visit furnished an appropriate occasion to raise the issue of bank loans on leases, effectively opening thereby the whole question of Hong Kong's post-1997 administration. His action remained highly confidential, because British officials feared that, should China rebuff him, confidence in Hong Kong's economy and currency would collapse. Soon after arriving in Beijing, MacLehose and several other prominent British China experts met Deng Xiaoping, who neither accepted nor rejected any British proposals, but simply deflected the issue of leases by declaring that neither Hong Kong residents nor investors had any cause for alarm. While expressing respect for Hong Kong's special status, Deng nonetheless stated clearly that Hong Kong was an integral part of China and must return to the PRC.[4]

The May 1979 British general election brought the Conservative leader Margaret Thatcher to power. In April 1981, Foreign Secretary Lord Carrington went to Beijing to reopen the subject of the New Territories leases, and to pave the way for a subsequent Thatcher visit to China, when Hong Kong's future would be the main item on the agenda. Although Deng told Carrington the matter was not yet urgent, he also clearly specified that eventually China would regain Hong Kong.

The year 1982 marked a crucial turning point. Firstly, China's reunification policy changed dramatically in January, as Hong Kong replaced Taiwan as Beijing's top priority in its drive to reunite all Chinese territories. Regaining Hong Kong represented a far more attainable goal, which Chinese leaders also hoped would serve as an example to encourage Taiwan to return. China's new constitution, promulgated in April, contained provisions for an autonomous Hong Kong SAR, which retained its own economic and legal system. Secondly, in Hong Kong the date was approaching when no more 15-year leases could be granted on properties within the New Territories, because these would expire after 1997. Thirdly, Britain declared war on Argentina over the Falkland Islands, a conflict many thousands of miles away yet nonetheless having significant consequences for Hong Kong. Only after the war ended that summer did Hong Kong's future and her impending visit to Beijing regain Thatcher's attention. Moreover, Britain's overwhelming victory against Argentina convinced Thatcher that Britain's military strength still sufficed to defend any British territory, no matter how distant, initially causing her to adopt a toughly nationalistic attitude when she began further discussions with Chinese leaders.[5]

On September 22, 1982, Thatcher, suffering from a cold but determined, arrived in Beijing resolved to take full charge of the talks, rescuing the negotiations from the Foreign Office's China hands, whom she considered virtual appeasers, so as staunchly to defend and preserve Hong Kong's freedom and values. The morning after her arrival she met Prime Minister Zhao Ziyang, who immediately told Thatcher that China would resume sovereignty over Hong Kong, but would maintain Hong Kong's stability and prosperity.[6] Furthermore, sovereignty and administration were inseparable. If forced to choose between Chinese sovereignty and Hong Kong's prosperity, China would give the former precedence, since as a matter of national pride China had to reclaim both sovereignty and administration.[7]

Deng and Thatcher met on September 24, 1982. Deng bluntly told Thatcher that China would take over Hong Kong in 1997, and sought British cooperation in the process so as to maintain the city-state's prosperity. For the first time, China had specified a date for Hong Kong's recovery. Thatcher retorted that Hong Kong was British by virtue of internationally recognized treaties, and while Britain was ready to concede sovereignty over Hong Kong to China after 1997, she stated emphatically that only continued British administration could guarantee Hong Kong's stability and prosperity. Deng flatly rejected her arguments, declaring that, with or without British assistance, China would resume full sovereignty and administration after 1997. The British flag and governor would have to depart, and China alone would decide what policies were suitable for Hong Kong. During this tough two-hour meeting both sides refused to compromise, and a furiously hostile Deng even absented himself from the farewell dinner banquet in Thatcher's honor. She finally realized she had been naïve in anticipating any speedy agreement on Hong Kong's future.

After leaving China, Thatcher arrived in Hong Kong on September 26, the first time any sitting Prime Minister had visited the tiny colony. While there she defended the legality of British treaty claims to Hong Kong, sharply reprimanding Deng for simply dismissing those rights under international law. "If countries try to abrogate treaties, it is very serious. If a country will not stand by one treaty, it will not stand by another."[8] Within Hong Kong confidence swiftly declined, as its people realized they were trapped between two intractable opponents, China and Britain, with little influence over their own future. The Hong Kong stock market and dollar both fell, leaving residents depressed over their uncertain prospects. Due to a lack of confidence in Thatcher's words, within a week of her departure from Hong Kong, the stock market fell by 25 percent, while the Hong Kong dollar depreciated some 12 percent.[9]

The assorted British, Chinese, and American interpretations of these crucial talks have become quite familiar.[10] Even as a reformist China opened to the outside world, knowing that a stable and prosperous Hong Kong would greatly facilitate the attainment of its objectives, the PRC was simply too proud and nationalistic to accept a continued formal British presence in Hong Kong. China never recognized the nineteenth-century "unequal treaties" ceding Hong Kong to Britain, and was determined to undo the "wrongs of history." On reflection, the Falklands victory notwithstanding, if China refused to extend the lease Britain realized it could not expect to retain Hong Kong, most of which was part of the Chinese mainland and indefensible against any determined Chinese assault. United States President Ronald Reagan would be unlikely to assist the British as he had in the Falklands, since the ongoing Soviet war in Afghanistan led American officials to seek deeper PRC involvement in an anti-Soviet front. American trade with China was also expanding rapidly, and the United States would not welcome instability in East Asia or serious conflict, let alone a war, between two such crucial states as China and Britain. The absence of viable options forced Thatcher to swallow her pride and negotiate the best attainable terms for post-1997 Hong Kong.

Until recently the Soviet attitude toward those talks remained unclear. Two documents recently made available at the AVP RF reveal Soviet sensitivities in some detail. Professor V. A. Krivtsov, Deputy Director of the Institute of Far Eastern Studies in Moscow, the principal Soviet think tank on China, wrote the first report, "The Problem of Xianggang (Hong Kong) and the Position of the USSR," for Igor A. Rogachev, the Head of the Far East Department at the MID, later Russian Ambassador to the PRC from 1992 to 2005. The other report, "Some New Tendencies in the British Approach to Relations with China," drafted by Ye. Safronov, a Second Secretary in the London Embassy, was also destined for the MID's Far East Department.[11]

The first document, written on June 20, 1983, discussed the Soviet position on Hong Kong's future status. Interestingly, Soviet officials perceived this primarily in the context of its implications for the Sino-Soviet border disputes that had bedeviled relations with the PRC during the 1960s and 1970s. Krivtsov mentioned that the Sino-British talks had raised matters directly affecting the Soviet Union, since China had attempted to declare that *all* treaties concluded by the Qing dynasty in the nineteenth century were unequal, which would naturally include treaties relating to the lengthy Chinese-Soviet border. "Although no official Chinese statement on Xianggang formally equated the unequal treaties between China and Great Britain with the Sino-Russian border treaties," unofficially it was clear that "the category of 'unequal treaties' comprises *all* international agreements entered into by Qing China during the nineteenth century." (italics added)

The problems over the relevant Sino-Russian treaties had deep historical roots. From the late seventeenth until the mid-nineteenth century Sino-Russian relations were stable, even relatively friendly. In 1689, the Treaty of Nerchinsk left undefined the Far Eastern border between China and the Russian Empire. Russian statesmen rarely paid attention to the Far East until the mid-nineteenth century, when various factors caused this perspective to change.[12] Firstly, after losing the 1839–1842 Opium War to Britain and suffering further weakening in the Taiping Rebellion, China was clearly a declining power. Secondly, Russia feared that increasing British and American naval and fishing activities in the Far East could bring those powers a permanent presence there. Thirdly, after losing the Crimean War Russia sought territorial expansion elsewhere. Fourthly, recent Russian explorations of Eastern Siberia made the government more conscious of the region's vast economic and strategic significance.

Within a few years Russia gained vast rich territories, negotiating two highly advantageous border treaties with China, the 1858 Treaty of Aigun and the 1860 Convention of Peking, which moved the Russian border far south and fixed the existing Manchurian border along the Amur and Ussuri Rivers.[13] In 1858, as British and French troops threatened Beijing, the Russians offered to mediate on China's behalf to obtain better terms. In return the Chinese very reluctantly agreed to the Treaty of Aigun, which fixed their border with Russia along the Amur River. The Russians remained unsatisfied, coveting the strategically crucial east coast bordering the Sea of Japan, where they could establish a warm water port at what is now the city of Vladivostok. While the Chinese argued that the Ussuri coast belonged to Manchuria, the Russians considered control of that shore crucial, fearing that otherwise Britain would annex it. During the Second Opium War of 1856–1860, Russia once again acted as a "moderate, neutral" intermediary between Britain and China. As Anglo-French forces again threatened Beijing, and Taiping rebels were also rumored to be approaching the capital, the Russians forced the Chinese to sign the Convention of Peking, confirming the validity of prior treaties and setting the coastal borders far to the south, close to the Korean frontier. Within three years Russia had acquired vast territories, totaling 665,000 square miles.[14]

Infuriated Chinese officials considered Russian claims to be China's good friend thoroughly disingenuous, and their territorial concessions a humiliating loss of face to foreign barbarians, whose zeal to acquire Chinese territory surpassed even that of the British and French. Among the Russians, by contrast, these agreements generated the myth that the Chinese considered the Russians, unlike other Europeans, friends rather than exploiters.[15] Except for the brief period 1918–1921, during and after the Russian Civil War, the Soviet Union never renounced its territorial gains or characterized these two treaties as unequal.[16] After Hong Kong returned to China in 1997 and Macao in 1999, Russia's acquisitions were the only remaining lands lost to China due to nineteenth-century imperialism, and the Amur and Ussuri frontiers in East Siberia and along the coast the only formerly Chinese territories still occupied by Europeans. Yet, while China considered its nineteenth-century treaties with Russia unequal, it also believed that, unlike those with Britain, these treaties were legitimate and recognized under international law. All border negotiations between the Soviet Union and the PRC accepted the legitimacy of these treaties, so that by the end of the twentieth century no outstanding territorial claims divided China and Russia.

As Soviet officials moved to normalize ties with the PRC after over 20 years of Sino-Soviet antagonism, they were forced to clarify Soviet views. On September 25, 1982, Margaret Thatcher stated in Beijing that all treaties between Britain and China were valid, and Hong Kong Island and the Kowloon Peninsula would remain permanently British unless and until a new treaty changed their status.[17] When negotiating with China, the British could employ the argument that both Soviet and Chinese officials considered their nineteenth-century treaties legal. Krivtsov therefore urged the Soviet government to adopt the position that further normalization of ties between the PRC and the Soviet Union required Soviet support for Chinese demands to reunify the whole country, including Taiwan. During the alliance period of the 1950s, the Soviet Union had given *full* support to the recovery of Hong Kong by China. Granted, however, their strained relations during the late 1970s and early 1980s, "the tactical line of *limited* and measured support for China's statements and actions on Xianggang [Hong Kong] is the most reasonable." (italics added) Soviet propaganda should make clear to other countries that the Soviets supported the return of Hong Kong, a territorial remnant of colonialism. The population of Hong Kong was heavily ethnically Chinese (over 95 percent); economically Hong Kong was closely linked to China; and even the British accepted that Hong Kong was basically Chinese. Hong Kong's prosperity rested on a strong and growing China. The Soviet Union therefore maintained that Hong Kong's future was entirely a Chinese internal matter.

As relations between the PRC and the Soviet Union deteriorated from the late 1950s onward, the Soviet media had often denounced China for its hypocrisy in criticizing European imperialism, yet refusing to move against those colonies, Hong Kong and Macao, literally on China's doorstep.[18] Now, however, continued criticism of China's procrastination in regaining Hong Kong should cease, since it would only impede the normalization of ties between the Soviet Union and the PRC. Krivtsov further suggested that, while the Soviets should continue on demographic and economic grounds to endorse Hong Kong's return to China, they should not mention that one basis of the Chinese claim was that the British had forced the Chinese to sign several unequal treaties, since: "Our official support of the Chinese view that the treaties concerning the status of Xianggang [Hong Kong] were unequal could give Beijing additional ammunition in its attempts to call into question the contractual and legal basis of the Sino-Soviet frontier."[19] While the Chinese claimed that even if the Soviets accepted their claim that the three treaties defining the Sino-Soviet border (1858, 1860, and 1881) were unequal, China would not seek to recover this huge tract of territory, they might subsequently reverse this position. Despite the fact that Chinese leaders currently stated that "China has never demanded the return of the Chinese territories taken over by Russia under some unequal treaties, the Chinese side has in no sense bound itself by any promise not to advance such demands in the future." Unless China clarified this issue, it was quite possible that at some point its leaders would announce that the PRC had "'decided not to be bound by such unequal treaties,' and demand the return of all territories allegedly 'detached' by Tsarist Russia."

Krivtsov urged that, when mentioning unequal treaties, the Soviet press should never suggest that any treaties signed between Russia and China were likewise "unequal," claiming that the treaties Britain and China concluded during the nineteenth century had nothing in common with those between Russia and China. First of all, the British had taken Hong Kong as the "result of British military aggression against China," whereas the treaties establishing the Russian-Chinese frontiers "were the result of diplomatic efforts by both parties." Secondly, Russia and China had merely clarified an undefined border, and the treaties defining those frontiers resulted from lengthy, amicable talks between two friendly states, a characterization that ignored the circumstances under which these agreements were negotiated. Thirdly, the report claimed the borders between Russia and China followed natural frontiers, the Amur and Ussuri Rivers, and respected the realities of the distribution of the respective Russian and Chinese populations. Again, this description was less than accurate, since in the mid-nineteenth century very few Russian civilians had inhabited that huge region, though it had a sizeable population of both Chinese people and Asian tribes, who had for centuries paid tribute to the Chinese. The Soviets therefore secretly hoped Margaret Thatcher would never concede that under international law the British-Chinese treaties were illegitimate.

The second document, dated June 20, 1983, some nine months after Thatcher met Deng in Beijing, during which no serious Sino-British negotiations took place, described the two countries' subsequent relations. China refused to grant Britain any formal role in a post-1997 Hong Kong, while Britain refused to concede both future sovereignty and control of Hong Kong's administration to China. As stock market, currency, and property values fell in unison, gloom pervaded Hong Kong.[20] The Soviet Embassy in London understandably characterized Sino-British relations as unstable. British experts doubted whether Deng Xiaoping and his reform policies enjoyed full control of China; British business leaders hesitated to invest in the PRC; while British sinologists queried American policy makers' conviction that China was a reliable ally against the Soviet Union. Soviet diplomats in London nonetheless warned the MID that the British Foreign Office did "not expect any 'dramatic' improvement in Sino-Soviet relations," and urged their government not to "'worry too much' about that."[21]

Interestingly, the Soviet Embassy expected Sino-British relations would soon improve. "In recent talks with us, British Foreign Office representatives ... noted the appearance of 'new optimism' in assessments of the prospects for Sino-British relations." Bolstering this optimism were the adoption by the Deng Xiaoping leadership "of 'pragmatism' in Beijing's international behavior and of an 'open policy' in its economic dealings with the West."[22] The PRC signed agreements with British firms to conduct oil exploration in the South China Sea, to construct a nuclear power plant near Hong Kong at Daya Bay, and to build two computer factories. Visits of British politicians and business leaders to China and by their counterparts to Britain increased. Hoping to encourage trade between their two countries, the British government anticipated opening a consulate in Shanghai, while the Chinese expected to open one in Manchester, both industrial cities.

Furthermore, the Soviets observed that both Britain and China were taking a new line on Hong Kong, noting the view of British informants that "in both countries the mass media treat Hong Kong largely as a business partner and an intermediary between Britain and China."[23] The British also moderated their disagreement with China over Hong Kong's sovereignty. Both China and Britain agreed temporarily to set aside the issue of who would administer Hong Kong after 1997 and tackle less contentious issues, so as to maintain Hong Kong's stability and prosperity in the approach to 1997. In return, China agreed to allow Governor Sir Edward Youde to participate in the talks over Hong Kong's future. The Soviet Embassy believed that Britain recognized that China would fully control Hong Kong after 1997, and Britain would focus increasingly on protecting its economic investments in the territory. Embassy officials cited the view of British China experts serving as government advisers, who "said quite openly that British recognition of the PRC's right to Hong Kong, including the two ceded colonial portions, Hong Kong Island and the Kowloon Peninsula, was 'inevitable,' but alleged that until recently the real problem was China's provision of firm guarantees to safeguard British business interests in this territory, which London would wish to receive as a written 'interim agreement.'" In return for ceding sovereignty and administration over all Hong Kong to China after 1997, British leaders believed that China would be willing to conclude a formal written agreement. Therefore, despite the prevailing pessimistic climate in relations between Britain and China, British officials believed "a mutually acceptable solution on Hong Kong may be reached even before the end of this year [1983]." Both sides wished to improve the political atmosphere. Britain would accept full Chinese control over Hong Kong, and would grant China access through Hong Kong to badly needed high technology. In return, China would increase its trade with Britain and allow more British investment in China, and would accept some British proposals on Hong Kong, guaranteeing a high degree of autonomy and freedom for Hong Kong.[24]

Soviet observers were astute. Within months, serious negotiations, which now included Governor Youde, began in Beijing, London, and Hong Kong itself. A few months after those talks opened, Britain recognized the inevitable, and agreed that it would play no formal role in Hong Kong after 1997. After that key concession, China was far more conciliatory in recognizing British economic interests in Hong Kong. On September 20, 1984, two years almost to the day after Thatcher visited Beijing, China and Britain signed a Joint Declaration providing the blueprint for the transition to Chinese rule for Hong Kong, and guaranteeing Hong Kong's people freedom and the maintenance of their existing way of life.[25]

On December 19, 1984, Britain and China ratified the Joint Declaration, officially proclaiming that on July 1, 1997, the PRC would take full control of Hong Kong. The Soviet Union observed that from the very beginning of Sino-British negotiations, China had made it extremely clear that Hong Kong and Macao were both Chinese territories, and that China had never recognized their colonial status. The Soviet Union had no difficulties with that position, but did face problems when China declared that the agreements between China with Britain and Portugal were unfair and implicitly non-binding because they were unequal treaties. Once again, China had raised the contention that so-called "unequal treaties" by definition violated international law, and therefore lacked any international validity. Soviet officials further noted that in a letter sent to the UN Special Committee on Decolonization in March 1972, with the specific purpose of denying the UN any jurisdiction over the status of either Hong Kong or Macao, the PRC had flatly stated that those three nineteenth-century treaties were illegal, and Hong Kong therefore did not have the status of a normal colony. In the Joint Declaration, signed on September 27, 1984, China again affirmed that it refused to acknowledge the validity of those nineteenth-century treaties. Prior Chinese assurances to the Soviets failed to dispel USSR fears that, if the nineteenth-century treaties between China and Britain were not valid, the same might be true of Russia's own nineteenth-century treaties with China.[26] Almost a decade after the handover, the Russian Federation quietly harbored the same misgivings as did its Soviet predecessor, worrying that China could easily repudiate these treaties, whereupon the huge Chinese population just across the lengthy shared border might easily move over and simply overwhelm the Russian Far East.

Following the signing of the Joint Declaration, Queen Elizabeth II of Great Britain paid a visit to Hong Kong and Macao in 1986, the first visit by an English monarch to the crown colony. The Soviet Union noted that her visit to Hong Kong did not go well as people in the territory were very nervous about their future under Chinese rule in little more than ten years' time. The Soviets also noted Hong Kong concerns over a nuclear plant that was being built right across the border from Hong Kong. Many people in

Hong Kong believed the power plant, despite all assurances, was not built according to the highest world safety standards, and feared another Chernobyl-like disaster, which could destroy Hong Kong.[27]

Only after the collapse of the Soviet Union in December 1991, did relations between Hong Kong and Russia warm significantly. Despite repeated efforts, throughout the 75 years of Soviet rule, the USSR was never allowed to establish any permanent diplomatic presence. However, its successor state, the Russian Federation, was permitted to do so. After a series of high-level negotiations, cleared on both sides with the Chinese, a Russian Consulate-General opened and in October 1994 the new Russian Consul-General, Kirill Ivanov, presented his credentials to Christopher Patten, the last British Governor. The Russian Consulate remained a small operation, occupying part of one floor of a high-rise building in the Wanchai district of Hong Kong Island, its full-time staff numbering no more than ten people, but its personnel cherished high hopes that trade, business, and cultural exchanges with Hong Kong would rapidly expand.

Carefully observing all diplomatic courtesies, the Russian Federation therefore sent a high ranking delegation, led by Foreign Minister Evgenii Primyakov, to attend the well-orchestrated joint Sino-British handover ceremony that took place on a very wet June 30–July 1, 1997 weekend in Hong Kong. President Yeltsin sent a congratulatory message to the Chinese government on the "occasion of the restoration of China's jurisdiction over Hong Kong," expressing confidence that Hong Kong would remain a "prosperous financial and economic center in Asia" and would "prove the effectiveness of Deng Xiaoping's 'one country, two systems' formula."[28] The newly free Russian press was, by contrast, far more critical and highly pessimistic, reflecting the view of newspaper columnists and the general population in Moscow, expressed repeatedly to a visiting Hong Kong academic that summer, that political and economic freedom would very speedily disappear as the Chinese government, backed up by its army and secret police, clamped down on Hong Kong. On July 2, Andrei Krushinsky proclaimed in the still Communist daily *Pravda*: "Hong Kong, whatever its political system, is now part of Communist China de facto. Geopolitically, this is the most serious event in East Asia since the Americans were driven out in the mid-1970s." Russian journalists even spoke appreciatively of the benefits of British colonial rule. The following day, on July 3, Fyodor Pogodin, writing in the reformist opposition business daily *Kommersant*, lamented:

"No matter what Beijing says or promises, the European-style democracy in Hong Kong is going to be replaced by a Communist regime, with the rulers customarily prevailing over the law and the state being in control of people's private life." On the same day, Vladimir Simonov wrote in the progressive daily *Moskovskii Komsomolets*, that "Britain looked good in her 156-year-old rule ... and when she decided to leave Hong Kong, she did so in a noble way."[29]

Whatever their apprehensions as to the future, expanding commercial and business opportunities became and remained the top priority for Russian diplomats in this city that epitomized business. Over successive years, trade between Russia and Hong Kong grew steadily. Hong Kong exports to Russia rose by 24 percent to US$149 million in the first four months of 2005, impressive growth that followed on an even larger increase of 52 percent to US$427 million in 2004. Major Hong Kong exports included parts and accessories for office machines and computers, toys, games, sporting goods, electronics, clothing, and watches. Trade in the reverse direction was, by contrast, less impressive. Hong Kong's total imports from Russia declined by 15 percent, to US$178 million in the first four months of 2005, after a prior 3 percent decline to US$482 million in 2004. Major commodities imported from Russia included oil, iron and steel, semi-precious stones, and furs.[30] While these figures were only a small fraction of the far greater US–Hong Kong trade, they represented a huge increase over the Soviet period.[31] By 2005, the Russian Trade Association in Hong Kong, established to facilitate commerce between the Russian Federation and Hong Kong, had over 100 members.[32] Major Russian companies in Hong Kong included Aeroflot Airlines, MMC Norilsk Nickel, and MMK, the huge Magnitogorsk Metalwork Company.

At the official level, a concrete affirmation of the deepening relationship between Russia and Hong Kong occurred when Igor Ivanov, who succeeded Primyakov as Foreign Minister, visited the city in July 2002. In return, Sir Donald Tsang, then Hong Kong's Chief Secretary, who subsequently became Chief Executive, visited Moscow in May 2004, becoming the first top Hong Kong official to go to Russia.[33] On the day-to-day basis, the Russian Consulate quickly became an active presence on the Hong Kong diplomatic scene. Like other such national representative offices, every year it hosted a National Day reception, attended by leading Hong Kong businessmen and politicians, as well as issuing visas to facilitate visits to Russia by businessmen and tourists. The Consulate also actively promoted the dissemination of information on Russian culture and educational exchanges with Hong Kong, efforts that ensured that Hong Kong officials and the general public knew more of Russia than at any time since at least World War II. During its first decade, it facilitated the appearances in Hong Kong of numerous Russian cultural groups, including the Bolshoi Opera and Ballet, the renowned Marinsky Opera and Ballet, various symphony orchestras, and circus troupes. In late October 2001, the Consulate promoted a weeklong Russian Film Festival. Working with the University of Hong Kong, in 1993, 1994, and 1999 the Consulate promoted educational exchanges involving extended research and teaching visits to each others' institutions by historians from the University of Hong Kong and the Russian State Pedagogical University in St. Petersburg. In summer 2000, under an exchange agreement signed between the two universities, the first ever educational field trip by University of Hong Kong undergraduates to St. Petersburg and Moscow took place.

Growing business and cultural ties were paralleled by the growth of a small but vital Russian community, consisting of around 300 people, mostly diplomats, academics, businessmen, their families, and wives of non-Russian foreign expatriates. This marked a change from the Soviet period, when the only Russians living in Hong Kong were émigré White Russians. The number of Russian tourists and businesspeople visiting Hong Kong, though again very small by comparison with those arriving from other European countries, has become significant. To accommodate them, Aeroflot makes three or four weekly flights in each direction between Hong Kong and Moscow, depending on the season, and most of these flights are fairly full, bringing some 15,000 Russians to Hong Kong each year.[34] Before 1997, Russians had to obtain visas for Hong Kong through the British Embassy in Moscow, or its Consulate in St. Petersburg. After 1997, the Chinese Embassy in Moscow or the Chinese Consulates elsewhere became the source for such visas. Paradoxically, even though the Russian Federation enjoyed excellent relations with the PRC, the visa situation for Russians coming to Hong Kong was no easier than during the last years of British rule. While post-1997 Russian visitors normally found these documents easy to obtain, as a rule they were only valid for two weeks and unless exceptionally good reasons were provided, could only be renewed once. One reason for this may have been that some

Russian tourists to Hong Kong were young women recruited, either voluntarily or against their will, into prostitution. Hong Kong's vigilant police force and strict immigration controls meant that few such young women remained in Hong Kong, but the city nonetheless acquired a reputation with international organizations as a transit point for Russian and other prostitutes, their travels often organized by Russian mobsters, who were journeying onward to work in Macao and other cities in China or Southeast Asia.[35] For Russians, the post-handover Hong Kong visa situation was nonetheless an improvement on the Soviet period, since Russians could travel to Hong Kong and, if they possessed appropriate documents, live and work there.

After 1997, the Russian media covered most major post-handover developments in Hong Kong. Significantly, the press noted that political freedom stood the test of time, and the more pessimistic predictions of many Russians were not fulfilled. Even so, Russian commentators bemoaned the lack of democracy in Hong Kong, producing decidedly factual articles on the various huge pro-democracy demonstrations of the early 2000s.[36] The Russian press also reported both the economic recession, which gripped Hong Kong for several years after the handover, and the subsequent economic recovery.[37] Russian newspapers and television likewise covered other major developments, such as the SARS epidemic of spring 2003 and the bird flu epidemic of subsequent years, both of which alarmed the Russian public, and even efforts to save a cake shop once patronized by former Hong Kong Governor Christopher Patten, as well as the highly publicized criminal trial of an American woman accused of murdering her husband in 2005.[38] Even so, most Russians' knowledge of Hong Kong remained limited, the popular image encompassing little more than *kung fu*, Jacky Chan, and other highlights of Hong Kong cinema productions, ensconced in a city of tall buildings.

Devoid of its past political overtones, the Hong Kong–Russian relationship of the early 21st century focused firmly on deepening commercial and economic ties, with a subsidiary emphasis on cultural activities. In Taiwan, unsettled issues as to the island's precise status still complicated Russian dealings with the island. This was not the case with Hong Kong. Stripped of the assorted international Cold War rivalries that had usually bedeviled their dealings, in Hong Kong as in Macao, both sides could concentrate on exploring the potential economic opportunities that Tsarist and Soviet-era officials and businessmen had coveted but rarely been able to develop. In many ways this more stable, less charged situation represented a return to the halcyon days of 1908 to 1914 when, briefly allied with Britain, Tsarist Russia no longer represented a threat to the security of colonial Hong Kong. For the first time in almost a century, mundane normality prevailed in Hong Kong–Russian relations.

Conclusion

Hong Kong, Taiwan, and Macao, component parts of the China periphery, are unquestionably ethnic Han Chinese territories, but politically, economically, and culturally speaking, great differences divide them from the PRC. Located either along or off the southeastern coast of China, all three are economically capitalist, while the PRC remains at least nominally Communist. To a much greater extent than present-day China, despite its recent huge economic growth, all three, though originally very poor, later became quite affluent. The populations of all three places enjoy significant political freedom and operate under a rule of law, while the PRC government accords its people only very limited political freedom. Culturally all three are far more westernized than the PRC. Hong Kong was a far outpost of some six million people administered by a once major European political and economic power, Great Britain. Despite considerable internationalization, Hong Kong still reflects the legacy of the British, who for 150 years settled and governed it. The much smaller and less populous Macao was likewise for 450 years a distant redoubt of a European country, Portugal, which several centuries ago possessed a great empire, and which was responsible for Macao's Mediterranean atmosphere. From 1895 to 1945, Taiwan was under Japanese rule, while its close post-1949 relationship with the United States has given the island a somewhat American atmosphere. All three places have been far less isolated from world developments than was true for much of its history of the PRC. Russian and Soviet relations with each of these entities were always very much a function of Russian-Soviet relations with other powers, including China, Great Britain, Japan, Portugal, and the United States.

Russia's relations with China originated during the late seventeenth century, rather earlier than those it developed with most European states. From that time onward Russia sought increased trade with China, and territorial expansion into lands long claimed by China. Russia and its successor state, the Soviet Union, quickly realized the potential economic and strategic value to themselves of the South China coast and the peripheral territories of Hong Kong, Macao, and Taiwan, all paradoxically in some way in China but not of China. As early as two centuries ago, before the establishment of British Hong Kong, Russia viewed the coastal periphery as a gateway to South China. From the time the colony was founded, Russia demonstrated interest in Hong Kong, seeking to expand trade and foreign investment there, as it also did with China itself and later in Taiwan, then often known as Formosa. Besides pursuing its political and economic objectives in China, Russia sought to acquire Western technology from rapidly developing Hong Kong and later also from Taiwan. Seeking to attain these goals, as early as 1860 Russia established a Consulate in Hong Kong, and another in 1895 in Formosa, which had just come under Japanese rule, but thought Macao too insignificant to merit one, leaving the Hong Kong organization to handle the few Russian dealings with the tiny territory. Its Consulates in Hong Kong and Guangzhou (Canton), together with its Embassy in Lisbon, provided any information needed on Macao, such as reports filed from Hong Kong during the Portuguese Revolution of 1910 discussing its impact on the tiny territory. The Hong Kong and Formosa Consulates closed shortly after the Bolshevik Revolution of 1917, once all governments involved recognized that the Bolsheviks had won firm control of Russia, which they were likely to retain for the foreseeable future.

From the early nineteenth century, Russia took advantage of the Qing dynasty's growing weakness to extract trade concessions from the Chinese government, obtaining low tariff benefits at least comparable to those China awarded other European states. During the mid-nineteenth century, Russia pressured China into signing three treaties, under whose terms China ceded to Russia hundreds of thousands of square miles of territory in the Far East along the Amur and Ussuri Rivers, and south along China's northeastern coast as far as what is today Vladivostok. Russia also established virtual protectorates over Outer Mongolia, Manchuria, and Xinjiang province in northwest China. In Manchuria, Russia built a railway line east to the newly established port of Vladivostok, and another line south to Port Arthur, which became a major Russian naval base for its Far East Fleet.

While the China periphery was a rather low priority for Russian policy makers, some Russian leaders, diplomats, and military officers recognized the area's geopolitical and commercial potential. Russian commanders noted the potential value of Hong Kong as both an economic gateway to South China and a strategic entrance to Southeast Asia, which was already attracting European colonization. Just south of Hong Kong, the French were already expanding into Indochina. Imperial Russia also coveted Hong Kong and Formosa as potential naval bases and at least twice, in 1854 and 1885, contemplated seizing Hong Kong by force of arms. Hong Kong's British rulers and inhabitants understandably mistrusted this Russian attention, fearing an outright Russian invasion attempt, as they realized that, in an era of slow and poor communications, Hong Kong was rather vulnerable to attack. Although Britain and Russia fought only one war during the nineteenth century, the Crimean conflict, relations between the two powers could at best be described as a "cold peace," a situation which continued until 1907. Just after the Crimean War ended, Admiral Efvim Putyatin visited Hong Kong and Macao, and in 1857 negotiated a commercial treaty with the British there. Subsequently, two members of the Russian royal family visited Hong Kong, Grand Duke Alexis in 1872, and the future Tsar Nicholas II in 1891, and the latter also very briefly visited Macao during his Far Eastern grand tour. Late nineteenth-century Russian officials also hankered after the island of Formosa, which was loosely governed by China. Despite their interest in the island, another nation, Japan, was swifter to take advantage of Chinese military weakness to launch the Sino-Japanese War, by the end of which in 1895, the island was ceded to Japan as a colony.

Following the Russo-Japanese War, Russia lost its special predominance in Manchuria, together with control of the railway lines and the Port Arthur naval base, to Japan. After the Bolshevik Revolution of 1917, the new Soviet regime temporarily renounced the unequal treaties whereby China had granted the Russian Empire special rights, particularly in Outer Mongolia. Seeking allies, the infant and internationally isolated Soviet regime also sought to demonstrate to the new Chinese Republic that it did not resemble other European countries. Once the Bolsheviks had defeated their anti-Communist opponents, the new Soviet government quietly rescinded its prior generous offer, and sought to reclaim all the old privileges and lands pertaining to Tsarist Russia. Chinese officials, however, had longer memories, and the unequal treaties were one of several reasons why during the twentieth century Sino-Russian relations repeatedly oscillated between friendship and antagonism.

Fundamental continuities characterized British views of Russia and its successor state, the Soviet Union. In both cases, the British government was hostile to an authoritarian and militaristic Tsarist or Soviet state and feared Russian territorial ambitions in East Asia, particularly in China. Throughout the nineteenth and twentieth centuries, the community of Russian residents in Hong Kong never numbered more than a few hundred individuals, and after 1917 it was not just small but also rather poor economically and generally apolitical, posing no danger to Britain as a fifth column. For most of the Tsarist period Russo-British political relations in Hong Kong were cool but correct, while throughout the entire period from the Bolshevik Revolution of 1917 until the dissolution of the Soviet Union, no official political relations existed between the Soviet state and Hong Kong. While Britain and Russia were allied during both world wars, at no time did either power trust the other or feel any great respect for its rival's political and economic system. Even when allied with it during World War I, the British government felt little affinity for authoritarian and militaristic imperial Russia. Throughout the entire period when it ruled Hong Kong, on the whole, Great Britain was suspicious or even hostile toward Russia and its post-1917 Soviet successor. The nature of British relations with Russia impacted on Hong Kong. When those two nations were at war or close to war, as occurred twice during the mid- to late nineteenth century, Hong Kong feared a seaborne invasion launched by Russia. Britain recognized Russian militaristic aspirations in the region, and feared that Russian territorial expansion could extend to South China and Hong Kong. When relations thawed, opportunities for Russia in the colony, especially economic ties, expanded.

After 1917, ideological suspicions bolstered Britain's distrust of Russia, as it confronted a revolutionary state pledged to overthrow and destroy its existing political and economic system. During the 1920s, Soviet support and financial assistance for several strikes in Hong Kong bolstered rather than allayed such fears, and over time ideological differences only exacerbated their already uneasy relationship. Britain refused to allow the Soviets to establish a consulate, trade office, news agency, travel office, or any other form of permanent presence. Even Soviet plans to build an oil refinery in 1933 fell through when the Soviet Union and Britain severed diplomatic relations that March. Despite Hong Kong's dependence on trade, Britain did not encourage any Soviet commercial expansion, fearing that would only encourage the Soviets to seek a permanent presence which, British officials firmly believed, would in turn enable and facilitate Soviet intelligence and subversive activities.

Unlike Tsarist Russia, the Soviet Union never considered any direct takeover of Hong Kong, Taiwan, or Macao, but actively supported the reverse, the return of all three to the PRC. Over time Soviet policy also became less radical. While during the 1920s, the Comintern sought to destabilize Hong Kong, during the 1930s it tried to encourage a militarily and economically strong Hong Kong that would offset the growing expansionist threat from Japan. Soviet officials considered Japanese rule in Taiwan strategically menacing, but Comintern efforts to destabilize the island were fruitless, as the local CPF was small, weak, and ineffective, and subject to severe Japanese repression. In interwar Macao, Soviet activities remained insignificant.

Throughout, Russian and Soviet policy makers tried to strike a balance between economic and strategic concerns, while at times, especially after 1949, considerations of ideological solidarity moderated other factors. Throughout the 1920s, Soviet policy toward Hong Kong revealed a certain tension between the MID and the Comintern, as each worked at cross purposes. During the 1920s, the MID followed a fairly cautious policy toward Hong Kong, seeking trade and western products for a devastated Russia, and also attempting to use commercial expansion to end Soviet Russia's near complete diplomatic isolation. The Comintern, by contrast, sought to promote international socialist revolution, and viewed relatively advanced Hong Kong as a potential vanguard site for a Chinese Marxist socialist revolution. There was perhaps some justification for this outlook. Ever since the late nineteenth century Hong Kong had given shelter to Chinese revolutionaries, such as Sun Yat-sen, opposed to the Qing dynasty. It was the most industrialized, educated, westernized, and—perhaps most significant—politically free of all Chinese cities, in these respects surpassing its most notable rival, Shanghai. Hong Kong workers, however, preferred economic to political gains, and held somewhat aloof from Communist agitation. By the end of 1927, moreover, Communist and workers' uprisings in several Chinese cities, including neighboring Guangzhou, had ended in failure, a fiasco for which Josef Stalin and his misguided foreign policies were largely responsible.

From then onward, the role of the Comintern declined and Soviet foreign policy concentrated almost solely on Soviet national interests. Initially, the encouragement of trade to propel Soviet industrialization once again became the primary focus of Soviet policy toward Hong Kong. Although Hong Kong served as a base during the 1930s for Southeast Asian and Chinese Communists and leftists, for the rest of the interwar period the pursuit of commercial advantage probably remained the most significant objective of Soviet policies toward not just the territory, but also Macao and Taiwan, although in all three cases trade with the Soviet Union never constituted more than a small fraction of total overseas commerce. For the Soviet Union, trading with and through Hong Kong was necessary to facilitate commerce with China. During the 1930s, as China became increasingly embroiled in a war with Japan that threatened its very survival, Hong Kong assumed greater importance as one of the few remaining Chinese ports not compromised by war, through which goods could still pass safely. While never officially recognizing British rule over Hong Kong, Soviet policy became more pragmatic, viewing the British garrison and fleet in Hong Kong as barriers to Japanese expansion.

Once the danger from an ambitious militaristic Japan had disappeared, as World War II reached its end in 1945 and the Cold War began, ideology once more came to the fore in Soviet dealings with Hong Kong, Taiwan, and Macao. It was official Soviet policy that all European colonies should enjoy the right of national self-determination, and should be speedily granted independence under governments of their own choice. According to Soviet logic, however, Hong Kong, Macao, and Taiwan fell into a different category, especially after 1949, when the Soviet government followed the PRC in declaring that all three territories were integral parts of China, which should therefore be returned immediately to their original sovereign, even if this required military force. Although Hong Kong and Macao were clearly European colonies, because they had been seized from China, an established sovereign state, they should not have the right to self-determination, whereby the local population would choose their own government, but should simply be restored to the mother country. Any attempt to introduce self-government was characterized as a "Western trick." In 1949 and 1950, immediately after the Communist victory in the Chinese Civil War, the Soviet Union also encouraged the PRC to retake not just Hong Kong and Macao, but also Taiwan. Ironically, while Mao Zedong was prepared to defer indefinitely regaining the first two, he actively sought to win back Taiwan, something that Soviet endorsement in spring 1950 of North Korean leader Kim Il-sung's plans to invade South Korea effectively shelved for well over half a century, if not permanently.

Soviet relations with Macao also provide interesting case studies of Soviet opposition to Western colonialism, and of the manner in which, where nominally Chinese territories were concerned, during the Sino-Soviet split these attitudes became embroiled in—but never fundamentally altered by—the ideological warfare the two Communist giants were waging against each other during the 1960s and 1970s. Although its intelligence about the enclave was very patchy, the Soviet Union approved virtually all PRC efforts to destabilize Macao to the detriment of Portuguese rule. Until the late 1960s, the Soviets also emphatically opposed the KMT government in Taiwan, treating it as a "renegade" and "illegitimate" regime and declaring that the island should also be returned to China. In other words, the Soviets supported the mainland Chinese position that there was only "one China," the PRC, whose capital was located in Beijing. Whatever the provocations and however poor its relations with China, the Soviets never compromised their fundamental ideological principles and always denied the legitimacy of both Portuguese control of Macao and British rule in Hong Kong.

Within those ideological constraints, during the 1960s, this position underwent a subtle evolution, shaped once more by developments in China. Again, different Soviet agencies pursued varying lines. As the Sino-Soviet alliance disintegrated into near warfare, many Soviet diplomats took a much more positive view of British Hong Kong, Portuguese Macao, and KMT-controlled Taiwan. As in the 1920s, MID officials recognized the potential benefits each place offered in terms of increased trade and access to advanced technology, and at least on an unofficial basis sought to improve relations. While trade with China itself was important to the Soviet Union, the ambivalent status of the marginal territories of Hong Kong, Taiwan, and Macao seemed to offer the Soviet Union the possibility of obtaining advanced western technology and products unavailable to them either in the West or from China itself. Hong Kong and later Taiwan, for example, supplied the Soviet Union with electronic products, Chinese medicines, ginseng, and other goods only available from East Asia. Whereas during the 1920s, Soviet officials sought to encourage a proletarian revolution in Hong Kong and Taiwan, they looked askance at the street violence that erupted in Hong Kong during 1967, disrupting trade and economic stability in the territory. Visiting Russian diplomats and journalists wrote much more positively on each territory, noting that each was far more affluent than the PRC and all, even Taiwan under martial law, possessed far greater freedoms than the mainland.

The International Department of the CPSU Central Committee was nonetheless still locked in the old ideological mindset, regarding all three territories as archaic relics of the past. The International Department blocked all efforts by the MID and the Ministry of Foreign Trade to open a Consulate or even a trade office in either Hong Kong or Taiwan. Once again Soviet policy was divided and uncoordinated, as Soviet diplomats and other officials sought a permanent presence in all three territories, which would not only facilitate the expansion of trade and investment, but also assist in gathering intelligence on developments within China, while the CPSU repeatedly ridiculed China's refusal to regain Hong Kong, Macao, and Taiwan by force of arms. At the height of the Sino-Soviet split, during the 1960s and 1970s, the Soviet Union also contemplated using Hong Kong, Macao, and Taiwan as bases for covert intelligence gathering on the PRC and developments throughout Southeast Asia. The Soviet Union even considered sending intelligence agents to Hong Kong and Macao, but whether such plans ever came to fruition is still unclear. It seems, however, that for at least a year or two in the late 1960s Soviet and Taiwanese officials repeatedly exchanged intelligence information on mainland China. The Soviet Union frequently lacked good intelligence gathering sites and agents in Cold War East and Southeast Asia, something that became very apparent when, for example, the Soviet Union wrongly predicted the PLA would not conquer all China in 1949, or that the North Vietnamese could not defeat the Americans and take South Vietnam in 1975.[1] Macao and Hong Kong could have served as invaluable sources of intelligence. Paradoxically, Macao's incompetent and inefficient colonial administration made it a more hospitable site for such undertakings than its more tightly controlled neighbor, British Hong Kong.

What similarities and what major differences characterized Soviet policy toward Hong Kong, Macao, and Taiwan? How did Soviet policy toward each change over time? What, finally, do Soviet dealings with the three territories reveal about Soviet policy toward China itself and, more broadly, the Northeast Pacific region? One continuity characterizing the entire course of Soviet policy toward Hong Kong, Taiwan, and Macao was that the Soviet Union always sought—at least rhetorically—to alter the status quo. Throughout the entire existence of the Soviet Union, its government never officially recognized British control of Hong Kong, where during the 1920s the Soviets hoped for and sought to encourage a revolution. During the later 1930s and after 1965, the Soviets accepted British control, and even thought it advantageous to themselves in terms of trade and defense, but they never officially recognized British colonial rule in Hong Kong as legitimate. Similar considerations of anti-colonialist ideology underpinned their formal repudiation of Portuguese control of Macao and Japanese sovereignty over Formosa.

While never very positive toward either the British or the Portuguese, as Sino-Soviet relations declined the Soviet Union's stance on continued colonial rule in Hong Kong and Macao became more complex, especially in connection with the more weighty territory of Hong Kong, which possessed an extremely vibrant economy and a stable currency. Yet, despite the dramatic and ever degenerating Sino-Soviet split, Moscow nonetheless still refused to abandon its ideologically driven anti-colonial and implicitly pro-PRC policy. Marxist-Leninist solidarity with even a deviant Communist country still took precedence over any attempt to improve formal economic, let alone political, relations with British-ruled Hong Kong or Portuguese-ruled Macao. During the 1960s, for instance, a movement existed in Hong Kong to grant the colony self-rule as an autonomous and self-governing territory within the British Commonwealth, essentially giving it dominion status. Whatever tensions divided it from the PRC, the Soviet Union fully supported China in rejecting moves toward self-rule as a western trick.[2] China and the Soviet Union staunchly and undeviatingly opposed all movements for political reform in Hong Kong as flagrant diversions to maintain continued western dominance over the colony. At least with regard to Hong Kong and Macao, the "one China" principle remained unchanged.

Until the very dissolution of the Soviet Union in 1991, Soviet policy in the region remained one of giving with one hand and taking with the other. These divisions and contradictions impeded Soviet efforts to develop economic or cultural ties with the region, making it extremely difficult for the authorities in Taiwan, Hong Kong, and Macao to understand the Soviet Union's true objectives. After 1956, Soviet foreign policy under the direction of Nikita Khrushchev sought to thaw the Cold War through his policy of "peaceful coexistence." Consequently, he queried China's belligerent stance toward Taiwan during the Second Strait Crisis in 1958 and toward India the next year, urging greater flexibility on the part of China. He even, for example, unsuccessfully urged China to consider allowing both China and Taiwan to participate in the Olympic movement, a suggestion China angrily rejected.

As the home base of a government the Soviet Union no longer recognized, Taiwan presented additional problems. Soviet and Taiwanese policies toward each other were both reactive, the result of changing geopolitical configurations, and their impact remained decidedly marginal. During the earlier Cold War, the Soviet Union and the PRC were close ideological, political, military, and commercial allies, as were Nationalist China and the United States. In the later 1950s, the Soviet-PRC alignment began to crumble, followed a few years later, albeit to a lesser degree, by the American-Taiwanese alliance. In the later 1960s, growing United States ties with the PRC led Taiwan, unnerved by its growing isolation, to approach the Soviets, who exhibited some interest, sending a top diplomatic intelligence operative to Taiwan in 1968. As a rule, Taiwan initiated gestures toward the Soviets, betraying its comparatively far more vulnerable international position. Yet, even after the United States switched diplomatic recognition to the mainland, it still remained Taiwan's patron and the guarantor of its security, and the ROC government feared compromising this all-important relationship, greatly inhibiting its freedom of maneuver, and limiting the scope of any moves in the Soviet direction. Its continuing desire to maintain good relations with the United States therefore narrowed Taiwan's scope for action. While the developing US rapprochement with mainland China and the visits of National Security Adviser Henry A. Kissinger and then of

President Richard Nixon to Beijing during the early 1970s alarmed and disturbed Taiwan leaders, they too recognized that ultimately they depended on the United States and its Seventh Fleet for protection from PRC attack. Even after the United States removed the sheltering naval flotilla from the Taiwan Strait, all knew that it could easily be redeployed. Although Taiwanese representatives were prepared to talk to the Soviets, develop commercial and cultural ties, and even at times exchange intelligence data on mainland China, they would not contemplate anything resembling a full political and military alliance with the Soviet Union. That move would have been far too extreme, and would have risked total American abandonment of the island. Although from the late 1960s onward, there was a progressive thaw in economic, cultural, and personal relations, throughout that entire period until the early twenty-first century, official political and diplomatic ties between the Soviet Union and Taiwan remained nonexistent.

Soviet responses to Taiwan were also somewhat ambivalent, illustrating the constraints its position as the world's leading Communist power imposed upon Soviet freedom of action. However acrimonious Sino-Soviet relations became, ideologically, the Soviets felt unable to abandon the PRC altogether and embrace Taiwan. Soviet policy toward Taiwan resembled its attitude toward Hong Kong, the last major British colony, whose government the Soviets likewise refused to recognize and condemned as a relic of Western colonialism. Soviet officials always hoped that the Sino-Soviet split was not final, and might end in ultimate reconciliation. Communist solidarity, together with concern to maintain Soviet leadership of the international socialist camp, trumped realpolitik, precluding for the Soviet Politburo's members, lifelong Communists all, the pragmatic but "counter-revolutionary" option of jettisoning Red China for its capitalist rival. However antagonistic its relationship with mainland China, publicly the Soviet Union doggedly contended that only one Chinese government existed, that in Beijing, though archival evidence suggests that Soviet officials might have acquiesced in international recognition of Taiwan, had the PRC found this acceptable. Over time, too, the Soviet Union and its satellites undoubtedly became more sympathetic to ROC participation in international organizations and meetings. Even so, despite Soviet recognition of Taiwan's increasing economic success and tolerance of its growing trade links with East European socialist states, every time the ROC sought to establish overt commercial relations, the

Soviets rejected these overtures, primarily for ideological reasons. Such Soviet ties with Taiwan as existed therefore remained discreet and low-profile; some Taiwan-Soviet trade apparently existed, but it was filtered through intermediaries, firms based in Eastern Europe and even in such capitalist locations as Austria, West Germany, Japan, and Hong Kong. Only after Russia abandoned Communism and the Soviet Union disappeared did its successor, the Russian Federation, open direct economic relations with Taiwan. The need to maintain its ideological credibility within the international Communist camp restricted the alternatives effectively available to Soviet leaders when dealing with Taiwan. Whereas ROC weakness and ultimate security dependence upon American protection limited any pro-Soviet moves from Taiwan, when the Soviet Union confronted the potential opportunities, strategic and economic, arising from the situation in Taiwan, the burden of Cold War leadership forced it into an equally confining ideological straitjacket.

One might, however, also argue that the Soviet Union decided to eschew the potential short-term benefits of wooing Taiwan in favor of the much larger prize of reestablishing positive and solid long-term relations with the PRC, a process that began during Gorbachev's presidency in the mid- and late 1980s. In other words, strategic pragmatism and ideology reinforced each other. This pattern continued even beyond the 1991 collapse of the Soviet Union. The successor Russian Federation invariably publicly endorsed the official Chinese stance on Taiwan's status, while from the early 1990s onward, massive Russian arms sales to China effectively bolstered the mainland military threat to the island and undercut any Taiwanese moves toward independence.

In contrast to the situation over Taiwan, in the case of Hong Kong, the Soviets were more eager than the British to develop closer ties, and therefore took a more proactive role. The British rebuffed virtually every Soviet approach, and longstanding Cold War suspicions precluded the development of any significant Soviet commercial or other permanent presence in Hong Kong. From the 1960s onward, the breakdown of Sino-Soviet relations gave the British colonial authorities still further reason to reject such overtures, since any permanent Soviet presence in Hong Kong might needlessly antagonize China. The maintenance of political and economic stability and the status quo in Hong Kong was a major concern for the British government, whose officials recognized that China, where for a crucial decade the unpredictable Cultural Revolution was at its volatile height, could at any time easily and almost painlessly take over Hong Kong. Not until after the collapse of the Soviet Union itself did Russia in 1994 obtain its long-coveted permanent diplomatic presence in Hong Kong.

Another basic feature of Soviet policy toward Taiwan, Hong Kong, and Macao was the question of identity. What exactly was Hong Kong? Taiwan? Macao? Since none were considered legitimate governments, the question of identity helped shape Soviet policy on the "one China" issue. To what extent did Taiwan's identity, in either a political or a cultural sense, differ from that of Beijing? The PRC claimed and still claims that Taiwan is and always has been an indivisible part of China. Yet the Taiwanese, Hong Kong, and Macao populations all possess strong and distinct local identities. In many ways, Soviet policy toward the China periphery—Hong Kong, Taiwan, and Macao—presents an interesting case study of one state's attempts to formulate rules for dealing with territories whose very existence it did not recognize. How does a country conduct trade, promote tourism and cultural ties, and even open offices, under such circumstances? This question posed many problems for the Soviet Union, especially from the 1960s onward, when Soviet officials genuinely desired to develop such ties. Their answer was to seek to expand trade and cultural ties on a business-to-business instead of on a country-to-country basis. When Aeroflot, for example, wished to discuss opening an air route from Moscow to Hong Kong or to Taiwan, it could only do so through negotiations with a Hong Kong or Taiwanese company, rather than with the Hong Kong authorities. Even when a Soviet company was state-controlled, agreements and contracts were always signed on a company-to-company basis. Furthermore, any contract between a Soviet company and a Hong Kong, Taiwanese, or Macanese counterpart had to include an explicit statement that the Soviet Union regarded all three territories as an integral part of the PRC. Entering into such an agreement in no way implied official Soviet recognition of British rule of Hong Kong, Portuguese administration of Macao, or KMT control of Taiwan. Whatever the provocations and however poor its relations with China, the Soviet Union never compromised its fundamental ideological principles and always denied the legitimacy of both Portuguese control of Macao and British rule in Hong Kong. In part because the Soviets insisted on so many conditions in such business agreements, whatever potential existed for the development of economic and other relations was never likely to be realized in full. External and ideological constraints greatly limited the potential for any real accomplishments in Soviet foreign policy toward the China periphery.

In sum, Russian and then Soviet foreign policy toward the China periphery resembled its policy toward China but possessed distinctive features that reflected the region's local characteristics. It was a policy shaped by Britain, Japan, the United States, and China itself. One can discern numerous continuities in Russian and Soviet policies toward Hong Kong, Taiwan, and Macao, which were always greatly affected by developments in neighboring China. In fact, prior to the collapse of relations between the Soviets and the Chinese, most information and even secret intelligence reports came from Chinese sources, and from the Soviet Embassy in Beijing or its Consulate in Guangzhou. Throughout the Soviet Union's entire history, its policies toward Hong Kong—and also toward Taiwan from the 1960s onward—were often divided and contradictory. During the 1920s and 1950s, Soviet policy was generally hostile to British rule of Hong Kong; while during the 1930s and 1960s onwards, the Soviets were quite conciliatory toward British rule. Generally both Russia and the Soviet Union considered Macao, by contrast, too small and unimportant to warrant any real policy of its own, though as with Hong Kong and Taiwan, Soviet officials gave rhetorical support to the future return of this colonial enclave to China. Stalin himself was aware of the existence of Macao, though he might have been unclear about its exact status.

The foreign policies toward the China periphery of imperial Russia and, for its first decade, likewise the USSR were quite proactive. During the Cold War years from 1945 to the early 1970s, by contrast, Russian foreign policy toward both Hong Kong and Taiwan was largely reactive, while the Soviet Union essentially had no policy toward Macao. In more than one sense, the three territories were peripheral, accorded a relatively low priority by both Russian and Soviet diplomats and other officials. Except, perhaps, when it rather unavailingly sought to obtain the economic and intelligence benefits that closer ties with Hong Kong might bring, the Soviet Union rarely initiated policy. On the fringes of China, in territories which were cultural and political borderlands, where Asia and the West encountered each other, as did the forces of doctrinaire communism and liberal capitalism, the Soviet Union generally simply responded to the initiatives and actions of the PRC, the ROC, and the United States. Soviet foreign policy toward the China periphery thus became increasingly complex, ambivalent, and even contradictory.

Russian and Soviet policy toward the China periphery was invariably shaped not only by China, but also by the state of Russian or Soviet relations with Britain, Portugal, and later with the United States as well. Very simply, when Russian and Soviet links with Britain and Portugal were good, links with Hong Kong and Macao were, at least, satisfactory; however when Russian and Soviet ties were poor, dealings with their colonies was either poor or completely non-existent. All parties concerned—the Russians or Soviets, the Hong Kong colonial government, and the Taiwanese—were therefore circumscribed in the options open to them. The PRC and the United States both shaped and defined those limits. First Russia and then the Soviet Union followed a regional policy in the China periphery—geographically Chinese but separated from China for lengthy periods of time, decades or even, in Macao's case, centuries—that resembled and was related to its policy toward China proper but also had significant differences, the product of the unique character of the China periphery. Ironically, the warming of Sino-Russian relations during the 1990s was a precondition for major increases in Russian commercial and cultural contacts with Taiwan, as the Russian rapprochement with mainland China convinced Beijing that unofficial Russian contacts with Taiwan did not undercut or threaten their own diplomatic position toward the island. As it became increasingly clear in the later twentieth century that the futures of Hong Kong and Macao lay with the PRC, highly attentive Soviet officials followed Chinese negotiations with Britain in 1984 and with Portugal in 1986, which soon resulted in agreements providing for each territory's return to full Chinese control as the twentieth century drew to a close. Once those events took place in 1997 and 1999, Russian economic ties with each newly created SAR increased, and for the first time since World War I Russian officials contemplated what they believed were bright future prospects for Russian relations with the China periphery.

Notes

Notes to Preface

1. Michael B. Share, "The Soviet Union, Hong Kong, and the Cold War, 1945–1970," *Cold War International History Project* Working Paper no. 41 (Washington, DC: Woodrow Wilson International Center for Scholars, 2003). The Russian Consulate-General in Hong Kong has placed a copy of this paper on their web site.
2. On the basis of those materials the author wrote an essay entitled: "The Enemy of My Enemy Is My Friend: The Soviet Union and Taiwan, 1943–1982," which was delivered at a conference of the Association of Third World Studies held in Costa Rica in October 2001. A very early version of the paper was published in a Taiwanese journal. "The Soviet Union and Taiwan, 1943–1982," *Tamkang Journal of International Affairs* 4, no. 4 (2000): 1–34. While conducting research in Taiwan, the author presented a paper on this topic at a seminar at the Academia Sinica in Taipei in October 2002. An extensively revised variant soon appeared in the journal *Cold War History*. "From Ideological Foe to Uncertain Friend: Soviet Relations with Taiwan, 1943–1982," *Cold War History* 3, no. 2 (January 2003): 1–34.

Notes to Introduction

1. S. A. Smith, *A Road Is Made: Communism in Shanghai, 1920–1927* (Honolulu: University of Hawaii Press, 2000); Leong Sow-Theng, *Sino-Soviet Relations: The First Phase, 1917–1920* (Canberra: Australian National University Press, 1971); Bruce A. Elleman, *Diplomacy and Deception: The Secret History of Sino-Soviet Relations* (London: M. E. Sharpe, 1997); Alexander Pantsov, *The Bolsheviks and the Chinese Revolution, 1919–1927* (Richmond, Surrey: Curzon Press, 2000); and William Rosenberg and Marilyn Young, *Transforming Russia and China: Revolutionary Struggle in the Twentieth Century* (New York: Oxford University Press, 1982).

2. Philip Snow, *The Fall of Hong Kong: Britain, China, and the Japanese Occupation* (New Haven, CT: Yale University Press, 2003); Gerhard Weinberg, *A World at Arms: A Global History of World War II* (Cambridge: Cambridge University Press, 1994); John W. Garver, *Chinese-Soviet Relations, 1937–1945: The Diplomacy of Chinese Nationalism* (New York: Oxford University Press, 1988); and Lee Chong-Sik, *Revolutionary Struggle in Manchuria: Chinese Communism and Soviet Interest, 1922–1945* (Berkeley: University of California Press, 1984).
3. Odd Arne Westad, *Cold War and Revolution: Soviet-American Rivalry and the Origins of the Chinese Civil War, 1944–1946* (New York: Columbia University Press, 1993); Dieter Heinzig, *The Soviet Union and Communist China 1945–1950: The Arduous Road to the Alliance* (Armonk, NY: M. E. Sharpe, 2004); and Chen Jian, *The Sino-Soviet Alliance and China's Entry into the Korean War* (Washington, DC: Cold War International History Project, 1992).
4. David Levine, *The Rift: The Sino-Soviet Conflict* (Jacksonville, IL: Harris-Wolfe, 1968); Tsui Tsien-hua, *The Sino-Soviet Border Dispute in the 1970's* (New York: Mosaic Press, 1983); and Gerald Segal, *Sino-Soviet Relations after Mao* (London: International Institute for Strategic Studies, 1988).
5. See Andreas Kappeler, *The Russian Empire: A Multiethnic History* (London: Longman, 2001); S. C. M. Paine, *Imperial Rivals: China, Russia, and Their Disputed Frontier* (Armonk, NY: M. E. Sharpe, 1996); Don C. Price, *Russia and the Roots of the Chinese Revolution, 1896–1911* (Cambridge, MA: Harvard University Press, 1974); and Rosemary Quested, *The Expansion of Russia in East Asia, 1857–1860* (Kuala Lumpur: University of Malaya Press, 1968).
6. Peter M. Ivanov, "Russian-Taiwanese Relations: Current State, Problems, and Prospects of Development," *Occasional Papers/Reprints Series in Contemporary Asian Studies* 133, no. 2 (1996): 1–76; Iu. M. Galenovich, *Samoutverzhdeniye sinovei Taivaniya* [Patriots of Taiwan] (Moscow: Muravei, 2002); and idem, *Moskva-Pekin, Moskva-Taipei* [Moscow-Peking, Moscow-Taipei] (Moscow: Izografius, 2002).
7. Peter M. Ivanov, *Gonkong* [Hong Kong] (Moscow: Nauka, 1990).
8. The best though very old work is Carlos Augusto Montalto de Jesus, *Historic Macao*, 3rd ed. (Hong Kong: Oxford University Press, 1984). The first edition appeared in 1902, and is only available in Portuguese.
9. Arnold L. Horelick, "Soviet Policy Dilemmas in Asia," *Asian Survey* 17, no. 6 (June 1977): 499–512; Reinhard Drifte, "European and Soviet Perspectives on Future Responses in Taiwan to International and Regional Developments," *Asian Survey* 25, no. 11 (November 1985): 1115–1122; and John W. Garver, "Taiwan's Russian Option: Image and Reality," *Asian Survey* 18, no. 7 (June 1978): 751–766.

10. P. E. Skachkov, *Ocherki istorii russkogo kitaevedeniia* [Outline of the History of Russian Sinology] (Moscow: Nauka, 1977); and Fedor Fedorovich Martens, *Rossiia i Kitai* [Russia and China] (St. Petersburg: A. Garten, 1881).
11. Paine, *Imperial Rivals*; John L. Evans, *Russian Expansion on the Amur, 1848–1860: The Push to the Pacific* (Lewiston, NY: Edwin Mellen Press, 1999); and Alexander Lukin, *The Bear Watches the Dragon: Russia's Perceptions of China and the Evolution of Russian-Chinese Relations since the Eighteenth Century* (Armonk, NY: M. E. Sharpe, 2003).
12. Elleman, *Diplomacy and Deception.*
13. Allen S. Whiting, *Soviet Policies in China, 1917–1924* (New York: Columbia University Press, 1954); and Conrad Brandt, *Stalin's Failure in China, 1924–1927* (Cambridge, MA: Harvard University Press, 1958).
14. Smith, *A Road Is Made*; idem, *Like Cattle and Horses: Nationalism and Labor in Shanghai, 1895–1927* (Durham, NC: Duke University Press, 2002); John King Fairbank, ed., *The Chinese World Order: Traditional China's Foreign Relations* (Cambridge, MA: Harvard University Press, 1968); Benjamin Isadore Schwartz, *Chinese Communism and the Rise of Mao* (Cambridge, MA: Harvard University Press, 1951); Maurice J. Meisner, *Li Ta-chao and the Origins of Chinese Marxism* (Cambridge, MA: Harvard University Press, 1967); and idem, *Mao's China and After: A History of the People's Republic*, 3rd ed. (New York: Free Press, 1999).
15. Pantsov, *The Bolsheviks and the Chinese Revolution*; and Odd Arne Westad, ed., *Brothers in Arms: The Rise and Fall of the Sino-Soviet Alliance, 1945–1963* (Washington, DC: Woodrow Wilson Center Press, 1998).
16. Garver, *Chinese-Soviet Relations*, p. 12.
17. Chan Lau Kit-ching, *From Nothing to Nothing: The Chinese Communist Movement and Hong Kong, 1921–1936* (London: Hurst, 1999), pp. 8, 189.
18. Heinzig, *The Soviet Union and Communist China.*
19. Westad, *Cold War and Revolution*, pp. 165–178.
20. Odd Arne Westad, *Decisive Encounters: The Chinese Civil War, 1946–1950* (Stanford, CA: Stanford University Press, 2003), pp. 232–234, 262–263.
21. Ibid., pp. 271–277.
22. Heinzig, *The Soviet Union and Communist China*; and Westad, *Cold War and Revolution.*
23. Ibid.; and also Thomas E. Stolper, *China, Taiwan, and the Offshore Islands: Together with an Implication for Outer Mongolia and Sino-Soviet Relations* (Armonk, NY: M. E. Sharpe, 1985).
24. Ilya V. Gaiduk, *The Soviet Union and the Vietnam War* (Chicago: Ivan R. Dee, 1996), p. 4.
25. Westad, ed., *Brothers in Arms*, "Preface," pp. xvii–xxii; Mark Mancall, *China at the Center: 300 Years of Foreign Policy* (New York: Free Press,

1984); and John King Fairbank, *The Great Chinese Revolution, 1800–1985* (New York: Harper & Row, 1986).

26. Heinzig, *The Soviet Union and Communist China*, Chapter 5, "Conclusions and Prospects," pp. 385–402.
27. Westad, ed., *Brothers in Arms*, "Preface."

Notes to Chapter 1

1. Among the best accounts of the early history of Hong Kong are: G. B. Endacott, *A History of Hong Kong*, 2nd ed. (London: Oxford University Press, 1964); Frank Welsh, *A History of Hong Kong*, 2nd ed. (London: HarperCollins, 1997); and Steve Tsang Yui-sang, *A Modern History of Hong Kong* (London: I. B. Tauris, 2004).
2. Curtis Keeble, *Britain, the Soviet Union, and Russia* (New York: St. Martin's Press, 2000), pp. 8–9.
3. AVP RI, f. 229, op. 776, d. 3, "Police Reports, 1891–1900"; AVP RI, f. 229, op. 776, d. 36, "Police Reports, 1905"; AVP RI, f. 229, op. 776, d. 45, "Police Circulars, 1907–1908"; AVP RI, f. 229, op. 776, d. 66, "Police Circulars, 1908–1910."
4. Two excellent recent descriptions of Russian relations with Britain in the Far East are Keeble, *Britain, the Soviet Union, and Russia*, Chapter 1, "Britain and Imperial Russia"; and Keith Neilson, *Britain and the Last Tsar: British Policy and Russia, 1894–1917* (Oxford: Clarendon Press, 1996).
5. PRO, CO 129/220, March 24, 1885, Government House to the Earl of Derby.
6. AVP RI, f. 143, op. 491, d. 407, "Reports from the Consulate, 1891–1907," pp. 70–109.
7. AVP RI, f. 229, op. 776, d. 394, September 1917.
8. The author received relatively good access to the AVP RI. The Director of the Reading Room provided him with catalogs of Russia's missions in Japan, Hong Kong, and Great Britain.
9. For a full description of Russian expansion into the Far East during the mid-nineteenth century, see John L. Evans, *Russian Expansion on the Amur, 1848–1860: The Push to the Pacific* (Lewiston, NY: Edwin Mellen Press, 1999); G. A. Lensen, *Russia's Eastward Expansion* (Englewood Cliffs, NJ: Prentice Hall, 1964); idem, *The Russian Push toward Japan: Russo-Japanese Relations, 1697–1875* (Princeton, NJ: Princeton University Press, 1959); and Andrew Malozemoff, *Russian Far Eastern Policy, 1881–1904: With Special Emphasis on the Causes of the Russo-Japanese War* (New York: Octagon Books, 1977).
10. F. A. Brokhaus and I. A. Efron, *Entsiklopedicheskii Slovar (Granat)* [Encyclopedic Dictionary (Granat)], 58 vols. (St. Petersburg: J. A. Efron,

1890–1907), vol. 25, pp. 817–818.

11. Winfried Baumgart, *The Crimean War, 1853–1856* (New York: Oxford University Press, 1999), Chapter 15, "The Minor Theatres of War: The White Sea and the Pacific," pp. 185–192; Barry M. Gough, "The Crimean War in the Pacific: British Strategy and Naval Operations," *Military Affairs* 37, no. 4 (December 1973): 130–136; and John Shelton Curtiss, *Russia's Crimean War* (Durham, NC: Duke University Press, 1979).
12. PRO, CO 129/46, June 5, 1854, pp. 76–114.
13. PRO, CO 129/50, June 1, 1855, Letter from Governor Bowring to Lord John Russell, pp. 114–147.
14. Admiral Evfim Putyatin (1803–1883) represented Russia on numerous diplomatic and military missions to Persia, the Ottoman Empire, China, and Japan. Putyatin is perhaps best known for the mission he led to Japan, on behalf of the Russian government, from 1852 to 1855, which successfully opened Japan to Russian trade. *Bolshaia Entsiklopediia* [Great Encyclopedia], vol. 16 (Moscow: Kirill I Mefodiya, 2000), pp. 15–16; *Entsiklopedicheskii Slovar (Granat)*, vol. 23, p. 674; and Mark Bassin, *Imperial Visions: Nationalist Imagination and Geographical Expansion in the Russian Far East, 1840–1865* (Cambridge: Cambridge University Press, 1999).
15. For a listing of Russia's major consular officials in Hong Kong, see G. A. Lensen, *Russian Diplomatic and Consular Officials in East Asia* (Tokyo: Sophia University, 1968).
16. AVP RI, f. 143, op. 491, d. 406 (1859–1888), "Reports from Hong Kong." In 1870, George F. Heard succeeded Silas E. Burrows as Consul, combining the post with that of Vice Consul. On January 14, 1875, Heard wrote to the MID, announcing that ill health forced him to resign his positions and return immediately to Europe, but later that year he died on the journey. Charles Edward Parker, another American citizen, replaced him, assisted by a Baltic German, Baron von Sodern, as Vice Consul. On Parker's resignation in March 1880, William Reimers, another American, became Russian Consul. During Reimers' absences his Vice Consul, Adolphe Andre, a German citizen, took charge of the Russian Consulate. In 1884, Reimers left Hong Kong permanently for Europe, and Max Grôte, a German merchant who had spent ten years in Hong Kong, was appointed Consul, assisted by Hermann Melchers as Vice Consul. In September 1887, another German, Stephen C. Michaelsen, was appointed both Russian and Austrian Consul, retaining both positions until 1900. During his frequent absences from Hong Kong, other Germans, including Johann Goosmann in 1891, the leading businessman Carl Jantzen in 1892, and Armin Haupt in 1898, all served as Acting Consuls. Count Bologovsky's successor, another Baltic German, Piotr H. Tiedemann, was appointed Consul in 1908. Suffering from an

unidentified blood disease under the hot, humid climate, in February 1909 he persuaded the MID to transfer him to Japan, whereupon Vice Consul W. Tratschild became Acting Consul. AVP RI, f. 229, op. 776, d. 84, 1909–1910.

17. The *Hong Kong Government Gazette*, the official publication of the Hong Kong government, listed every new appointment. The *Gazette* also listed various new Hong Kong Government proclamations and laws.
18. AVP RI, f. 143, op. 491, d. 406, p. 79.
19. AVP RI, f. 143, op. 491, d. 406.
20. AVP RI, f. 143, op. 491, d. 406, "Reports from the Consulate, 1859–1888"; and AVP RI, f. 229, op. 776, d. 81, 1909, "Russian Trade."
21. AVP RI, f. 143, op. 491, d. 407, "Reports from the Consulate, 1908," pp. 97–109; and AVP RI, f. 229, op. 776, d. 81, 1909.
22. AVP RI, f. 143, op. 491, d. 406, "Reports from the Consulate, 1859–1888."
23. AVP RI, f. 143, op. 491, d. 407, "Reports from the Consulate, 1891–1907," pp. 97–109.
24. AVP RI, f. 143, op. 776, d. 1, May 26, 1901, Interior Ministry, St. Petersburg, to Russian Consul, pp. 26–27.
25. AVP RI, f. 143, op. 491, d. 407, pp. 91–99.
26. AVP RI, f. 143, op. 491, d. 407, pp. 75–90; and AVP RI, f. 229, op. 776, d. 73, 1909, "London Letters," copies of documents sent to Beijing and Russia.
27. AVP RI, f. 143, op. 491, d. 406, Letter from Director, Asian Department, MID, to the Foreign Minister.
28. PRO, CO, 129/160, March 20, 1872, pp. 322–325.
29. PRO, CO, 129/160, March 20, 1872, pp. 330–331.
30. NA, Dispatch no. 138–140, September 19, 1872, US Consul David Barclay to Charles Kale, Assistant Secretary of State, "American Consul Reports from Hong Kong."
31. PRO, CO 129/159, September 13, 1872; PRO, CO 129/162, January 30, 1873, pp. 130–132; and PRO, CO 129/162, April 22, 1873, pp. 397–398.
32. AVP RI, f. 143, op. 491, d. 406, "Reports from the Consulate, 1859–1888."
33. PRO, CO 129/89, March 1, 1882, pp. 89–91.
34. PRO, CO 129/220, March 24, 1885, Government House to the Earl of Derby.
35. Ibid.
36. PRO, CO 129/220, March 24, 1885, Government House to the Earl of Derby; PRO, CO 129/221, April 30, 1885, pp. 186–192; and PRO, CO 129/221, May 7, 1885, pp. 221–226.
37. William Boyd, "A Chekhov Lexicon," *The Guardian Unlimited Books: Review*, http://books.guardian.co.uk/review/story/0,12084,1252154,00.html, July 3, 2004 (accessed March 30, 2006).
38. "Anton Chekhov to Alexei S. Suvorin, December 9, 1890," in *Anton*

Chekhov and His Times, comp. Andrei Turkov, trans. Cynthia Carlile and Sharon McKee (Fayetteville: University of Arkansas Press, 1995), p. 289. On this visit, see also Donald Rayfield, *Anton Chekhov: A Life* (Evanston, IL: Northwestern University Press, 1997), p. 234; and Daniel Gilles, *Chekhov: Observer Without Illusion*, trans. Charles Lam Markmann (New York: Funk and Wagnalls, 1968), p. 148.

39. Ronald Hingley, *A New Life of Anton Chekhov* (London: Oxford University Press, 1976), p. 142.
40. Esper Ukhtomskii, *Travels in the East of Nicholas II, Emperor of Russia When Cesarewitch 1890–1891*, 2 vols., ed. Sir George Birdwood (London: Constable, 1896), vol. 2, pp. 289–299. On Nicholas II's tour of Asia, see also David Schimmelpenninck van der Oye, *Toward the Rising Sun: Russian Ideologies of Empire and the Path to War with Japan* (DeKalb: Northern Illinois University Press, 2001), pp. 15–23.
41. Ukhtomskii, *Travels in the East*, vol. 2, pp. 290–299, quotations from pp. 290, 293–294.
42. Ibid., pp. 142–143, 299, 444–446, quotations from pp. 142, 143, 299, 445. On Ukhtomskii's views regarding the opportunities for Russian policy in Asia, see also van der Oye, *Toward the Rising Sun*, pp. 42–60.
43. AVP RI, f. 143, op. 491, d. 407, "Reports from the Consulate, 1891–1907."
44. Neilson, *Britain and the Last Tsar: British Policy and Russia, 1894–1917.*
45. PRO, CO 129/271, March 3–April 1, 1896, Report from Governor Robinson to Joseph Chamberlain.
46. Ibid., pp. 504–512; and PRO, CO 129/274, April 22, 1896, pp. 64–66.
47. AVP RI, f. 229, op. 776, d. 1, "Reports from the Consulate, 1897."
48. Endacott, *A History of Hong Kong*, p. 260.
49. Gillian Bickley, *Hong Kong Invaded! A '97 Nightmare* (Hong Kong: Hong Kong University Press, 2001); also Endacott, *A History of Hong Kong*, p. 260.
50. Neilson, *Britain and the Last Tsar: British Policy and Russia, 1894–1917.*
51. PRO, CO 129/293, August 1899, pp. 136–138; and PRO, CO 129/302, November 17, 1900, pp. 828–833.
52. The Russian-Chinese Bank (after 1910 the Russo-Asiatic Bank) was chartered in St. Petersburg on November 24, 1895, to further Russian imperial interests in China. It was conceived by Minister of Finance Sergei Witte, headed by Nicholas II's former traveling companion Prince Esper Ukhtomskii, and backed financially by the French as a joint French and Russian operation. It became Tsarist Russia's largest financial institution. Far more than just a bank, it issued currency and coined money, collected taxes, financed commercial enterprises, and bribed Chinese officials to respond favorably to Russian requests. Branches of the bank were established in major Chinese cities and foreign colonies in China, such as Hong Kong. It

owned the Chinese Eastern Railroad, which ran through Manchuria to the Pacific Ocean. The bank transmitted French capital to Russia, and maintained numerous connections with various industrial firms in Russia and in China as both a bank and an investment trust. In 1910, the bank merged with the *Banque du Nord de Paris*, and became the Russo-Asiatic Bank. For further information on the bank, see Joseph Wieczynski, ed., *The Modern Encyclopedia of Russian and Soviet History*, vol. 32 (Gulf Breeze, FL: Academic International Press, 1983), pp. 82–85.

53. Bickley, *Hong Kong Invaded!*, p. 21.
54. NA, Dispatch no. 138, September 27, 1899, from the Consulate-General in Hong Kong to the US State Department, "Possibilities of War between Japan and Russia."
55. *The Hong Kong Government Gazette*, no. 92, February 12, 1904, pp. 165–169.
56. *The Hong Kong Government Gazette*, no. 285, April 26, 1904, p. 734.
57. *The Hong Kong Government Gazette,* no. 399, May 31, 1904, p. 999; and *The Hong Kong Government Gazette*, no. 100, February 14, 1905, p. 149.
58. PRO, CO 129/325, April 8, 1904, pp. 24–28; and PRO, CO 129/326, February 25, 1904, pp. 91–96, 438–457.
59. PRO, CO 129/322, May 1904, pp. 641–648.
60. PRO, CO 129/323, August 1, 1904, pp. 167–168.
61. AVP RI, f. 143, op. 491, d. 407, "Reports from the Consulate, 1891–1907," pp. 108–109.
62. AVP RI, f. 229, op. 776, d. 83, pp. 3–13. The Faculty of Arts and the Department of History are currently housed in the Main Building of the University of Hong Kong.
63. Interestingly Stolypin has emerged as a popular figure in today's post-Soviet Russia. Two recent books in English on him are: Alexandra Shecket Korros, *A Reluctant Parliament: Stolypin, Nationalism, and the Politics of the Russian Imperial State Council, 1906–1911* (Lanham, MD: Rowman & Littlefield, 2002); and Abraham Ascher, *P. A. Stolypin: The Search for Stability in Late Imperial Russia* (Stanford, CA: Stanford University Press, 2001).

Notes to Chapter 2

1. Of the huge quantity of World War I literature, very little deals with military operations in East Asia and the Pacific Ocean. Three recent books which do to some extent cover that vast territory are: Spencer C. Tucker, *The Great War, 1914–1918* (London: UCL Press, 1998), pp. 194–198; Herman Joseph Hiery, *The Neglected War: The German South Pacific and the Influence of*

World War I (Honolulu: University of Hawaii Press, 1995); and Hew Strachan, *The First World War*, vol. 1 (Oxford: Oxford University Press, 2001), Chapter 6, "The War in the Pacific," pp. 441–494.

2. Only Strachan, *The First World War*, Chapter 6, covers Hong Kong's role in the war to any extent.
3. PRO, FO 371, F1928, 1914, "Proposal to Withdraw Some British Troops from Hong Kong."
4. AVP RI, f. 229, op. 776, d. 3329, "War News from Hong Kong, 1914."
5. PRO, GA, August 28, 1914, p. 346; PRO, GA, August 25, 1915, p. 415; PRO, GA, March 13, 1916, p. 267; and PRO, GA, September 28, 1917, pp. 556–567.
6. AVP RI, f. 229, op. 776, d. 410, 1915, Secret Telegram from Malevsky, Russian Ambassador to Japan, "Weapons Shipments to Russia." Sesame oil, derived from the seeds, was very useful for cooking.
7. AVP RI, f. 229, op. 776, d. 83, pp. 11–13.
8. AVP RI, f. 229, op. 776, d. 83, June 15, 1915, Letter from *Mitsui Kaisha* to the Russian Consul-General, Hong Kong, p. 11.
9. PRO, CO 129/422, May 28, 1915, pp. 380–382.
10. PRO, CO 129/437, December 14, 1916, pp. 738–743; and PRO, CO 129/439, May 31, 1916, pp. 237–238, 300–307, 368–371.
11. PRO, CO 129/440, December 9, 1916, pp. 12–13.
12. AVP RI, f. 229, op. 776, d. 394, May 29, 1915, Consul-General to British headquarters, China Command.
13. AVP RI, f. 229, op. 776, d. 394, September 23, 1915.
14. AVP RI, f. 229, op. 776, d. 394, October 2, 1915.
15. Ibid.
16. Ibid.
17. PRO, CO 129/435, December 11, 1916, pp. 456–498.
18. AVP RI, f. 229, op. 776, d. 424, 1917, "Announcing the New Government in Russia."
19. AVP RI, f. 229, op. 776, d. 394, September 1917.
20. PRO, GA, April 24, 1918, no. 152, p. 139.
21. AVP RI, f. 229, op. 776, d. 422, 1917, "Political Emigrants."
22. PRO, GA, April 5, 1918, no. 126, p. 120.
23. AVP RI, f. 229, op. 776, f. 503, 1918, "White Army Officers."
24. John Albert White, *The Siberian Intervention* (Princeton, NJ: Princeton University Press, 1950), p. 221.
25. R. H. Ullman, *Anglo-Soviet Relations*, vol. 1, *Intervention and the War* (Princeton, NJ: Princeton University Press, 1961), pp. 90–91. See also J. F. N. Bradley, *Allied Intervention in Russia* (London: Weidenfeld & Nicolson, 1968), p. 24.
26. Serge P. Petroff, *Remembering a Forgotten War: Civil War in Eastern*

European Russia and Siberia, 1918–1920 (Boulder, CO: East European Monographs, 2000), pp. 43, 51, 118; "The Long, Long Trail: The British Army in the Great War of 1914–1918. The Duke of Cambridge's Own (Middlesex Regiment)," http://www.1914–1918.net/msex.htm (accessed March 16, 2006); and "The Royal Hampshire Regiment: The 37th and 67th Foot," http://www.Pauljerrard.com/ww1/Battalions/1_9th.html (accessed March 16, 2006).

27. Patrick J. Rollins, "Russian Commerce Raiders in the Red Sea and Indian Ocean, 1904," *Naval War College Review* 47, no. 3 (Summer 1994): 86–105.
28. AVP RI, f. 229, op. 776, d. 97, 1909, "Russian Volunteer Fleet."
29. HK PRO, Carl Smith Collection, 1013/001/2072/GIF; and AVP RI, f. 184, op. 761, d. 900, 1900–1915.
30. PRO, CO 129/451, March 1918, "Requisitioning of Vessels of the Russian Volunteer Fleet," p. 35.
31. PRO, CO 349, WO 19421, April 26, 1918, Cypher Telegram from the Russian Consul-General, Hong Kong, to the British Government.
32. PRO, CO 129/451, April 20, 1918, pp. 735–737.
33. It is not clear from the source which Russian government protested the British requisition. It may have been either the Bolshevik government in Moscow, or one of a number of White Russian regimes.
34. PRO, CO 129/448, April 12, 1918, pp. 108–114.
35. PRO, CO 129/447, March 20, 1918, pp. 528–535.
36. AVP RF, f. 0100, op. 2/a, por. 5, d. 133, March 5–May 25, 1918, "Department Committee, Training for Sailors, Foreign Department of Siberian Fleet," p. 5.
37. AVP RF, f. 0100, op. 2/a, por. 5, d. 133, March 5, 1918, Telegram from the Far East Committee of Foreign Affairs, Khabarovsk, to Petrograd. Nikolai Markovich Lubarsky (1887–1938) joined the Bolshevik Party in 1917. During 1918 he edited the Vladivostok Soviet newspaper *Krasnoe Znamya* or *Red Banner*, and in March 1919 Lubarsky helped organize the founding Congress of the Comintern. Lubarsky left the Communist Party in 1923, was arrested during the purges, and deported to the *Gulag*, where he died in 1938.
38. AVP RF, f. 0100, op. 2/a, por. 5, d. 441, 1917–1920, p. 7.
39. Ibid.
40. PRO, FO 371/10496, September 9, 1924, Letter from G. Grindle, Undersecretary of State, to the Foreign Secretary.
41. PRO, CO 129/451, March 6, 1918, pp. 308–312.
42. PRO, CO 129/476, November 13, 1922, pp. 349–359.
43. PRO, FO 371/11910, November 22, 1922, Letter from Russian Volunteer Fleet, Hong Kong Agency, to the Colonial Secretary, Hong Kong, pp. 132–133.
44. PRO, FO 371/9350, 1923, pp. 24–25.

45. PRO, GA, January 24, 1919, no. 46, p. 62.
46. PRO, GA, February 29, 1924, no. 100, p. 76.
47. In January 1918, the new Soviet government nationalized all Russian banks, including the Russo-Asiatic Bank. A counter Russo-Asiatic Bank opened its headquarters in Paris that same year. For several years there were competing banks, each claiming to be the true Russo-Asiatic Bank. As the Soviet Union normalized relations with European states, that state of affairs had to end. In September 1926, the Paris headquarters directed that all its branches, including those in China and Hong Kong, enter into voluntary liquidation. For further information on the bank, see Rosemary Quested, *The Russo-Chinese Bank: A Multinational Financial Base of Tsarism in China* (Birmingham: Department of Russian Language and Literature, University of Birmingham, 1977); Olga Crisp, "The Russo-Chinese Bank: An Episode in Franco-Russian Relations," *Slavonic and East European Review* 52, no. 127 (April 1974): 197–212; and D. R. Watson, "The Rise and Fall of the Russo-Asiatic Bank: The Problems of a Russian Enterprise with French Shareholders, 1910–1926," *European History Quarterly* 23, no. 1 (January 1993): 39–49.
48. PRO, FO 371/12587, November 9, 1926, Letter from the Manager of the Russo-Asiatic Bank, Hong Kong Branch, to the Hong Kong Colonial Secretary, p. 208.
49. PRO, FO 371/10496, September 20, 1924, Letter from the Russian Chargé d'affaires, London, to the British Foreign Secretary, and October 9, 1924, Letter from J. D. Gregory, Foreign Office, to Foreign Secretary Ramsay MacDonald.
50. AVP RF, f. 0100, op. 12, d. 96, pap. 155, 1923–1928, "Report of July 24, 1928, *Secret*."
51. PRO, FO 371/12587, March 25, 1927, Letter from Governor C. Clementi to the Foreign Secretary, Hong Kong, p. 207.
52. AVP RF, f. 0100, op. 12, d. 96, pap. 155, 1923–1928, July 24, 1928, "Report by the Head of the Economics and Law Section, MID, Sabanin, to the Head of the Far East Department, MID, Kozlovsky."
53. AVP RI, f. 229, op. 776, d. 422, 1917, "Political Emigrants."

Notes to Chapter 3

1. For further information on the Comintern, see Fernando Claudín, *The Communist Movement: From Comintern to Cominform* (London: Penguin, 1975); Robert V. Daniels, *A Documentary History of Communism*, vol. 2 (Hanover, NH: University Press of New England, 1984); and Kevin McDermott and Jeremy Agnew, eds., *The Comintern: A History of*

International Communism from Lenin to Stalin (Basingstoke, Hampshire: Macmillan, 1996).

2. An excellent survey of Comintern activities in China is given in Michael Weiner, "Comintern in East Asia, 1919–1939," in *The Comintern*, eds. McDermott and Agnew, pp. 158–190.
3. Until the Russian Revolution of 1917, Grigori Voitinsky (1893–1953) lived in the United States and Canada. After the Bolshevik triumph, he returned to Russia, joined the Communist Party, and fought against White Russian forces in Siberia. Voitinsky joined the Comintern in 1920, and was assigned to its Far East Department. As its representative to China, during the 1920s he had three assignments in Beijing and Shanghai, between which he served in Moscow as the Chief of the Comintern's Far East Secretariat. In 1927 he returned to China, witnessing Chiang Kai-shek's break with the CCP and subsequent massacre of Chinese Communists. After that crisis Voitinsky was recalled to Moscow, left the Comintern, and died a natural death in 1953. For further information on him and other Comintern figures, see Branko Lazitch and Milorad Drachkovitch, eds., *Biographical Dictionary of the Comintern* (Stanford, CA: Hoover Institution Press, 1973), pp. 429–430.
4. Adolf Ioffe (1883–1927) early on became a close ally of Leon Trotsky, and would remain such for the rest of his life. In June 1917, Ioffe joined the Communist Party, and was elected to the Central Committee, and then to the Petrograd Military Revolutionary Committee, which organized the Bolshevik Revolution in that city. Afterwards Ioffe began a diplomatic career, and from 1922 to 1923 he served as the Soviet government's emissary to China. There Ioffe concluded the accord with Sun Yat-sen, and facilitated the alliance between the KMT and the CCP. After Trotsky's expulsion from the Communist Party in 1927, Ioffe committed suicide. Lazitch and Drachkovitch, eds., *Biographical Dictionary of the Comintern*, pp. 165–166.
5. The founding of the CCP and the reasons for the formation of the United Front fall largely outside the bounds of this chapter. Details can be found in any good survey of modern Chinese history or the CCP. Among the best in English are Immanuel C. Y. Hsü, *The Rise of Modern China*, 6th ed. (New York: Oxford University Press, 2000); Chang Kuo-t'ao, *The Rise of the Chinese Communist Party*, 2 vols. (Lawrence: University Press of Kansas, 1971–1972); and Robert C. North, *Chinese Communism* (London: Weidenfeld & Nicolson, 1966).
6. Mikhail Borodin (1884–1951) joined the Russian Social Democratic Party in 1903, and immediately became close to the Bolshevik wing. When the Comintern first organized in 1919, Borodin became its representative successively to the United States, Mexico, Germany, and eventually Great

Britain, where he was arrested in 1922 and imprisoned for six months. In September 1923 Borodin was sent to China as the Comintern representative to the CCP and the Soviet representative to Sun Yat-sen. Borodin played a crucial role in organizing the United Front between the CCP and the KMT. Following the 1927 split, Borodin was recalled to Moscow. Dropped from further Comintern activities, Borodin edited foreign-language publications, and managed to survive Stalin's purges of the 1930s. However, in 1949 Borodin, then editor of the English-language daily newspaper *Moscow News*, was arrested and died in a camp two years later. Lazitch and Drachkovitch, eds., *Biographical Dictionary of the Comintern*, p. 34.

7. RGASPI, f. 514, op. 1, d. 50, "Report of M. M. Borodin about the Situation in South China," p. 329.
8. PRO, CO 129/492, March 22, 1926, "Situation in Canton," pp. 122–162.
9. Curtis Keeble, *Britain, the Soviet Union, and Russia* (New York: St. Martin's Press, 2000), pp. 84–119. Sir Curtis Keeble was British Ambassador to the Soviet Union from 1978 to 1982.
10. PRO, CO 129/457, December 12, 1919, "Labour Conditions in Canton and Bolshevism in the Far East," pp. 643–662.
11. PRO, CO 129/457, December 12, 1919, "Labour Conditions in Canton and Bolshevism in the Far East," pp. 643–656.
12. RGAE, f. 7795, op. 1, d. 203, "Report of Operations by the Soviet Trade Fleet *(Sovtorflot)* of its Activities in China in 1926," pp. 1–32.
13. RGASPI, f. 514, op. 1, d. 40, April 4, 1923, pp. 28–35.
14. PRO, FO 371/10242, 1924, "Shipment of Arms," p. 161.
15. G. B. Endacott, *A History of Hong Kong,* 2nd ed. (London: Oxford University Press, 1964), p. 289. The 1921 census gave its population as 625,000 of whom 610,000 were Chinese.
16. For a discussion of Comintern and MID differences in Western Europe, see McDermott and Agnew, eds., *The Comintern*, pp. 95–99.
17. RGASPI, f. 514, op. 1, d. 40, April 4, 1923, Letter from G. I. Safronov, Head of the Far East Section of the Comintern, to the Politburo of the CPSU, pp. 28–35.
18. Keeble, *Britain, the Soviet Union, and Russia*, pp. 84–101; and R. H. Ullman, *Anglo-Soviet Relations*, vol. 3, *The Anglo-Soviet Accord* (Princeton, NJ: Princeton University Press, 1972).
19. RGASPI, f. 627, op. 1, d. 4, February 13, 1924, Letter from L. M. Karahkan to M. M. Borodin, pp. 20–21.
20. G. O. Kheniuoi and M. L. Titarenko, eds., *Komintern i Kitai, Dokumenti* [The Comintern in China, Documents], vol. 1, 1920–1925 (Moscow: Nauka, 1994), August 30, 1922, Telegram of A. A. Ioffe to L. M. Karakhan, p. 110.
21. RGASPI, f. 495, op. 154, d. 233, "Comintern Views of Hong Kong," p. 4.
22. Ibid. See also Chan Lau Kit-ching, *From Nothing to Nothing: The Chinese*

Communist Movement and Hong Kong, 1921–1936 (London: Hurst, 1999), pp. 27–36.
23. Chan Lau, *From Nothing to Nothing*, pp. 32–33.
24. Ibid., p. 70.
25. RGASPI, f. 514, op. 1, d. 103, February 19, 1924, "Report from Borodin about the Situation," p. 88.
26. RGASPI, f. 514, op. 1, d. 26, Victor Chen, "Report from Hong Kong Written for the Comintern on the Contemporary Situation in China and Hong Kong," pp. 27–31.
27. RGASPI, f. 514, op. 1, d. 26, p. 65. Henk Sneevliet (pseudonym Maring) (1883–1942) served on the Comintern's Executive Committee from 1920. Sneevliet was an expert on national and colonial questions following his revolutionary experiences in the Dutch East Indies. The Comintern appointed Sneevliet its representative in China from 1920 through 1923. A member of the Trotskyist faction of the Comintern, Sneevliet was a victim of the power struggle between Trotsky and Stalin. The Comintern expelled Sneevliet in 1928, and he returned to his native Holland. During World War II, the Germans executed him in Amsterdam. Alexander Pantsov, *The Bolsheviks and the Chinese Revolution, 1919–1927* (Richmond, Surrey: Curzon Press, 2000).
28. Frank Welsh, *A History of Hong Kong*, 2nd ed. (London: HarperCollins, 1997), p. 369.
29. Ibid.
30. PRO, FO 371/8030, 1922, pp. 44–45.
31. Chan Lau, *From Nothing to Nothing*, pp. 21–26.
32. Ibid., pp. 57–63.
33. Ibid., pp. 85–95.
34. RGASPI, f. 514, op. 1, d. 26, 1922, Lam Wai Man, "Report on the Chinese Seamen's Movement to the Comintern," pp. 78–83.
35. Kheniuoi and Titarenko, *Komintern i Kitai, Dokumenti*, vol. 1, 1920–1925, May 20, 1922, "From a Report of Di Lin to the Far East Section of the Comintern," pp. 82–83.
36. PRO, CO 129/512/2, 1929, pp. 11–31.
37. RGASPI, f. 495, op. 154, d. 233, June 23, 1924, "Organization Resolution passed by the Organization Commission of the Transport Conference of the Orient," p. 31.
38. Ibid., p. 32.
39. Chan Lau, *From Nothing to Nothing*, pp. 37–52. Chan Lau points out that the membership of the Hong Kong Communist Party was transient, fluctuating, and fast changing, and also predominantly working class.
40. PRO, FO 371/12494, 1927, "Survey of Russian-Chinese Relations," pp. 312–316.

41. S. A. Smith, *A Road Is Made: Communism in Shanghai, 1920–1927* (Honolulu: University of Hawaii Press, 2000).
42. AVP RF, f. 0100, op. 10, d. 32, pap. 15, July 26, 1926, "Report from the Soviet Embassy in China to the Foreign Ministry, Moscow."
43. RGASPI, f. 514, op. 1, d. 350, March 1928, Letter from V. I. Soloviev to N. I. Bukharin, Moscow, p. 347.
44. PRO, FO 371/10950, 1925, p. 132.
45. PRO, FO 371/11679, 1926, p. 19.
46. RGAE, f. 7795, op. 1, d. 203, 1926, "Political Struggle between the Soviet Union and Britain in South China," p. 2.
47. Ibid., pp. 16–17.
48. RGAE, f. 7795, op. 1, d. 35, 1926, "Report from the Far East regarding the Soviet fleet in China," p. 243.
49. PRO, CO 349/56063, November 28, 1924. The Soviet reports were in MID, as per details in the next footnote.
50. AVP RF, f. 0100, op. 11, d. 8, pap. 12, September 1927, Telegram from MID to Beijing, p. 30.
51. AVP RI, f. 0100, op. 12, d. 96, pap. 155, 1923–1928, October 13, 1927, Letter to the Chinese Consul, Nikolaevsk-Ussurisk, p. 6.
52. Ibid., October 29, 1927, "Consul of China in Nikolaevsk-Ussurisk," p. 5.
53. PRO, FO 371/10949, 1925, p. 95–98.
54. Ibid., p. 61.
55. AVP RF, f. 0100, op. 11, d. 8, pap. 12, May 19, 1926, Report by Musine to MID.
56. PRO, CO 129/491, September 23, 1924, pp. 44–50.
57. PRO, FO 371/10949, p. 50.
58. Ibid., p. 66.
59. Ibid., p. 168.
60. PRO, CO 129/492, March 22, 1926, pp. 122–162.
61. PRO, FO 371/120660, 1925, Report Written by British Embassy Employee Sir Ronald MacKay to Austen Chamberlain, p. 52.
62. AVP RF, f. 0100, op. 10, d. 111, pap. 133, January–July 1926, Nikolai Rogachev, Moscow, pp. 7–9.
63. AVP RF, f. 0100, op. 10, d. 88, pap. 130, June 4–December 6, 1926, "Reports from the Soviet Consulate-General in Guangzhou," pp. 54–60.
64. AVP RF, f. 0100, op. 11, d. 8, pap. 12, May 19, 1926.
65. RGAE, f. 7795, op. 1, d. 203, "Report of Operations by the Soviet Trade Fleet (*Sovtorflot*) of Its Activities in China in 1926," p. 29; AVP RF, f. 0100, op. 11, d. 136, pap. 147, March 14, 1927, "Note from the Consul-General in Guangzhou to Eugene Chan, Minister of Foreign Affairs," p. 129.
66. AVP RF, f. 0100, op. 11, por. 134, pap. 147, April 12, 1927, Letter from M.

Rozengol'ts, London, to Sir. Austen Chamberlain, p. 2.

67. AVP RF, f. 0100, op. 10, d. 88, pap. 130, September 1, 1926, "Report from the Consul-General, Guangzhou, to Ambassador Karakhan," pp. 74–76.
68. PRO, FO 371/12494, June 14, 1927, Letter by G. Grindle of the Foreign Office, p. 323; and RGAE, f. 7795, op. 1, d. 203, "Political Struggle between Britain and the Soviet Union in South China," p. 15.
69. Keeble, *Britain, the Soviet Union and Russia*, p. 110.
70. Ibid., p. 100.
71. AVP RF, f. 0100, op. 11, d. 8, pap. 12, 1927, May 19, 1926, Report Filed by Musine.
72. Welsh, *A History of Hong Kong.*
73. Hsü, *The Rise of Modern China.*
74. RGASPI, f. 514, op. 1, d. 123, December 1925, Letter from Fedor F. Roskolnikov, Moscow, to G. N. Voitinsky, pp. 213–216.
75. RGASPI, f. 17, op. 162, d. 2, December 3, 1925, "Stalin Protocol."
76. AVP RF, f. 0100, op. 10, d. 111, pap. 133, May 14, 1926, Letter from Chicherin, Moscow, to Stalin.
77. PRO, CO 129/497, December 7, 1926, "Foreign Policy with relation to Japan and Russia," pp. 423–438.
78. AVP RF, f. 0100, op. 10, d. 111, pap. 133, March 20, 1926, "Brief Reference to the March Events in Guangzhou," pp. 7–9.
79. Ibid., "Further Description of March Events in Guangzhou," p. 10.
80. PRO, CO 129/499/3, March 10, 1927, "Secret Service Report," pp. 2–9.
81. Weiner, "Comintern in East Asia, 1919–1939," in *The Comintern*, eds., McDermott and Agnew, pp. 170–173.
82. RGASPI, f. 514, op. 1, d. 123, December 1925, Letter from Fedor F. Roskolnikov, Moscow, to G. N. Voitinsky, pp. 666–669.
83. AVP RF, f. 0100, op. 10, d. 111, pap. 133, January–July 1926, December 16, 1925, "Letter from Kisanok," pp. 4–6.
84. AVP RF, f. 0100, op. 10, d. 88, pap. 130, "Report by the Soviet Consul-General, Guangzhou, to Karakhan."
85. RGASPI, f. 17, op. 162, d. 2, December 3, 1925, "Protocol of the Politburo, no. 93, Central Committee, CPSU," signed by Stalin, pp. 202–205.
86. AVP RF, f. 0100, op. 10, d. 111, pap. 133, January 11, 1926, "Extract of a Letter from Kisanok, Guangzhou."
87. Heinz Neumann (1902–1937?) was a young activist in the German Communist movement, who went to Moscow in 1922. While remaining active in the German Communist Party, Neumann became a member of the CPSU and the Comintern. In the struggle against Trotsky and Zinoviev, Neumann supported Stalin. Stalin sent Neumann to China in 1927, where he helped organize the Guangzhou Uprising in December. Despite his loyalty to Stalin, in 1937

Neumann was dismissed from all his Comintern and Communist Party posts and arrested, dying in the *Gulag*. Lazitch and Drachkovitch, eds., *Biographical Dictionary of the Comintern*, pp. 288–289.

88. PRO, FO 371/12422, 1927.
89. PRO, CO 129/493, June 28, 1926, pp. 138–154.
90. Smith, *A Road Is Made*, pp. 190–208.
91. PRO, FO 371/12498, 1927.
92. AVP RF, f. 0100, op. 11, d. 136, pap. 147, 1927, "Reaction to the Guangzhou Uprising," pp. 10–11.
93. PRO, CO 129/499, March 10, 1927, "Secret Service Report," pp. 10–12.
94. Chan Lau, *From Nothing to Nothing*, pp. 78–82.
95. Arif Dirlik, "The Guangzhou Uprising in Workers' Perspective," *Modern China* 23, no. 4 (October 1997): 363–397. The quotation is taken from a diary entry of a teacher in Guangzhou at that time, Earl Swisher, on May 29, 1927. Dirlik's well-researched article is based on Chinese and British sources. This section focuses on Soviet archival material, which presents the Soviet perspective on the uprising.
96. Harold Isaacs, *The Tragedy of the Chinese Revolution*, 3rd ed. (Stanford, CA: Stanford University Press, 1966), quoted in Dirlik, "The Guangzhou Uprising," pp. 369, 379.
97. PRO, FO 371/13221, 1928.
98. PRO, CO 129/508, 1928, "Canton Situation," pp. 19–20.
99. AVP RF, f. 0100, op. 11, d. 136, pap. 147, 1927, "Reaction to the Guangzhou Uprising," p. 20.
100. Ibid., p. 21.
101. AVP RF, f. 0100, op. 12, d. 93, pap. 155, "Destruction of the Soviet Consulate-General in Guangzhou," 1928, pp. 10–29. After his return to Moscow, Consul-General Boris Pokhvalinsky filed his report to the MID.
102. Ibid.
103. PRO, CO 129/508/1, 1928, "Canton Situation," p. 12.
104. AVP RF, f. 0100, op. 11, d. 136, pap. 147, Telegram from the Soviet Consul-General to Moscow, sent from Hong Kong.
105. Ibid., "Reaction to the Guangzhou Uprising," p. 24. Those who boarded the *Kinshan* included the Consul-General, his wife, and their two children; Mrs. Malamed and her child; Mr. Vershinin; Mrs. Markevich; Mr. Berman; Mrs. Madyar and her child; Mr. Oshanin and his child; Miss Osvpechetko; Miss Kosivsky; Mr. and Mrs. Ozhekhinsky; Mr. and Mrs. Pereudoth; Mrs. Kush; Mr. Portnov; Mr. Eschenko; and Mrs. Ulyanov. The remainder, who traveled on the SS *Zasma*, were Mr. and Mrs. Ploche and their child; Mr. and Mrs. Minin; Josinin; Savak; Mrs. Mastizky; G. Vinogradov; A. Vinogradov and his child; Mr. and Mrs. Musallor; and Gonerov.

106. PRO, FO 371/12494, 1927, "Survey of Russian-Chinese Relations," pp. 323–347; and PRO, CO 129/508/1, 1928, "Canton Situation," pp. 19–20.
107. PRO, CO 129/508, 1928, Letter from Ian Maxton to W. G. Ormsby-Gore, Under Colonial Secretary, Hong Kong, p. 24.
108. AVP RF, f. 0100, op. 12, d. 93, pap. 155, 1928, Consul-General Pokhvalinsky, "Destruction of the Russian Consulate-General in Guangzhou," pp. 10–29.
109. Ibid.
110. AVP RF, f. 0100, op. 11, d. 136, pap. 147, "Reaction to the Guangzhou Uprising," p. 21.
111. AVP RF, f. 0100, d. 8, pap. 12, 1927, p. 47.
112. Dirlik, "The Guangzhou Uprising," p. 387.
113. Chan Lau, *From Nothing to Nothing*, pp. 95–104.
114. International Red Day is a Chinese Communist holiday. On August 1, 1927, Chinese Communist leaders, including Zhou Enlai, Zhu De, He Long, and Liu Bocheng led 30,000 troops from the Northern Expedition in an uprising in Nanching, Jiangxi province. This was considered the first assault on the KMT, and also the beginning of the CCP's independent leadership of the revolutionary war and army. The CCP decided that August 1 would be commemorated as the "Glorious Birthday of the Chinese Worker Peasant Army" (predecessor of the Chinese PLA). He Xixiang, *365 tian: Zhong wai jieri jinian ri daquan* [365 Days] (Beijing: Zhongguo zhuoyue chubanshe, 1990), pp. 258–259.
115. PRO, CO 129/512/2, 1929, pp. 30–31.

Notes to Chapter 4

1. Steve Tsang Yui-sang, *A Modern History of Hong Kong* (London: I. B. Tauris, 2004), Chapter 8, "Imperial Grandeur," pp. 102–115. Tsang takes a fairly positive view of British rule.
2. Philip Snow, *The Fall of Hong Kong: Britain, China, and the Japanese Occupation* (New Haven, CT: Yale University Press, 2003). The first chapter, "Pre-War Hong Kong: The British and Their Subjects," gives an excellent portrait of Hong Kong society on the eve of the war. See also Frank Welsh, *A History of Hong Kong*, 2nd ed. (London: HarperCollins, 1997), Chapter 13, "A Colonial Backwater."
3. For further information on International Red Day, please refer to n.114 in Chapter 3.
4. RGASPI, f. 514, op. 1, d. 487, May 30, 1929, "Resolution of the Far East Department, Comintern," p. 568. Chan Lau Kit-ching gives an excellent account of the Hong Kong Communist Party in *From Nothing to Nothing:*

The Communist Movement and Hong Kong, 1921–1936 (London: Hurst, 1999). See especially Part III, "The Frustrated Years, 1928–1930."

5. PRO, CO 129/512/2, 1929, pp. 11–31.
6. PRO, CO 1030/1124, 1960–1962, "Communist Activities in Hong Kong," p. 13.
7. Colin Crisswell and Mike Watson, *The Royal Hong Kong Police, 1841–1945* (Hong Kong: Macmillan, 1982), p. 123.
8. Dennis J. Duncanson, "Ho-chi-Minh in Hong Kong, 1931–32," *The China Quarterly*, no. 57 (January–March 1974): 94–100.
9. Sophie Quinn-Judge, *Ho Chi Minh: The Missing Years, 1919–1941* (London: Hurst, 2002), pp. 150–200.
10. Chan Lau, *From Nothing to Nothing*, p. 189.
11. HK PRO, Carl Smith Collection, 1018/00177461/GIF.
12. FBI History, "Famous Cases: Vonsiatsky Espionage," http://www.fbi.gov/lib ref/historic/famcases/vonsiatsky/espionage.htm (accessed March 20, 2006). On June 10, 1942, the FBI (US Federal Bureau of Investigation) indicted the pro-fascist Vonsiatsky for conspiracy to commit treason. He was found guilty and sentenced to five years in afederal prison. Vonsiatsky was released after the war in 1947, subsequently stayed out of politics, and died in 1965.
13. Kevin Sinclair, *Asia's Finest Marches on: Policing Hong Kong from 1841 into the 21st Century: An Illustrated Account of the Hong Kong Police* (Hong Kong: Kevin Sinclair Associates, 1997), p. 46.
14. Crisswell and Watson, *The Royal Hong Kong Police*, p. 125.
15. PRO, CO 129/521/3, 1930, pp. 25–135.
16. RGAE, f. 8045, op. 3, d. 762, 1941.
17. Ibid., d. 570, 1933, p. 79.
18. RGAE, f. 413, op. 13, d. 211, October 1, 1932, Soviet Trade Office, London, p. 22.
19. RGAE, f. 413, op. 13, 1935, d. 569, p. 12.
20. PRO, CO 129/544, 1933.
21. PRO, FO 371/16238, 1932.
22. Ibid., p. 26.
23. Ibid., pp. 21, 24.
24. For additional information on the reasons for the break in relations, see Curtis Keeble, *Britain, the Soviet Union, and Russia* (New York: St. Martin's Press, 2000), Chapter 6, "Approach to War."
25. PRO, CO 129/541/12, 1933, p. 64.
26. Kevin McDermott and Jeremy Agnew, eds., *The Comintern: A History of International Communism from Lenin to Stalin* (Basingstoke, Hampshire: Macmillan), p. 184.
27. Ibid., pp. 98–119.
28. Ibid., pp. 7–9.

29. Due to a non-aggression pact signed with the Japanese in spring 1941, for virtually the entire war the Soviet Union maintained diplomatic and other relations with Japan, only breaking the pact and joining the war in August 1945, after Germany had surrendered in Europe.
30. AVP RF, f. 100, op. 18, d. 38, pap. 41, 1934, "China and England," *Tass* Clippings.
31. AVP RF, f. 100, op. 18, d. 63, pap. 41, March 29, 1934, "Dossier on China and Britain," p. 5.
32. AVP RF, f. 100, op. 19, d. 42, pap. 45, 1935, "China and England," *Tass* Clippings.
33. AVP RF, f. 100, op. 20, d. 52, pap. 52, 1936, "China and England," *Peking and Tientsin Times*, August 29, 1936.
34. AVP RF, f. 100, op. 21, d. 50, pap. 60, 1937, Part 3, "China and England," *Tass* clippings.
35. AVP RF, f. 100, op. 21, d. 48, pap. 60, 1937, "China and England."
36. AVP RF, f. 100, op. 21, d. 49, pap. 60, 1937, Part 2, "China and England."
37. AVP RF, f. 100, op. 21, d. 48, pap. 60, 1937, "China and England," *Canton Daily Sun*, March 17, 1937; and AVP RF, f. 100, op. 21, d. 49, pap. 60, 1937, Part 2, "China and England."
38. AVP RF, f. 100, op. 21, d. 49, pap. 60, 1937, Part 2, "China and England."
39. AVP RF, f. 100, op. 21, d. 51, pap. 61, 1937, Part 4, "China and England."
40. PRO, CO 129/571/6, 1938.
41. AVP RF, f. 100, op. 22, d. 74, pap. 80, 1938, "China and England," *Tass* report.
42. PRO, CO 129/575/3, January–December 1939, pp. 98–119. For further information on the Battle of Nomonhan, see Alvin D. Coox, *Nomonhan: Japan Against Russia, 1939*, 2 vols. (Stanford, CA: Stanford University Press, 1985); Gerhard Weinberg, *A World at Arms: A Global History of World War II* (Cambridge: Cambridge University Press, 1994), pp. 56, 81; and Peter Calvocoressi and Guy Wint, *Total War: Causes and Courses of the Second World War*, 2nd ed. (New York: Viking Press, 1989), pp. 892–901.
43. Snow, *The Fall of Hong Kong*.
44. Richard Overy and Andrew Wheatcroft, *The Road to War* (London: Macmillan, 1989), p. 252.
45. AVP RF, f. 100, op. 28, d. 11, pap. 209, 1941–1942, Part I, "China and England," *Tass* accounts.
46. AVP RF, f. 100, op. 30, d. 616, pap. 224, 1943, Part 1, *Tass* Intelligence Reports; AVP RF, f. 100, op. 30, d. 16, pap. 225, 1943, Part 2, *Tass* Intelligence Reports; and AVP RF, f. 100, op. 30, op. 35a, d. 13, pap. 238, 1944, Part 1, "China and England."
47. Snow, *The Fall of Hong Kong*, p. 141.

48. Crisswell and Watson, *The Royal Hong Kong Police*, p. 181.
49. Stephen Verralls, "The Tragic Story of Sergeant H. W. Jackson, Hong Kong Police," *Hong Kong Disciplined Service Collectibles*, http://www.hkdsc.co m/life/jackson.html (accessed March 20, 2006).
50. Geoffrey Charles Emerson, "Stanley Internment Camp, Hong Kong, 1942–1945: A Study of Civilian Internment during the Second World War" (M.Phil. thesis, University of Hong Kong, 1973), p. 26.
51. Chan Lau, *From Nothing to Nothing*, p. 8.
52. Ibid.
53. AVP RF, f. 100, op. 35a, d. 13, pap. 239, 1944, Part 2, "China and England," *Tass* Intelligence Reports.
54. For details on these negotiations, see subsequent chapters of this book, and also Michael B. Share, "The Soviet Union, Hong Kong, and the Cold War, 1945–1970," *Cold War International History Project* Working Paper no. 41 (Washington, DC: Woodrow Wilson International Center for Scholars, 2003).

Notes to Chapter 5

1. The American Consulate-General was the largest in the world, devoted mainly to "listening in" on developments in China. The American government was especially concerned with Chinese development of nuclear weapons, troop movements within the PRC, and levels of political dissent. Some 280 people, of whom 42 were Vice Consuls, worked at the Consulate-General, as the Soviet Union and local Hong Kong newspapers noted. Many of America's most experienced sinologists served there. During the 1950s the CIA station, located in the Consulate-General, also expanded rapidly. In fact Hong Kong remained an intelligence center of outstanding importance until the British withdrawal from the territory in 1997. See AVP RF, f. 1dvo, op. 42, d. 50, 1955, "Report by Vice Consul V. Kapralov, Guangzhou," p. 36; *Ta Kung Pao*, January 12, 1958; "Activities of US Agents," *South China Morning Post*, September 26, 1954; NA, RG 84, December 12, 1958, State Department to US Consulate, Hong Kong; James Lilley with Jeffrey Lilley, *China Hands: Nine Decades of Adventure, Espionage, and Diplomacy in Asia* (New York: Public Affairs Press, 2004), esp. Chapters 6 and 8; and Richard J. Aldrich, *The Hidden Hand: Britain, America, and Cold War Secret Intelligence* (London: John Murray, 2001), pp. 293–314.
2. NA, 746g.00, *Die Kronkolonie und der Kalte Krieg: Kleiner politischer Reiseführer durch Hongkong* [The Crown Colony and the Cold War: A Short Political Guidebook to Hong Kong], document prepared for the German Consulate-General in Hong Kong by Mr. Klaus H. Pringsheim. The document was then made available to the American Consulate-General. For

British policy in Hong Kong, see Zhai Qiang, *The Dragon, the Lion, and the Eagle: Chinese-British-American Relations, 1949–1958* (Kent, OH: Kent State University Press, 1994); for American policy, see Nancy Bernkopf Tucker, *Taiwan, Hong Kong, and the United States, 1945–1992: Uncertain Friendships* (New York: Twayne, 1994); and for Chinese policy, both Nationalist and Communist, see Steve Tsang Yui-sang, "Strategy for Survival: The Cold War and Hong Kong's Policy toward Kuomintang and Chinese Communist Activities in the 1950s," *Journal of Imperial and Commonwealth History* 25, no. 2 (May 1997): 294–317.

3. The only Russian history of Hong Kong is by Peter M. Ivanov, *Gonkong* [Hong Kong] (Moscow: Nauka, 1990). Prof. Ivanov's account contains surprisingly little on Russian and Soviet activities in the colony, only a ten-page description in one chapter on Russian activities during the late nineteenth century up through the Russian Revolution of 1917. Prof. Ivanov's book says nothing of Soviet activities or policies in Hong Kong, but focuses on political, economic, and social developments within the crown colony.
4. NA, RG 84, March 31, 1948, Airgram from US Consulate-General, Hong Kong, to State Department.
5. PRO, FO 371/1018, 1948; and AVP RF, f. 1dvo, op. 42, d. 116, p. 6. In late 1949, Hong Kong had a total population of 1.8 million people, of whom 14,000 were foreigners, excluding British troops.
6. AVP RF, f. 1dvo, op. 42, d. 75, May 19, 1949.
7. PRO, FO 371/177697, February 17, 1964, Letter by E. G. Willan, Hong Kong government, to the Colonial Office; NA, March 8, 1948, Circular Airgram.
8. NA, RG 84, 846G.00, September 26, 1946, US Consulate-General Report: "Relations between British Authorities and the Chinese in Hong Kong"; NA, RG 84, 846G.00, March 31, 1948, "Soviet Personnel in Hong Kong." The reason for US State Department concern over the possible pro-Communist sympathies of Hong Kong workers was largely because 30 years earlier, during the 1920s, Hong Kong workers had engaged in a series of militant, partly political strikes, culminating in a large general strike that lasted for 16 months. For further information, see Chapter 3 above.
9. PRO, FO 371/1018, "Report on Soviet Activities in Hong Kong, 1948"; and NA, RG 84, May 31, 1948, Telegram sent from Consul-General Hopper, Hong Kong, to the State Department.
10. AVP RF, f. 1dvo, op. 41, d. 125, April 25, 1948, Letter to V. M. Molotov, p. 41.
11. AVP RF, f. 1dvo, op. 34a, d. 15, p. 11.
12. AVP RF, f. 1dvo, op. 41, d. 125, April 12, 1948, Letter to Ya. Malik, p. 40.
13. AVP RF, f. 1dvo, op. 41, d. 125, Letter to V. S. Kamenev, Head of VOKS,

from G. Tiunkin, Head, Far East Department, MID, p. 42.

14. AVP RF, f. 1dvo, op. 41, d. 125, 1948, "Report about the Work of VOKS," p. 100.
15. Ibid.
16. NA, RG 84, 1946, Telegram from G. D. Hopper, Consul-General, Hong Kong, to the State Department, p. 3.
17. PRO, FO 371/N 3238/1018/38, 1948.
18. AVP RF, f. 1dvo, op. 41. d. 125, 1948, "Report about the Work of VOKS," p. 100.
19. RGASPI, f. 17, op. 128, d. 994, April 1946, p. 268.
20. AVP RF, f. 1dvo, op. 34a, d. 15, November 24, 1946, "Information about Hong Kong," p. 6.
21. Steve Tsang Yui-sang, *Hong Kong: An Appointment with China* (London: I. B. Tauris, 1997), pp. 34–35.
22. "Gazeta 'Jinvanbao' trebiuet vozvrashcheniya Gonkonga kitaiu [Newspaper "Sinvanbao" demands the return of Hong Kong to China]," *Pravda*, May 15, 1946, p. 4; and PRO, FO 371/53598. Unfortunately, no documents could be retrieved in the Russian archives to bolster the *Pravda* articles.
23. "Trebovaniye o vozvrashchenni Gonkonga, Kouloona, i Amoya Kitaiu [Demands for the return of Hong Kong, Kowloon, Macao to China]," *Pravda*, February 16, 1946, p. 4.
24. RGASPI, f. 17, op. 128, d. 994.
25. AVP RF, f. 1dvo, op. 34a, d. 15, p. 9.
26. For a fuller description of Hong Kong at the close of World War II, see G. B. Endacott, *A History of Hong Kong*, 2nd ed. (London: Oxford University Press, 1964); Frank Welsh, *A History of Hong Kong*, 2nd ed. (London: HarperCollins, 1997); and Steve Tsang Yui-sang, *A Modern History of Hong Kong* (London: I. B. Tauris, 2004).
27. RGASPI, f. 17, op. 128, d. 994.
28. AVP RF, f. 1dvo, op. 34a, d. 15, p. 6.
29. AVP RF, f. 1dvo, op. 34a, d. 15, p. 8.
30. PRO, FO 371/1018, "Report on Soviet Activities in Hong Kong, 1948."
31. NA, RG 84, September 2, 1947, Letter to the US Ambassador, Nanjing, from the US Consulate-General, Shanghai. The British made similar allegations regarding Soviet opium trafficking during the 1920s, allegations the Soviets unofficially admitted. PRO, CO 349/56063; AVP RF, f. 0100, op. 11, d. 8, pap. 12; and AVP RF, f. 0100, op. 12, d. 96, pap. 155, 1923–1928.
32. NA, RG 84, April 2, 1947, Airgram from the US Consulate-General, Hong Kong, to the State Department; and NA, RG 84, Hong Kong Consulate-General, 1948, 110.2–800.

33. NA, RG 84, August 1, 1947, US Consulate-General, Hong Kong, to Washington.
34. *Guardian* and *Le Figaro*, September 22, 1950.
35. NA, RG 84, Dispatch no. 346, December 29, 1950, US Consulate-General, Shanghai.
36. PRO, FO 371/83264, 1950.
37. AVP RF, f. 1dvo, op. 44, d. 147, May 12, 1951, D. Savostin, Soviet Consulate, Guangzhou, "Some Information on Hong Kong," p. 15.
38. Robert Boardman, *Britain and the People's Republic of China, 1949–74* (New York: Barnes & Noble, 1976); and RGASPI, f. 17, op. 137, d. 720, May 12, 1951, "Some Facts about Hong Kong."
39. AVP RF, f. 1dvo, op. 42, d. 118, September 26–December 10, 1949, "American and British Policies in China."
40. AVP RF, f. 1dvo, op. 42, d. 116, September 26, 1949, M. Safronov, Soviet Embassy, Beijing, "Hong Kong—Survey of the Modern Economic Situation."
41. "Conversation between Mao and Stalin," December 16, 1949, AVP RF, f. 45, op. 1, d. 329, ll. 9–17; translation by Danny Rozas, *Cold War International History Project Bulletin* 6/7 (Winter 1995): 6; and Dieter Heinzig, *The Soviet Union and Communist China 1945–1950: The Arduous Road to the Alliance* (Armonk, NY: M. E. Sharpe, 2004), pp. 278–279.
42. Heinzig, *The Soviet Union and Communist China*, p. 299; and S. N. Goncharov, John Wilson Lewis, and Xue Litai, *Uncertain Partners: Stalin, Mao, and the Korean War* (Stanford, CA: Stanford University Press, 1993), pp. 99–100.
43. AVP RF, f. 1dvo, op. 44, d. 147, May 12, 1951, D. Savostin, Soviet Consulate, Guangzhou, "Some Information on Hong Kong," p. 13.
44. AVP RF, f. 1dvo, op. 44, d. 147, May 12, 1951, D. Savostin, Soviet Consulate, Guangzhou, "Some Information on Hong Kong."
45. AVP RF, f. 1dvo, op 42, d. 116, September 26, 1949, M. Safronov, Soviet Embassy, Beijing, "Hong Kong—Survey of the Modern Economic Situation."
46. AVP RF, f. 1dvo, op. 44. d. 147, December 1951, N. Matkov, Soviet Consulate, Guangzhou, "Political and Economic Position of Hong Kong"; and AVP RF, f. 1dvo, op. 43, d. 148, December 1951, Maliukin, Soviet Consul in Guangzhou, "England Supplies Ammunition from Hong Kong to Korea."
47. AVP RF, f. 1dvo, op. 49, d. 119, March 1956, L. Grachev, Soviet Consulate, Guangzhou, "Political and Economic Position of Hong Kong," pp. 11–12.
48. RGASPI, f. 17, op. 137, d. 722, A. Sergiev, "Reports about the Situation in Hong Kong in the First Half of 1951," p. 242.
49. AVP RF, f. 1dvo, op. 42, d. 50, 1955, "Report Filed by V. Kapralov, Vice Consul, Guangzhou," p. 37.

50. AVP RF, f. 1dvo, op. 44, d. 147, May 12, 1951, D. Savostin, Soviet Consulate, Guangzhou, "Some Information on Hong Kong," pp 16–18.
51. AVP RF, f. 1dvo, op. 43, d. 148, December 28, 1951, G. I. Tiunkin, Soviet Consulate, Guangzhou, "Report to the MID," p. 159; and AVP RF, f. 1dvo, op. 47, d. 106, p. 29.
52. Aldrich, *The Hidden Hand*, pp. 293–314.
53. AVP RF, f. 1dvo, op. 47, d. 106, October 10–November 15, 1953, p. 7.
54. AVP RF, f. 1dvo, op. 47, d. 105, 1954, I. V. Kalabukhov, Soviet Consul, Guangzhou, "Hostile Activities by the United States toward China," pp. 50–53.
55. AVP RF, f. 1dvo, op 42, d. 50, 1955, p. 149.
56. AVP RF, f. 1dvo, op. 49, d. 119, L. Grachev, Soviet Consulate, Guangzhou, "Survey of the Political and Economic Position of Hong Kong in 1956," p. 11.
57. Ibid., p. 14.
58. Aldrich, *The Hidden Hand*, pp. 313–314. See also Chapter 7, n.41.
59. Thomas J. Christensen, *Useful Adversaries: Grand Strategy, Domestic Mobilization, and Sino-American Conflict, 1947–1958* (Princeton, NJ: Princeton University Press, 1996), pp. 198–199.
60. AVP RF, f. 1dvo, op. 44, d. 147, May 12, 1951, D. Savostin, Soviet Consulate, Guangzhou, "Some Information on Hong Kong," p. 15.
61. RGASPI f. 17, op. 137, d. 722, 1951, "Report about the Situation in Hong Kong"; AVP RF, f. 1dvo, op 44, d. 147, N. Matkov, Staff Attaché, Guangzhou, "Political and Economic Position of Hong Kong," p. 4; AVP RF, f. 1dvo, op. 44, d. 147, D. Savostin, Soviet Consulate, Guangzhou, "Some Information on Hong Kong," p. 15; and AVP RF, f. 1dvo, op 45, d. 148, 1952, "Information about Hong Kong and Macao."
62. AVP RF, f. 1dvo, op. 44, d. 147, May 1951, D. Savostin, Soviet Consulate, Guangzhou, "Some Information on Hong Kong," p. 13.
63. AVP RF, f. 1dvo, op. 49, d. 119, L. Grachev, Soviet Consulate, Guangzhou, "Political and Economic Situation of Hong Kong in 1956," p. 11.
64. Hope Millard Harrison, *Driving the Soviets up the Wall: Soviet-East German Relations, 1953–1961* (Princeton, NJ: Princeton University Press, 2003), pp. 78–80.
65. AVP RF, f. 1dvo, op. 43, d. 145, 1950, T. Skvortsov and E. Shalunov, Soviet Embassy, Beijing, "Report on Hong Kong and Macao," p. 3.
66. PRO, CO 1030/380, 1954, "European Refugees through Hong Kong," p. 33.
67. PRO, CO 1030/385, 1956.
68. AVP RF, f. 1dvo, op. 49, d. 119, March 2, 1956, L. Grachev, Soviet Consulate, Guangzhou, "Political and Economic Position of Hong Kong in 1956," p. 6.
69. AVP RF, f. 1dvo, op. 42, d. 50, 1955, V. Kapralov, Vice Consul, Guangzhou, p. 29.

70. Ibid., p. 28.
71. Ibid., pp. 30–34.
72. AVP RF, f. 1dvo, op. 42, d. 117, December 27, 1948–September 15, 1949, N. Shesterikov, "American and British Hopes for a Resurgence of Nationalism in a Communist China," p. 35.
73. AVP RF, f. 1dvo, op. 47, d. 106, January 5, 1954, "Provocative Propaganda of the English in Hong Kong," pp. 8, 21–23.
74. NA, RG 306, March 1954, "Little Moe." "Little Moe" was the name of a cartoon figure featured in the pamphlet.
75. NA, RG 306, March 11, 1954, "Telegram from State to USIS."
76. RGASPI, f. 17, op. 137, d. 720, May–November 1951, p. 11; AVP RF, f. 1dvo, op. 47, d. 106, January 1954, p. 8; AVP RF, f. 1dvo, op. 48, d. 135, 1955, pp. 37–38; and AVP RF, f. 1dvo, op. 42, d. 50, 1955, V. Kapralov, Vice Consul, Guangzhou, pp. 26, 38.
77. NA, RG 306, June 1, 1950, Communist Propaganda Materials.
78. PRO, CO 1030/326, October–November 1954, "Political Allegiance of Hong Kong Citizens," p. 5.
79. NA, RG 84, January 25, 1952, Telegram from Hong Kong Consulate-General to the State Department; and NA, RG 84, January 4, 1953, Telegram from Hong Kong Consulate-General to the State Department.
80. PRO, CO 1030/250, "Fortnightly Intelligence Reports from Hong Kong," pp. 34–36.
81. RGASPI, f. 17, op. 137, d. 720, May 12, 1951, D. Savostin, Consul-General, Guangzhou, "Some Facts about Hong Kong," Briefing Background for Stalin and Molotov; AVP RF, f. 1dvo, op. 44, d. 147, D. Savostin, Soviet Consulate, Guangzhou, "Some Information on Hong Kong," p. 18; AVP RF, f. 1dvo, op. 48, d. 135, 1955, "Hong Kong and Macao," p. 50; and AVP RF, f. 1dvo, op. 42, d. 50, 1955, V. Kapralov, Vice Consul, Guangzhou, p. 45.
82. NA, RG 306, April 26, 1954, Telegram from USIS, Hong Kong, to the State Department.
83. AVP RF, f. 1dvo, op. 42, d. 50, September 1955, "Articles of Interest to the Soviet Union in the Hong Kong Press," p. 114; and AVP RF, op. 49, d. 119, L. Grachev, Soviet Consulate, Guangzhou, March 2, 1956, "Political and Economic Position of Hong Kong in 1956," p. 16.
84. RGASPI, f. 17, op. 137, d. 720, May–November 1951, Soviet Consulate, Guangzhou, "Political and Economic Situation in Hong Kong," p. 11; and RGASPI, f. 17, op. 137, d. 722, June–October 1951, Soviet Consulate, Guangzhou, p. 117.
85. PRO, FO 371, 129053, 1957.
86. AVP RF, f. 1dvo, op. 44, d. 147, D. Savostin, Soviet Consulate, Guangzhou, "Some Information on Hong Kong," p. 13.

87. AVP RF, f. 1dvo, op. 49, d. 119, March 2, 1956, L. Grachev, Soviet Consulate, Guangzhou, "Political and Economic Position of Hong Kong."
88. AVP RF, f. 1dvo, op. 51, d. 28, March 22, 1958, Letter to Andrei Gromyko, from N. Fedorenko and M. Zimyatin, Soviet Embassy, Beijing, p. 1.
89. AVP RF, f. 1dvo, op. 51, d. 28, May 13, 1958, Response by Andrei Gromyko, p. 2.
90. AVP RF, f. 1dvo, op. 51, d. 28, Subsequent Circular Report, pp. 13–15.

Notes to Chapter 6

1. RGANI, f. 5, op. 49, d. 131–133, June 18, 1958, "Diary of P. N. Verashagin, Adviser to the Soviet Embassy in Beijing," pp. 164–165.
2. PRO, FCO 21/661, 1220067, 1970.
3. AVP RF, f. 1dvo, op. 53, d. 25, February 16, 1966, R. Iskandrov, Third Secretary, Far East Department, MID, USSR, "Broad Survey of Hong Kong and Macao," p. 5.
4. AVP RF, f. 1dvo, op. 54, d. 31, February 11, 1967, Far East Department, MID, USSR, "General Report on Hong Kong and Macao," no. 440, p. 8.
5. PRO, FCO 21/716, 1219443, 1970.
6. Aleksandr Fursenko and Timothy Naftali, *Khrushchev's Cold War: The Inside Story of an American Adversary* (London: W. W. Norton, 2006), pp. 412–416.
7. PRO, FCO 21/73, Russian newspaper articles on Hong Kong and Macao.
8. Elizabeth Wishnick, *Mending Fences: The Evolution of Moscow's China Policy, from Brezhnev to Yeltsin* (Seattle: University of Washington Press, 2001), p. 28.
9. Ibid.
10. PRO, FCO 21/73, Russian articles.
11. AVP RF, f. 1dvo, op. 54, d. 31, December 11, 1967, "Political Economics of the KNP (Chinese Communist Party) and Its Relations with Hong Kong and Macao," pp. 108–138.
12. Ibid., p. 105.
13. Steve Tsang Yui-sang, *Hong Kong: An Appointment with China* (London: I. B. Tauris, 1997), p. 70.
14. AVP RF, f. 1dvo, op. 54, d. 31, December 11, 1967, "Political Economics."
15. Ibid., p. 133.
16. AVP RF, f. 1dvo, op. 53, d. 25, February 12, 1966, R. Iskandarov, Far East Department, MID, USSR, "Broad Survey of Hong Kong and Macao," p. 5.
17. Richard J. Aldrich, *The Hidden Hand: Britain, America, and Cold War Secret Intelligence* (London: John Murray, 2001), p. 310.
18. AVP RF, f. 1dvo, op. 54, d. 31, December 11, 1967, "Political Economics," pp. 108–138.

19. Stephen Dorril, *MI6: Fifty Years of Special Operations* (London: Fourth Estate, 2000), pp. 719–720. This information appeared originally in Stephen Merret, "British help to US in Vietnam," *Red Camden*, April/May 1969; and in *Lobster*, no. 4, 1984.
20. AVP RF, f. 1dvo, op. 49, d. 41, June 27–September 1, 1962, Ye. Brezhneva, "Report on Refugees from China," p. 2.
21. AVP RF, f. 1dvo, op. 44, d. 147, December 31, 1951, N. Matkov, "Political and Economic Position of Hong Kong," p. 5; and AVP RF, f. 1dvo, op. 43, d. 145, 1950, T. Skvortsov and E. Shalunov, "Information about Hong Kong and Macao," p. 3.
22. AVP RF, f. 1dvo, op. 49, d. 41, June 27–September 1, 1962, Ye. Brezhneva, "Report on the Refugees from China," pp. 2–6.
23. RGASPI, f. 17, op. 137, d. 720, May 12, 1951, D. Savostin, Soviet Consulate, Guangzhou, "Some Facts about Hong Kong," Briefing Background for Stalin and Molotov.
24. PRO, FCO 21/876, 1971, "Release of Confrontation Prisoners." Most prisoners were quickly released. By the end of 1971, only eight remained in custody, all of whom had been convicted on terrorism and murder charges. In a gesture of goodwill to the PRC, the Hong Kong government promised to release even those few fairly quickly. PRO, FCO 21/1025, 1971, "Release of Prisoners."
25. AVP RF, f. 1dvo, op. 54, d. 31, June 10, 1967, V. Azariushkin, Soviet Embassy, Bangkok, "About Events in Hong Kong," pp. 19–21.
26. AVP RF, f. 1dvo, op. 54, d. 31, June 17, 1967, B. Chiudinov, Soviet Embassy, London, "Events in Hong Kong and Deteriorating Chinese-British Relations," pp. 25–33.
27. AVP RF, f. 1dvo, op. 54, d. 31, August 3, 1967, "Further Developments on the Events in Hong Kong and on English-Chinese Relations," pp. 35–43.
28. Ibid.
29. Ibid.
30. AVP RF, f. 1dvo, op. 54, d. 31, June 17, 1967, "Events in Hong Kong and Deteriorating Chinese-British Relations."
31. Ibid., p. 43.
32. AVP RF, f. 69, op. 59, d. 31, pap. 239, July 4–October 11, 1967, B. Chiudinov, Third Secretary, London Embassy, "Report about Affairs in England."
33. PRO, FCO 21/202, May 28, 1968, Translation of an *Izvestiya* article entitled: "The Story of a Betrayal," September 16, 1967.
34. PRO, FCO 21/122, June 16, 1967, From Phnom Penh to the Foreign Office.
35. AVP RF, f. 1dvo, op. 53, d. 25, February 16, 1966, R. Iskandarov, Far East Department, MID, USSR, p. 3.
36. AVP RF, f. 1dvo, op. 54, d. 31, June 10, 1967, V. Azariushkin, Soviet

Embassy, Bangkok, "About Events in Hong Kong," pp. 19–21.

37. AVP RF, f. 100, op. 59, d. 23, pap. 255, February 8–December 11, 1972, "Taiwan, Hong Kong, and Macao." In 1967, Hong Kong exported only US$670,000 to the Soviet Union, while importing US$6,699,000. By 1970, trade had grown significantly between the two states. Hong Kong exported US$7.96 million, while importing US$12.3 million.
38. At that time, the exchange rate was roughly HK$5 to US$1.
39. HK PRO, HKRS 70-3-556, October 14, 1968.
40. Ibid.
41. AVP RF, f. 1dvo, op. 51, d. 30, August 1964, p. 1.
42. Ibid., V. Lebedev, "Information on Herman Travel."
43. AVP RF, f. 1dvo, op. 53, d. 25, February 1, 1966, Letter to N. G. Sudarikov, Far East Department, MID, USSR, from Department of International Air Services, Ministry of Civil Aviation, p. 1. Currently, and for the past several years, Aeroflot has operated direct non-stop flights from Moscow to Hong Kong. Very recently, Aeroflot has increased the numbers of flights from three to six times a week, and has signed a co-share agreement with Hong Kong's flagship carrier Cathay Pacific.
44. Ibid., July 13, 1966, Letter to N. G. Sudarikov, Far East Department, MID, USSR, from A. Besedin, Chief, Department of International Air Services, Ministry of Civil Aviation.
45. AVP RF, f. 1dvo, op. 54, d. 31, January 12, 1967, Letter to N. G. Sudarikov, Far East Department, MID, USSR, from A. Besedin, Chief, Department of International Air Services, Ministry of Civil Aviation, p. 1.
46. Ibid., February 1, 1967, Letter to A. Besedin, Chief, Department of International Air Services, Ministry of Civil Aviation, from N. G. Sudarikov, Far East Department, MID, USSR, p. 2.
47. Ibid., February 11, 1967, Far East Department, MID, USSR, no. 440, "General Report on Hong Kong and Macao," p. 9.
48. Ibid., Translation into Russian of Letter Written in English by the Hong Kong Corporation "Shop-Buy-Mail" to MID, February 1967.
49. Ibid., May 1967, Letter to V. I. Likhachev, Head, Far East Department, MID, USSR, from A. Besedin, Chief, Department of International Air Services, Ministry of Civil Aviation.
50. Ibid., May 29, 1967, Letter to A. Besedin, Chief, Department of International Air Services, Ministry of Civil Aviation, from V. Likachev, Head, Far East Department, MID, USSR.
51. HK PRO, HKRS 70-2-264, 1968, "Communism in Hong Kong."
52. PRO, FCO 28/9, February 25, 1967.
53. Ibid., FCO 21/874, 1971, "Attempts by the USSR to Gain a Foothold."
54. "There's Something about Soviet Labor," *The Economist*, February 27, 1971.

55. *Politisches Archiv des Auswärtigen Amts*, Bonn, Germany, B 37/592: Hong Kong, 1971, October 2, 1971, Consul-General von Heyden to Foreign Office, "About the Activities of the Soviet Union in Hong Kong." Document located, translated, and graciously given to the author by Dr. Bert Becker, Visiting Professor at the University of Hong Kong.
56. *Politisches Archiv des Auswärtigen Amts*, Bonn, B 37/592: Hong Kong, 1971, October 2, 1971, von Heyden to Foreign Office.
57. PRO, FCO 21/1021, 1972 (FEH 3/303/1), November 14, 1972, "Attempts by the Soviet Union to Gain a Foothold in Hong Kong."
58. Ibid.
59. Ibid.
60. HK PRO, HKRS 70-3-556, October 1968.
61. "Analysis of Evergrowing Russian Maritime Power," *South China Morning Post*, August 24, 1971, p. 9.
62. PRO, FCO 21/874, April 30, 1971, J. A. L. Morgan, British Embassy, Moscow.
63. AVP RF, f. 1dvo, op. 54, d. 31, February 11, 1967, Far East Department, MID, "General Report on Hong Kong and Macao," no. 440.
64. PRO, FO 371, 177697, NS 1161/2, February 17, 1964, Letter from E. G. Willan, Hong Kong Government, to J. D. Higham, Colonial Office, London.
65. Ibid.
66. Ibid.
67. PRO, FO 371, 177697, NS 1161/4, 1964.
68. PRO, FO 371, 177697, NS 1161/6, April, 1964.
69. PRO, FO 371, 177697, NS 1161/5, March 23, 1964, Letter from E. G. Willan, Hong Kong Government, to J. D. Higham, Colonial Office, London.
70. PRO, CO 1030/1717, April 6, 1964, p. 3.
71. PRO, FCO 21/73, Russian articles.
72. PRO, FCO 21/202, "Foreign Views on Hong Kong, 1967."
73. PRO, FCO 21/716, 1970, "Effect on Hong Kong of Relations between China and the USSR."
74. PRO, FCO 21/1021, 1972, FEH 3/303/1. Only after the collapse of the Soviet Union in December 1991 were Russian citizens allowed to visit Hong Kong on tourist or business visas. Even then, however, each visa was issued for a maximum of two weeks, easily renewable only once.
75. PRO, FCO 21/874, 1971, "Secret."
76. PRO, FCO 21/716, 1970, April 8, 1970, G. G. H. Walden, Eastern European and Soviet Department, Foreign Office, "Soviet Interest in Hong Kong," pp. 11–12.
77. Professor Ronald Hill (Professor Emeritus, University of Hong Kong) in discussion with the author, March 8, 2006.
78. Jane Moir, "Discovery Mystery," *South China Morning Post*, January 22, 2005,

http://web.lexis-nexis.com/universe/document? (accessed March 17, 2006).

79. C. K. Lau, "When the Cold War Hit Discovery Bay," *South China Morning Post*, December 11, 2004, http://72.14.203.104/search?q=cache:dzQ8cq UjhucJ (accessed March 17, 2006).
80. Colum Murphy, "Spy Fear Led to Disco Bay," *Hong Kong Standard*, January 13, 2005, http://www.thestandard.com.hk (accessed March 17, 2006).
81. David Akers-Jones, *Feeling the Stones: Reminiscences* (Hong Kong: Hong Kong University Press, 2004), p. 70.

Notes to Chapter 7

1. Nancy Bernkopf Tucker, *Taiwan, Hong Kong, and the United States, 1945–1992: Uncertain Friendships* (New York: Twayne, 1994); Ralph N. Clough, *Island China* (Cambridge, MA: Harvard University Press, 1978); and Robert Accinelli, *Crisis and Commitment: United States Policy toward Taiwan, 1950–1955* (Chapel Hill: North Carolina University Press, 1996).
2. Thomas J. Bellows, "Normalization: A Taiwan Perspective," *Asian Affairs* 6, no. 6 (July–August 1979): 339–358; and John Franklin Copper, "Taiwan's Options," *Asian Affairs* 6, no. 5 (May–June 1979): 282–294.
3. Arnold L. Horelick, "Soviet Policy Dilemmas in Asia," *Asian Survey* 17, no. 6 (June 1977): 499–512; Reinhard Drifte, "European and Soviet Perspectives on Future Responses in Taiwan to International and Regional Developments," *Asian Survey* 25, no. 11 (November 1985): 1115–1122; and John W. Garver, "Taiwan's Russian Option: Image and Reality," *Asian Survey* 18, no. 7 (July 1978): 751–766. For a Russian perspective, albeit a very limited one for the Soviet period, see the early section in Peter M. Ivanov, "Russian-Taiwanese Relations: Current State, Problems, and Prospects of Development," *Occasional Papers/Reprints Series in Contemporary Asian Studies* 133, no. 2 (1996): 1–76.
4. RGASPI, f. 495, op. 128, d. 14, "Survey."
5. PRO, FCO 21/703 (1219434), 1970, "Political Reports from Taiwan." The entire document is an excellent background piece.
6. Immanuel C. Y. Hsü, *The Ili Crisis: A Study of Sino-Russian Diplomacy, 1871–1881* (Oxford: Clarendon Press, 1965).
7. AVP RI, f. 148, op. 487, d. 1426, 1887–1902, "Formosa," Russian Consulate, Fuzhou, Fujian province, China.
8. RGASPI, f. 495, op. 128, d. 14, July 5, 1928, "Formosa under the Yoke of Japanese Imperialism."
9. Ibid., March 6, 1896, Note, unsigned, pp. 25–27.
10. John Franklin Copper, *Taiwan: Nation State or Province?* 4th ed. (Boulder, CO: Westview Press, 2003), p. 37.

11. PRO, FCO 21/703 (1219434), 1970.
12. Ramon H. Myers and Mark R. Peattie, eds., *The Japanese Colonial Empire, 1895–1945* (Princeton, NJ: Princeton University Press, 1984), p. 352.
13. W. G. Beasley, *Japanese Imperialism, 1894–1945* (Oxford: Clarendon Press, 1987), p. 149.
14. PRO, FO 371/10965, 1925, "Formosa Year Book," F 1871/1871/23, p. 54.
15. Copper, *Taiwan: Nation State or Province?*, p. 43.
16. AVP RI, f. 143, op. 491, d. 407, "Reports from the Consulate, 1891–1907."
17. RGASPI, f. 495, op. 128, d. 14, July 5, 1928, "Formosa under the Yoke of Japanese Imperialism."
18. RGASPI, f. 495, op. 128, d. 4, June 30, 1934, "Economic Survey of Formosa."
19. RGASPI, f. 495, op. 128, d. 14, July 5, 1928, "Formosa under the Yoke of Japanese Imperialism."
20. RGASPI, f. 495, op. 128, d. 14, "Great Aborigine Uprising in Formosa."
21. RGASPI, f. 495, op. 128, d. 1, May 27, 1932, "Letter to Revolutionary Workers in Formosa."
22. RGASPI, f. 495, op. 128, d. 14, February 7, 1931, Agnes Smedley, "The Formosan Revolt."
23. Ibid.; and PRO, FO 371/10965, 1925, "Formosa Annual Report," p. 54.
24. RGASPI, f. 495, op. 128, d. 1, May 27, 1932, "Letter to Revolutionary Workers in Formosa."
25. RGASPI, f. 495, op. 128, d. 4, June 30, 1931, "Economic Survey of Formosa."
26. RGASPI, f. 495, op. 128, d. 14, July 5, 1928, "Formosa under the Yoke of Japanese Imperialism."
27. RGASPI, f. 495, op. 128, d. 4, June 30, 1931, "Economic Survey of Formosa."
28. RGASPI, f. 495, op. 128, d. 11, June 12, 1930, Ah-Sao, "Present Situation in Formosa." During the interwar period, two yen were equivalent to one US dollar.
29. RGASPI, f. 495, op. 128, d. 6, July 7, 1930, "Recent Economic and Political Situation in Formosa."
30. RGASPI, f. 495, op. 128, d. 11, June 12, 1930, Ah-Sao, "Present Situation in Formosa."
31. RGASPI, f. 495, op. 128, d. 6, April 1932, Ong Ding Chuan, "Uprising Against White Terror." 100 sen equaled one yen, which was worth US 50 cents at that time.
32. RGASPI, f. 495, op. 128, d. 10, April 10, 1931, Comrade Chan, Letter to Far East Bureau, Comintern.
33. RGASPI, f. 495, op. 128, d. 6, May 12, 1930, Ong Ding Chuan, "Situation of

the CPF in Formosa." Comintern agent Ong Ding Chuan, who was hardly literate, dictated her series of bimonthly letters and reports to a British subject, S. T. Baer, who wrote them in her excellent native English.

34. RGASPI, f. 495, op. 128, d. 10, April 2, 1931, Ong Ding Chuan, "Objective Situation for Formation of CPF."
35. RGASPI, f. 495, op. 128, d. 1, April 13, 1931, "Letter to Formosan Communists."
36. Ibid.
37. Ibid.
38. RGASPI, f. 495, op. 128, d. 1, July 7, 1931, "Letter to Formosan Communists."
39. RGASPI, f. 495, op. 128, d. 13, September 20, 1931, "Materials from the Minsuta Party CC Program"; and RGASPI, f. 495, op. 128, d. 6, April 1932, "Program of the CPF."
40. RGASPI, f. 495, op. 128, d. 1, September 25, 1932, "Letter to Revolutionary Workers in Formosa."
41. Frank S. T. Hsiao and Lawrence R. Sullivan, "The Chinese Communist Party and the Status of Taiwan, 1928–1943," *Pacific Affairs* 52, no. 3 (Autumn 1979): 446–454.
42. RGASPI, f. 495, op. 128, d. 1, July 7, 1931, "Letter to Formosan Communists."
43. RGASPI, f. 495, op. 128, d. 1, September 25, 1932, "Letter to Revolutionary Workers in Formosa."
44. AVP RF, f. 100, op. 21, d. 49, pap. 60, 1937, Part 2, "China and England," Press Clippings.
45. John W. Garver, *Chinese-Soviet Relations, 1937–1945: The Diplomacy of Chinese Nationalism* (New York: Oxford University Press, 1988), pp. 18–22, 37–50; and Charles B. McLane, *Soviet Policy and the Chinese Communists, 1931–1946* (New York: Columbia University Press, 1958), pp. 128–137.
46. Garver, *Chinese-Soviet Relations*, pp. 40–41; and Claire Lee Chennault, *Way of a Fighter: The Memoirs of Claire Lee Chennault*, ed. Robert Hotz (New York: G. P. Putnam's Sons, 1949), pp. 61–67, quotation from p. 63.
47. S. V. Slyusarev, "Protecting China's Air Space," in *Soviet Volunteers in China 1925–1945: Articles and Reminiscences*, trans. David Fidlon (Moscow: Progress, 1980), pp. 252–254.
48. Chennault, *Way of a Fighter*; Martha Byrd, *Chennault: Giving Wings to the Tiger* (Tuscaloosa: University of Alabama Press, 1987); and Daniel Ford, *Flying Tigers: Claire Chennault and the American Volunteer Group* (Washington, DC: Smithsonian Institution Press, 1991).
49. AVP RF, f. *komissiya Litvinova*, op. 7, d. 6, September–October 1943—Study of American Interests in the postwar world regarding Taiwan: Secret

#88-44, September 1, 1943, Vzh. 26, January 25, 1944, p. 2.

50. Ibid., p. 9.
51. AVP RF, f. *komissiya Litvinova*, op. 7, d. 6, #348 (secret), H-44 (revised) October 19, 1943, p. 2.
52. PRO, FO 371/105216, 1953, "Future of Taiwan."
53. Hsiao and Sullivan, "The Chinese Communist Party and the Status of Taiwan," pp. 465–467.
54. PRO, FO 371/69621, 1948, "Taiwan."
55. HK PRO, RS 70, 22/2091/1949, July 15, 1949.
56. AVP RF, f. 56, op. 16, d. 227, 1950, p. 123.
57. Brian Murray, "Stalin, the Cold War, and the Division of China: A Multi-Archival Mystery," Working Paper no. 12, June 1995, *The Cold War International History Project Virtual Archive*, http://wilsoncenter.org/index.cfm?topic_id=1409&fuseaction=va2.browse&sort=Collection.
58. PRO, FO 371/75833, October 12, 1949, F. Cheng, Chinese Embassy, London.
59. PRO, FO 371/75804, 1949, Consulate to Foreign Office.
60. Tucker, *Taiwan, Hong Kong, and the United States*, p. 30.
61. Dieter Heinzig, *The Soviet Union and Communist China 1945–1950: The Arduous Road to the Alliance* (Armonk, NY: M. E. Sharpe, 2004), pp. 277–279.
62. Chen Jian, *China's Road to the Korean War: The Making of the Sino-American Confrontation* (New York: Columbia University Press, 1994), pp. 96–102.
63. AVP RF, f. 4, op. 1, d. 329, pp. 9–17. Chen Jian, Vojtech Mastny, Odd Arne Westad, and Vladislav Zubok, translators and commentators, *Talks with Mao Zedong and Zhou Enlai, 1949–1953*, "Conversation between Mao and Stalin," December 16, 1949, *Cold War International History Project Virtual Archive*, pp. 298–299, http://www.wilsoncenter.org/index.cfm?topic_id=1409&fuseaction=va2.document&identifier=5034F49F-96B6-175C-9FCF896060A0A734&sort=Collection&item=Sino-Soviet%20Relations (accessed March 27, 2006); and Heinzig, *The Soviet Union and Communist China*.
64. AVP RF, f. 56, op. 17, d. 343, 1950, p. 18.
65. Chen Jian, *Mao's China and the Cold War* (Chapel Hill: North Carolina University Press), pp. 50, 107.
66. Ibid., p. 54.
67. Ibid., pp. 30–35.
68. Ibid., pp. 126–130.
69. AVP RF, f. 56, op. 17, d. 344, pp. 87, 104.
70. Tucker, *Taiwan, Hong Kong, and the United States*, p. 34.
71. Ibid., pp. 167–168.
72. Hope Millard Harrison, *Driving the Soviets up the Wall: Soviet-East German*

Relations, 1953–1961 (Princeton, NJ: Princeton University Press, 2003), "Similar Chinese and East German Responses to Khrushchev's Twentieth Congress' New Course," pp. 78–80.

73. PRO, FO 371/133506, 1958, Moscow Embassy to Foreign Office, London.
74. Ivanov, "Russian-Taiwanese Relations," pp. 7–11.
75. RGANI, f. 2, op. 30, d. 51, December 29, 1954, pp. 14–15.
76. PRO, FO 371/110242, December 1954, Statement by the MID of the USSR.
77. Chen, *Mao's China and the Cold War*, pp. 167–170.
78. PRO, FO 371/115032, 1955; and PRO, FO 371/115031, 1955.
79. Appu K. Soman, *Double-Edged Sword: Nuclear Diplomacy in Unequal Conflicts: The United States and China, 1950–1958* (Westport, CT: Praeger, 2000), p. 146.
80. Gordon H. Chang, "To the Nuclear Brink: Eisenhower, Dulles, and the Quemoy-Matsu Crisis," *International Security* 12, no. 4 (Spring 1988): 96–123.
81. Richard J. Aldrich, *The Hidden Hand: Britain, America, and Cold War Secret Intelligence* (London: John Murray, 2001), pp. 313–314.
82. Thomas J. Christensen, *Useful Adversaries: Grand Strategy, Domestic Mobilization, and Sino-American Conflict, 1947–1958* (Princeton, NJ: Princeton University Press, 1996), pp. 198–199.
83. RGANI, f. 5, op. 49, d. 131, January 20, 1958, Report by Yuri Andropov to the CPSU Central Committee.
84. RGANI, f. 5, op. 49, d. 131, February 5, 1958, Telegram from the Soviet Embassy, Beijing, to the Vice Minister of Foreign Affairs, N. Fedorenko.
85. RGANI, f. 5, op. 49, d. 131, January 1958, p. 9.
86. RGANI, f. 5, op. 49, d. 131–133, p. 78.
87. William Taubman, *Khrushchev: The Man and His Era* (New York: W. W. Norton, 2003), pp. 389–392.
88. "Stenogram: Meeting of the Delegations of the Communist Party of the Soviet Union and the Chinese Communist Party," July 5–20, 1963, *Cold War International History Project Virtual Archive*, http://wilsoncenter.org/index.cfm?topic_id=1409&fuseaction=va2.browse&sort=Collection.
89. Odd Arne Westad, ed., *Brothers in Arms: The Rise and Fall of the Sino-Soviet Alliance, 1945–1963* (Washington, DC: Woodrow Wilson Center Press, 1998), p. 236.
90. Czeslaw Tubilewicz, "Taiwan and the Soviet Union during the Cold War: Enemies or Ambiguous Friends?" *Cold War History* 5, no. 1 (February 2005): 78.
91. Chen, *Mao's China and the Cold War*, p. 175.
92. Mark Kramer, "The USSR Foreign Ministry's Appraisal of Sino-Soviet Relations on the Eve of the Split, September 1959," *Cold War International History Project Virtual Archive*, pp. 7–9, http://wilsoncenter.org/index.cfm?t

opic_id=1409&fuseaction=va2.browse&sort=Collection; and Wu Lengxi, "Memoir: Inside Story of the Decision Making during the Shelling of Jinmen," *Cold War International History Project Virtual Archive*, pp. 3–18, http://wilsoncenter.org/index.cfm?topic_id=1409&fuseaction=va2.browse&sort=Collection.

93. Taubman, *Khrushchev*, p. 392.
94. Chen, *Mao's China and the Cold War*, p. 202.
95. Ibid., pp. 182–185.
96. Soman, *Double-Edged Sword*, p. 183.
97. PRO, FO 371/133526, 1958, *Pravda*, September 1958.
98. Westad, ed., *Brothers in Arms*, p. 274.
99. Ibid., p. 151.
100. Soman, *Double-Edged Sword*, p. 183.
101. PRO, FO 371/133528.
102. Chen, *Mao's China and the Cold War*, p. 201.
103. Mark Kramer, "The USSR Foreign Ministry's Appraisal of Sino-Soviet Relations," pp. 7–10.
104. AVP RF, f. 0100, op. 51, d. 28, pap. 435, Far East Department, MID, 1958, October 21, 1958, "Discussion between Liu Sao and G. Zhukov," p. 65.
105. RGANI, f. 5, op. 49, d. 131, September 23, 1958.
106. NA, RG 84, July 6, 1974, Telegram from Beijing to Washington.
107. Westad, ed., *Brothers in Arms*, p. 151.
108. Harrison, *Driving the Soviets up the Wall*, pp. 132–135.
109. Vladislav M. Zubok, "The Mao-Khrushchev Conversations," July 2–August 3, 1958 and October 2, 1959, *Cold War International History Project Virtual Archive*, pp. 3–5, http://wwics.si.edu/index.cfm?topic_id=1409&fuseaction=library.document&id=14656.
110. United States Department of State, "Memorandum of Conference with President Eisenhower, Washington, DC, September 25, 1959," in *Foreign Relations of the United States, 1958–60*, Vol. X, Part I, *Eastern Europe Region, Soviet Union, Cyprus* (Washington, DC: US Government Printing Office, 1993), pp. 1–19.
111. Sergei N. Khrushchev, *Nikita Khrushchev and the Creation of a Superpower*, trans. Shirley Benson (University Park: Pennsylvania State University Press, 2000), p. 268.
112. PRO, FCO 21/709 (1219440), 1970, "UK Recognition of Taiwan." As part of the agreement between the United Kingdom and the PRC, when full diplomatic relations were established at the ambassadorial level, the United Kingdom Consulate outside Taipei was closed in March 1972. The Consulate's buildings and all property were put up for sale. PRO, FCO 21/867 (1656405), "Closure of UK Consulate in Taiwan"; and PRO, FCO

21/1266, 1974, "Disposal of the British Consulate in Taiwan."

113. AVP RF, f. 100, op. 49, por. 38, d. 208, Excerpt from a Lecture by Fairbank on November 21, 1960, at the University of Connecticut, Storrs, Connecticut, pp. 2–7.
114. PRO, FO 371/133526, December 30, 1957, British Consulate, Tamsui, Taiwan to the Foreign Office, "Future of Taiwan: Two Chinas Issue." See also Priscilla Roberts, "William Clayton and the Recognition of China, 1945–66: More Speculations on 'Lost Chances in China,'" *Journal of American-East Asian Relations* 7, no. 1–2 (Spring–Summer 1998): 5–37.
115. AVP RF, f. 100, op. 49, por. 38, d. 208, p. 25.
116. AVP RF, f. 100, op. 48, por. 36, pap. 202, February 21, 1961, Soviet Embassy, Beijing, pp. 20–25.
117. AVP RF, f. 0100, op. 51, d. 28, pap. 435, April 18, 1958, Far East Department, MID, Letter from P. Chernishev to M. V. Zimyanin, "References about China, 1958," pp. 5–7. Copies of this directive were sent to the MID for each Soviet republic, and to the Ministries of Communication, Sea Fleet, and Culture, the State Committee for Cultural Ties with Foreign Countries, *Tass*, the Central Trade Union Organization, the Academy of Sciences, the Executive Committee of the CPSU, and several youth and "solidarity" organizations.
118. RGANI, f. 5, op. 49, d. 131, April 19, 1958, Letter to the CPSU Central Committee by G. Zhukov, pp. 52, 54.
119. RGANI, f. 5, op. 49, d. 131–133, Diary of K. A. Chrugikov, pp. 171–186.
120. AVP RF, f. 100, op. 51, d. 5, pap. 531, September 4, 1958, "Memo from the Ministry of Foreign Affairs of the PRC to the Soviet Embassy, Beijing."
121. AVP RF, f. 100, op. 51, d. 28, pap. 435, October 1958, Far East Department, Letter from M. Kapitsa to A. A. Zolutukhin, p. 57.
122. Ilya V. Gaiduk, *Confronting Vietnam: Soviet Policy toward the Indochina Conflict, 1954–1963* (Stanford, CA: Stanford University Press, 2003), pp. 84–87. See also Ang Cheng Guan, *Vietnamese Communists' Relations with China and the Second Indochina Conflict, 1956–1962* (London: McFarland, 1997); and idem, *The Vietnam War from the Other Side: The Vietnamese Communists' Perspective* (London: RoutledgeCurzon, 2002).
123. RGANI, f. 5, op. 49, d. 131–133, Letter of the CPSU, Central Committee, Vice Chief, Section with Socialist Countries and Parties, E. I. Vinogradov, to the Vice Chief of Science and Mathematics, D. Kiutkin, pp. 182–188.
124. RGANI, f. 5, op. 49, d. 131–133, Pushkov's Report, pp. 189–195.
125. AVP RF, f. 0100, op. 51, d. 28, pap. 435, August 19, 1958, Far East Department, China Sector, Letter of Athletic Association of PRC, p. 45.
126. AVP RF, f. 0100, op. 51, d. 28, pap. 435, January 8, 1958, "Letter from Avery Brundage to Tong Shui-Ye," p 52.
127. AVP RF, f. 0100, op. 51, d. 28, pap. 435, April 25, 1958, "Letter from Tong

Shui-Ye to Avery Brundage," p. 53.

128. AVP RF, f. 0100, op. 51, d. 28, pap. 435, June 1, 1958, "Letter from Brundage to Tong," p. 56.
129. AVP RF, f. 0100, op. 51, d. 28, pap. 435, August 19, 1958, "Letter from Tong to Brundage," p. 51.
130. AVP RF, f. 0100, op. 51, d. 28, pap. 435, August 19, 1958, "Declaration of Athletic Association of PRC"; and AVP RF, f. 0100, op. 51, d. 28, pap. 435, August 19, 1958, "Declaration of the China Olympic Committee," p. 47.
131. AVP RF, f. 0100, op. 51, d. 28, pap. 435, September 4, 1958, Memo from the Chinese Ambassador to the USSR State Committee for Cultural Ties with Foreign Countries, p. 25. Copies of this memo were sent to Yuri Andropov, Central Committee of the CPSU, as well as to numerous Soviet embassies and organizations.
132. AVP RF, f. 0100, op. 51, d. 28, pap. 435, August 8, 1958, Letter and Report from Deputy Head of Physical Education and Sports to Deputy Foreign Minister N. S. Patolichev. A copy of each was also sent to the CPSU Central Committee, International Department.
133. AVP RF, f. 0100, op. 51, d. 28, pap. 435, September 1958, "Meeting of Sports Organizations in Berlin," p. 36.
134. AVP RF, f. 0100, op. 51, d. 28, pap. 435, September 1958, "Letter from the IOC, Lausanne Switzerland," pp. 87–89.
135. AVP RF, f. 0100, op. 51, d. 28, pap. 435, November 1958, "Draft of a Letter from the Soviet Olympic Committee."
136. AVP RF, f. 0100, op. 51, d. 28, pap. 435, November 13, 1958, "Letter from M. Zimyanin to D. Postnikov."
137. PRO, FO 371/141407, 1959, British Consulate, Tamsui, Taiwan, A. Veitch.
138. AV RF, f. 52, op. 1, d. 499, S. Antonov and R. Kudashev, "Memorandum of Conversation of N. S. Khrushchev with Mao Zedong, Beijing, October 3, 1959," *Cold War International History Project Virtual Archive*, p. 2, http://wilsoncenter.org/index.cfm?topic_id=1409&fuseaction=va2.browse&sort=Collection.
139. RGANI, f. 5, op. 49, d. 435, July 5, 1961, Information from the Soviet Embassy, Beijing, to MID, Moscow, pp. 113–117.
140. PRO, FO 371/170725 and 170731, 1963, p. 33.

Notes to Chapter 8

1. RGANI, f. 5, op. 49, "Annual Report from the Beijing Embassy on Taiwan Developments, 1961," p. 249; and also AVP RF, f. 100, op. 49, pap 38, d. 208, April 1962–January 1963, Soviet Embassy, Beijing, translation and analysis of *South China Morning Post* article, "So Called Agreement about Cease Fire

between Taiwan and the PRC," September 8, 1962, Translator—E. Brezhneva.

2. AVP RF, f. 100, op. 48, d. 36, pap. 202, February 1961, Soviet Embassy, Beijing, "Foreign and Internal Position of Taiwan," pp. 1–55.
3. AVP RF, f. 100, op. 49, por. 38, d. 208, April 1962–January 1963, April 1962, Soviet Embassy, Beijing, "About Visits by Harriman and Other Prominent Americans to Taiwan," pp. 8–12.
4. AVP RF, f. 100, op. 50, d. 36, pap. 213, January–October 1963, Soviet Embassy, Beijing, V. Tsarenko, and V. Trifonov, pp. 6–10.
5. NA, RG 59, Box 3864, October 25, 1963, "Chi-Com-USSR."
6. AVP RF, f. 100, op. 52, d. 27, pap. 222, March 1965, Letter from French Embassy, Moscow, to MID, and Bulgarian Note, pp. 1–2.
7. AVP RF, f. 100, op. 54, d. 32, pap. 231, January–September 1967, pp. 1–4.
8. AVP RF, f. 100, op. 49, por. 38, d. 208, April 1962–January 1963, September 20, 1962, Letter from Soviet Embassy, Tokyo.
9. AVP RF, f 100, op. 52, d. 27, pap. 222, March–September 1965, pp. 1–6.
10. AVP RF, f. 100, op. 54, d. 32, pap. 231, January–September 1967, "Position of Taiwan," pp. 5–10.
11. PRO, FCO 21/520, December 30, 1969, British Consulate, Tamsui, Taiwan.
12. NA, Central Foreign Policy Files 1967–1969, RG 59/1613/1982, September 6, 1967, US Embassy, Taipei, "Summary of Recent Developments on Taiwan," p. 5.
13. The Sino-Soviet dispute, which essentially lies outside the parameters of this book, has generated an extensive literature, including John Gittings, *Survey of the Sino-Soviet Dispute: A Commentary and Extracts from the Recent Polemics, 1963–1967* (London: Oxford University Press, 1968); Klaus Mehnert, *Peking and Moscow* (New York: Putnam, 1963); Donald S. Zagoria, *The Sino-Soviet Conflict, 1956–1961* (Princeton, NJ: Princeton University Press, 1962); O. Edmund Clubb, *China and Russia: The "Great Game"* (New York: Columbia University Press, 1971); Herbert J. Ellison, ed., *The Sino-Soviet Conflict: A Global Perspective* (Seattle: University of Washington Press, 1982); Roy Aleksandrovich Medvedev, *China and the Superpowers*, trans. Harold Shukman (Oxford: Blackwell, 1986); Robert S. Ross, ed., *China, the United States, and the Soviet Union: Tripolarity and Policy Making in the Cold War* (Armonk, NY: M. E. Sharpe, 1993); and Vladislav Zubok and Constantine Pleshakov, *Inside the Kremlin's Cold War: From Stalin to Khrushchev* (Cambridge, MA: Harvard University Press, 1996).
14. Nancy Bernkopf Tucker, *Taiwan, Hong Kong, and the United States, 1945–1992: Uncertain Friendships* (New York: Twayne), p. 102.
15. NA, RG 59/1613/1983, April 29, 1969, US Department of State Intelligence Note.

16. NA, RG 84, June 11, 1969, US Embassy, Sofia, Bulgaria.
17. AVP RF, f. 718, op. 56, d. 37, January 24, 1969, "Taiwan and the Problem of Two Chinas."
18. Peter M. Ivanov, "Russian-Taiwanese Relations: Current State, Problems, and Prospects of Development," *Occasional Papers/Reprints Series in Contemporary Asian Studies* 133, no. 2 (1996): 3–4.
19. Czeslaw Tubilewicz, "Taiwan and the Soviet Union during the Cold War: Enemies or Ambiguous Friends?" *Cold War History* 5, no. 1 (February 2005): 80. Tubilewicz bases his claim on the memoirs, published in the Taipei-based *Lianhe Bao* in October 1995, of Wei Jingmeng (Wei Ching-meng), who organized Louis' trip to Taipei.
20. NA, RG 59, Pol 32-1, Pol Chicom-USSR, July 30, 1969, "Research Memorandum: Communist China; Sinkiang—Weak Spot in the West," REA-29.
21. NA, RG 59/1613/1983, December 11, 1967, US Embassy, Moscow. This embassy report on Chiang Ching-kuo's background noted that Chiang only reluctantly returned to China after the war with Japan began. Subsequently, the American Embassy in Taipei commented that Chiang was "rumored to have espoused Communism." NA, RG 59/1613/2203, April 10, 1970, US Embassy, Taipei, p. 3.
22. Unfortunately the author was denied access to possible relevant documents at the RGANI, which might have resolved this mystery.
23. Stanley Karnow, "Rare Soviet Visit to Taiwan," *Washington Post,* November 2, 1968.
24. NA, RG 59, November 6, 1968, US State Department Intelligence Note, November 6, 1968; and Dick Wilson, "Kremlin Woos Taiwan," *Bangkok Post*, January 13, 1969.
25. John W. Garver, "Taiwan's Russian Option: Image and Reality," *Asian Survey* 18, no. 7 (July 1978): 755.
26. PRO, FCO 21/520, British Embassy, Washington, Victor Louis, "Soviet Writer Tells of Visit to Taiwan," article found in *Washington Post*, March 19, 1969.
27. Jay Taylor, *The Generalissimo's Son: Chiang Ching-kuo and the Revolutions in China and Taiwan* (Cambridge, MA: Harvard University Press, 2000), pp. 287–289.
28. PRO, FCO 21/520, March 10, 1969, British Embassy, Beijing.
29. John Franklin Copper, "Taiwan's Options," *Asian Affairs* 6, no. 5 (May–June 1979): 290. Tubilewicz claims, though he gives no evidence for this, that Louis made three further visits to Taiwan, in November 1971, December 1974, and June 1975. Tubilewicz, "Taiwan and the Soviet Union," p. 80.
30. PRO, FCO 21/520, 1969, British Embassy, Moscow, dispatch written by J. O. Kerr.

31. PRO, FCO 21/518, June 5, 1969, British Consulate, Tamsui, Taiwan.
32. NA, RG 59/1613/2202, POL CHINAT, 1970–1973, April 1973, US Embassy, Taipei.
33. PRO, FCO 21/520, 1968–1969, "Soviet Relations with Taiwan."
34. Ivanov, "Russian-Taiwanese Relations," p. 4.
35. NA, RG 84, February 13, 1970, US Embassy, Taipei.
36. Tucker, *Taiwan, Hong Kong, and the United States*, p. 105.
37. PRO, FCO 21/520, 1968–1969, "Soviet Relations with Taiwan."
38. NA, RG 84, April 3, 1972, US Embassy, Taipei, p. 6.
39. William C. Kirby, Robert S. Ross, and Li Gong, eds., *Normalization of US-China Relations: An International History* (Cambridge, MA: Harvard University Press, 2005), pp. 239–240.
40. NA, RG 84, March 16, 1972, US Embassy, Taipei.
41. NA, RG 59/1613/2203, POL 7 to 15-2 CHINAT, 1970–1973, June 1, 1972, State Department Memo from Assistant Secretary of State Marshall Green to Secretary Rogers.
42. NA, RG59/1613/2207, POL 17-1 CHINAT-US to POL 2 Col, June 1972, US Embassy, Taipei. The US Embassy in Moscow reported similar rumors.
43. NA, RG 59/1613/2202, POL CHINAT-US, 1970–1973, April 12, 1972, State Department Intelligence Note, p. 2.
44. AVP RF, f. 100, op. 59, d. 23, February 8–December 11, 1972, "Taiwan and the Problem of Two Chinas," pp. 1–8.
45. Ibid., p. 6.
46. Ibid., p. 8.
47. NA, RG 59/1613/2205, POL H-J, CHINAT to POL CHINAT-US, March 10, 1971, State Department Memo.
48. NA, RG 59/1613/2207, January 25, 1972, US Embassy, Tokyo.
49. AVP RF, f. 100, op. 59, d. 23, pap. 255, December 1972, Soviet UN representative, New York, pp. 33–42.
50. PRO, FCO 21/1412, 1975, "Disposal of the Former British Consulate."
51. NA, RG 59/1613/2204, May 21, 1973, US Embassy, Taipei, to US State Department. The transit of Soviet naval vessels was also described in Garver, "Taiwan's Russian Option," p. 757.
52. NA, RG 59/1613/2207, June 1973, US Embassy, Tokyo.
53. NA, RG 59/1613/2203, POL 7 to 15-2 CHINAT, 1970–1973, March 30, 1973, US State Department Memo, East Asian Desk, "Foreign Policy Options for Taiwan."
54. NA, RG 59/1613/2202, POL CHINAT, 1970–1973, June 1973, American Embassy, Taipei.
55. Ivanov, "Russian-Taiwanese Relations," p. 5.
56. PRO, FCO 21/1263, "Relations between Taiwan and China," 1974.

57. "Evaluation by the Soviet Party Central Committee of the Normalization of US-Chinese Ties," August 30, 1978, *Cold War International History Project Virtual Archive*.
58. AVP RF, f. 100, op. 66, d. 27, January 7–December 29, 1979, "Reports on Relations with Third Countries," Far East Department, MID, pp. 1–70.
59. Ibid., p. 72.
60. AVP RF, f. 100, op. 67, d. 295, 1980, Soviet Embassy, Japan.
61. AVP RF, f. 100, op. 68, d. 9, January 13, 1982, Soviet Embassy, Japan, p. 10.
62. AVP RF, f. 100, op. 68, d. 9, September 14, 1982, p. 137.
63. AVP RF, f. 100, op. 71, d. 20, pap. 314, December 12, 1984, "Problem of Macao," pp. 114–120.
64. AVP RF, f. 100, op. 71, d. 20, pap. 314, March 13, 1984, Soviet Embassy, Netherlands, P. Spiredonov, Adviser to the Embassy, "International Relations with the PRC and Taiwan," pp. 15–26. Unfortunately, later articles relating to Taiwan in MID remained closed. These included two potentially useful articles from 1986, entitled "Position of Taiwan Today by the Chinese Leadership" and "Perspectives on the Situation in Taiwan." AVP RF, f. 100, op. 73, d. 18, pap. 324, 1986.
65. Ivanov, "Russian-Taiwanese Relations," p. 10.
66. Ibid., p. 18.
67. Ibid., pp. 8–13.
68. Stephanie Mann, "International Reaction to Taiwan's Election," *Voice of America*, March 19, 2000, *Federation of American Scientists: News*, http://www.fas.org/news/taiwan/2000/000319-taiwan2.htm (accessed March 25, 2006).
69. Rian Jensen and Erich Marquardt, "The Sino-Russian Romance," *China Brief*, March 21, 2006, *Asia Times Online*, http://www.atimes.com/atimes/Central_Asia/HC21Ag02.html (accessed March 28, 2006).
70. For further information on Russian-Chinese relations during the Gorbachev and Yeltsin eras, see Elizabeth Wishnick, *Mending Fences: The Evolution of Moscow's China Policy, from Brezhnev to Yeltsin* (Seattle: University of Washington Press, 2001).
71. Andrew Locher, "China's War on Obsolescence," January 1999, *The Trumpet.com*, http://www.thetrumpet.com/index.php?page=article&id=521 (accessed March 22, 2006).
72. Wishnick, *Mending Fences*, p. 144.
73. Claire Bigg, "Russia: Joint Military Exercises with China: A Result of a New Strategic Partnership," August 18, 2005, *Radio Free Europe/Radio Liberty*, http://www.rferl.org/featuresarticle/2005/08/40554110-295C-4760-9635-BCC86A121F45.html (accessed March 23, 2006).

74. Eric Koch, "The Increasingly Intertwined Bear & Dragon: Russia and China Overcome Historic Animus in the Face of Modern Ambitions," April 7, 2005, *Jewish Institute for National Security Affairs*, http://www.jinsa.org/articles.html/function/view/categoryid/884/documented/2905/history/3,884,2905 (accessed March 23, 2005).
75. Ibid.
76. Rian Jensen and Erich Marquardt, "The Sino-Russian Romance."
77. Information provided by Dr. Kirill M. Barsky, then Head of China Section of Division of Hong Kong, Macao, and Taiwan, MID, June 2004.
78. Bevin Chu, "The Big Lie of Taiwan's Election: A Lie Heard Halfway around the World," January 25, 2004, *Pravda.ru Online*, http://english.pravda.ru/world/2002/01/25/26007.html (accessed March 25, 2006).
79. "Russia Comes Out Against Taiwan's Independence," March 29, 2004, *Pravda.ru Online*, http://newsfromrussia.com/main/2004/03/29/53079.html (accessed March 25, 2006).
80. "Russian Lawmakers: China Has Right to Safeguard Territorial Integrity," *Xinhua News Agency*, March 16, 2005, *China Daily Online*, http://www.chinadaily.com.cn/english/doc/2005-03/16/content_425530.htm (accessed March 25, 2006).
81. A. A., "China to Mark World War II Anniversary of Taiwan's Liberation," October 24, 2005, *Pravda.ru Online*, http://newsfromrussia.com/china/2005/10/24/65941.htm (accessed March 25, 2006).
82. D. M., "Russia Tilts Taiwan over Scrapping of Unification Body," January 3, 2006, *Pravda.ru Online*, http://english.pravda.ru/news/russia/01-03-2006/76727-0 (accessed March 25, 2006).
83. Christopher Bodeen, "Taiwan's Opposition Leader Arrives in China on Historic Trip," April 26, 2004, *Pravda.ru Online*, http://newsfromrussia.com/china/2005/04/26/59424.html (accessed March 25, 2006); and "Taiwan and China: People Must Be Put First," May 11, 2005, *Pravda.ru Online*, http://newsfromrussia.com/world/2005/05/11/59678.html (accessed March 25, 2006).
84. Chandler Rosenberger, "Russian Legislators Introduce Bill to Strengthen Ties to Taiwan," *Central News Agency WWW (Taiwan)*, October 3, 1997, *Institute for the Study of Conflict, Ideology, and Policy*, http://www.bu.edu/iscip/digest/vol2/ed19.html (accessed March 25, 2006).
85. "Zhirinovsky in Taipei," *Monitor* 4, no. 193 (October 1998), *The Jamestown Foundation*, http://www.jamestown.org/publications_details.php?volume_id=21@issue_id=1404&article_id=14297 (accessed March 25, 2006).
86. "Li Peng Holds Talks with Russian Counterpart," *Xinhua News Agency*, December 11, 2001, *People's Daily Online*, http://english.people.com.cn/200112/11/eng20011211_86349.shtml (accessed March 25, 2006). Also see

"China Protests Zhirinovsky's Visit to Taiwan," *RFE/RL Newsline* 2, no. 206, Part I (October 23, 1998), *Friends & Partners: Linking US-Russia Across the Internet*, http://www.fplib.org/friends/news/omri/1998/10/981023I.html (opt,mozilla,mac,english,,new (accessed March 25, 2006).

87. Information provided by Barsky, June 2004.
88. Ibid.
89. Ivanov, "Russian-Taiwanese Relations," p. 55.
90. Information provided by Barsky, June 2004.
91. Ibid.
92. Ibid.
93. Stephen A. McDonald, "Made in China: Bad…Made in Taiwan: Good," March 20, 2002, *Pravda.ru Online*, http://newsfromrussia.com/world/2002/03/20/27107.html (accessed March 25, 2006).
94. Svetlana Anina, "Two-Headed Creatures," *NGN newspaper*, November 29, 2003, *Pravda.ru Online*, http://english.pravda.ru/science/tech/4201-1/ (accessed March 25, 2006).

Notes to Chapter 9

1. Perhaps appropriately, given Macao's much smaller size, population, and significance, the literature on Macao is far less extensive than that on Hong Kong. Some relevant titles include: Rosmarie Wank-Nolasco Lamas, *History of Macao: A Student's Manual* (Macao: Institute of Tourism Education, 1998); Cesar Guillen-Nuñez, *Macao* (Hong Kong: Oxford University Press, 1984); Jean A. Berlie, "Macao's Overview at the Turn of the Century," *American Asian Review* 18, no. 4 (Winter 2000): 25–68; R. D. Cremer, ed., *Macao: City of Commerce and Culture, Continuity and Change,* 2nd ed. (Hong Kong: API Press, 1991); Austin Coates, *A Macao Narrative* (Hong Kong: Heinemann, 1978); and last but not least, the classic work by Carlos Augusto Montalto de Jesus, *Historic Macao*, 3rd ed. (Hong Kong: Oxford University Press, 1984).
2. R. D. Cremer, "From Portugal to Japan: Macao's Place in the History of Trade," in *Macao: City of Commerce and Culture*, pp. 23–38.
3. Guillen-Nuñez, *Macao*, pp. 35–42.
4. Philippe Pons, *Macao*, trans. Sarah Adams (Hong Kong: Hong Kong University Press, 2002), p. 8.
5. Ivan Fedorovich Kruzenshtern, *Voyage round the World, in the Years 1803, 1804, 1805, and 1806,* trans. Richard Belgrave Hoppner (London: John Murray, 1813), pp. xviii–xxxii; "Voyages around the World," *The History of the Russian Navy*, http://www.navy.ru/history/hrn7-e.htm (accessed April 1, 2006); and A. V. Borodin, "From the History of Russia's Pacific Navy: Era

of Discoveries," *Russia's Pacific Navy*, http://www.fegi.ru/prim/flot/flot1_2.htm (accessed April 1, 2006). On the broader significance of such Russian voyages of circumnavigation, see Ilya Vinkovetsky, "Circumnavigation, Empire, Modernity, Race: The Impact of Round-the-World Voyages on Russia's Imperial Consciousness" (presented at the "Meeting of Frontiers" conference, Library of Congress, Washington, DC, May 18, 2001), *Library of Congress*, http://www.loc.gov/rr/european/mofc/vinkovetsky.html (accessed April 1, 2006).

6. Kruzenshtern, *Voyage round the World*, pp. 289–290; and information provided by Kirill M. Barsky, Head of the China Section of Division of Hong Kong, Macao, and Taiwan, MID, June 2004.
7. Urey Lisiansky, *A Voyage round the World, in the Years 1803, 4, 5, & 6: Performed, by Order of His Imperial Majesty Alexander the First, Emperor of Russia, in the Ship Neva* (London: John Booth, 1814), pp. 269–270.
8. Kruzenshtern, *Voyage round the World*, pp. 281–287, quotations from pp. 283, 286.
9. Ibid., pp. 286–287.
10. V. R. K., "Otryki iz pisem morskogo ofitsera [Fragment from a Letter of a Naval Officer]," *Morskoi Sbornik* [Naval Collection] 29, no. 5 (May 1857): 5–27, quotation from p. 6, translated and quoted in Mark Bassin, *Imperial Visions: Nationalist Imagination and Geographical Expansion in the Russian Far East, 1840–1865* (Cambridge: Cambridge University Press, 1999), p. 147.
11. AHM, AH/AC/P-00246 (microfilm A0685), no. 45, April 2, 1880, "Problems between China and Other Nations." The document in the Macao archive unfortunately never identified the Russian admiral.
12. AHM, CO 755, March 31, 1879, "Document from the Overseas Historical Archive," Lisbon, Portuguese Consulate in Hong Kong.
13. AHM, AH/AC/P-00247 (microfilm A0685), April 8, 1880, Governor's Office, Macao to Lisbon.
14. AHM, CO 755. The internal difficulties the Portuguese Consul referred to in his report to Lisbon were growing unrest on the part of Russian Populists, which culminated in the assassination of Tsar Alexander II on March 1, 1881.
15. Lamas, *History of Macao*, p. 56.
16. Esper Ukhtomskii, *Travels in the East of Nicholas II, Emperor of Russia When Cesarewitch 1890–1891*, 2 vols., ed. Sir George Birdwood (London: Constable, 1896), vol. 2, pp. 299–300.
17. AHM, CO 740, 1889–1892, March 1892, "Forthcoming Visit in Early April of Grand Duke Nicholas to Macao," Government Palace, Macao.
18. For a fuller account of Hong Kong's involvement in the Russo-Japanese War, see Chapter 1 above.

19. BO, no. 9, February 27, 1904; and BO, no. 14, April 2, 1904.
20. James M. Anderson, *The History of Portugal* (Westport, CT: Greenwood Press, 2000), pp. 141–142; David Birmingham, *A Concise History of Portugal* (Cambridge: Cambridge University Press, 1993), pp. 145–150; Antonio Henrique R. de Oliveira, *History of Portugal* (New York: Columbia University Press, 1976); H. V. Livermore, *A New History of Portugal* (Cambridge: Cambridge University Press, 1969); and Jose H. Saraiva, *Portugal: A Companion History* (Manchester: Carcanet Press, 1997).
21. AVP RI, f. 113, op. 776, 1910–1911, November 22, 1910, "Macao Revolution, Report from Consul-General in Hong Kong to M. Koroshovts, Russian Mission, Beijing," pp. 1–10. Earlier that year the Russian Consul-General had written to the Portuguese Consul-General in Hong Kong requesting information on an ancestor of his who had visited and stayed in Macao over a century earlier, in 1772, and to the best of his knowledge had died in the territory. The Portuguese Consul wrote back responding that the only information his government possessed on Tiedemann's ancestor was that he had arrived in the territory. AHM, AH/AC/P-02551 (microfilm A0768), March–May 1910.
22. AVP RI, f. 113, op. 776, 1910–1911, December 18, 1910, Report from Consul-General Tiedemann to M. Korosovts, Russian Mission, Beijing, pp. 10–12.
23. AHM, AH/AC/P-13569 (microfilm A1182), October 23, 1931, "Exterminate Communist Activities in Macao," Police Chief to the Director of Civil Administration.
24. Lamas, *History of Macao*, p. 99.
25. AHM, AH/AC/P-16027 (microfilm A1278), March 1937, "Internal Circular from the Colonial Minister in Lisbon to All Governors of All Colonies."
26. AHM, AH/AC/P-16027 (microfilm A1278), May 10, 1940, "Confidential Memo," no. 814/797/38-M.
27. Pons, *Macao*, p. 94. Georgy Vitalovich Smirnov (1903–1947) was arguably the most famous White Russian to settle in Macao and Hong Kong. He was born in Vladivostok, but fled Russia at the time of the Revolution of 1917 for the Manchurian city of Harbin, then still largely Russian. After the Japanese invasion of 1931, Smirnov fled China for Hong Kong. Very poor, Smirnov painted anything he could—matchbooks, soap-boxes, postcards—to provide for himself and his family. When the Japanese conquered Hong Kong in December 1941, the family lost everything. Penniless and facing constant harassment by the Japanese, Smirnov fled once again, this time to Macao. There he painted numerous street scenes of the enclave, supplementing that meager income by giving painting and music lessons. Eventually the Portuguese recognized his abilities and gave him a regular allowance. This was perhaps the only time in Smirnov's life when he enjoyed some peace

and security. At the end of the war, the reluctant Smirnov family had to return to Hong Kong. Only 44 years old, the depressed Smirnov died in 1947 and was buried at Happy Valley cemetery in Hong Kong, possibly an inappropriate final resting place for such an unhappy individual.

28. Pons, *Macao*, p. 121.
29. Lamas, *History of Macao*, p. 103.
30. See Chapter 5.
31. AVP RF, f. 45, op. 1, d. 343, pp. 97–103. Reproduced in "Talks with Mao Zedong and Zhou Enlai, 1949–1953," *Cold War International History Project Virtual Archive*, p. 21.
32. AVP RF, f. 100, op. 43, d. 145, pap. 315, 1950, T. Skvortsov, Consultant, Far East Department, MID, "Macao–Background."
33. AVP RF, f. 100, op. 45, d. 148, pap. 358, 1952, "Position in Macao," October–November 1951, translated from Chinese Military Intelligence by A. Sergiev, pp. 164–169.
34. AVP RF, f. 100, op. 45, d. 148, pap. 358, December 1951, "Position in Macao," pp. 170–176; AVP RF, f. 100, op. 45, d. 148, pap. 358, January 1952, "Position in Macao," pp. 178–183; and AVP RF, f. 100, op. 45, d. 148, pap. 358, March 1952, "Position in Macao," pp. 198–209. All reports translated from Chinese Military Intelligence by A. Sergiev.
35. AVP RF, f. 100, op. 45, d. 149, pap. 358, 1952, "Position in Macao, Part II"; AVP RF, f. 100, op. 45, d. 149, pap. 358, May–June 1952, "Position in Macao," pp. 52–62; and AVP RF, f. 100, op. 45, d. 149, pap. 358, September 1952, "Position in Macao," pp. 133–145. All reports translated by A. Sergiev.
36. AVP RF, f. 100, op. 46, d. 133, pap. 375, 1953, "Hong Kong and Macao," pp. 21–24.
37. AVP RF, f. 100, op. 47, d. 106, pap. 388, 1954, "Position of Hong Kong and Macao," pp. 12–15. Translated by I. Kriuchkov.
38. AVP RF, f. 100, op. 48, d. 135, pap. 408, 1955, "Situation in Hong Kong and Macao," pp. 2–9; AVP RF, f. 100, op. 48, d. 135, pap. 408, December 1954, B. Kupralov, "Situation in Hong Kong and Macao," Bulletin no. 10, pp. 10–15; and AVP RF, f. 100, op. 48, d. 135, pap. 408, November 13, 1955, I. Kriuchkov, "To the Intentions of the Portuguese Powers," Soviet Consulate, Guangzhou, pp. 157–162.
39. AVP RF, f. 100, op. 60, d. 37, pap. 535, 1967, V. Kiuzmin, "Use of Hong Kong and Macao by China and the US," pp. 1–13.
40. AVP RF, f. 100, op. 53, d. 25, pap. 226, 1966, P. Iskandarov, "About the Position of China toward Hong Kong and Macao," pp. 2–6.
41. Elizabeth Wishnick, *Mending Fences: The Evolution of Moscow's China Policy, from Brezhnev to Yeltsin* (Seattle: University of Washington Press,

2001), p. 28. See Chapter 6, n.7 for further information.

42. AVP RF, f. 100, op. 56, v. 1, d. 62, pap. 504, 1963, "Macao: A Survey," pp. 1–3.
43. AVP RF, f. 100, op. 60, d. 37, pap. 535, 1967, V. Kiuzmin, "Use of Hong Kong and Macao by China and the US," pp. 1–13; and AVP RF, f. 100, op. 54, d. 31, pap. 233, 1967, Far East Department, MID, "Macao," pp. 4–6.
44. Ho Yin's son Edmund Ho Hau Wah is currently Chief Executive of the Macao SAR.
45. PRO, FCO 21/641, 1970, *Secret*, "Evacuation of Macao."
46. Lamas, *History of Macao*, pp. 107–108.
47. PRO, FCO 21/961, 1972, "Situation in Macao," British Embassy, Lisbon.
48. Chapter 6 provides greater detail on the riots and their impact on Hong Kong.
49. Lamas, *History of Macao*, p. 108.
50. AVP RF, f. 100, op. 64, d. 22, pap. 279, June 21, 1977, P. M. Medvedovskii, Soviet Embassy, Lisbon, "Status of Macao," First European Section, MID, pp. 1–3.
51. The causes and events of the Portuguese Revolution fall outside the bounds of this chapter. See Anderson, *The History of Portugal*, pp. 163–177; and Birmingham, *A Concise History of Portugal*, pp. 179–192.
52. Lamas, *History of Macao*, p. 109.
53. AVP RF, f. 100, op. 62, d. 28, pap. 268, 1975, "About the Question of Macao," pp. 1–3.
54. AVP RF, f. 100, op. 62, d. 28, pap. 268, 1975, "Hong Kong and Macao," USSR opinion, Far East Department, MID.
55. AVP RF, f. 100, op. 62, d. 28, pap. 268, 1975, "About the Question of Macao," pp. 1–3.
56. Ibid.
57. PRO, FCO 21/1218, 1974, "Internal Situation in Macao," *Secret*.
58. AVP RF, f. 100, op. 71, d. 20, pap. 314, December 12, 1984, V. A. Krivtsov, Vice Director, Institute of Far East, to the Head of the Far East Department, MID, Igor Rogachev, "Problem of Macao," pp. 114–120.
59. Lamas, *History of Macao*, p. 114.
60. AVP RF, f. 100, op. 73, d. 9, pap. 322, October 22, 1986, "Portuguese-Chinese Talks on Macao," pp. 70–71.
61. Ibid., f. 100, op. 74, d. 17, pap. 328, 1987, Soviet Embassy, Singapore, Iu. V. Parfenov, "Information on Hong Kong, Taiwan and Macao," pp. 29–32.
62. BO, no. 18, May 2, 1989, Government Office #62/GM/89, p. 2374.
63. BO, no. 18, April 30, 1990, microfilm B0099, p. 1575.
64. *Macau: City of Culture Guide, 1998*, http://home.macau.ctm.net/~liox0001/travel/macau/mo_talk.shtml (accessed March 27, 2006); and Bertil Lintner, "The Russian Mafia in Asia," February 3, 1996, *Asia Pacific Media*

Services Limited, http://www.asiapacificms.com/articles/russian_mafia/ (accessed March 27, 2006).

65. Antonio Nicaso, "The Fire within Russia's Gang Warfare: Part 11—Organized Crime Reaches Gigantic Proportions in Yeltsin Territory," June 24, 2001, *Tandem Online Magazine*, http://www.tandemnews.com/viewstory.php?storyid=92&page=1 (accessed March 27, 2006).
66. Bruce Michael Bagley, "Globalization and Transnational Organized Crime: The Russian Mafia in Latin America and the Caribbean," October 31, 2001, *Mama Coca*, http://www.mamacoca.org/feb2002/art_bagley_globalization_organized_crime_en.html (accessed March 27, 2006); and see also Lintner, "The Russian Mafia in Asia."
67. "Macao Rocked by Gangland Violence ahead of Handover," October 1999, *Gambling Magazine*, http://gamblingmagazine.com/articles/22/22-97.htm (accessed March 27, 2006).
68. "Russian, Ukrainian Crime Groups Set to Corner Global Drug Market," April 8, 2002, *Stratfor.com*, http://www.stratfor.com/products/premium/read_article.php?id=203770&selected=Country%20Profiles&showCountry=1&channelId=14&showMore=1 (accessed March 27, 2006).
69. Minwoo Yun, "Understanding Russian Organized Crime: Its Causes, Present Situations, and Significances," April 16, 2003, pp. 50, 51, *Sam Houston State University: Journal of Doctoral and Research Studies in Educational Leadership, Issue # 3*, http://www.shsu.edu/~edu_elc/journal/research%20online/54Russian%20organized%20crimeunderstanding%20of%20Russian%20organiz..pdf (accessed November 4, 2006).
70. Vladimir Isachenkov, "Soviet Women Slavery Flourishes," *Associated Press*, November 6, 1997, *Factbook on Global Sexual Exploitation: Macao*, http://www.uri.edu/artsci/wms/hughes/macau.htm (accessed March 27, 2006).
71. Amy O'Neill Richard, "International Trafficking in Women to the United States: A Contemporary Manifestation of Slavery and Organized Crime," *DCI Exceptional Intelligence Analyst Program: An Intelligence Monograph*, April 2000, p. 58, *Center for the Study of Intelligence*, http://www.cia.gov/csi/monograph/women/trafficking.pdf (accessed November 4, 2006).
72. Louise I. Shelley, "The Changing Position of Women: Trafficking, Crime, and Corruption," in *The Legacy of State Socialism and the Future of Transformation*, ed. David Lane (Lanham, MD: Rowman & Littlefield, 2002), p. 211; Lintner, "The Russian Mafia in Asia"; and Peter Gordon, review of *The Living Room of the Dead*, by Eric Stone, December 15, 2005, *The Asian Review of Books on the Web*, http://www.asianreviewofbooks.com/arb/article.php?article=630 (accessed March 27, 2006).
73. United Nations Press Release, "Secretary-General's Representative for Children in Armed Conflicts Says Translating Commitments into

Action Most Pressing Challenge," April 22, 1998, *United Nations: Office of the Special Representative of the Secretary-General for Children and Armed Conflict*, http://www.un.org/special-rep/children-armed-conflict/Press Releases/PR1998-04-22-HR-CN-867.html (accessed March 27, 2006); and TED Case Studies, "Trafficking in Russian Women: Sexual Exploitation as a Growing Form of International Trade," June 2000, *The Trade Environment Database*, http://www.american.edu/TED/traffic.htm (accessed March 27, 2006).

74. "Beginners Trade Union Guide to Macao," October 2005, *Hong Kong Liaison Office of the International Trade Union Movement*, http://www.ihlo.org/HKM/Macau_Background.pdf (accessed March 27, 2006); and "Human Trafficking & Modern-Day Slavery: Russian Federation (Russia)," June 2005, *Human Trafficking & Modern-Day Slavery*, http://gvnet.com/humantrafficking/Russia.htm (accessed March 27, 2006).
75. United States Department of State, "Country Reports on Human Rights Practices: China (includes Tibet, Hong Kong, and Macau), released by the Bureau of Democracy, Human Rights, and Labor," February 28, 2005, *United States Department of State*, http://www.state.gov/g/drl/rls/hrrpt/2004/41640.htm#macau (accessed March 27, 2006).
76. "Human Trafficking & Modern-Day Slavery: Russian Federation (Russia)," *Human Trafficking & Modern-Day Slavery*, http://gvnet.com/humantrafficking/Russia.htm (accessed March 27, 2006).
77. "Human Trafficking & Modern-Day Slavery: Macau (Macao)," June 2005, *Human Trafficking & Modern-Day Slavery*, http://gvnet.com/humantrafficking/Macau.htm (accessed March 27, 2006).
78. Information provided by Barsky, June 2004.

Notes to Chapter 10

1. Frank Welsh, *A History of Hong Kong*, 2nd ed. (London: HarperCollins, 1997), pp. 101–131.
2. Robert Cottrell, *The End of Hong Kong: The Secret Diplomacy of Imperial Retreat* (London: John Murray, 1993), pp. 58–76.
3. AVP RF, f. 100, op. 62, d. 28, pap. 268, 1975, V. Zarkov, Senior Adviser, Soviet Mission, UN, New York, "Relations between China and Hong Kong."
4. Ibid.
5. Gerald Segal, *The Fate of Hong Kong* (London: Simon & Schuster, 1993), pp. 32–40.
6. Zhao Ziyang opposed the military suppression of the student demonstrators at Tiananmen Square on June 4, 1989. As a result, the hard-line rulers

removed Zhao from his position as Premier, and placed him under house arrest, where he languished, forbidden to talk to any foreigners, until his death on January 17, 2005.

7. Cottrell, *The End of Hong Kong*, pp. 85–87.
8. Ibid., pp. 92–93.
9. Ibid., p. 94.
10. Those works cited above give detailed analyses of the British, Chinese, and American interpretations.
11. AVP RF, f. 100, op. 70, d. 9, pap. 307, January 20–December 12, 1983, "Correspondence on Political Issues Concerning Third Countries 1983"; and AVP RF, f. 100 , op. 70, d. 21, pap. 309, February 9–December 16, 1983, "Reports about Relations with Third Countries."
12. Andreas Kappeler, *The Russian Empire: A Multiethnic History* (London: Longman, 2001), p. 35.
13. For a fuller account, see S. C. M. Paine, *Imperial Rivals: China, Russia, and Their Disputed Frontier* (Armonk, NY: M. E. Sharpe, 1996); John L. Evans, *Russian Expansion on the Amur, 1848–1860: The Push to the Pacific* (Lewiston, NY: Edwin Mellen Press, 1999); and Mark Bassin, *Imperial Visions: Nationalist Imagination and Geographical Expansion in the Russian Far East, 1840–1865* (Cambridge: Cambridge University Press, 1999).
14. Evans, *Russian Expansion on the Amur*, pp. 96–97.
15. An excellent new and well researched study of the perceptions and misperceptions by each side is Alexander Lukin, *The Bear Watches the Dragon: Russia's Perceptions of China and the Evolution of Russian-Chinese Relations since the Eighteenth Century* (Armonk, NY: M. E. Sharpe, 2003).
16. William Rosenberg and Marilyn Young, *Transforming Russia and China: Revolutionary Struggle in the Twentieth Century* (New York: Oxford University Press, 1982), pp. 72–95.
17. Mark Roberti, *The Fall of Hong Kong: China's Triumph and Britain's Betrayal* (New York: John Wiley & Sons, 1996), pp. 48–51.
18. For further details, see Chapter 6.
19. The third treaty was the Treaty of St. Petersburg in February 1881. It did not pertain to the Russian-Chinese frontier in the Far East, but instead to the border between the two empires in Central Asia, and was far more favorable to the Chinese government. Russia abandoned most of its gains in the rugged and remote Ili Valley, east of Almaty (formerly Alma Ata), Kazakhstan. That treaty defined the frontier between the current independent nation of Kazakhstan and the Chinese province of Xinjiang. In return, Russia received a nine million ruble indemnity, the right to open up to seven more consulates in China, and duty free trade in the area.

20. Segal, *The Fate of Hong Kong*, pp. 40–44. In the year after Margaret Thatcher's visit to Beijing and Hong Kong, the Hong Kong dollar lost one-third of its value, and property values fell even more.
21. AVP RF, f. 100, op. 70, d. 21, pap. 309, Ye. Safronov, Second Secretary, Soviet Embassy, London, England, "Information about New Tendencies in English Relations with China," p. 6.
22. Ibid.
23. Ibid., p. 7.
24. Ibid., p. 10.
25. Roberti, *The Fall of Hong Kong*, pp. 115–126.
26. AVP RF, f. 100, op. 73, d. 18, pap. 324, September 26, 1986, "Hong Kong and the Problem of Unfair Treaties."
27. AVP RF, f. 100, op. 73, d. 9, pap. 322, January–December, 1986, November 13, 1986, Soviet Mission, UN, Geneva, Switzerland, "About the Visit of Queen Elizabeth to China," pp. 67–69.
28. "Yeltsin Congratulates China over Hong Kong", *RFE/RL* 1, no. 64, Part I (July 1997), *Friends & Partners: Linking US-Russia Across the Internet*, http://fplib.org/friends/news/omri/1997/07/970701I.html(opt,mozilla,pc,English.,new) (accessed March 28, 2006).
29. US Information Agency: Foreign Media Reaction: Daily Digest, "Hong Kong Joins China: Can 'One Country, Two Systems' Work for Taiwan," July 3, 1997, *US Information Agency*, http://www.fas.org/news/taiwan/1997/97wwwh0703.htm (accessed March 27, 2006).
30. Hong Kong Trade Development Council, "Hong Kong/Russia Bilateral Trade," June 14, 2005, *Hong Kong Trade Development Council*, http://www.tdctrade.com/mktprof/Europe/mprussia.htm (accessed March 28, 2006).
31. See Chapter 6, p. 150 for trade figures during the 1960s.
32. L. M. Gudoshnikov, *Gonkong Spravochni* [Hong Kong Guide] (Moscow: Institute of Far East Studies Press, 2004), p. 168.
33. Information provided by Kirill M. Barsky, Head of the China Section, Division of Hong Kong, Macao, and Taiwan, MID, June 2004.
34. Dmitri Prosvirkin, Cultural Attaché, Russian Consulate-General, Hong Kong, in discussion with the author on April 3, 2006.
35. United States Department of State, "Trafficking in Persons Report: Hong Kong," July 2001, *United States Department of State*, http://www1.umn.edu/humanrts/usdocs/traffickingreport-2001.html (accessed March 27, 2006); United States Department of State, "Country Reports on Human Rights Practices, China (Includes Hong Kong and Macau), 2001, released by the Bureau of Democracy, Human Rights and Labor, March 4, 2002," *United States Department of State*, http://www.state.gov/g/drl/rls/hrrpt/2001/eap/8289.htm (accessed March 27, 2006); and United States Department of State,

"Trafficking in Persons Report, released by the Office to Monitor and Combat Trafficking in Persons, June 14, 2004," *United States Department of State*, http://www.state.gov/g/tip/rls/tiprpt/2004/33191.htm (accessed March 27, 2006).

36. V. A., "Tens of Thousands March for Full Democracy in Hong Kong," December 5, 2005, *Pravda.ru Online*, http://newsfromrussia.com/china/2005/12/05/69176.html (accessed March 23, 2006); I. L., "China Condemns U.S. Support for Full Democracy in Hong Kong," December 1, 2005, *Pravda.ru Online*, http://newsfromrussia.com/world/2005/12/01/68913.html (accessed March 23, 2006); and "British Man Gets 21 Days in Hong Kong Jail," March 15, 2006, *Pravda.ru Online*, http://english.pravda.ru/news/world/15-03-2006/77297-British-0 (accessed March 23, 2006).
37. D. M., "Economists Say, Hong Kong Consumer Prices Seem to Remain Steady", January 17, 2006, *Pravda.ru Online*, http://newsfromrussia.com/world/2006/01/17/71254.html (accessed March 23, 2006).
38. See, for example, "Hong Kong Scientists Believe SARS Virus Is Spread by African Wild Cat–Viverra," May 23, 2003, *Pravda.ru Online*, http://newsfromrussia.com/science/2003/05/23/47380.html (accessed March 23, 2006); "SARS Under Control," May 28, 2003, *Pravda.ru Online*, http://english.pravda.ru/world/asia/28-05-2003/2928-sars-0 (accessed March 23, 2006); T. E., "Hong Kong Residents to Be Given Guns to Shoot Birds Suspected of Carrying Flu," October 28, 2005, *Pravda.ru Online*, http://newsfromrussia.com/world/2005/10/28/66457.html (accessed March 23, 2006); I. L., "Hong Kong Closes Bird Parks after Chicken Test Positive for Bird Flu," February 1, 2006, *Pravda.ru Online*, http://newsfromrussia.com/world/2006/02/01/72183.html (accessed March 23, 2006); "Hong Kong to Reduce Chicken Population," March 7, 2006, *Pravda.ru Online*, http://english.pravda.ru/news/world/07-03-2006/76950-chicken%20population-0 (accessed March 23, 2006); AP, "Hong Kong Legislator Launches Plan to Save Last British Governor's Favorite Cake Shop," May 12, 2005, *Pravda.ru Online*, http://newsfromrussia.com/society/2005/05/12/59710.html (accessed March 23, 2006); and "American Housewife Killed Husband in Hong Kong," August 3, 2005, *Pravda.ru Online*, http://newsfromrussia.com/accidents/2005/08/03/60958.html (accessed March 23, 2006).

Notes to Conclusion

1. Steven J. Morris, "The War We Could Have Won," *The New York Times*, May 1, 2005, p. 15.
2. AVP RF, f. 1dvo, op. 51, d. 28, May 13, 1958, "Circular Report Issued by Foreign Minister Andrei Gromyko," pp. 13–15.

Bibliography

ARCHIVES AND LIBRARY COLLECTIONS

1. Russia

- The State Archive of the Russian Federation (GARF), Moscow
- The Russian State Archive of Socio-Political History (RGASPI), Moscow. Up to March 1999, it was known as the Russian Center for Preservation and Study of Records of Modern History (RTsKhIDNI).
    - CPSU, Central Committee files
        - f. 17 (*mezhdiunarodnyi department*) [International Department, China]
    - *Arkhiv kominterna* (*Comintern fond*) [Comintern Archive]
        - f. 495
        - f. 514
        - f. 627
- The Russian State Archive of Contemporary History (RGANI), Moscow. Up to March 1999, it was known as the the Center for Preservation of Contemporary Documentation (TsKhSD).
    - CPSU, Central Committee, International Department
        - f. 2 (*CC Plenum*) [CC Plenums], 1941–1966
        - f. 5 (*Apparat*) [CC Apparatus], 1952–1991
- The Archive of Foreign Policy of the Russian Empire (AVP RI), Moscow
    - f. 143 (*Kitaiskii Stol*) [Chinese Section]
    - f. 148 (*Tikan Okeansky*) [Pacific Department]
    - f. 229 (*k-vo v Gonkong*) [Hong Kong Consulate]
- The Archive of Foreign Policy of the Russian Federation (AVP RF), Moscow.
    - f. 1dvo (Ki-118 or Ki-718) *(Dal'nevostochnoye Otdelenie—Kitaiskii sektor)* [Far East Section—China Sector]
    - f. 56-B (*gazeti otdel*) [press section]
    - f. 0100 (*Ref-ra po kitaiu*) [China Sector—*secret*]
    - f. 100 (*Ref-ra po kitaiu*) [China Sector—*confidential*]

f. 69 (*Ref-ra po Angliu)* [British Section]
f. *komissiya Litvinova* [Litvinov Commission]

- The Russian State Archive of the Economy (RGAE), Moscow
  f. 7795 (*Sovtorflot)* [Soviet Trade Fleet]
  f. 8045 (*Ministerstvo Morskovo Transporta)* [Ministry of Sea Transport]
  f. 413 (*Narkom Vestok)* [People's Commissariat of Foreign Trade]
- The Institute of Far East Studies Library (IFES), Moscow

2. Great Britain

- The Public Records Office, London (PRO)
  CO (Colonial Office): CO129, CO 349, CO 740, CO 1030
  FCO (Foreign and Colonial Office): FCO 21, FCO 28
  FO (Foreign Office): FO 371
  GA (General Division)
  WO (War Office)

- The British Library, London

3. The United States

- The National Archives II at College Park, Maryland (NA)
  Record Group 59 (General Records of the Department of State)
  US Department of State, Central Policy Files
  Record Group 84 (Foreign Service Post Files)
  US Consulate-General, Hong Kong Files
  US Embassy, Moscow, Russia Files
  US Embassy, Sofia, Bulgaria Files
  US Embassy, Taipei, Taiwan Files
  US Embassy, Tokyo, Japan Files
  Record Group 306 (Records of the US Information Agency)
- Davis Center for Russian and Eurasian Studies Collection, H. C. Fung Library, Harvard University, Cambridge, MA
- Memorial Library, The University of Wisconsin, Madison
- The Widener Library, Harvard University, Cambridge, MA

4. Taiwan

- The Foreign Ministry Archive, Taipei
- The Kuomintang Party Archive, Taipei

5. Hong Kong

- The Hong Kong Public Records Office (HK PRO)
  Carl Smith Collection
  HKRS 70
- Main Library, The University of Hong Kong
- *Hong Kong Government Gazette* (official publication of the Hong Kong government)

6. Macao

- *Arquivo Histórico de Macau* [Macao Historical Archive] (AHM)
- *Boletim Official* [Official Bulletin] (BO)

7. Germany

- *Politisches Archiv des Auswärtigen Amts* [German Foreign Ministry Archive], Berlin
  B 37 (German Consulate-General, Hong Kong)

8. Oral History Interviews

- Professor Ronald Hill, Professor Emeritus of Geography, University of Hong Kong, March 9, 2006
- Professor Andrei Ledovsky, Former Soviet Consul in Beijing and Nanjing, China, March 9, 2001
- Mr. Dmitri Prosvirkin, Cultural Attaché, Russian Consulate-General, Hong Kong, April 3, 2006

9. Journals and Newspapers

American Asian Review
Asian Affairs
Asian Survey
Diplomacy & Statecraft
Cold War History
European History Quarterly
Izvestiya
Journal of Imperial and Commonwealth History
Military Affairs
Modern China
Naval War College Review
Pravda
The Round Table
Slavonic and East European Review
South China Morning Post

PUBLISHED DOCUMENTS COLLECTIONS

Antonov, S., and R. Kudashev. "Memorandum of Conversation of N. S. Khrushchev with Mao Zedong." October 2, 1959, *Cold War International History Project Virtual Archive*, http://wwics.si.edu/index.cfm?topic_id=1409&fuseaction=library.document&id=14857.

Chen, Jian, Vojtech Mastny, and Odd Arne Westad, et al. (translators and commentators). "Talks with Mao Zedong and Zhou Enlai, 1949–1953." December 16, 1949, *Cold War International History Project Virtual Archive*, http://wwics.si.edu/index.cfm?topic_id=1409&fuseaction=library.document&id=528.

Daniels, Robert V. *A Documentary History of Communism*, vol. 2. Hanover, NH: University Press of New England, 1984.

"Evaluation by the Soviet Party Central Committee of the Normalization of US-Chinese Relations." August 30, 1978, *Cold War International History Project Virtual Archive*, http://wwics.si.edu/index.cfm?topic_id=1409&fuseaction=library.document&id=63653.

Foreign Relations of the United States, 1958–1960, Vol. X, Part 1, *Eastern Europe Region, Soviet Union, Cyprus*. Washington, DC: US Government Printing Office, 1993.

Kheniuoi, G. O., and M. L. Titarenko, eds. *Komintern i Kitai, Dokumenti* [The Comintern in China, Documents]. Vol. 1, 1920–1925. Moscow: Nauka, 1994.

Kramer, Mark. "The USSR Foreign Ministry's Appraisal of Sino-Soviet Relations on the Eve of the Split, September 1959." *Cold War International History Project Virtual Archive*, http://wwics.si.edu/index.cfm?topic_id=1409&fuseaction=library.document&id=328.

"Stenogram: Meeting of the Delegations of the Communist Party of the Soviet Union and the Chinese Communist Party." July 5–20, 1963, *Cold War International History Project Virtual Archive*, http://wwics.si.edu/index.cfm?topic_id=1409&fuseaction=library.document&id=57.

Wu, Lengxi. "Memoir: Inside Story of the Decision Making during the Shelling of Jinmen." Li Xiaobing, Chen Jian and David Wilson (translators and annotators). *Cold War International History Project Virtual Archive*, pp. 3–18, http://wwics.si.edu/index.cfm?topic_id=1409&fuseaction=library.document&id=182.

Zubok, Vladislav M. "The Mao-Khrushchev Conversations." July 2–August 3, 1958 and October 2, 1959, *Cold War International History Project Virtual Archive*, pp. 3–5, http://wwics.si.edu/index.cfm?topic_id=1409&fuseaction=library.document&id=14656.

PRINTED SECONDARY SOURCES

Accinelli, Robert. *Crisis and Commitment: United States Policy toward Taiwan, 1950–1955*. Chapel Hill: North Carolina University Press, 1996.

Akers-Jones, David. *Feeling the Stones: Reminiscences*. Hong Kong: Hong Kong University Press, 2004.

Aldrich, Richard J. *The Hidden Hand: Britain, America, and Cold War Secret Intelligence*. London: John Murray, 2001.

Anderson, James M. *The History of Portugal.* Westport, CT: Greenwood Press, 2000.

Ang, Cheng Guan. *Vietnamese Communists' Relations with China and the Second Indochina Conflict, 1956–1962*. London: McFarland, 1997.

________. *The Vietnam War from the Other Side: The Vietnamese Communists' Perspective*. London: RoutledgeCurzon, 2002.

Ascher, Abraham. *P. A. Stolypin: The Search for Stability in Late Imperial Russia*. Stanford, CA: Stanford University Press, 2001.

Baryshnikov, V. N. "Principal Position of the USSR on the Taiwan Question." *Problemi dal'nevo vostoka* [Problems of Far East], no. 3 (1982): 40–49.

Bassin, Mark. *Imperial Visions: Nationalist Imagination and Geographical Expansion in the Russian Far East, 1840–1865*. Cambridge: Cambridge University Press, 1999.

Baumgart, Winfried. *The Crimean War, 1853–1856*. New York: Oxford University Press, 1999.

Beasley, W. G. *Japanese Imperialism, 1894–1945*. Oxford: Clarendon Press, 1987.

Bellows, Thomas J. "Normalization: A Taiwan Perspective." *Asian Affairs* 6, no. 6 (July–August 1979): 339–358.

Berlie, Jean A. "Macao's Overview at the Turn of the Century." *American Asian Review* 18, no. 4 (Winter 2000): 25–68.

Bickley, Gillian. *Hong Kong Invaded! A '97 Nightmare*. Hong Kong: Hong Kong University Press, 2001.

Birmingham, David. *A Concise History of Portugal*. Cambridge: Cambridge University Press, 1993.

Boardman, Robert. *Britain and the People's Republic of China, 1949–74*. New York: Barnes & Noble, 1976.

Bolshaia Entsiklopediia [Great Encyclopedia]. Moscow: Kirill I Mefodiya, 2000.

Bradley, J. F. N. *Allied Intervention in Russia*. London: Weidenfeld & Nicolson, 1968.

Brandt, Conrad. *Stalin's Failure in China, 1924–1927*. Cambridge, MA: Harvard University Press, 1958.

Brokhaus, F. A., and I. A. Efron, eds. *Entsiklopedicheskii Slovar (Granat)* [Encyclopedic Dictionary (Granat)]. 58 vols. St. Petersburg: J. A. Efron, 1890–1907.

Byrd, Martha. *Chennault: Giving Wings to the Tiger*. Tuscaloosa: University of Alabama Press, 1987.

Calvocoressi, Peter, and Guy Wint. *Total War: Causes and Courses of the Second World War*. 2nd ed. New York: Viking Press, 1989.

Chan Lau, Kit-ching. *From Nothing to Nothing: The Chinese Communist Movement and Hong Kong, 1921–1936*. London: Hurst, 1999.

Chang, Kuo-t'ao. *The Rise of the Chinese Communist Party*. 2 vols. Lawrence: University Press of Kansas, 1971–1972.

Chang, Gordon H. "To the Nuclear Brink: Eisenhower, Dulles, and the Quemoy-Matsu Crisis." *International Security* 12, no. 4 (Spring 1988): 96–123.

Chekhov, Anton Pavlovich. *Letters of Anton Chekhov*. Translated from Russian by Michael Henry Heim in collaboration with Simon Karlinsky. London: Bodley Head, 1973.

Chen, Jian. *The Sino-Soviet Alliance and China's Entry into the Korean War*. Washington, DC: Cold War International History Project, 1992.

________. *China's Road to the Korean War: The Making of the Sino-American Confrontation*. New York: Columbia University Press, 1994.

________. *Mao's China and the Cold War*. Chapel Hill: North Carolina University Press, 2001.

Chennault, Claire Lee. *Way of a Fighter: The Memoirs of Claire Lee Chennault*. Edited by Robert Hotz. New York: G. P. Putnam's Sons, 1949.

Christensen, Thomas J. *Useful Adversaries: Grand Strategy, Domestic Mobilization, and Sino-American Conflict, 1947–1958*. Princeton, NJ: Princeton University Press, 1996.

Claudín, Fernando. *The Communist Movement: From Comintern to Cominform*. London: Penguin, 1975.

Clough, Ralph N. *Island China*. Cambridge, MA: Harvard University Press, 1978.

Clubb, O. Edmund. *China and Russia: The "Great Game."* New York: Columbia University Press, 1971.

Coates, Austin. *A Macao Narrative*. Hong Kong: Heinemann, 1978.

Coox, Alvin D. *Nomonhan: Japan Against Russia, 1939*. 2 vols. Stanford, CA: Stanford University Press, 1985.

Copper, John Franklin. "Taiwan's Options." *Asian Affairs* 6, no. 5 (May–June 1979): 282–294.

________. *Taiwan: Nation-State or Province?* 4th ed. Boulder, CO: Westview Press, 2003.

Cottrell, Robert. *The End of Hong Kong: The Secret Diplomacy of Imperial Retreat*. London: John Murray, 1993.

Cremer, R. D., ed. *Macao: City of Commerce and Culture, Continuity and Change*. 2nd ed. Hong Kong: API Press, 1991.

Crisp, Olga. "The Russo-Chinese Bank: An Episode in Franco-Russian Relations." *Slavonic and East European Review* 52, no. 127 (April 1974): 197–212.

Crisswell, Colin, and Mike Watson. *The Royal Hong Kong Police, 1841–1945*. Hong Kong: Macmillan, 1982.

Curtiss, John Shelton. *Russia's Crimean War*. Durham, NC: Duke University Press, 1979.

De Oliveira, Antonio Henrique R. *History of Portugal*. New York: Columbia University Press, 1976.

Dirlik, Arif. "The Guangzhou Uprising in Workers' Perspective." *Modern China* 23, no. 4 (October 1997): 363–397.

Dorril, Stephen. *MI6: Fifty Years of Special Operations*. London: Fourth Estate, 2000.

Drifte, Reinhard. "European and Soviet Perspectives on Future Responses in Taiwan to International and Regional Developments." *Asian Survey* 25, no. 11 (November 1985): 1115–1122.

Duncanson, Dennis J. "Ho-chi-Minh in Hong Kong, 1931–32." *The China Quarterly*, no. 57 (January–March 1974): 84–100.

Elleman, Bruce A. *Diplomacy and Deception: The Secret History of Sino-Soviet Relations*. London: M. E. Sharpe, 1997.

Ellison, Herbert J., ed. *The Sino-Soviet Conflict: A Global Perspective*. Seattle: University of Washington Press, 1982.

Emerson, Geoffrey Charles. "Stanley Internment Camp, Hong Kong, 1942–1945: A Study of Civilian Internment during the Second World War." M.Phil. thesis, University of Hong Kong, 1973.

Endacott, G. B. *A History of Hong Kong*. 2nd ed. London: Oxford University Press, 1964.

Evans, John L. *Russian Expansion on the Amur, 1848–1860: The Push to the Pacific*. Lewiston, NY: Edwin Mellen Press, 1999.

Fairbank, John King, ed. *The Chinese World Order: Traditional China's Foreign Relations*. Cambridge, MA: Harvard University Press, 1968.

Fairbank, John King. *The Great Chinese Revolution, 1800–1985*. New York: Harper & Row, 1986.

Ford, Daniel. *Flying Tigers: Claire Chennault and the American Volunteer Group*. Washington, DC: Smithsonian Institution Press, 1991.

Fursenko, Aleksandr, and Timothy Naftali. *Khrushchev's Cold War: The Inside Story of an American Adversary*. London: W. W. Norton, 2006.

Gaiduk, Ilya V. *The Soviet Union and the Vietnam War*. Chicago: Ivan R. Dee, 1996.

________. *Confronting Vietnam: Soviet Policy toward the Indochina Conflict, 1954–1963*. Stanford, CA: Stanford University Press, 2003.

Galenovich, Iu. M. *Tszyn Chzhunchzhyen ili neizvestnii chan kaishi* [The Unknown Chiang Kai-shek]. Moscow: Muravei, 2000.

________. *Moskva-Pekin, Moskva-Taipei* [Moscow-Peking, Moscow-Taipei]. Moscow: Izografus, 2002.

________. *Samoutverzhdeniye sinovei Taivaniya* [Patriots of Taiwan]. Moscow: Muravei, 2002.

Garver, John W. "Taiwan's Russian Option: Image and Reality." *Asian Survey* 18, no. 7 (July 1978): 751–766.

________. *Chinese-Soviet Relations, 1937–1945: The Diplomacy of Chinese Nationalism*. New York: Oxford University Press, 1988.

Gilles, Daniel. *Chekhov: Observer Without Illusion*. Translated by Charles Lam Markmann. New York: Funk and Wagnalls, 1968.

Gittings, John. *Survey of the Sino-Soviet Dispute: A Commentary and Extracts from the Recent Polemics, 1963–1967*. London: Oxford University Press, 1968.

Goncharov, S. N., John Wilson Lewis, and Xue Litai. *Uncertain Partners: Stalin, Mao, and the Korean War*. Stanford, CA: Stanford University Press, 1993.

Gough, Barry M. "The Crimean War in the Pacific: British Strategy and Naval Operations." *Military Affairs* 37, no. 4 (December 1973): 130–136.

Gudoshnikov, L. M. *Gonkong Spravochni* [Hong Kong Guide]. Moscow: Institute of Far East Studies Press, 2004.

Guillen-Nuñez, Cesar. *Macao*. Hong Kong: Oxford University Press, 1984.

Harrison, Hope Millard. *Driving the Soviets up the Wall: Soviet-East German Relations, 1953–1961*. Princeton, NJ: Princeton University Press, 2003.

He Xixiang. *365 tian: Zhong wai jieri jinian ri daquan* [365 Days]. Beijing: Zhongguo zhuoyue chubanshe, 1990.

Heinzig, Dieter. *The Soviet Union and Communist China 1945–1950: The Arduous Road to the Alliance*. Armonk, NY: M. E. Sharpe, 2004.

Hiery, Herman Joseph. *The Neglected War: The German South Pacific and the Influence of World War I*. Honolulu: University of Hawaii Press, 1995.

Hingley, Ronald. *A New Life of Anton Chekhov*. London: Oxford University Press, 1976.

Horelick, Arnold L. "Soviet Policy Dilemmas in Asia." *Asian Survey* 17, no. 6 (June 1977): 499–512.

Hsiao, Frank S. T., and Lawrence R. Sullivan. "The Chinese Communist Party and the Status of Taiwan, 1928–1943," *Pacific Affairs* 52, no. 3 (Autumn 1979): 446–467.

Hsü, Immanuel C. Y. *The Ili Crisis: A Study of Sino-Russian Diplomacy, 1871–1881*. Oxford: Clarendon Press, 1965.

________. *The Rise of Modern China*. 6th ed. New York: Oxford University Press, 2000.

Isaacs, Harold. *The Tragedy of the Chinese Revolution*. 3rd ed. Stanford, CA: Stanford University Press, 1966.

Ivanov, Peter M. *Gonkong* [Hong Kong]. Moscow: Nauka, 1990.

________. "Russian-Taiwanese Relations: Current State, Problems, and Prospects of Development." *Occasional Papers/Reprints Series in Contemporary Asian Studies* 133, no. 2 (1996): 1–76.

Kappeler, Andreas. *The Russian Empire: A Multiethnic History*. London: Longman, 2001.

Keeble, Curtis. *Britain, the Soviet Union, and Russia*. New York: St. Martin's Press, 2000.

Khrushchev, Sergei N. *Nikita Khrushchev and the Creation of a Superpower*. Translated by Shirley Benson. University Park: Pennsylvania State University Press, 2000.

Kirby, William C., Robert S. Ross, and Gong Li, eds. *Normalization of US-China Relations: An International History*. Cambridge, MA: Harvard University Press, 2005.

Korros, Alexandra Shecket. *A Reluctant Parliament: Stolypin, Nationalism, and the Politics of the Russian Imperial State Council, 1906–1911*. Lanham, MD: Rowman & Littlefield, 2002.

Kruzenshtern, Ivan Fedorovich. *Voyage round the World, in the Years 1803, 1804, 1805, and 1806*. Translated by Richard Belgrave Hoppner. London: John Murray, 1813.

Lamas, Rosmarie Wank-Nolasco. *History of Macao: A Student Manual*. Macao: Institute of Tourism Education, 1998.

Lazitch, Branko, and Milorad Drachkovitch, eds. *Biographical Dictionary of the Comintern*. Stanford, CA: Hoover Institution Press, 1973.

Lee, Chong-Sik. *Revolutionary Struggle in Manchuria: Chinese Communism and Soviet Interest, 1922–1945*. Berkeley: University of California Press, 1984.

Lensen, G. A. *The Russian Push toward Japan: Russo-Japanese Relations, 1697–1875*. Princeton, NJ: Princeton University Press, 1959.

________. *Russia's Eastward Expansion*. Englewood Cliffs, NJ: Prentice Hall, 1964.

________. *Russian Diplomatic and Consular Officials in East Asia*. Tokyo: Sophia University, 1968.

Leong, Sow-Theng. *Sino-Soviet Relations: The First Phase, 1917–1920*. Canberra: Australian National University Press, 1971.

Levine, David. *The Rift: The Sino-Soviet Conflict*. Jacksonville, IL: Harris-Wolfe, 1968.

Lilley, James, with Jeffrey Lilley. *China Hands: Nine Decades of Adventure, Espionage, and Diplomacy in Asia*. New York: Public Affairs Press, 2004.

Lisiansky, Urey. *A Voyage round the World, in the Years 1803, 4, 5, & 6: Performed, by Order of His Imperial Majesty Alexander the First, Emperor of Russia, in the Ship Neva*. London: John Booth, 1814.

Livermore, H. V. *A New History of Portugal*. Cambridge: Cambridge University Press, 1969.

Lukin, Alexander. *The Bear Watches the Dragon: Russia's Perceptions of China and the Evolution of Russian-Chinese Relations since the Eighteenth Century*. Armonk, NY: M. E. Sharpe, 2003.

Malozemoff, Andrew. *Russian Far Eastern Policy, 1881–1904: With Special Emphasis on the Causes of the Russo-Japanese War*. New York: Octagon Books, 1977.

Mancall, Mark. *China at the Center: 300 Years of Foreign Policy*. New York: Free Press, 1984.

Martens, Fedor Fedorovich. *Rossiia i Kitai* [Russia and China]. St. Petersburg: A. Garten, 1881.

McDermott, Kevin, and Jeremy Agnew, eds. *The Comintern: A History of International Communism from Lenin to Stalin*. Basingstoke, Hampshire: Macmillan, 1996.

McLane, Charles B. *Soviet Policy and the Chinese Communists: 1931–1946*. New York: Columbia University Press, 1958.

Medvedev, Roy Aleksandrovich. *China and the Superpowers*. Translated by Harold Shukman. Oxford: Blackwell, 1986.

Mehnert, Klaus. *Peking and Moscow*. New York: Putnam, 1963.

Meisner, Maurice J. *Li Ta-chao and the Origins of Chinese Marxism*. Cambridge, MA: Harvard University Press, 1967.

________. *Mao's China and After: A History of the People's Republic*. 3rd ed. New York: Free Press, 1999.

Montalto de Jesus, Carlos Augusto. *Historic Macao*. 3rd ed. Hong Kong: Oxford University Press, 1984.

Murray, Brian. "Stalin, the Cold War, and the Division of China: A Multi-Archival Mystery." Working Paper no. 12, June 1995, *The Cold War International History Project Virtual Archive*, http://wilsoncenter.org/index.cfm?topic_id=1409&fuseaction=va2.browse&sort=Collection.

Myers, Ramon H., and Mark R. Peattie, eds. *The Japanese Colonial Empire, 1895–1945*. Princeton, NJ: Princeton University Press, 1984.

Neilson, Keith. *Britain and the Last Tsar: British Policy and Russia, 1894–1917*. Oxford: Clarendon Press, 1996.

North, Robert C. *Chinese Communism*. London: Weidenfeld & Nicolson, 1966.

Overy, Richard, and Andrew Wheatcroft. *The Road to War*. London: Macmillan, 1989.

Pantsov, Alexander. *The Bolsheviks and the Chinese Revolution, 1919–1927*.

Richmond, Surrey: Curzon Press, 2000.

Paine, S. C. M. *Imperial Rivals: China, Russia, and Their Disputed Frontier*. Armonk, NY: M. E. Sharpe, 1996.

Petroff, Serge P. *Remembering a Forgotten War: Civil War in Eastern European Russia and Siberia, 1918–1920*. Boulder, CO: East European Monographs, 2000.

Pons, Philippe. *Macao*. Translated by Sarah Adams. Hong Kong: Hong Kong University Press, 2002.

Price, Don C. *Russia and the Roots of the Chinese Revolution, 1896–1911*. Cambridge, MA: Harvard University Press, 1974.

Quested, Rosemary. *The Expansion of Russia in East Asia, 1857–1860*. Kuala Lumpur: University of Malaya Press, 1968.

________. *The Russo-Chinese Bank: A Multinational Financial Base of Tsarism in China*. Birmingham: Department of Russian Language and Literature, University of Birmingham, 1977.

Quinn-Judge, Sophie. *Ho Chi Minh: The Missing Years, 1919–1941*. London: Hurst, 2002.

Rayfield, Donald. *Anton Chekhov: A Life*. Evanston, IL: Northwestern University Press, 1997.

Roberti, Mark. *The Fall of Hong Kong: China's Triumph and Britain's Betrayal*. New York: John Wiley & Sons, 1996.

Roberts, Priscilla. "William Clayton and the Recognition of China, 1945–1966: More Speculations on 'Lost Chances in China.'" *Journal of American-East Asian Relations* 7, no. 1–2 (Spring–Summer 1998): 5–37.

Rollins, Patrick J. "Russian Commerce Raiders in the Red Sea and Indian Ocean, 1904." *Naval War College Review* 47, no. 3 (Summer 1994): 86–105.

Rosenberg, William, and Marilyn Young. *Transforming Russia and China: Revolutionary Struggle in the Twentieth Century*. New York: Oxford University Press, 1982.

Ross, Robert S., ed. *China, the United States, and the Soviet Union: Tripolarity and Policy Making in the Cold War*. Armonk, NY: M. E. Sharpe, 1993.

Saraiva, Jose H. *Portugal: A Companion History*. Manchester: Carcanet Press, 1997.

Scammell, G. V. "After Da Gama: Europe and Asia after 1498." *Modern Asian Studies* 34, no. 3 (July 2000): 513–543.

Schwartz, Benjamin Isadore. *Chinese Communism and the Rise of Mao*. Cambridge, MA: Harvard University Press, 1951.

Segal, Gerald. *Sino-Soviet Relations after Mao*. London: International Institute for Strategic Studies, 1988.

________. *The Fate of Hong Kong*. London: Simon & Schuster, 1993.

Share, Michael B. "The Soviet Union and Taiwan, 1943–1982." *Tamkang Journal of International Affairs* 4, no. 4 (2000): 1–34.

________. "The Soviet Union, Hong Kong, and the Cold War, 1945–1970." *Cold*

War International History Project Working Paper no. 41. Washington, DC: Woodrow Wilson International Center for Scholars, 2003.

________. "From Ideological Foe to Uncertain Friend: Soviet Relations with Taiwan, 1943–1982." *Cold War History* 3, no. 2 (January 2003): 1–34.

________. "Red Star Ascending, Flagging Union Jack: Soviet Views on the Handover of Hong Kong." *Diplomacy and Statecraft* 15, no. 1 (March 2004): 57–78.

________. "Along the Fringes of 'the Great Game': Imperial Russia and Hong Kong, 1841–1907." *The Round Table* 93, no. 377 (October 2004): 725–737.

________. "Clash of Worlds: The Comintern, British Hong Kong and Chinese Nationalism, 1921–1927." *Europe-Asia Studies* 57, no. 4 (June 2005): 601–624.

________. "The Bear Yawns? Russian and Soviet Relations with Macao." *Journal of the Royal Asiatic Society* 16, no. 1 (January 2006): 1–16.

Shelley, Louise I. "The Changing Position of Women: Trafficking, Crime, and Corruption." In *The Legacy of State Socialism and the Future of Transformation*, edited by David Lane, pp. 207–224. Lanham, MD: Rowman & Littlefield, 2003.

Simmons, Ernest J. *Chekhov: A Biography*. London: Jonathan Cape, 1963

Sinclair, Kevin. *Asia's Finest: An Illustrated Account of the Hong Kong Police*. Hong Kong: Unicorn, 1983.

________. *Asia's Finest Marches on: Policing Hong Kong from 1841 into the 21st Century: An Illustrated Account of the Hong Kong Police*. Hong Kong: Kevin Sinclair Associates, 1997.

Skachkov, P. E. *Ocherki istorii russkogo kitaevedeniia* [Outline of the History of Russian Sinology]. Moscow: Nauka, 1977.

Slyusarev, S. V. *Soviet Volunteers in China 1925–1945: Articles and Reminiscences*. Translated by David Fidlon. Moscow: Progress, 1980.

Smith, S. A. *A Road Is Made: Communism in Shanghai, 1920–1927*. Honolulu: University of Hawaii Press, 2000.

________. *Like Cattle and Horses: Nationalism and Labor in Shanghai, 1895–1927*. Durham, NC: Duke University Press, 2002.

Snow, Philip. *The Fall of Hong Kong: Britain, China, and the Japanese Occupation*. New Haven, CT: Yale University Press, 2003.

Soman, Appu K. *Double-Edged Sword: Nuclear Diplomacy in Unequal Conflicts; The United States and China, 1950–1958*. Westport, CT: Praeger, 2000.

Stolper, Thomas E. *China, Taiwan, and the Offshore Islands: Together with an Implication for Outer Mongolia and Sino-Soviet Relations*. Armonk, NY: M. E. Sharpe, 1985.

Strachan, Hew. *The First World War*. Vol. 1. Oxford: Oxford University Press, 2001.

Swettenham, John. *Allied Intervention in Russia, 1918–1919*. London: George Allen & Unwin, 1967.

Taubman, William. *Khrushchev: The Man and His Era*. New York: W. W. Norton, 2003.

Taylor, Jay. *The Generalissimo's Son: Chiang Ching-kuo and the Revolutions in China and Taiwan*. Cambridge, MA: Harvard University Press, 2000.

Tsang, Yui-sang, Steve. "Strategy for Survival: The Cold War and Hong Kong's Policy towards Kuomintang and Chinese Communist Activities in the 1950s." *Journal of Imperial and Commonwealth History* 25, no. 2 (May 1997): 294–317.

________. *Hong Kong: An Appointment with China*. London: I. B. Tauris, 1997.

________. *A Modern History of Hong Kong*. London: I. B. Tauris, 2004.

Tsui, Tsien-hua. *The Sino-Soviet Border Dispute in the 1970's*. New York: Mosaic Press, 1983.

Tubilewicz, Czeslaw. "Taiwan and the Soviet Union during the Cold War: Enemies or Ambiguous Friends?" *Cold War History* 5, no. 1 (February 2005): 75–86.

Tucker, Nancy Bernkopf. *Taiwan, Hong Kong, and the United States, 1945–1992: Uncertain Friendships*. New York: Twayne, 1994.

Tucker, Spencer C. *The Great War, 1914–1918*. London: UCL Press, 1998.

Turkov, Andrei, comp. *Anton Chekhov and His Times*. Translated by Cynthia Carlile and Sharon McKee. Fayetteville: University of Arkansas Press, 1995.

Ullman, R. H. *Anglo-Soviet Relations*. Vol. 1, *Intervention and the War*. Princeton, NJ: Princeton University Press, 1961.

________. *Anglo-Soviet Relations*. Vol. 2, *Britain and the Russian Civil War, 1918–1920*. Princeton, NJ: Princeton University Press, 1968.

________. *Anglo-Soviet Relations*. Vol. 3, *The Anglo-Soviet Accord*. Princeton, NJ: Princeton University Press, 1972.

Ukhtomskii, Esper. *Travels in the East of Nicholas II, Emperor of Russia When Cesarewitch 1890–1891*. 2 vols. Edited by Sir George Birdwood. London: Constable, 1896.

Van der Oye, David Schimmelpennick. *Toward the Rising Sun: Russian Ideologies of Empire and the Path to War with Japan*. DeKalb: Northern Illinois University Press, 2001.

Watson, D. R. "The Rise and Fall of the Russo-Asiatic Bank: The Problems of a Russian Enterprise with French Shareholders, 1910–1926." *European History Quarterly* 23, no. 1 (January 1993): 39–49.

Weinberg, Gerhard. *A World at Arms: A Global History of World War II*. Cambridge: Cambridge University Press, 1994.

Weiner, Michael. "Comintern in East Asia, 1919–1939." In *The Comintern: A History of International Communism from Lenin to Stalin*, edited by Kevin McDermott and Jeremy Agnew, pp. 158–190. Basingstoke, Hampshire: Macmillan, 1996.

Welsh, Frank. *A History of Hong Kong*. 2nd ed. London: HarperCollins, 1997.

Westad, Odd Arne. *Cold War and Revolution: Soviet-American Rivalry and the Origins of the Chinese Civil War 1944–1946*. New York: Columbia University Press, 1993.

________. *Decisive Encounters: The Chinese Civil War, 1946–1950*. Stanford, CA: Stanford University Press, 2003.

Westad, Odd Arne, ed. *Brothers in Arms: The Rise and Fall of the Sino-Soviet Alliance, 1945–1963*. Washington, DC: Woodrow Wilson Center Press, 1998.

White, John Albert. *The Siberian Intervention*. Princeton, NJ: Princeton University Press, 1950.

Whiting, Allen S. *Soviet Policies in China, 1917–1924*. New York: Columbia University Press, 1954.

Wieczynski, Joseph, ed. *The Modern Encyclopedia of Russia and Soviet History*, vol. 32. Gulf Breeze, FL: Academic International Press, 1983.

Wishnick, Elizabeth. *Mending Fences: The Evolution of Moscow's China Policy, from Brezhnev to Yeltsin*. Seattle: University of Washington Press, 2001.

Zagoria, Donald S. *The Sino-Soviet Conflict, 1956–1961*. Princeton, NJ: Princeton University Press, 1962.

Zhai, Qiang. *The Dragon, the Lion, and the Eagle: Chinese-British-American Relations, 1949–1958*. Kent, OH: Kent State University Press, 1994.

Zubok, Vladislav, and Constantine Pleshakov. *Inside the Kremlin's Cold War: From Stalin to Khrushchev*. Cambridge, MA: Harvard University Press, 1996.

INTERNET SOURCES

Asia Pacific Media Services Limited: The Russian Mafia in Asia.
http://www.asiapacificms.com/articles/russian_mafia/

Asia Times Online.
http://www.atimes.com/atimes/Central_Asia/HC21Ag02.html

The Asian Review of Books on the Web.
http://www.asianreviewofbooks.com/arb/article.php?article=630

Center for the Study of Intelligence.
https://www.cia.gov/csi/monograph/women/trafficking.pdf

China Daily Online.
http://www.chinadaily.com.cn/english/doc/2005-03/16/content_425530.htm

Cold War International History Project Virtual Archive.
http://wilsoncenter.org/index.cfm?topic_id=1409&fuseaction=va2.browse&sort=Collection

Factbook on Global Sexual Exploitation: Macao.
http://www.uri.edu/artsci/wms/hughes/macau.htm

FBI History: Famous Cases: Vonsiatsky Espionage.
http://www.fbi.gov/libref/historic/famcases/vonsiatsky/espionage.htm
Federation of American Scientists: News.
http://www.fas.org/news/taiwan/2000/000319-taiwan2.htm
Friends and Partners: Linking US-Russia across the Internet.
http://www.fplib.org
Gambling Magazine.
http://gamblingmagazine.com/articles/22/22-97.htm
The Guardian Unlimited Books Review.
http://books.guardian.co.uk/review/story/0,12084,1252154,00.html.
The History of the Russian Navy.
http://www.navy.ru/history/hrn7-e.htm
Hong Kong Disciplined Service Collectibles.
http://www.hkdsc.com/life/jackson.html
Hong Kong Liaison Office of the International Trade Union Movement.
http://www.ihlo.org/HKM/Macau_Background.pdf
Hong Kong Standard.
http://www.thestandard.com.hk
Hong Kong Trade Development Council.
http://www.tdctrade.com/mktprof/Europe/mprussia.htm
Human Trafficking & Modern-Day Slavery.
http://gvnet.com/humantrafficking/Russia.htm, c
Institute for the Study of Conflict, Ideology, and Policy.
http://www.bu.edu/iscip/digest/vol2/ed19.html
The Jamestown Foundation.
http://jam.newvillagemedia.com/publications_details.php?volume_id=21&issue_id=1404&article_id=14297
Jewish Institute for National Security Affairs.
http://www.jinsa.org/articles.html
Library of Congress.
http://www.loc.gov/rr/european/mofc/vinkovetsky.html
"The Long, Long Trail: The British Army in the Great War of 1914–1918. The Duke of Cambridge's Own (Middlesex Regiment)."
http://www.1914-1918.net/msex.htm
Macau: City of Culture Guide, 1998.
http://home.macau.ctm.net/~liox0001/travel/macau/mo_talk.shtml
Mama Coca.
http://www.mamacoca.org/feb2002/art_bagley_globalization_organized_crime_en.html
People's Daily Online.
http://english.people.com.cn

Pravda.Ru Online.
http://english.pravda.ru
Radio Free Europe/Radio Liberty.
http://www.rferl.org/featuresarticle/2005/08/40554110-295C-4760-9635-BCC86A121F45.html
The Royal Hampshire Regiment: The 37th and 67th Foot.
http://www.Pauljerrard.com/ww1/Battalions/1_9th.html
Russia's Pacific Navy.
http://www.fegi.ru/prim/flot/flot1_2.htm
Sam Houston State University: Journal of Doctoral and Research Studies in Educational Leadership, Issue # 3.
http://www.shsu.edu/~edu_elc/journal.htm
South China Morning Post.
http://72.14.203.104/search?q=cache:dzQ8cqUjhucJ
Stratfor.com.
http://www.stratfor.com/products/
Tandem Online Magazine.
http://www.tandemnews.com/viewstory.php?storyid=92&page=1
The Trade Environment Database.
http://www.american.edu/TED/traffic.htm
The Trumpet.Com.
http://www.thetrumpet.com/index.php?page=article&id=521
United Nations: Office of the Special Representative of the Secretary-General for Children and Armed Conflict.
http://www.un.org/special-rep/children-armed-conflict/PressReleases/
United States Department of State.
http://www.state.gov/g/drl/rls/hrrpt/2004/41640.htm#macau
United States Information Agency.
http://www.fas.org/news/taiwan/1997/97wwwh0703.htm
Wikipedia: The Free Encyclopedia.
http://en.wikipedia.org/wiki

Index